All-Age Lectionary Services

Year C

All-Age Lectionary Services

Year C

Resources for all-age worship

These service outlines were originally published by Scripture Union as *Light for the Lectionary* 2009/2010. They have been fully revised with new material added or available online.

Copyright © Scripture Union 2012
ISBN 978 1 84427 641 7

Scripture Union England and Wales
207–209 Queensway, Bletchley,
Milton Keynes, MK2 2EB, England

Email: info@scriptureunion.org.uk

Website: www.scriptureunion.org.uk

All rights reserved. No part of this publication may be reproduced, stored in a retrieval system, or transmitted in any form or by any means, electronic, mechanical, photocopying, recording or otherwise, without the prior permission of Scripture Union.

Scripture quotations are taken from: THE HOLY BIBLE, NEW INTERNATIONAL VERSION (Anglicised edition) Copyright © 1979, 1984, 2011 by Biblica (formerly International Bible Society). Used by permission of Hodder & Stoughton Publishers, an Hachette UK company; or from The Bible, Contemporary English Version, published by HarperCollins *Publishers,* © American Bible Society 1991, 1992, 1995. Used by permission. Anglicisations © British and Foreign Bible Society 1997.

British Library Cataloguing-in-Publication Data: a catalogue record of this book is available from the British Library

Printed and bound in India by Thomson Press

Cover design: Grax Design

Internal design: Helen Jones

Typesetting: Georgina Pensri

Scripture Union is an international Christian charity working with churches in more than 130 countries.

Thank you for purchasing this book. Any profits from this book support SU in England and Wales to bring the good news of Jesus Christ to children, young people and families and to enable them to meet God through the Bible and prayer.

Find out more about our work and how you can get involved at:

www.scriptureunion.org.uk
(England and Wales)

www.suscotland.org.uk (Scotland)

www.suni.org (Northern Ireland)

www.scriptureunion.org (USA)

www.su.org.au (Australia)

Foreword

'Children belong with the worshipping congregation because the body of Christ has no age requirements. Christianity is age-inclusive.' David Ng and Virginia Thomas (1981)

'Help – it's all-age worship this week! What can I do?'

As a Diocesan Children's Adviser, I heard that cry over and over again! In our heads we know that all ages coming together to worship God, confess sin, hear Scripture together, pray and be strengthened by the Holy Spirit to live Jesus' way in the world, is what we are called to – but it's very hard work! And for many people, it's daunting to think of creative ways to engage across the generations whilst leading worship that is focused on God.

That's why I welcome the third volume of the *All-Age Lectionary Services* series. In it there are yet again resources which will find a permanent home in the toolbox of any all-age worship leader. Firmly rooted in the scriptures set for each week, creative ideas are offered for every aspect of the liturgy to engage children and adults alike in prayer, worship and response to God.

As someone who serves in a church which uses the Lectionary, I'm looking forward to using the ideas in this book to widen my horizons and help me become more creative in both leading and speaking when all-ages are together.

'Incorporating children into our corporate worship services is counter-cultural and disquieting, but churches truly interested in the soul-care of their children need to grapple with this issue.' Ivy Beckwith (2004)

I thank God for those who have contributed to this book and pray that it will help you grapple with all-age worship so that your worship may be truly age-inclusive.

Mary Hawes
National Children's Adviser for the Church of England

Contents

10	Leading all-age worship	
13	What's in All-Age Lectionary Services Year C?	
14	Advent Sunday	1 Thessalonians 3:9–13; Luke 21:25–36
19	Second Sunday of Advent	Malachi 3:1–4; Luke 3:1–6
24	Third Sunday of Advent	Zephaniah 3:14–20; Luke 3:7–18
29	Fourth Sunday of Advent	Micah 5:2–5a; Luke 1:39–45
34	Christmas Day	Isaiah 52:7–10; Luke 2:1–14
39	First Sunday of Christmas	Colossians 3:12–17; Luke 2:41–52
44	Second Sunday of Christmas	Ephesians 1:3–14; John 1:10–18
49	Epiphany (nearest Sunday to 6th January)	Ephesians 3:1–12; Matthew 2:1–12
54	The Baptism of Christ (First Sunday of Epiphany)	Isaiah 43:1–7; Luke 3:15–17,21,22
59	Second Sunday of Epiphany	Psalm 36:5–10; John 2:1–11
64	Third Sunday of Epiphany	Nehemiah 8:1–3,5,6, 8–10; Psalm 19
69	Fourth Sunday of Epiphany	1 Corinthians 13:1–13; Luke 2:22–40
74	Second Sunday before Lent (CW)	Genesis 2:4–9,15–25; Psalm 65
79	Second Sunday before Lent (RCL)	Isaiah 6:1–8; Luke 5:1–11
84	Sunday before Lent	Exodus 34:29–35; Luke 9:28–36
89	First Sunday of Lent	Psalm 91:1,2,9–16; Luke 4:1–13
94	Second Sunday of Lent	Genesis 15:1–12,17,18; Psalm 27
99	Third Sunday of Lent	Isaiah 55:1–9; Psalm 63:1–8
104	Fourth Sunday of Lent	2 Corinthians 5:16–21; Luke 15:1–3,11–32
109	Mothering Sunday	Exodus 2:1–10; Luke 2:33–35
114	Fifth Sunday of Lent	Philippians 3:4–14; John 12:1–8

119	Palm Sunday	Psalm 118; Luke 19:28–40
124	Good Friday	Psalm 130; John 18,19
129	Easter Day	Luke 24:1–12; 1 Corinthians 15:19–26
134	Second Sunday of Easter	Acts 5:27–32; John 20:19–31
139	Third Sunday of Easter	Psalm 30; John 21:1–19
144	Fourth Sunday of Easter	Psalm 23; Acts 9:36–43
149	Fifth Sunday of Easter	Acts 11:1–18; Revelation 21:1–6
155	Sixth Sunday of Easter	Psalm 67; Acts 16:9–15
160	Ascension Day	Acts 1:1–11; Luke 24:44–53
165	Seventh Sunday of Easter	Acts 16:16–34; John 17:20–26
170	Pentecost	Acts 2:1–21; John 14:8–17,25–27
175	Trinity Sunday	Romans 5:1–5; John 16:12–15
180	Proper 4	1 Kings 18:20,21,30–39; Luke 7:1–10
185	Proper 5	1 Kings 17:17–24; Luke 7:11–17
190	Proper 6	2 Samuel 11:26 – 12:10,13–15; Luke 7:36 – 8:3
195	Proper 7	Psalm 22:19–29; Luke 8:26–39
200	Proper 8	1 Kings 19:15,16,19–21; Luke 9:51–62
205	Proper 9	Galatians 6:7–16; Luke 10:1–11,16–20
210	Proper 10	Psalm 25:1–10; Luke 10:25–37
216	Proper 11	Genesis 18:1–10a; Luke 10:38–42
222	Proper 12	Genesis 18:20–32; Luke 11:1–13
227	Proper 13	Ecclesiastes 1:2,12–14; 2:18–23; Luke 12:13–21
232	Proper 14	Genesis 15:1–6; Luke 12:32–40
237	Proper 15	Hebrews 11:29 – 12:2; Luke 12:49–56
242	Proper 16	Hebrews 12:18–29; Luke 13:10–17

247	Proper 17	Proverbs 25:6,7; Luke 14:1,7–14
252	Proper 18	Philemon 1–21; Luke 14:25–33
257	Proper 19	1 Timothy 1:12–17; Luke 15:1–10
262	Proper 20	Amos 8:4–7; 1 Timothy 2:1–7
267	Proper 21	1 Timothy 6:6–19; Luke 16:19–31
272	Harvest (CW)	Deuteronomy 26:1–11; Psalm 100
277	Proper 22	2 Timothy 1:1–14; Luke 17:5–10
282	Proper 23	2 Kings 5:1–3,7–15; Luke 17:11–19
286	Proper 24 (suitable for Bible Sunday)	Genesis 32:22–31; 2 Timothy 3:14 – 4:5
291	Proper 25	2 Timothy 4:6–8,16–18; Luke 18:9–14
295	All Saints' Day	Ephesians 1:11–23; Luke 6:20–31
300	Fourth Sunday before Advent	2 Thessalonians 1:1–12; Luke 19:1–10
305	Third Sunday before Advent (Remembrance Day)	2 Thessalonians 2:1–5,13–17; Luke 20:27–38
310	Second Sunday before Advent	2 Thessalonians 3:6–13; Luke 21:5–19
315	Sunday next before Advent/ Christ the King	Colossians 1:11–20; Luke 23:33–43

Leading all-age worship

Leading all-age worship that is focused around the lectionary is a privilege, as leaders introduce God to people of all ages, of various abilities, learning styles, spiritual maturity and backgrounds.

In Scripture Union, we believe that the ministry of all-age services is vitally important for the following reasons:

- Children and young people benefit because they experience being part of God's new community, as everyone contributes, learns and worships together. Children realise that they matter. Church really is for all ages. Incidentally, children build relationships with a much wider range of people through church than is normally likely in contemporary society. In these services there is a culture where everyone can make a suggestion, have a go, make a mistake and try again.

- Adults benefit as they learn from children and young people, often with a greater variety of approaches than are usually on offer. (All-age services are not an opportunity for Sunday group leaders or people with no responsibility for children to have a Sunday off.)

- Visitors or people on the fringe often feel more comfortable because fewer assumptions are made of them. (It should be OK to just sit and watch. Often churches offer an all-age service at festival times, welcoming to all, free from jargon and appropriate.)

- People with a variety of learning styles and abilities benefit because the interactivity and creativity in evidence in all-age worship require a variety of approaches and responses.

- The team that leads all-age services benefits because the components to a service call for a variety of gifts, encouraging people to take risks, grow in maturity and enjoy being part of a team, since it is a great opportunity for discipleship of team members. Few people can realistically create all-age worship for every Sunday on their own. Most just run out of ideas. What is more, they require a lot of planning and preparation in advance.

- The church is making a statement about the nature of 'church' – everyone matters, all can know and belong to God, all can be included and all can contribute, whatever their age, ability or spiritual maturity. (All-age services, however messy they may be, are one of the most exciting opportunities for church leaders to nurture faith, from any starting point.)

All-age services could be one of three different styles of a meal. All have value but which do you find the most satisfying? Which of these styles best suits your church?

Type of meal	What motivates this choice?	How it is consumed	What's good	What's not so good	How to describe
Soup only	the cook – wants a quick, easy meal	easily digestible	satisfying on a cold day	everyone eats the same whatever their needs or preferences	everything together and comfortable
Buffet meal	the diner – eats whatever takes their fancy	at least one dish for everyone	tasty with variety	not necessarily well balanced	join in when you want to
Three-course meal	the cook – promotes healthy eating, adventurous new dishes	eat in order: starter, main course, dessert	variety, guarantees nurture	hard work for the cook	balanced and nourishing long-term

- How do you make decisions about what happens in your all-age services?
    - [ ] Whatever is easiest
    - [ ] What you have always done
    - [ ] What church members want
    - [ ] What visiting parents and carers want
    - [ ] What the leadership perceives people need spiritually
    - [ ] Who is available at any one time
    - [ ] Other

- What are the good things about your all-age services?
    - [ ] They make the majority of people happy
    - [ ] Children and young people enjoy them
    - [ ] Provide choice
    - [ ] A Sunday off for Sunday group leaders
    - [ ] Encourage spiritual growth
    - [ ] Reach out to those on the fringe
    - [ ] Enable people to grow their gifts
    - [ ] Other

The service outlines in this book assume that the leaders of all-age services are committed to the spiritual growth of everyone present and that ideally every activity should be relevant to some degree for everyone. We have to be honest – this is not always possible, but that, at least, is the aim.

The congregation may include people with disabilities or poor eyesight, those who find reading a challenge, those with strong views on music, the very young or the outsider. In trying to include one group of people, you may connect with several others. For example, using a variety of approaches to learning, those with reading difficulties may feel catered for. As very young children worship with adults who are welcoming, trustworthy and joyful, they will be experiencing something of who God is. The Scripture Union website provides an especially wide range of options for younger children. The *Big Bible Storybook* and the *Tiddlywinks* material, both from SU, are also invaluable resources for this age group.

May God continue to bless you in this vital ministry!

'Tricia Williams

All-age editor

What's in All-Age Lectionary Services Year C?

ACTIVITIES

Bible foundations: a guide to the issues involved in at least two of the set passages for the day plus background information.

Bible reading: suggestions for preparing and presenting the reading of the Bible to the congregation.

Bible retelling: ideas for drama, storytelling and other suggestions for alternative ways of presenting the Bible passage.

Bible talk: engaging ways to share the Bible and discover the message for today in a mixed-age congregation.

Beginning the service and Ending the service: a recognition of how important these are in holding a service together.

Prayer activity: creative ideas for praying in response to the message of the Bible.

Prayers of intercession: suggestions for talking with God on behalf of our world in need.

Prayer of confession: a guide not only to recognising our need of God's forgiveness, but also asking for forgiveness and cleansing.

Helpful extras: a number of additional features including Music and song ideas, Game, Statement of faith and download suggestions.

Notes and comments: further advice or background information on adapting the material for your purposes.

WRITERS

Andy Bell, Janet Berkovic, Sarah Bingham, Vanessa Cato, Matt Campbell, Andrew Chuter, Andrew Clark, Michael Dawson, Jean Elliott, Ian Gooding, Andy Gray, Nick Harding, Darren Hill, Gill Hollis, Lisa Holmes, Nigel Hopper, Mike Law, Eric Leese, Joel Lewis, Jane Maycock, Tim Norwood, Rona Orme, Amy Robinson, Sera Rumble, Hil Sewell, Matt Stone, Ali Walton, John Wilks, Pam Williams, Ro Willoughby, Robert Willoughby, Ruth Wills

WEBSITE

Free downloadable additional resources are presented as follows: (YearC.Proper6_3) – the lectionary year, the specific Sunday and the number of the download for that day. All are available from www.scriptureunion.org.uk/light. Other resources are also available on www.lightlive.org.

ADVENT SUNDAY

READINGS: 1 Thessalonians 3:9–13; Luke 21:25–36
Jeremiah 33:14–16; Psalm 25:1–10

Bible foundations
Aim: to explore how we wait for the Lord's promised return

Jeremiah 33 points towards a time of fulfilled promise while Luke 21:25–36 describes an escalated global picture of what Jesus had previously predicted in verses 20–24. Jesus has been focusing on the events facing Jerusalem and its destruction but now turns his attention to a time of worldwide upheaval that ushers in the judgement of the nations. This is merely the precursor to the main event, the return of the Son of Man and the deliverance he brings. The imagery of the heavenly bodies alludes to Old Testament texts, such as Isaiah 13:10, where they accompany God's judgement of the nations. Another Old Testament allusion is in verse 27, with the phrase, 'Son of Man'.

Jesus' use of the fig tree in his parable was highly appropriate as it was one of the few trees in Israel that loses its leaves in winter. Despite Jesus' words in verse 32 about 'this generation' the emphasis was on God's kingdom and the salvation it brings. 'This generation' was at a climax point in history as Jesus stands among them. The fabric of existence could change and disappear but they would still be left with the truth of God. The only way to get through to the end was to be constantly vigilant and to pray for strength. If not, the end would come as a total surprise.

In 1 Thessalonians 3:9–13 Paul is overjoyed at the way the Christians in Thessalonica were living out their faith and he thanks God for them. It would appear that Paul's desire to be with the church wasn't due to faithless behaviour on their part but is more likely due to some errant teaching, although it did not as such appear to be affecting the way they lived. Paul closes by praying that the believers would remain holy and blameless, until Jesus returns.

Beginning the service

As they come into church, give a few people a slip of paper on which is written this instruction: Count how many signs or indications you observe that the service is about to begin.

Do what you usually do in preparation but ensure that the music group and PA people are very busy getting ready, the welcomers look as though most people have arrived, the leader fusses over arranging their books, furniture is checked to be in the right place; make a lot of fuss. The leader waits without saying anything until everyone is ready. If those involved in the service normally enter from the back or side of the building (such as a choir), let them stand more in evidence than usual.

Welcome everyone and comment that you gave signs that the service was about to begin. Eventually everyone recognised this! Ask how many of these signs were spotted. In this service we'll be looking at the signs that indicate the promised return of Jesus, exploring how we should respond as we wait for him.

Bible reading

Luke 21:25–36 could be accompanied by some powerful sound effects. These are available as an audio download (YearC.Advent1_1) and include the sounds of roaring waves (verse 25), frightened people (verse 26), a trumpet (for the coming Son of Man) (verse 27), summer wind in the trees (verse 30), crashing cymbals (verse 35). Encourage the congregation to open a Bible to follow it. Explain that these words of Jesus contain a series of signs. Ask the congregation to count how many signs are mentioned. See if the congregation can list them all, recording the answers. You will need this list for the **Bible talk.**

Read 1 Thessalonians 3:9–13 and display the following three bullet points as you do so, available as a download (YearC.Advent1_2). These could be shown again towards the end of the **Bible talk.**

- Be strong in faith.
- Love one another.
- Keep yourselves pure and innocent.

Bible retelling

This short play expands upon the **Bible reading** from Luke 21. Two angels (Gladriel and Rebus) have been charged with setting up the signs that point to the fact that Jesus is about to return. We meet them in the early planning stage. Introduce the two angels, who need not be dressed as 'angels'.

Gladriel: Right, item one on the agenda: Get the sun, moon and stars to participate. Rebus, how is that progressing?

Rebus: I can report that we have the union that represents fusion-powered celestial bodies on board: that means the sun and the stars.

Gladriel: I know all about that! Don't take me for a fool just because I don't have an astral diploma in physics.

Rebus: Sorry, I was just pointing out that we are having a little trouble with the moon. It is a bit of a rogue element, neither planet nor

Gladriel: star. So it's holding out for a good deal.

Gladriel: Hmmm. Make sure you find a solution to that. The moon is important as it holds such a prominent place in the night sky. We need all the astral bodies to be involved, otherwise the people who think they are so tough may not faint from terror.

Rebus: That leads me on to my next window of opportunity. The clouds are being a little awkward.

Gladriel: The clouds? They are normally so accommodating – a rain shower here, a torrential downpour there – they even help us out when we need a little fog.

Rebus: Normally, yes, but they seem to be kicking up a fuss. Carrying the Son of Man is not included in their job description.

Gladriel: Why not use the global warming bargaining chip? Promise that as the temperature of the earth increases we'll let them increase precipitation. It'll get warmer but there'll also be more rain. That should persuade them.

Rebus: I'll propose that and see what response I get. But I'm worried that people will still carry on as normal and not understand what is being said.

Gladriel: Apparently the Son of God is going to use one of those stories, those parables, that he tells so well, to make the point.

Rebus: But will we get it all sorted out in time? I am worried that I just don't have the angel power to get it all arranged.

Gladriel: Let me give you some inside information. Apparently everything will be ready at the right time – all part of the great plan. No one actually knows when these things will happen. The point is that we should all make sure we are ready for them and live in the right way.

Bible talk

With: the list of signs from the **Bible reading** activity; three bullet points to display (see the **Bible reading**)

Ask younger members of the congregation what important event is coming up in a few weeks' time. Then ask them: what are the signs to show that Christmas is coming? Most signs will be man-made, such as displays in the windows and fairy lights. At this point, light the first candle in the Advent ring, as a sign that Christians have begun the season of Advent.

Signs of the seasons – so get ready

Ask if anyone can think of signs which signal an event that happens in nature, such as milder winters or wetter summers that might signal global warming, or leaves falling off trees and darker evenings to signal that winter is coming. How do we get ready for the different seasons?

Refer back to the list of signs in the **Bible reading** from Luke 21. Some of the signs may sound frightening such as the strange talk of the sun, moon and stars. It sounds a bit like a film about the end of the world. These signs are not to scare us but are in fact just like the signs that Christmas will soon be here. They show us that Jesus will return to make everything right.

Signs of Christmas – so get ready

Ask younger members to suggest what needs to be done to prepare for Christmas. Answers might include preparing Christmas cards, making or buying presents, or practising for a Christmas event. If you have a carol service, assemblies in a local school or some other special event planned, ask one of the key organisers of it to describe their preparations. (You could pause to pray for this.) If we see the signs that something is about to happen, we need to make sure we are ready. Imagine what it would be like if the date arrived for the Christmas event you have just talked about and no one was ready. Encourage as much audience speculation as possible.

Signs that Jesus will return – so get ready

Invite someone to read 1 Thessalonians 3:9–13. Explain that Paul wrote this letter to a church in the city of Thessalonica some years after Jesus had spoken about the signs that would happen. He wanted to make sure that the church would be ready for when Jesus returned.

Comment that to drive safely we should all know the process of mirror, signal and manoeuvre. Or in first aid one of the rules is the process of airway, breathing and circulation. Paul lays down an equally useful three-way process to living a godly life (see verses 10, 12 and 13). Show the three bullet points from the **Bible reading**. Briefly explain what these mean – that we should keep our lives dependent upon God, that we should love those who also love God and that we should make sure that our lives are holy and acceptable to God. Jesus has promised to return. We shouldn't be afraid or worried because Paul has given us some pretty good advice on how we should act in preparation.

Prayers of intercession

With: enough pieces of A5 card for everyone – these could be prepared beforehand using the text and images as below or available as a download (YearC.Advent1_3); pens or pencils

Remind the congregation of the three-way process from the **Bible talk**. You are going to use the cards to pray for the three ways of getting ready for Jesus' return. Each person should fold their A5 piece of card in half to make a simple A6 booklet.

On the front cover everyone writes something about God that helps them have faith in him, such as 'God cares', or 'God protects me'.

On the inside left page, everyone draws a large heart shape, inside of which they write 'Dear God, help me to love…' and then add the name of someone they want to show more love to – an individual or a group.

On the inside right page create a flash shape and write 'Dear God, help me be pure by…' and then one thing that they can do to be more godly. Explain that this is a private prayer card that no one else needs to see. Give people some ideas such as watching what we say or spending time with God.

On the back page everyone should write 'Amen, until Jesus returns' followed by their name and the date. The card could be decorated and covered with glitter or stickers.

Once the cards have been made, allow a few moments of silent prayer and reflection. Encourage everyone to use the prayer cards throughout the week.

Ending the service

Hold up your card and remind people to put their own card in a conspicuous place all week. Sing a song that emphasises why we can have a strong faith in God.

Helpful extras

Music and song ideas

'Purify my heart'; 'Holy, holy, holy'; 'Holy, holy, holy, Lord God almighty'; 'I am a new creation'; 'Faithful one'; 'Our God is an awesome God'.

Statement of faith

You could use actions to accompany this well-known statement of faith: arms outstretched as in a cross-shape for 'Christ has died'; arms raised up and outwards for 'Christ is risen'; arms held high for 'Christ will come again'.

Christ has died,
Christ is risen,
Christ will come again.

Notes and comments

This is a challenging passage; however, the emphasis is on being ready and prepared for the return of Jesus rather than on becoming obsessed with the predicted signs. There are many references in the New Testament to the fact that the specific time of Jesus' return is known only to the Father.

If the church supports someone working in another part of the country or the world, you could create a large Advent card similar to the one in the **Prayer activity** and encourage everyone to sign it and then send it off in time for Christmas.

Make sure that if you have an Advent ring, you give it a prominent place in the service throughout Advent. Explain that the candles have various meanings, one of which is that the four candles stand for: the prophets; John the Baptist; the Bible; the angels – all of whom brought the good news of Jesus. The large candle stands for Jesus himself.

Alternative online options

Visit www.lightlive.org for additional activities for children, young people and adults.

SECOND SUNDAY OF ADVENT

READINGS: **Malachi 3:1–4; Luke 3:1–6**
Luke 1:68–79 (Benedictus); Philippians 1:3–11

Bible foundations
Aim: to prepare our hearts and lives for the coming of Jesus

John the Baptist bursts upon the scene in a way reminiscent of Elijah – out in the desert, a fiery prophet, set against the rulers of his time, positioning himself clearly within the prophetic tradition (Luke 3:4–6) and bringing God's word of judgement to the people of his day (vs 7–14). His arrival certainly caused a stir since it was a common belief that no prophet had been seen in Israel since Malachi. Luke's language 'the word of God came to John' (v 2) is almost technical language for a prophet appearing. For a prophet to arise seemed to indicate the arrival of the last days, the Day of the Lord and the coming of the Messiah (vs 15–18). This is what had been predicted in Malachi. God will send a messenger who will prepare for God's coming to his people. Malachi seems to be echoing the promise of Isaiah 40:3–5 as Luke does in 3:4–6. Both Malachi and Luke are profoundly eschatological.

Luke is very keen to position John historically in the fifteenth year of Tiberius when Herod Antipas, his brother Philip and Lysanias were the power brokers in the territory, with Annas and Caiaphas as the high priests. We already know of John's birth from Luke 1 and his relationship to Jesus. Luke's Gospel follows his career right to the end, through his imprisonment and uncertainties (7:18–35), including the compliments paid to him by Jesus (7:24–28). His death seems to prefigure that of Jesus and certainly fits in with the fate of prophets who preceded him (13:34,35). Luke, strangely, does not record John's death. (Compare Matthew 14:1–12.) Not that John's death rendered him less of a threat, apparently. Herod seems to have feared that he could be reached by John from beyond the grave (9:7–9). Now that is an admission of real power!

Beginning the service

With: a list of washing or cleaning opportunities that might have occurred today, with the least likely being called out first. For example: washing the dog, cleaning the car, washing the kitchen floor, using the dish washer, washing hair, having a shower, cleaning teeth

Ask everyone to stand and then read out the list, instructing anyone to sit down when a cleaning task they have done today is called out. By the end only a few people will be left and you can declare them the people in the church most in need of deep cleansing! Make sure that this is done in a light-hearted manner. Explain that in the service you will be looking at how the wrong or painful things in our lives need to be 'washed away' as we get ready to welcome Jesus in Advent.

Note: you could light the Advent candles at this point, especially as the second candle is often linked to John the Baptist (see **Notes and comments** from last week) Talk about how light shows up dirt and cobwebs in the darkness.

Bible reading

With: statements from Malachi 3:1–4 (see below and available as a PowerPoint download (YearC.Advent2_1)

Explain that the prophet Malachi was speaking to God's people after they had returned from exile in Babylon to Jerusalem, and the Temple had been rebuilt (although Ezra and Nehemiah had not yet returned) – but times were hard and the people were running out of hope. This led them to make wrong sacrifices and disobey God.

Show the six statements and, after each, check that people understand its broad sense. Then ask everyone to decide whether the statement is a warning or a promise, taking a vote.

When completed, read the Bible verses from Malachi 3 once more to reinforce them. (There are some strong warnings but more promises of God's love and presence.)

Statement cards

> A. I, the Lord All-Powerful, will send my messenger to prepare the way for me.
> B. Then suddenly the Lord you are looking for will appear in his temple.
> C. The messenger you desire is coming with my promise, and he is on his way.
> D. On the day the Lord comes, he will be like a furnace that purifies silver or like strong soap in a washbasin. No one will be able to stand up to him.
> E. The Lord will purify the descendants of Levi, as though they were gold or silver.
> F. Then they will bring the proper offerings to the Lord, and the offerings of the people of Judah and Jerusalem will please him, just as they did in the past.
>
> Malachi 3:1–4 (CEV)

Luke 3:1–6 is a detailed but dramatic reading.

Bible talk

With: a messy task; appropriate floor coverings; bowl of hot water; strong soap; towels; two pieces of white cloth

In advance, find a volunteer to demonstrate a

messy task, something that they would do in normal daily life such as changing a bike tyre or chain, cleaning muddy boots or a sticky saucepan. As the volunteer does their messy task, establish that this is part of their normal life. Ask them to pause to wipe their hands on one piece of cloth and show just how messy their hands have got.

Invite them then to clean their hands thoroughly in warm water with the strong soap (invite children to smell this). Comment on the strength of the soap and the effort needed to ensure their hands are totally clean – they may need more than one bowl of water. Invite them to wipe their hands on the other white cloth. There should be no noticeable marking.

Show the two cloths and contrast them. In our everyday lives, we do some things that make us messy and dirty, so we need to be careful and make sure that we are clean. (Refer to **Beginning the service**.) Explain that this picture helps us understand something about what it is like to follow God. God is good and pure. When we forget him or disobey him, it is as though our clean hands (or a clean piece of cloth) have become messy and dirty. But God is merciful. He wants to make us ready to worship him again. Christians often talk about God's mercy 'washing us clean'.

The different promises and warnings in this prophecy from Malachi are meant to encourage the people of Malachi's time to return to God and give up the wrong things they were doing which were making them messy and dirty in God's eyes. God's message and his coming, which Malachi also predicts, will be 'like strong soap in a washbasin',

getting people ready to obey God again. (Link this to the volunteer's hands being washed with strong soap.)

Conclude by making a link to the message of Luke 3 and the work of John the Baptist. He came to get people ready for God's coming in Jesus, which Malachi foretold. John asked the people of his time, whoever they were, to look at their lives and think about how they were disobeying God. They needed to make a clear change. John knew that the one sent from God would give God's Holy Spirit to people, who would enable them to really be made clean and purified as if they had been washed by strong soap. (Show your cloths again to show the difference.)

Prayer activity

With: paper; coloured pens or pencils

Before the service, identify specific needs for prayer within the church or in the wider world.

Remind people that the prophet Malachi used picture language from real life to talk about God – as a furnace or strong soap. Thinking of God in pictures can help us get ready to welcome Jesus into our lives and can remind us that God wants us to follow him in all of our life.

Distribute pens and pencils and ask adults, young people and children to work together as groups sitting near each other, to think of ideas for pictures that show God's mercy and ability to change or cleanse us. Suggest people either write or draw these. See below for some ideas.

Once back together again, invite people one at a time to call out an idea based on the pictures they have drawn. Follow each statement by a simple prayer asking God to work in one of the situations you have identified before the service. For example:

'God is like a bright street light that suddenly shines in a dark place.' *Lord, we pray for (country name) where there is much darkness – bring healing and peace.*

'God is like a house painter decorating a dirty house and making it beautiful.' *Lord, we pray for (a person's name) who is struggling. May they know that you love them.*

After several pictures, join together in saying the Lord's Prayer.

Prayer of confession

With: bath bombs that change colour or fizz when they touch hot water (divided into smaller portions without crumbling, with enough portions for one each); several large bowls of hot water; a copy of the prayer below, available as a PowerPoint download (YearC.Advent2_2)

Bring the bowls of hot water and the bath bombs to the front. Explain that the bombs are a kind of soap. Refer to today's **Bible reading**, where people need to be 'washed' or changed by God, to get rid of things that are hurtful to themselves or others.

Ask people to think about situations in their lives that they would like to see God change, or actions they have done that they feel need to be 'washed away'. Invite people to come forward and cast a piece of bath bomb into a bowl of hot water. They can stay to pray silently, watching the water change and transform as the bath bomb dissolves. (You could play music or sing a song or hymn emphasising God's forgiveness and healing during this time.)

Invite everybody to speak the following emboldened statements, displayed on the screen or in the notice sheet.

Father God, we have heard your promise to wash us clean, like strong soap.
Take our lives and empower us to know and welcome your Son Jesus, who came as 'God with us'.
John the Baptist said to people who wanted to live God's way, 'Turn back to God and be baptised. Then your sins will be forgiven.' In Jesus, God comes with love to help us and teach us the right way to live.
Amen. Praise to God who washes us pure and clean.

Ending the service

With: a can of air freshener

Walk up and down the church spraying air freshener and declaring, 'Make us clean and pure, Lord God! Make us ready to welcome you!' Conclude by singing a song such as 'Purify my heart' or 'Light of the world'.

Helpful extras

Music and song ideas

Declaring Jesus' coming: 'Christ is the world's light'; 'Lord Jesus Christ, you have come to us'; 'Long ago, prophets knew'. Becoming right with God: 'Be still and know'; 'Change my heart, O God'; 'Breathe on me, breath of God'; 'Purify my heart'. Acting justly to others: 'Beauty for brokenness'; 'For the healing of the nations'; 'Great is the darkness'. Stuart Townend's song 'Light of the world' is a marvellous statement about Christ coming as light for the world to show up darkness and dirt for what it is. There are many other light-focused songs.

Notes and comments

Instead of a psalm, the lectionary recommends using the song of Zechariah known as the 'Benedictus', which Zechariah was inspired by God to pray over his son, John the Baptist, at his birth. In the **Prayer of confession** you could use phrases from the song, instead of the responses suggested:

Leader: John the Baptist was told to tell God's people that they could be saved and all their sins forgiven. God's love and kindness will shine upon us like the sun that rises in the sky.
All: **On us who live in the dark shadow of death, this light will shine to guide us into a life of peace. Amen!**

Alternative online options

For your convenience the following activity is available as a download: YearC.Advent2_3 Songs of praise (based on Luke 1:67–80). Visit www.lightlive.org for additional activities for children, young people and adults.

Christmas Wrapped Up!
(978 1 85999 795 6)

More Christmas Wrapped Up!
(978 1 84427 261 7)

- All-age Advent, Christmas Day and Nativity services
- Assembly outlines
- Christmas quizzes and dramas
- Songs, raps and rhymes

Everything you need to get the most out of Christmas!

For more details, visit www.scriptureunion.org.uk

THIRD SUNDAY OF ADVENT

READINGS: **Zephaniah 3:14–20; Luke 3:7–18**
Isaiah 12:2–6 (Canticle); Philippians 4:4–7

Bible foundations

Aim: to proclaim the good news of repentance and forgiveness as we wait for Jesus to come

Looking at Zephaniah 1, it is clear that Zephaniah belonged to the royal house of Judah. He was prophesying during the reign of Josiah (640–609 BC), a time of religious renewal for the people. In 3:1–8 he speaks of a time when Jerusalem is punished for refusing to fear God and so God punishes the city for her sins. Verses 9–13 look at how God purifies the city from all those who live without God, leaving those who trust in him. Now, in verses 14–20 we see those people celebrating, rejoicing and singing because God has stopped punishing them. He has defeated their enemies. They can stop being afraid. God, as a mighty warrior, has saved them. He is also gentle, rejoicing over them and refreshing them with his love. He heals the lame, gathers everyone back together and brings them safely home. They will prosper again and be able to hold their heads up among other nations. Here is a wonderful picture of God's restoration and renewal of his people as they repent of their sins.

In Luke 3:7–18 John the Baptist speaks of the same theme of repentance and forgiveness, but he does so in the light of the coming of Jesus. He challenges people to 'do something to show that [they] really have given up [their] sins' (CEV), and to 'produce fruit in keeping with repentance' (NIV). The challenge is for those with plenty to share it with those who have little, and for those who are cheating others to stop. As we prepare to celebrate the coming of Jesus into our world, we too are challenged to ask God's forgiveness for living to please ourselves. Then we can know the joy of coming home to our heavenly father, as the people of Jerusalem came home. However, as John the Baptist reminds us, we too are challenged to show that we have given up what causes us to sin in the way that we live.

Beginning the service

With: an opening response based on Zephaniah 3:17 as given below:

Leader: The Lord your God wins victory after victory.
All: He is always with us.
Leader: He celebrates and sings because of you.
All: He will refresh us with his love.

Ask questions such as, 'What happens when we do something wrong?' You're looking for the answer along the lines of having to say sorry or being punished. Or, 'What happens if we do something wrong and we say sorry for doing it?' You're looking for an answer along the lines of making it up with the person we've hurt and being forgiven for it.

Today's service is looking at what happens when we do things that let God down. We'll find out about some people who were happy and who came home when God forgave them and some people who changed the ways they lived after they'd said sorry to God and found his forgiveness. We'll then think about the wrong things we do that let God down, but he forgives us and helps us to live in the way he wants us to live.

Bible reading

A scripted form of Zephaniah 3:14–20 (CEV) is available as a download (YearC.Advent3_1). The words in ordinary type are for the leader to say, while the words in bold are for everyone to say.

A dramatised form of Luke 3:7–18 (CEV) is available as a download (YearC.Advent3_2).

Bible talk

With: several people prepared in advance to mime the actions as below, suitable for all ages

You are going to think about some people who didn't live as God wanted them to. He punished them for a while, but then he sent them a special messenger, Zephaniah, with the promise that he would stop punishing them. Zephaniah would go on to have a reason to celebrate, because God would defeat their enemies and take them back home, because he loved them and they were his.

Explain that you are going to play a game of charades in which some actors will mime actions from Zephaniah chapter 3 and everyone else can put up their hands or call out what the mime stands for. After each mime there are a few words of explanation.

'Celebration' (3:14) **and 'Shout out'** (3:14)
Run these two mimes straight after each other. Explain that Zephaniah told the people of Jerusalem and Judah they would celebrate and shout out because their punishment would be over. The people had all lived just how they wanted to. They had ignored God and hadn't worshipped him. Because of this he would punish them by sending an army from another country to take them away from their home. God has promised them, through Zephaniah, that their enemies would retreat (verse 15).

'King' (3:15)
Mime a king acting in a regal, yet kind way. God, their king would be with his people, so they wouldn't need to worry any more. Their troubles would be over.

25

'Fear' (3:16)
Mime a group of people really afraid. Zephaniah told the people that they wouldn't need to be afraid any more, or worry about what was going to happen next.

'Love' (3:17)
God would comfort the people with his love. He is so big, and strong and mighty (use these words here, if later you're going to sing the song 'My God is so big, so strong and so mighty') that he can defeat their enemies. Eventually, he would comfort all the people with his love, because they pleased him. He takes great pleasure because of them.

'The whole world' (3:19)
The whole world would know that God loves his people. Their enemies would be defeated. The lame and the outcasts whom everyone has despised would be praised. All the people of Jerusalem and Judah would be able to celebrate because God had forgiven their sins and brought their time of sadness to an end.

'Coming home' (3:20)
You could include spoken words as this could be challenging to mime. The Lord promised that because he had forgiven them he would take his people back to their home. He tells them that they will see him with their own eyes and that they will tell him they love him. The people can trust this promise because it is God himself who has made it.

John the Baptist declares a message of hope and challenge
In the New Testament reading, Luke 3:7–18, John the Baptist told people about what Jesus was coming to do. Zephaniah promised the people that one day they would see God with their own eyes. This came true because those who saw Jesus saw God with their own eyes. John the Baptist told people they had to get ready for Jesus to come by showing they were sorry for their sins. Those who had two coats were told to give one away. Those who had lots to eat were told to share it with those who were hungry. The tax collectors were told not to charge people more than they owed. The soldiers were told not to force people to pay them in order to be left alone.

As we get ready for Christmas to celebrate Jesus' coming, we need to get ready by saying sorry to him for the wrong we've done. If we do, we too can shout and celebrate just like the people of Jerusalem and Judah were told to do. Then God will refresh us with his love, like he did for them. But we also need to do what John the Baptist said; we need to do something to show that we are sorry for our sins. We need to ask God for strength to live in the way that he wants us to. And let's say thank you to him for refreshing us with his love.

Prayer of confession
With: either a laptop, data projector and PowerPoint; or an overhead projector, acetate and water erasable pen; or a flipchart stand, flipchart, marker pens, wide decorator's paint brush and white poster paint made up to a thick consistency

John the Baptist said, 'Turn back to God … Then your sins will be forgiven' (Luke 3:3 CEV). We're going to say sorry to God for the things we do which let him down. Suggest what we may need to say sorry to God for, or ask for suggestions. Write these up in a column on one side of the page on the computer screen, acetate or flipchart page. Then ask for suggestions of the opposite: the good, positive ways that God wants us to live. Write those up in a column opposite each of the things to confess.

Lead the congregation in an extempore prayer of confession, bringing to God the things on the list. Conclude by reading 1 John 1:8,9: 'If we say that we have not sinned, we are fooling ourselves, and the truth isn't in our hearts. But if we confess our sins to God, he can always be trusted to forgive us and take our sins away' (CEV).

As a sign that God has kept his promise and taken our sins away, either delete the list of wrong things we have done from the computer or rub them out from the list on the acetate, or paint over them with white paint on the flipchart. Explain that the list of good ways to live will be used in the prayer time later in the service.

Prayer activity

With: the list of good ways to live from the **Prayer of confession**; cut-out shapes of apples in red and green paper, large enough for people to write on; pens or pencils for most people to have one; a tree of some sort (a small Christmas tree or some bare twigs in a pot – big enough for people to place their paper apples on during the prayer time)

John the Baptist said that we should do something to show that we really have given up our sins – 'produce fruit in keeping with repentance' (Luke 3:8 NIV). John said that those who had two coats should give one away, those who had enough to eat should share it with someone else, tax collectors shouldn't make people pay more than they owed, soldiers shouldn't force people to pay them to leave them alone – lots of practical actions. In the prayer time, we're going to pray that God will help us to do the things which show that we really have given up our sins.

Encourage everyone, using things on the list of good ways to live, to write or draw prayers for troubled parts of the world on the apple-shaped paper, asking God to help them perform practical actions. Children may need some help.

Play some quiet music (live or recorded – perhaps the song 'Father, I place into your hands the things I cannot do'). Ask everyone to bring their apples to the 'tree' to place them on it as a way of requesting the things they've prayed for.

When everyone has brought up their apples, lead in a closing prayer to bring all these prayers to God.

Ending the service

With: the following prayer on display available as a download (YearC.Advent3_3)

Everyone joins in with the closing response.

Heavenly Father,
Thank you for forgiving us when we let you down.
Please refresh us with your love.
Pour out your Holy Spirit on us
so that we can show in our lives
the good ways you want us to live.
Be with us as we get ready to celebrate the coming of your Son, Jesus.
We ask these things in his name.
Amen.

The Lord is coming to baptise us with the Holy Spirit and with fire.

Everyone: Come, Lord Jesus!

Helpful extras

Music and song ideas

'My God is so big, so strong and so mighty'; 'The Father's Song (I have heard so many songs)' picks up the idea from Zephaniah 3:17 about God delighting in us – this could be used when people bring their prayers to the front, during the **Prayer activity**; 'Therefore the Redeemed of the Lord' picks up on the people of God returning to Zion with singing; 'The King is among us' relates to the presence of God with his people; 'Light of the World' ('Fire of God') looks forward to Jesus coming with the fire of his Holy Spirit; 'On Jordan's bank' (a more formal hymn) relates to the themes from Luke 3.

Notes and comments

During the **Prayer activity**, use 'Father, I place into your hands' or 'The Father's Song' or any quiet, instrumental piece or recorded music.

If the service contains a baptism of a child, concentrate more on the reading about John the Baptist from Luke 3:7–18 and make the link between baptism, repentance and bearing fruit, pointing out that the child's parents are going to help the child to grow up living the way that God wants us all to live.

If this is a service of Holy Communion ensure that the **Prayer of confession** comes after the **Bible talk**.

In July 2011 a conference of church leaders was held to look into the position of Christians in the Holy Land. Sixty years ago as many as 25 per cent of the population was Christian, many from ancient traditions. The number is now around 1.5 per cent and most Christian activity revolves around western tourism and pilgrimage! It would be appropriate in the light of today's theme to pray for Christians living in Israel/Palestine. An Internet search will yield up-to-date information.

Alternative online options

For your convenience the following activity is available as a download: YearC.Advent3_4 Christmas brainstorm. Visit www.lightlive.org for additional activities for children, young people and adults.

FOURTH SUNDAY OF ADVENT

READINGS: **Micah 5:2–5a; Luke 1:39–45 [46–55]**
Luke 1:46b–55 (Magnificat) or Psalm 80:1–7; Hebrews 10:5–10

Bible foundations
Aim: to celebrate the good news that God is drawing near to us in Jesus

Micah was a prophet who came from the foothills of Judah. He was prophesying at some point between 750 and 686 BC. He brought messages of destruction and messages of hope to the people. Micah 5:2–5a is a prophecy of hope. He looks forward to the coming of a ruler from Bethlehem who will be a caring shepherd for the people. This ruler will bring peace and the whole world will know of his greatness.

In Luke 1:39–56 Elizabeth and Mary look forward to the births of their promised sons. Elizabeth has the eyes of faith, given to her by the Holy Spirit, to see that the child that Mary is carrying is, in fact, her Lord. Her words are a huge encouragement to Mary who has gone to her cousin perhaps seeking peace and quiet after the upheaval in her own home as a result of her unexpected pregnancy.

Mary's song of praise (often referred to as the 'Magnificat', after the Latin translation of its opening word) is a reflection of Luke's concern to bring good news to the poor, oppressed and needy. Mary sings God's praises because he has done great things for her. He has overcome the proud and dragged down kings and princes. Instead, he gives power to the humble and feeds the hungry. Mary celebrates God's faithfulness because he has kept the promise he made to Abraham and he will continue to keep it.

As Christmas approaches we celebrate with Micah, Elizabeth and Mary, the promise of the gift of Jesus, God's Son. We celebrate the fact that, as Hebrews 10:10 reminds us, we have been made holy because Jesus gave his body in sacrifice for us. We are reminded to look forward to Christmas with excitement and anticipation because we have good news that God is drawing near to us in giving us his Son, Jesus.

Beginning the service

With: an Advent calendar or Advent crown

Ask the congregation (especially the children) how long it is until Christmas. Ask how people are feeling as Christmas gets closer and closer. People may say they feel stressed because there's so much to do, or they're sad because someone they love has died since last Christmas. Make sure that you end on a positive note of excitement and anticipation.

Either open the door in the Advent calendar, or light the candles on the Advent crown. Remind everyone that the purpose of Advent calendars and crowns is to help us to look forward to celebrating Jesus' coming at Christmas. Set the scene of the service by saying that we'll be hearing from three Bible characters who celebrated the good news of someone whose task would be to draw people nearer to God.

Bible reading

Read Micah 5:2–5a in three parts and display the verses if appropriate – a CEV version is given below and is available as a download (YearC.Advent4_1)

> **Voice 1 or one section of the congregation:**
> Bethlehem Ephrath, you are one of the smallest towns in the nation of Judah. But the Lord will choose one of your people to rule the nation – someone whose family goes back to ancient times.
>
> **Voice 2 or a second section of the congregation:**
> The Lord will abandon Israel only until this ruler is born, and the rest of his family returns to Israel.

> **Voice 3 or a third section of the congregation:**
> Like a shepherd taking care of his sheep, this ruler will lead and care for his people by the power and glorious name of the Lord his God. His people will live securely, and the whole earth will know his true greatness,
>
> **All voices or the whole congregation together:**
> because he will bring peace.
>
> Micah 5:2–5a (CEV)
>
> **Leader:** This is the word of the Lord.
> **Response:** Thanks be to God.

Luke 1:39–56 could be read as a script in three parts followed by the singing of the Magnificat or the hymn 'Tell out my soul'. The CEV version below is available as a download (YearC.Advent4_2).

> **Narrator:** A short time later Mary hurried to a town in the hill country of Judea. She went into Zechariah's home, where she greeted Elizabeth. When Elizabeth heard Mary's greeting, her baby moved within her. The Holy Spirit came upon Elizabeth. Then in a loud voice she said to Mary:
>
> **Elizabeth:** God has blessed you more than any other woman! He has also blessed the child you will have. Why should the mother of my Lord come to me? As soon as I heard your greeting, my baby became happy and moved within me. The Lord has blessed you because you believed that he will keep his promise.

Narrator: Mary sang a song of praise:
(At this point either continue the reading from Luke 1, or sing Mary's song of praise, in the hymn 'Tell out my soul'.)

Mary: With all my heart
I praise the Lord, and I am glad
because of God my Saviour.
He cares for me, his humble servant.
From now on, all people will say
God has blessed me.
God All-Powerful has done
great things for me, and his name is holy.
He always shows mercy
to everyone who worships him.
The Lord has used his powerful arm
to scatter those who are proud.
He drags strong rulers from their thrones
and puts humble people in places of power.
God gives the hungry good things to eat,
and sends the rich away with nothing.
He helps his servant Israel
and is always merciful to his people.
The Lord made this promise to our ancestors, to Abraham and his family forever!

Narrator: Mary stayed with Elizabeth for about three months. Then she went back home.

Luke 1:39–56 (CEV)

Bible talk

With: the pictures or descriptions of Christmas Day that everyone did in the **Game**, see below

Ask a few children and adults to bring their pictures or descriptions to the front. Show them or read them to everyone else. Ask what it is about Christmas that people really look forward to. People may mention negative aspects of Christmas – feeling stressed because of all that needs doing, the elderly being lonely, quarrels in the family, children squabbling, toys being broken, people being sad because people they love are no longer alive at this family time. Whether we are really looking forward to it, or whether it makes us feel sad for some reason, Christmas is actually all about God drawing near to us by giving his Son Jesus to be born as one of us.

Micah told of a ruler to draw people closer to God

Ask people what they can remember from the reading from Micah. In particular, what was the person like whose arrival Micah was looking forward to? Draw out the fact that, through Micah, God promised his people a ruler who would be a shepherd to care for his people so that they could live in safety and security. He would bring them peace and the whole earth would know how great he was. Everyone looked forward to the coming of this shepherd. We know what Micah didn't know, when he had this message from God, that the shepherd they were expecting was Jesus.

Elizabeth's son would draw people closer to God

Elizabeth and Mary were also looking forward to something exciting happening. Ask people about this – they were both expecting baby sons. Elizabeth knew that her son would be great in God's sight, and that he would get people ready for the Lord to come (Luke 1:14–17). Mary knew that her Son would be called Jesus and that his kingdom would never end (Luke 1:31–33).

Mary's Son would draw people closer to God

When Mary went to see Elizabeth (Luke 1:39–45), Elizabeth's baby jumped for joy and Elizabeth felt him jump. Mary was so happy at what God had done for her that, while she was with Elizabeth, she sang a song of praise to God. Ask if anyone can remember any of the things that Mary said about God in her song of praise. As Mary got ready to celebrate Jesus' birth she knew that God would keep his promises to her and that he would show mercy to everyone who worships him.

So with Micah, Elizabeth and Mary we celebrate the good news that God is drawing near to us in giving us his Son. As we look forward to celebrating the birth of Jesus, we trust God to keep his promises to us, just as he did for Mary, and we thank him for being kind to us because we worship him. Like Micah and his people who celebrated the good news of the loving shepherd, and like Elizabeth and Mary who celebrated the good news that they were expecting their sons to be born, so we celebrate the good news that God is drawing near to us by giving us Jesus.

Prayers of intercession

With: the Taizé chant, 'Magnificat'. If you use the chant, make sure that you explain what the words mean so that people understand what they're singing. Sing the chant to replace the alternative spoken response below, at the end of each section of the intercessions. The spoken response is:
Leader: With all my heart
All: I will praise the Lord.

Leader: Mary said, 'I am glad because of God my Saviour. He cares for me.'
Heavenly Father, thank you for caring for us and loving us, even when we don't love you as much as we could.
With all my heart: **I will praise the Lord**.

Leader: Mary said, 'God drags strong rulers from their thrones and puts humble people in places of power.'
Heavenly Father, thank you for those in government and everyone who leads us in this country. Please give them humble hearts in all that they do.
With all my heart: **I will praise the Lord**.

Leader: Mary said, 'God gives the hungry good things to eat.'
Heavenly Father, we thank you for providing us with all that we need to eat. Help us never to take your generosity for granted. Be with those who are hungry and in need and help us to play our part in providing what they need.
With all my heart: **I will praise the Lord.**

Leader: Mary said that God 'is always merciful to his people'.
Heavenly Father, we thank you that you are merciful to us. We pray today for those who need your special help at this time (at this point pray for any in the church who are ill, bereaved or in need).
With all my heart: **I will praise the Lord**.

Leader: Heavenly Father, we bring you all these prayers in the name of your Son, Jesus Christ, whose coming we are ready to celebrate. Amen.

Ending the service

Heavenly Father,
Thank you for the good news that you have given us your Son Jesus.
Help us to look forward to celebrating his

birth with excitement.
Please fill us with your Holy Spirit
so that we can praise you for your precious gift.
We ask this in the name of Jesus
who came to save us and make us holy.
Amen.

Helpful extras

Music and song ideas

'Come on and celebrate'; 'Tell out my soul'; Taizé chant: 'Magnificat'; 'We declare your majesty'; 'Oh come, oh come, Emmanuel'; 'Emmanuel'.

Game

With: large sheets of paper; crayons and pencils

This isn't a game as such, but is an activity which should be included at some point before the **Bible talk**. Begin by asking people what it is about Christmas that they are looking forward to. Make sure you get answers from children and adults. After a short time of discussion, ask people to either draw a picture or write a brief description of what one thing they are looking forward to. People in mixed-age groups could work on something together. Ask people to keep their writing/drawing until later in the service.

Notes and comments

If there is a baptism of a child, or a dedication or thanksgiving, draw out from the reading from Luke 1 more of the elements of Elizabeth's excitement at being pregnant and her happiness at the reaction of her child to Mary.

If you're using Psalm 80:1–7 draw out the links between the shepherd ruler whom Micah was looking forward to and the shepherd whom the psalmist speaks of, with the promise of restoration. If you use Hebrews 10:5–10, make links between Mary being willing to do God's will and offering herself up to him, and Jesus being willing to do God's will. You could point out that looking forward to Christmas is important because it was Jesus' birth as a human being that enabled him to give himself as a sacrifice so that we can be made holy.

Don't worry if this service is simpler than some of your all-age services. Christmas is such a busy time for everyone that having a slightly simpler, quieter, more reflective service is probably no bad thing.

Alternative online options

For your convenience the following activity is available as a download: YearC.Advent4_3 Adult sermon. Visit www.lightlive.org for additional activities for children, young people and adults.

CHRISTMAS DAY

READINGS: **Isaiah 52:7–10; Luke 2:1–14**
Psalm 98; John 1:1–14

Bible foundations
Aim: to proclaim the good news that Jesus is born

Nothing recorded in the Gospels is there by accident. Everything is there for a purpose. As with the beginning of John the Baptist's ministry, Jesus' birth is placed very specifically during the reign of the Roman emperor, Augustus, and at the time of an imperial census. It is this which caused Jesus to be born in Bethlehem, his ancestral home, rather than in Nazareth where he then lived after his return from Egypt (Luke 2:1–5). Luke cares for history and getting his facts right (Luke 1:1–4).

But why record the dramatic proclamation of Jesus' birth to a bunch of common shepherds, who hardly seem to be geared up for what was to happen to them? It could simply be that Luke wishes to demonstrate how the coming of Jesus turns all expectations of significance and status upside down. After all, Jesus' mother had said this very thing (Luke 1:51–53). Shepherds did not have a particularly good reputation among town dwellers. They could, however, trace their heritage back to a certain King David (see Psalm 23) and God is sometimes spoken of as a shepherd (Ezekiel 34).

It could also be that the revelation to the shepherds recalls the prophecy of Isaiah 52:7–10. The picture here is of watchmen in Jerusalem looking out over the hillsides and seeing the fantastic good news being brought to them from that quarter. This is not so unusual. After all, Israel had met with God in the most significant but perhaps unexpected way in Sinai, following the Exodus from Egypt. That God should herald his good news from the mountains and wastelands beyond Jerusalem is a fairly solid biblical tradition – and one which is amply fulfilled when the shepherds encounter the angels and become the messengers of good news.

Beginning the service

With: a large gift-wrapped box, containing an individually wrapped baby doll (or the figure of Jesus from your crib), a Good News Bible and a heart shape

Wish everybody a happy Christmas, then declare that the church has been sent a gift! Ask the children to help you unwrap it. As the children produce each item, name it and hold it up for everyone to see. Explain that we have been sent the good news that God loves us and gave us his Son.

If you have a nativity scene, ask children to place the three items there, the baby in the manger with the Bible and the heart beside it, to act as a focal point for the service. Sing a carol that features the word 'joy' or 'good news'.

Bible reading

Read Isaiah 52:7–10 and encourage the congregation to listen out for the word 'joy' (which comes twice in the NIV) and to give a shout of joy when they hear it. You could ask them to cheer, applaud or shout alleluia! The reader, or a leader, will need to lead the shouting so that everyone joins in.

During the reading of Luke 2:1–14 children could perform a nativity scene, by miming the various movements. There can be enough shepherds and angels for every child to get involved, including any visitors. Provide suitable simple props. The reader should read slowly, leaving pauses for the action'.

Bible talk

With: eight large cards on which are written one of the letters to spell 'GOOD NEWS' – a PowerPoint version of these letters arranged to spell the different words/phrases is available as a download (YearC.Christmas_1)

Ask everyone to turn to somebody near them and share the best piece of news they have heard all year. It could be personal news like the birth of a grandchild, or a wedding; or it could be national or international news. Ask for a few examples. Then ask people to comment on how many people they shared their good news with. How did they do it? How did they feel about sharing it?

Remind the congregation of **Beginning the service**, asking children if they can remember what was found in the box and what it meant. One of the gifts was a Good News Bible. Why is a Bible called 'Good News'? Usually when we have good news we tell lots of people, but first we have to know what the good news is that we have been given.

Read the message of the angels from Luke again: 'Don't be afraid! I have good news for you, which will make everyone happy. This very day in King David's home town a Saviour was born for you. He is Christ the Lord. You will know who he is, because you will find him dressed in baby clothes and lying on a bed of hay.' (CEV)

So where is the good news in the Christmas story? Ask eight volunteers of all ages to come to the front and give each of them one of the letter cards. Explain that these cards spell several words which connect with Christmas and include some of the most important things. Ask if anyone can work out the Christmassy words that they spell, and eventually arrange them so that the letters spell the following:

'SNOW!'
Give the clue: white stuff that falls from the sky. Christmas cards, songs and carols often mention snow at Christmas, but we don't often get to see it! It's probably not the most important thing about Christmas.

'NEW GOODS'
Give the clue: presents that are new. Ask how many people have already opened their presents. Did they get what they wanted? If they haven't opened them yet, what are they hoping to unwrap later? We like to give and receive 'new goods' at Christmas because it reminds us of a special gift God gave us – but presents aren't the most important part of Christmas.

'GOD NOW' and 'GOES DOWN'
Give the clues: God is not just for yesterday or tomorrow and has only six letters. We're getting closer, but the E and the S have been left out, so we'll have to put them back although Christmas is all about God with us, Emmanuel. Rearrange the cards to spell 'GOES DOWN' with the clue: Jesus came down to earth.

'GOOD NEWS'
Jesus was God incarnate – he came down to earth from heaven so that we could know him. Finally, arrange the cards to spell 'GOOD NEWS'. Jesus was the good news that Isaiah predicted in today's reading, and that the angels sang about: the good news of salvation. Through him, our sins are forgiven and we have eternal life.

To end, explain that the gift of good news is not just for us. Once we have been given it, we can give it to other people. It's the most important thing that we can give at Christmas or at any time. The reading from Isaiah shows how welcome the good news is to people who have been waiting for it. The final two lines of the reading from Isaiah are repeated in Psalm 98: 'All the ends of the earth will see the salvation of our God.' That is what the shepherds did, as they rushed to see the Saviour and then went back praising God and inevitably sharing the news with others. Encourage the congregation to see those words from the Old Testament as a prophecy of hope and a challenge – the good news of Christ's salvation is ours to give.

Prayer activity

With: candles and holders, or tapers, one for everyone; one lit candle

Ask a child, 'If I gave you ten pounds, and you gave it to your mum, would you then be able to spend it?' Explain that the good news is not like something that you have to give up to give it away. Instead, it's like a candle flame – however many candles you light with it, your flame is still the same size.

Explain that you are going to represent the spreading of the good news by filling the church with light from your one candle flame. Ask people to pass the flame on when they receive it, but to do it slowly and prayerfully. As they pass the flame, they can think of a person, country or situation that needs the good news, and pray that God would use them to help share it. As they receive the flame, they thank God for sending Jesus into our lives, and for the people who were instrumental in their own faith.

There are some suggestions for music while this is going on, in **Music and song ideas** below.

Prayer of confession

With: the objects from **Beginning the service**

Introduce these prayers by referring back to the gifts that were opened in **Beginning the service**, and explain that when we open a great present, we don't just put it straight down and forget about it – we use it! The time of confession is an ideal time to use the gift of love and the good news of forgiveness that we have been given.

Ask everyone to quietly think of something that they would like to be forgiven for, and allow a few moments of silence before saying the general confession, or using this prayer all together. It is available as a download (YearC. Christmas_2).

Father God, we know that we have done many wrong things that have hurt you, your world and other people.

We are very sorry.

Thank you for sending us the gift of your Son, and showing us how much you love us.

Thank you for the good news of your forgiveness – please forgive us now. Amen.

Ending the service

With: the nativity scene; copies of Gospels to give away; chocolate!

The shepherds who visited the stable may not have brought any gifts with them, but they received a gift when they were there – the good news that the angels had been singing about. Encourage the congregation to visit the 'stable' (or some other suitable place) before they leave. There they can collect a gift to take away with them: a copy of a Gospel and something sweet! Explain that these are to remind us of the gift of the good news that God gave us and that we now have to give. Members of the congregation may wish to pass on their Gospel and the good news to someone else over Christmas.

Many Christian bookshops sell little cards telling the Christmas story, which may be more suitable to give to children than a whole Gospel; or you could print your own to include the words 'Good news' as a heading. Scripture Union publishes four *Bauble books* and *Happy Christmas*, all of which would be suitable for this.

Helpful extras
Music and song ideas

You will probably want to sing traditional carols today, especially if you expect people to be in church who do not usually attend but may know traditional carols. *Carol Praise* (HarperCollins*Publishers*) is a valuable collection of Christmas carol arrangements, new and old. Here are suggestions of child-friendly songs linked to the readings: 'How lovely on the mountains' ('Our God reigns') Isaiah 52; 'Go tell it on the mountain' Isaiah 52; 'You shall go out with joy' Psalm 98; 'The candle song' by Graham Kendrick, John 1; 'The Calypso Carol' Luke 2; 'Come and join the celebration' Luke 2.

If you have a choir, you may wish to include the choral carol, 'This is the truth sent from above' which is about spreading the good news.

During the **Prayer activity**, sing or play background music with themes of light such as 'The candle song' (above). Other carols include 'Torches'; 'O little town of Bethlehem'; 'Silent night'; the Taizé song 'The light of Christ (has come into the world)'.

Statement of faith

This is also available as a download (YearC.Christmas_3).

Leader: We have the good news.

Child: What is the good news?

All: That there is one God, who is our Father and made the world and everything in it.

Leader: We have the good news.

Child: What is the good news?

All: That the Lord Jesus Christ, the only Son of God, the Light, came down from heaven to save us and was born of the Virgin Mary on the first Christmas day.

Leader: We must spread the good news.

Child: What is the good news?

All: That Jesus was crucified for us, died and was buried: but three days later he came to life again and ascended into heaven where he reigns as king. His kingdom is everlasting.

Leader: We can spread the good news.

Child: How can we spread the good news?

All: **Because Jesus sent us a helper, the Holy Spirit, who is one with the Father and with Jesus, who spoke through the prophets and speaks to us today. This is our good news for all the world.**

Notes and comments

For a Christmas Communion service, the Gospel reading could become the focus as the song of the angels is repeated in the Gloria and at the end of the **Statement of faith** suggested above.

As an alternative or an addition to the **Prayer activity**, the spreading of the good news could also be represented by passing the bread and wine round the congregation; alternatively, coming up to the altar rail could be linked to coming to receive from the Christ child, and tied in with the suggestion for **Ending the service**.

If you use John 1:1–14 as the Gospel reading option, make reference in the **Bible talk** to Jesus as the Word (linking to good news), John the Baptist as the messenger (spreading the good news) and Jesus as the Light (linking to the **Prayer activity**).

Don't forget to light the central candle in the Advent ring/crown.

Alternative online options

For your convenience the following activity is available as a download: YearC.Christmas_4 Good news march for 5s and under. Visit www.lightlive.org for additional activities for children, young people and adults.

FIRST SUNDAY OF CHRISTMAS

READINGS: **Colossians 3:12–17; Luke 2:41–52**
1 Samuel 2:18–20,26; Psalm 148

Bible foundations

Aim: to set out to follow the example of Jesus in goodness and wisdom

The New Testament fairly frequently presents Jesus in terms of Old Testament Wisdom. This Wisdom is sometimes personified, though scholars differ over whether Wisdom was ever thought of as an actual person. (See Proverbs 8:22–31.) Writing about Wisdom became even more common between the Old Testament and the New. So Jesus' statement in Matthew 11:28–30 clearly reflects Ecclesiasticus (or Sirach) 51:23–27 (found in the Apocrypha), contrasting the 'yoke' of discipleship to him with that of Jewish legalism. John 1:1–18 also picks up many Wisdom motifs, applying them to Jesus. The visit of the Magi in Matthew 2:1–12 suggests how oriental wisdom travels to Bethlehem to find its ultimate fulfilment in the Christ child. In Luke 2:41–52 there is a kind of equivalent passage describing Jesus' discussion with the wise elders of his time. He is already moving beyond the control of his parents and confounds the assembled rabbis with his insight (vs 41–47). His parents may not have understood what was going on but this rather self-possessed child is an embodiment of Wisdom which far outstrips his peers. The Sermon on the Mount and much of the rest of Jesus' teaching can be read largely as Wisdom teaching.

Colossians also draws heavily upon what the Old Testament says about wisdom, to describe the majesty and significance of Christ. For example, Wisdom's role in creation described in Proverbs 8:22–31 is transferred to Christ, in Colossians 1:15–20: the 'image of God' (v 15) and the agent of creation (vs 16,17). This is contrasted in chapter 2 with other forms of death-dealing 'wisdom' involving rules and regulations (vs 16–19). This belongs to an old life which has to be put to death (3:5) to allow for the beauty of life lived by the Spirit and for spiritual wisdom to thrive. The characteristics described in Colossians 3:12–17 are all about goodness and wisdom. Christians can foster that life, putting on suitable 'clothes' (v 12) and behaving in ways that promote wise and holy living (vs 15–17).

Beginning the service

With: the crib scene

Spend a few moments comparing Christmas memories of gifts, fun moments or bad cracker jokes with the congregation. Recognise that after Christmas we pack away the decorations, find shelves for all the new toys and then start thinking about other things. Point out the church's nativity scene (if you have one) and show that Jesus is still there, in the manger. Not only is the Christmas season not over in the church's year, but the story of Jesus in our lives is certainly not over. The season of Epiphany has yet to begin.

After Christmas we have a choice – do we pack Jesus away with the crib scene, or do we follow him into the rest of his story? Explain that today's theme is all about following Jesus, finding out more about the person he grew up to be and seeing if we can be like him.

An alternative service starter can be found under **Game** in **Helpful extras**.

Bible reading

While reading Colossians 3:12–17, volunteers could 'clothe' a Christmas tree (or decorate the pulpit, lectern or church) with the many words mentioned. These would have to be printed onto card, large enough to be legible, and coloured or decorated in some way. They could be handed out to volunteers of all ages before the reading begins and added to the display by each person as they hear their word in the reading. This would illustrate Paul's metaphor of clothing in the reading. In the NIV version (given below), the words needed for the first half of the reading would be: compassion, kindness, humility, gentleness, patience, forgiveness and love. If you wished to continue after verse 14 you could add gratitude, although this is not part of Paul's original clothing metaphor!

> Therefore, as God's chosen people, holy and dearly loved, clothe yourselves with **compassion, kindness, humility, gentleness** and **patience**. Bear with each other and forgive whatever grievances you may have against one another. Forgive as the Lord forgave you. And over all these virtues put on love, which binds them all together in perfect unity. Let the peace of Christ rule in your hearts, since as members of one body you were called to peace. And be thankful. Let the word of Christ dwell in you richly as you teach and admonish one another with all wisdom, and as you sing psalms, hymns and spiritual songs with **gratitude** in your hearts to God. And whatever you do, whether in word or deed, do it all in the name of the Lord Jesus, giving thanks to God the Father through him.
>
> Colossians 3:12–17 (NIV)

Bible talk

With: a plant; three cards with the following lines on: a wavy line, a speech bubble and 'Belongs to…'/name label on one side, and the words PEACE, WORD and NAME on the other

Show a green plant and ask what is needed for it to grow. Older children should be able to list water, soil and sunlight, and have some idea of what each one is useful for. As you talk about them, ask three volunteers to hold up the cards, the word-side first and then the picture-side facing the congregation.

In the Gospel reading today, Jesus grew in wisdom, and if we want to follow him and be like him, then we need to grow in wisdom too. The reading from Paul's letter to the Colossians mentioned three things that, just like the plant, we need in order to be able to grow and live: The PEACE of Christ, the WORD of God and the NAME of the Lord Jesus. These words will be repeated, and to sustain involvement, you could encourage everyone to perform an action each time they hear one of the words. You could use British Sign Language, or point to the heart for 'peace', the mouth for 'word', and the head for 'name'. Go through these three words as follows, asking each volunteer to turn their picture card around as you do so.

Peace

Ask what is meant by this. You may get answers such as stillness and calm or absence of war and chaos. Jesus' death means that we can be at peace in our relationship with God, and also that we can live with one another (in the world and in the church family) without fighting. There is order not chaos, calm not riots and kindness not anger. Just like the gentle waves of the sea. (Show the wavy line.)

Word

Jesus is called the Word of God. You could refer to John 1:1 which may have been read during the Christmas period. The message about him is also called the Word. He spoke words of truth. We call the Scriptures the Word of God too. Hearing and responding to what we know of Jesus and what we have heard him say needs to fill our lives. Knowing God and sharing him is top priority. (Show the speech bubble.)

Name

A name identifies who we are or where we are. Give some examples, ending with a name label on school uniform or in a book. If we belong to the Lord Jesus, we go by his name and we live our lives in his name. People discover him by what they see of him in those who bear his name. (Show the 'Belongs to' card.)

The Gospel reading about the 12-year-old Jesus in the Temple shows us that Jesus was demonstrating all these things as he grew in wisdom. Jesus was obedient to his parents and grew up as an ordinary boy. His message did bring division to families where there were those who served him and those who did not – that is still the case – but it is not Jesus who produced the lack of peace. Talk about how we can bring peace within families, communities and in the wider world. Include how we can proclaim the peace that Jesus brings between all people and God. Refer to the message of the angels to the shepherds. We need to grow in our ability and willingness to love and forgive.

Then talk about how the Word of God can fill our lives. Jesus was asking questions in the Temple as well as giving answers. He wanted to find out what the priests and teachers there could tell him about God's Word. He read the Scriptures as all Jewish boys did. He grew in his understanding of his identity. Talk about the opportunities at the start of a new year to get to know God better – new year's resolutions that last. We need to teach each other in a variety of ways as suggested by Paul in Colossians 3.

Finally, talk about how Jesus lived in a way that pleased God, in a way that was what was expected of anyone who goes by the name of God. Jesus told his parents that he was in his Father's house. He knew exactly who he was. Talk about how others might see Christ by the way that we live. Give some specific examples.

Prayer activity

With: blank cards or sticky notes, one for everyone; pens or pencils

Remind the congregation of Psalm 148 or read a short part of it, or leave it until this point in the service to read it all. Then read Colossians 3:16, commenting that Paul recommends, as a means to let the Word of Christ dwell in us richly, that people 'sing psalms …with gratitude in your hearts to God'. Gather into groups (or, with smaller numbers, this could be done as a whole congregation) to create a psalm of praise and gratitude in the style of Psalm 148. Each person has a card or sticky note on which they write or draw a part of God's creation. These are laid out beside each other and a reader from each group can 'read' the psalm by adding 'Praise the Lord, you…' before each word or picture. The reader could finish by adding verses 13 and 14 of the original psalm.

The finished cards could be kept and displayed somewhere to create a song of praise to which the whole congregation has contributed.

Prayer of confession

With: words from Colossians 3 (see **Bible reading**)

As an introduction to a liturgical prayer of confession, read through Colossians 3:12–17 again slowly, or use the key words that were displayed during the **Bible reading** to 'clothe' the Christmas tree. Encourage people to think quietly of examples in their own lives when they have not been kind, humble, compassionate, gentle, patient, forgiving and loving. These could then be spoken one by one with a congregational response, or the general confession could be said.

Ending the service

With: printed cards in a basket

Read Colossians 3:15–17 as part of the dismissal. Baskets of cards are available as people leave, containing cards with these Bible verses and either 'The Peace of Christ', 'The Word of God' or 'The name of the Lord Jesus' printed on them. The three symbols would be a good reminder of the points made in the **Bible talk**. Invite people to pick up the card or cards that they feel are most relevant to take home with them.

Helpful extras

Music and song ideas

You will probably wish to sing Christmas carols today, but here are some suggestions for hymns and songs with the theme of following Jesus: 'O Jesus, I have promised'; 'The Servant King'; 'Will you come and follow me?'; 'Give me oil in my lamp'.

The full version of 'Once in royal David's city' includes verses about children following Jesus in the way that he grew up, which are particularly appropriate to the Gospel reading and the season.

The following two hymns are inspired by Psalm 148 and could be sung as well as, or instead of, the reading, or sung or played during the **Prayer activity**: 'O praise ye the Lord'; 'All creatures of our God and King'.

Game

The following variation on a Victorian parlour game, 'Do as I do' could be used for **Beginning the service**, or as an illustration later on.

Two people are chosen to be the leaders. Each chooses a different continuous action, for example nodding the head or tapping a foot – although they can be sillier than that!

The leaders have to approach somebody else and say 'My master says do as I do' while demonstrating their action. The person being spoken to starts performing the action, and finds another person and says 'My master says, do as I do' to them. This is repeated many times. The object of the game is a competition between the two actions, each leader aiming to have everybody performing their action at the same time, so the moment an action is passed on, the recipient must pass it to as many people as possible without being stopped by someone telling them to do the other action.

This game can lead into a discussion about whose example we follow, and how we know that what they are doing is good. Sometimes it can seem very confusing, with people giving us different messages. When someone says, as in the game, 'My master says, do as I do', we need to check carefully which master they are following! We can trust Jesus because of who he is. He speaks with God's authority. He is the Master whose message we then pass on.

Notes and comments

The theme of following Jesus is very appropriate for a baptism. If an infant baptism is taking place during this service, the theme of growth could be developed, comparing the Gospel reading with the reading from 1 Samuel. The **Bible talk** could be illustrated by the water, oil and candle used in the baptism, rather than using the plant imagery.

Alternative online options

Visit www.lightlive.org for additional activities for children, young people and adults.

SECOND SUNDAY OF CHRISTMAS

READINGS: **Ephesians 1:3–14; John 1: [1–9] 10–18**
Jeremiah 31:7–14; Psalm 147:12–20

Bible foundations
Aim: to celebrate God's big plan for his world and his people

The world is a place of bewildering complexity, with a rich and varied past and an uncertain future. In order to make sense of both reality and our place within it, human beings have often sought to understand history (past, present and future) in terms of a 'big story'. This can be expressed as a religion, an ideology, for example Marxism, or a secular belief in human progress.

The Bible contains the Christian's 'big story', revealed to us by God himself. As Ephesians 1 makes clear, the key events in this amazing story do not occur by chance; rather they reflect God's 'plan' for both his people and the whole created order (1:10). This plan began before the creation of the world (v 4; John 1:1) and has been worked out in human history, reaching its focal point with the coming of Jesus into the world (v 9). Jesus' life and his death on the cross bring forgiveness and freedom (or 'redemption') from the sin which enslaves us (v 7).

This story of God's salvation and love becomes our story, when we believe in Jesus (v 13). God has good things in mind for his people (Psalm 147:12–14; Jeremiah 31:7–14), for at the heart of his purposes is a community who will be his children (Ephesians 1:5). We await the future grand climax of God's big plan and our full and completed salvation (v 14), when we will take our place as part of a renewed and unified creation under the Lordship of Christ (v 10). As we reflect on this story of God's lavish and glorious grace in Christ (vs 7,8), we too join with Paul in this celebratory hymn of praise. It will also motivate us to 'live for the praise of his glory' (v 12), for every person present in this all-age service has a part to play in God's great plan.

Beginning the service

Each new year we often make plans and resolutions. (Ask for some examples.) Experience suggests that on average such human resolutions last for only five days. At the start of this year we are celebrating God's plan to save his people. We are celebrating God's purposes which lasted not merely for days but centuries. He planned for everything to come under Jesus' control. It is not surprising therefore that this service will be full of praise.

Bible reading

Ephesians 1:3–14 is available as a download (YearC.Christmas2_1). If you use this option from the NIV, create an effect of praise with one voice or half of the congregation stating truths which are then echoed and amplified. This also has the advantage of simplifying the grammar to make the passage more accessible.

Slowly and meditatively read John 1:10–18 (and 1–9 if you choose) accompanied by the following images: verse 10 (a globe or view of earth from space); verse 11 (a cross); verse 12 (the name 'Jesus'); verse 13 (a picture representing adoption or Adoption Day Card or the word Adoption); verse 14 (footprints); verse 15 (an arm giving directions); verse 16 (an overflowing glass or picture of abundance); verse 17 ('Grace and truth' – there are images of this on the Internet where the 't' of the word 'truth' is designed as a cross); verse 18a (the word 'God' out of focus); verse 18b (the word 'God' in focus).

Alternatively, for a vigorous and forceful version of this passage, use *The Street Bible* by Rob Lacey.

Bible talk

With: five large card jigsaw pieces to form a rectangular jigsaw (four corners and central piece), assembled on a board with sticky tack/pins. (The centre piece is labelled 'in Christ', the four corner pieces are 'us'; 'from before creation'; 'forgiveness' and 'the praise of his glory'. The pieces 'from before creation', 'forgiveness' and 'the praise of his glory' to be the same colour card indicating they belong together – the three story elements of beginning, middle and end.) This is available as a download (YearC.Christmas2_2). Alternatively, these five words/phrases could be stuck inside the pages of a very large book, which connects with the idea of a storybook.

We are often asked to write stories at school. In planning a story, a number of decisions have to be made. We choose the characters, decide on the plot or story itself (which has a beginning, a middle and an end) and settle on the climax or resolution at the end. You could refer to your favourite story.

God has a plan which is for us to live life to the full. This plan is referred to in the reading from Ephesians 1.

God chose his characters
Amazingly, God chose us (verse 11) to work with him. There was no casting and choosing of film stars and famous celebrities. He chose us! (Put the first corner of the jigsaw in place.)

God decided on the beginning
There was a beginning and verse 4 tells us that God's plan was taking shape from before the creation of the world. We often seem to live from day to day, minute by minute, but God had an overview. (Put the second corner, 'from before creation' in place.)

The middle of the story
The middle of the story is that now we can enjoy his forgiveness – verse 7. (Put the third corner, 'forgiveness' in position.) Briefly explain what forgiveness is and why it was necessary, using language that is easy for people of all ages to understand.

The end of the story
The end of the story is referred to in verses 12 and 14. It is that we shall live for the praise of his glory. (Put in place the fourth corner, 'the praise of his glory'.)

God's solution
The key part of this plan that holds everything together is Jesus Christ. (The central interlocking section that holds the four corners in place is positioned. It is labelled 'in Christ'.) This plan was not small in scale. It was a plan for the world, for all time and for God's people.

Prayer activity

With: pieces of paper with 'Thank you, God' written at the top; pens/pencils

After Christmas we often write thank you letters, emails or texts to thank people who have given us presents. We are now going to do the same to God.

Read John 1:16: From the fullness of his grace we have all received one blessing after another. Then read Ephesians 1:8: He lavished on us the riches of his grace.

Invite everyone to write down or draw some of the presents God has given to them, we could even say, lavished on them. The 'thank you notes' are collected and offered to God.

Alternatively, signing can be used to emphasise key ideas in the following prayer. The signs suggested are from British Sign Language: www.britishsignlanguage.com/words/list.php. The signs for 'good', 'Jesus', 'guide', 'children' and 'thank you' need to be introduced and practised in a lively, friendly way. The instructions can be shown on a screen and/or you may have a member of the congregation who can sign. (The sign for 'Guide' is not included on the suggested website so use the following sign: right hand grasps the tip of the left fingers and pulls the left hand forward.)

The leader uses the following prayer:

At the beginning of a new year we praise God for his goodness. **(Good)**

Lord God, you sent us a teacher. You sent Jesus. **(Jesus)**

You sent us the Saviour to die for our wrongs.

You sent us light to guide us. **(Guide)**

You gave us truth.

You gave us the right to become children of God. **(Children)**

You gave us one another for support and help.

From you we have received one blessing after another.

We praise you, God, for the good things you have lavished on us. **(Good)**

good things in our own life,

in our own family,

in our own church.

Lord, we thank you. **(Thank you)**

A song of praise could immediately follow, or the congregation could listen to a song such as 'Saviour, I must sing (Saviour of the World)'.

Prayer of confession

This is based on Ephesians 1.

Lord God, you chose us to be holy and blameless in your sight.
Yet so often we fall short of your standards.
Lord, we are sorry that we let you down.
At times we go our own way, do our own thing and ignore you.
We are to blame.
We need you to forgive us and make us clean and make us new.
We thank you that you had a plan.
You sent Jesus and in him we have forgiveness of sins.
In him we are made clean.
Thank you.

Prayers of intercession

With: the pictures used to illustrate the reading from John as a focus for intercessions

The person leading these intercessions needs to provide relevant information.

Lord, we remember the troubled places of the world *(show the picture of a globe or view of earth from space)*, especially…

We remember those who work to bring aid and help but are persecuted and misunderstood *(show a picture of the cross)*. In particular we pray for…

We pray for those who work as missionaries bringing the light of the knowledge of Jesus *(look at the name 'Jesus')*. We think of…

We pray for our families, asking that we can appreciate one another *(show the picture representing adoption or Adoption Day Card)*. We ask for…

We pray for those who provide role models for others *(show the footprints)*. We ask for help as we, in our turn, model godly living to others.

We pray for our teachers *(show an arm giving directions)*. Especially we pray for schools and those who work in schools in this congregation…

We pray for a thankful heart *(show the picture of an overflowing glass or a picture of abundance)*. We bring to mind those people who are bitter…

We pray for our church leaders *(look at picture of 'Grace and truth')*. May they teach accurately and speak out against the injustices of our time…

Lord, we are so preoccupied with our physical health: our hearts, our hearing, our sight *(look at the word 'God' out of focus then the word 'God' in focus)*. May we have hearts devoted to you and eyes and ears for you this week.

Ending the service

With: a memory verse on display, either John 1:14 or 1:18 or whatever verse is relevant for the church in the coming year

We have remembered that new year's resolutions are quickly broken. We have thought of God's resolve to bring all things together in Christ. Many individuals (and churches) choose a Bible verse to act as a memory verse for the year. In today's reading John 1:14 (or verse 18) is central. Have you thought of having a memory verse for the year? One of these two verses would be appropriate. A simpler verse that talks about Jesus as light may be more appropriate for children, such as 'Jesus said, "I am the light of the world."' John 8:12

'The Word became flesh and made his dwelling among us. We have seen his glory, the glory of the one and only Son, who came from the Father, full of grace and truth.' John 1:14 (NIV)

We can resolve to honour God's 'one and only' this coming year.

Helpful extras
Music and song ideas

For the start of a year: 'Lord, for the years'; 'O God beyond all praising' in which we trust God for our 'tomorrows'; 'Be thou my vision'.

God's plan: 'Long ago, prophets knew' celebrates God's timeless plan; 'God is working his purpose out'; 'Who would think that what was needed' compares a human plan with God's surprising plan in sending Jesus; 'Love divine' celebrates new creation, great salvation and restoration.

Songs to listen to: 'Saviour, I must sing' praises God for his gifts of life and liberty and Jesus the Saviour, available on *Focus on… Redemption* Kingsway Music CD; 'There is a Redeemer' picks up the ideas of the name of Jesus and the gift of the Holy Spirit; 'Oh, the mercy of God' (based on the Ephesians reading) by Geoff Bullock, Kingsway Thank you Music.

Statement of faith
This is based on John and is available as a download (YearC.Christmas2_3).

Notes and comments
There is a visual presentation of John 1:1–5,14 which is available on *Just Worship DVD Video Resources Volume 1*. The clip can be embedded in a PowerPoint presentation.

Alternative online options
Visit www.lightlive.org for additional activities for children, young people and adults.

EPIPHANY

READINGS: **Ephesians 3:1–12; Matthew 2:1–12**
Isaiah 60:1–6; Psalm 72:[1–9] 10–15

Bible foundations

Aim: to celebrate the way God reveals himself to people of different races and nationalities – Jews and Gentiles

In Ephesians 3:1–12, Paul continues to elaborate upon God's big plan for his world, which he introduced to his readers in chapter 1. This plan is described as a 'mystery' (1:9; 3:3–6,9). When we hear this word, we instinctively think in terms of something secret and inexplicable as in, say, an Agatha Christie murder mystery. In the New Testament, however, a 'mystery' refers to a truth which was once concealed and beyond human understanding but which has now been revealed by God himself (3:3,5). The 'mystery of Christ' (3:4) is concerned with how Gentiles (non-Jews), as well as Jews, are welcomed by God into his family.

While the Old Testament focuses primarily on God's love and goodness towards Jews, we do get glimpses of a time when he will reveal himself to all nations (see Isaiah 60:3 and Psalm 72:8–11). The picture of pilgrimage and of different races worshipping God that is found in these two Old Testament references is echoed in a startling way by the experience of the Gentile 'Magi' who travelled to meet the newly born Jesus (Matthew 2:1–12). However, the 'mystery of Christ' (Ephesians 3:4) which lay at the heart of Paul's gospel far exceeded such hopes. Through the gospel of Christ, God has brought a new international community into existence so anyone who believes, whatever race or nationality, can enter into the full privileges and benefits of salvation. This means being a member of God's family (3:6) and enjoying the 'boundless riches of Christ' (3:8). The Church is a multi-racial humanity (2:15) and as such it is a key dimension in God's plan for a renewed and united creation (1:10). Here is a challenge to everyone present in this service, to be as one people to make this mystery known to others (3:9).

Beginning the service

With: Christmas cards that portray the Wise Men

Talk about receiving Christmas cards showing the visit of the Magi (traditionally the Wise Men) to see Jesus. You could hold up some cards or display them in a PowerPoint. Explain that you are going to look at the significance of this visit, for it holds one of the first clues in the gospel story that non-Jews would worship Jesus.

Bible reading

To highlight the international appeal, choose readers from different cultural backgrounds or use two contrasting British accents to highlight the geographical range of discipleship.

Introduce Ephesians 3:1–12 by saying that Paul was given the task of taking the good news of Jesus to the non-Jewish Gentiles.

Matthew 2:1–12 could be read by different voices: a narrator (N), Herod (H), a Chief Priest (CP) and one of the Magi (M). The version below, based on the TNIV, is also available as a download (YearC.Epiphany_1).

> N After Jesus was born in Bethlehem in Judea, during the time of King Herod, Magi from the east came to Jerusalem. These astrologers asked for directions.
>
> M Where is the one who has been born king of the Jews? We saw his star in the east and have come to worship him.
>
> N When King Herod heard this he was disturbed, and all the people of Jerusalem were puzzled too. When he had called together all the people's chief priests and teachers of the law, he asked them the question the Magi had posed.
>
> H Where is the Christ to be born?
>
> CP In Bethlehem in Judea, for this is what the prophet has written: 'But you, Bethlehem, in the land of Judah, are by no means least among the rulers of Judah; for out of you will come a ruler who will be the shepherd of my people Israel.'
>
> N Then Herod called the Magi secretly and found out from them the exact time the star had appeared. He sent them to Bethlehem and gave them orders.
>
> H Go and make a careful search for the child. As soon as you find him, report to me, so that I too may go and worship him.
>
> N After they had heard the king, they went on their way, and the star they had seen in the east went ahead of them until it stopped over the place where the child was. When they saw the star, they were overjoyed. On coming to the house, they saw the child with his mother Mary, and they bowed down and worshipped him. Then they opened their treasures and presented him with gifts of gold and of incense and of myrrh. And having been warned in a dream not to go back to Herod, they returned to their country by another route.

Matthew 2:1–12 (TNIV)

For a more contemporary reading of Matthew 2, look at *The Street Bible* by Rob Lacey and read 'almost overcome with excitement' instead of the translation given for that idea in verses 9–11.

Bible retelling

An imaginative retelling of the story can be found as a download (YearC.Epiphany_2).

Bible talk

With: nine candles (be very safety conscious); eight images as indicated below – five contemporary images of Christians from 1 Israel, 2 India, 3 Europe, 4 Africa, 5 Australia or New Zealand – (visit Scripture Union International's website www.suinternational.org for appropriate pictures), 6 the badge of the Diocese of the Arctic with its igloo (do an Internet search), 7 rough seas with a ship in sight, 8 the Canadian Christmas stamp showing the Magi in early American terms, available as a download (YearC.Epiphany_3)

Light the first candle. One of the Hanukkah candles is known as the servant light because it is used to light up all the others. Christians see Jesus as the servant, the light of the world. As we light the servant candle, which will then be used to light the other candles, we remember that Jesus came to serve.

Light the second candle, taking the light from the servant candle. Jesus came to Jewish people. *(Show picture of people in Israel.)* But even when Jesus was a young baby, the old man Simeon told his parents that Jesus had also come as a light to the Gentiles.

Light the third candle. *(Show a picture of people in India.)* The Magi came from Asia and were non-Jews who came to worship Jesus. We do not know where exactly. Their presence in the birth narratives of Jesus was an early hint that the gospel was for all peoples.

Light the fourth candle. After Jesus' death, the good news of Jesus was brought to Jews and non-Jews on the continent of Europe by the apostle Paul. *(Show a picture of people in Europe.)* Christian groups were set up in Rome and parts of Greece such as Corinth.

Light the fifth candle. The good news of Jesus was also taken to Africa. People from Africa were present in Jerusalem at the time of Pentecost and Philip met the man from Ethiopia on the road from Jerusalem to Gaza. *(Show a picture of people in Africa.)*

Light the sixth candle. Centuries later, missionaries took the gospel to North and South America. The Canadian Government authorised a Christmas stamp which shows the Magi in early American terms. The Magi are seen as three native American warriors or braves. They follow the star to a tent or tepee. *(Show this image.)*

Light the seventh candle. The gospel was also taken to Australia and New Zealand from where the Christian church has sent many people to spread the good news of Jesus around the world. *(Show a picture of people in Australia or New Zealand.)*

Light the eighth candle. Then there are Antarctica and the Arctic. The church in the Diocese of the Arctic reaches out to the Inuit peoples. *(Show the badge of the Diocese of the Arctic with its igloo.)* Because different peoples live in different environments, Christians have to reinterpret parts of the Bible. The Inuit peoples do not have sheep. To them it makes sense to think of Jesus as 'the baby seal of God'. Translators of the Bible are used by God to make the Christian message understandable to peoples living in widely differing countries.

Light the ninth candle. Finally we think of the seas and all those sailing on the ocean. The Mission to Seamen supports sailors when they arrive in foreign ports far away from home by offering a Christian welcome and hospitality. People are often 'loved' into God's kingdom by acts of caring compassion and consideration. *(Show a picture of the seas.)*

The Magi knelt before the child Jesus to worship him. Their three gifts were gold, frankincense and myrrh. These were costly substances. All Christians are called to share the good news of Jesus with others, wherever they find themselves. Sometimes it is costly to worship and serve King Jesus. But it is the most important task given to anyone.

Prayer of confession

This is available as a download (YearC. Epiphany_4).

Prayers of intercession

With: images of gold, frankincense and myrrh to show on a screen or a piece of gold; an incense stick; a flask labelled myrrh to be held as the prayer focus progresses; one reader to read the emboldened sentences below while someone else leads in prayer

Gold is for the King.
In the past year there were some golden experiences in the church. (Recall the births of babies, marriages, anniversaries, new jobs, holidays, fun times together, etc.) Invite everyone to think of a golden time in the past year and to thank God for it.
We pray for wisdom and integrity for world leaders and governments.
We pray for justice and right motives for those taking decisions that affect other people's lives. We pray for peace in our world.
The King of kings brings salvation; let loving hearts enthrone him.

Myrrh is for suffering.
Christmas cards often bring news from family and friends, sometimes news of illness, hospital treatment or sadness. (Recall any sad times for people within the church in the past year.) Invite everyone to think of a sad or tough experience. Thank God that he was there with them.
We pray for those on the church prayer list. We remember those who are precious to us and are suffering.
We pray for wisdom, patience and calmness for hospital staff and carers.
Nails and a spear shall pierce him through, the cross be borne for me, for you. Lord, bring healing, wholeness, tranquillity, hope and peace.

Frankincense is for worship.
In the past year there have been special spiritual moments when a new truth was understood or we grew closer to Jesus. Maybe some people met him for the first time or experienced his power and holiness. (Recall any significant events for the church.) Invite everyone to think of someone who helps them and supports them in their Christian life. Thank God for them. Think of a special time spent in God's presence in the past year. Thank God for his faithfulness.
Bring him incense, gold and myrrh. Come

rich and poor to own him.
Accept these prayers
For the sake of your Son, our Saviour, Jesus
Christ, Amen.

Ending the service

With: picture of Lego crib scene, available as a download (YearC.Epiphany_5)

Today we have focused on the spread of Christianity across the continents and throughout the world. A few years ago, Churches Together in Warwick organised 105 cribs displayed throughout the town. They were in shops and schools, hotels and houses. An 8-year-old boy designed one from Lego. Jedd Morgan presented the Magi not as kings, not as warrior braves but as space travellers. One of the Lego space visitors carried a video camera to record the event! Jesus is good news for our world. But he is not just limited to the world; he is Lord of creation and he is Lord of the cosmos. (Show the images.)

Helpful extras

Music and song ideas

Hymns highlight our own offering to the King: 'In the bleak midwinter' ends with 'If I were a wise man I could do my part, yet what I can I give him: give my heart'; 'King of kings, majesty' includes the lines 'I lay my all before you now'; 'When I survey the wondrous cross' ends with God's love demanding 'my soul, my life, my all'; 'All I once held dear' speaks of putting Jesus first, before 'all this world reveres and wars to own'; 'As with gladness men of old' expresses the wish that we may bring 'our costliest treasures' before Christ the King; 'Father, I place into your hands'.

Other hymns can focus on the international scope of the gospel: 'God is working his purpose out'; 'All over the world'; 'He's got the whole world in his hands'.

Songs can be chosen from different musical traditions across the world to reflect the universal appeal of Christianity. Make this connection explicit in the introduction of the song: 'The Virgin Mary had a baby boy' uses traditional Afro-Caribbean music and ends with the Wise Men seeing Jesus; 'The Cowboy Carol' is popular in schools; 'Silent Night' is Austrian; 'Little Jesus, sweetly sleep' is a traditional Czech carol. A church choir could sing a carol from another country.

Statement of faith

This is available as a download (YearC. Epiphany_6).

Notes and comments

According to *Common Worship*, Epiphany can be celebrated on 10 January. This is also the day to celebrate the baptism of Jesus. You will need to choose whether to focus on the first Sunday of Epiphany or the baptism of Jesus.

'Celebrate the feasts' by M. Zimmerman and G. Getz looks at how Jewish festivals such as Hanukkah can be used in Christian worship.

In the **Bible talk**, acknowledge all the nationalities present in the congregation.

Alternative online options

Visit www.lightlive.org for additional activities for children, young people and adults.

BAPTISM OF CHRIST

READINGS: **Isaiah 43:1–7; Luke 3:15–17,21,22**
Psalm 29; Acts 8:14–17

Bible foundations

Aim: to recognise that at his baptism Jesus' identity and his role were made clear

The prophet Isaiah's reference to the servant in later chapters of Isaiah could refer to King Cyrus who came to the rescue of God's people in exile in Babylon, or could refer to God's people, Israel, or could (and this is how Christians most frequently understand it) refer to Christ, the Messiah. So what is the identity of the servant? In Isaiah 43, the writer refers to Jacob and Israel as a people and yet as a person, as one who has been redeemed (v 1), called by name (v 1), suffers (v 2), is known and saved by God as part of a transaction (v 3), loved (v 4); protected (v 5) and scattered (v 6). This connects with the later understanding of the servant as 'Israel'. God's plan was that his people should share the truth about himself with all peoples.

In his baptism (Luke 3:15–17, 21–22) Jesus identified with the sins of the people and in a sense the people themselves, becoming as one with them. He also identified with John's message since John declared he himself was not the Messiah, but was pointing to Jesus as the promised one. Jesus also received the affirmation that he was the loved one of God and God's power came upon him. There are resonances with the Isaiah 43 reading, including the 'passing through the waters' (v 3). Luke records that the people wanted to know John's identity. He deflected any grandiose expectations away from himself. The one to come would baptise with the Holy Spirit and would separate the godly from the ungodly, to cleanse and gather together. People were wise to wonder who this Messiah would be.

Acts 8:14–17 draws on the image in Isaiah 43:5–7 of people coming from far and wide, as the Holy Spirit came to those in Samaria, north of Jerusalem. (Their initial baptism in the name of Jesus was not sufficient (v 16).

Beginning the service

Ask who has had to wear an identity badge as part of a conference or children's club, or in visiting a building, or every day at work? How many recent incidences of badge-wearing can you count in the congregation? Let two or three children count them. Talk about why we need identity badges. Explain that you will be exploring identities in the service.

Bible reading

In introducing Isaiah 43, remind everyone of the theme of the service and ask them to listen out for what God said to his people about their identity. What the prophet Isaiah is saying to God's people is relevant to them as they are living in Babylon, far away from their home in Jerusalem. They had been taken away as captives, a result of failing to live as God wanted them to. They had worshipped other gods and had done many immoral things. Living in Babylon had been very hard for them so God was reminding them who they are – and who he is. There would have been the temptation for them to lose their identity and become like the Babylonian communities they were living in. God wanted them to resist and remain distinctly different.

This could be read by two people, taking it in turns to read what is essentially a list of God's characteristics and powerful deeds.

> A But now, this is what the LORD says—
> he who created you, Jacob,
> B he who formed you, Israel:
> A "Do not fear, for I have redeemed you;
> B I have summoned you by name; you are mine.

A When you pass through the waters,
 I will be with you;
B and when you pass through the rivers,
 they will not sweep over you.
A When you walk through the fire,
 you will not be burned;
B the flames will not set you ablaze.
A For I am the LORD your God,
 the Holy One of Israel, your Saviour;
B I give Egypt for your ransom,
 Cush and Seba in your stead.
A Since you are precious and honoured in my sight,
 and because I love you,
 I will give nations in exchange for you,
B and peoples in exchange for your life.
A Do not be afraid, for I am with you;
B I will bring your children from the east
A and gather you from the west.
B I will say to the north, 'Give them up!'
A and to the south, 'Do not hold them back.'
B Bring my sons from afar
A and my daughters from the ends of the earth—
A&B everyone who is called by my name,
B whom I created for my glory,
A whom I formed and made."

Isaiah 43:1–7 (TNIV)

The Gospel reading, Luke 3:15–17,21,22, is short. Ask people to listen to it being read. What does John the Baptist say about Jesus? As they listen, let people look at a picture of Jesus' baptism on the screen or copied onto the notice sheet. This will help to focus minds and imaginations. For example: the 'Baptism of Jesus' by Fra Angelico or a stained glass window by William Morris or a picture of Jesus and John by a non-European painter.

Bible talk

With: two very large circles/rectangles of card (to form two badges), with five phrases about God's identity from Isaiah 43 (see below) on different coloured card to be stuck on one circle and four phrases about Jesus (see below) on card to be stuck on the other (these are available as a PowerPoint slide on a download (YearC.BaptismChrist_1))

What's your identity?
Introduce a member of the congregation who has many roles in life – eg a parent, a partner, a position at work, a son/daughter, a brother/sister, the supporter of a charity or club, a church member, a vehicle driver, a neighbour, a musician, a pet owner, a friend. It would help if some of these roles are not already known to those in the service.

Ask everyone what roles/names they think could be written on this person's ID badge. If the congregation finds this a challenge, give some of the relevant suggestions above.

The identity of God's people
In the reading from Isaiah, the prophet explained the privileged position that God's people, Israel, had. Remind them – for example: **God had created them, called them by name, been with them in disasters, been their God, treated them as precious/very dear** (CEV) etc. Explain how God's people were living in exile in Babylon and wonder together what it would have meant to them to know how much they mattered to God. Ask children to stick these five phrases above on the 'God's people' ID card/badge.

Jesus' identity
Give a brief explanation of the details of John's role as a baptiser and Jesus' baptism. (Matthew 3:13–17 and Mark 1:9–11 give fuller versions of the event.) Comment that in Luke's Gospel people were asking who John the Baptist was but ended up discovering far more about Jesus' identity. Luke records several phrases that identify who Jesus was. Ask children to stick these four phrases below on the big badge as you explain them.

More powerful than John – the coming Messiah (Jesus, although John did not identify Jesus as such at this point) was more powerful than John himself. This must have been shocking (but exciting) for John's audience since John himself already had celebrity status!

Able to baptise with the Holy Spirit – Jesus would do more then baptise with water as John did, but would pour the Holy Spirit upon people.

A judge – Jesus would also pour fire upon people (not necessarily literally) as he came to judge and purify people.

A voice from heaven called him, 'My son, my beloved' – God the Father recognised Jesus as his much-loved Son.

Jesus was no ordinary man and his baptism set him upon the start of his ministry. He knew who he was in God's eyes. He now knew what he had been called to be and do – although he may not have known all the details.

Lead onto the **Prayer activity**.

Prayer activity

With: a round/rectangular piece of card, with a safety pin stuck on the back or two-sided sticky tape stuck on the back (as a badge), one for each person; pens/pencils

Who does God think you are?
Ask everyone to imagine God giving them an identity badge. What would they write on it? Suggest this could be their name or a nickname, their role, or their relationship to God, bearing in mind what the prophet Isaiah wrote about God's people, Israel. Give people time to write on their badge-shaped card. After people have written what they think God would write on their identity badge, lead with the following prayers:

We thank you, Lord God, that you call us by name. (In silence thank God for the name or identity that he has given you.)

We thank you, Father God, that you called Jesus your much-loved Son. At the start of his ministry, when he was baptised, he knew who he was and what role he had to play. Help us to listen to you, and to obey you. This week help us to show others that we belong to you, at school, work, home or play. (Invite people to think of something they will be doing this week, when they will have the opportunity to live for God.)

Prayers of intercession

Invite everyone to hold out one hand and take hold of each finger with the other hand and pray as follows:

Hold up the thumb: we give a 'thumbs up' when something is good. Thank God for something about yourself that you are pleased with.

Hold the index finger: the index finger is sometimes called the pointing finger for when someone shows the way. Think of something that you have just learnt about Jesus and ask God to help you to go on learning.

Hold the middle finger: this is the tallest finger. Pray for someone who is younger or smaller than you are who may look up to you as an example; someone to help them.

Hold the ring finger: this is the ring finger, so think of someone in your family, or a friend, who often calls you by name or uses a special nickname. Thank God for this person.

Hold the little finger: this is the weakest finger so pray about how you may feel weak in a certain situation and ask God to give you his strength.

Place your hand into the palm of the other hand: God has called us by name and holds us safe. Thank God that he has called you by name and ask him to keep you safe this week. Amen.

Ending the service

With: a bowl of water at the front or by the exit

Jesus was baptised in the river and would have got very wet. His baptism was not only a sign of identity (loved by God the Father and belonging to him) but also a sign of having turned to God and been washed clean. Jesus himself had done no wrong so did not need to be forgiven but he was identifying with John's message about the sins of all people, the people Jesus himself came to save.

As a final action, invite people to say how sorry they are for the wrong that they have done, for the times this week when they have not lived as God wanted them to. Then invite them to come to the front (or to do this as they leave the building) to dip a finger in the bowl of water and feel the wetness of the cleansing water. This is not an act of baptism but a symbolic reminder of what baptism stands for. This suggestion could be incorporated into a **Prayer of confession**.

Helpful extras

Music and song ideas

'Beloved and blessed'; 'Abba, Father'; 'Be still and know that I am God' (and amend the words appropriately, such as 'You are my child, I call you by name' or 'I will be with you, in the good times and bad'); 'I, the Lord of sea and sky'.

Notes and comments

The **Ending the service** suggestion could be used as a **Prayer of confession**.

The idea of using the hand to prompt prayer in the **Prayers of intercession** is well known. You can adapt it to use in a service that focuses on many other themes and you can change the reasoning behind using a certain digit of the hand. For example, if the hand is held with the thumb pointing to the nose, the thumb can be used to pray for those who are closest to us; from a pianist's perspective, the fourth finger is the weakest finger so can be used to pray for those who are in need, while the little finger is the finger when we pray for ourselves.

If there is a baptism in this service, there are obvious links to make with the God-identity of those being baptised or of those who are their sponsors and their relationship to God. If there is a service of Holy Communion, the suggestion to remind us of the cleansing role of baptism in **Ending the service** could be used before people receive the bread and the wine.

Alternative online options

Visit www.lightlive.org for additional activities for children, young people and adults.

SECOND SUNDAY OF EPIPHANY

READINGS: **Psalm 36:5–10; John 2:1–11**
Isaiah 62:1–5; 1 Corinthians 12:1–11

Bible foundations
Aim: to explore the way God transforms lives

The Psalter begins by introducing us to 'two ways': the way which leads to life and the way which leads to death (see Psalm 1). While Psalm 36 stands firmly within this 'two ways' tradition, the striking contrast developed here is between human sinfulness at its blackest (v 4), and the goodness of God in all its wonderful diversity (vs 5–10).

The faithless person is, above all, marked by a failure to fear the living God (v 1). The psalmist, however, is characterised by a healthy fear of God which bursts into a hymn of praise. In verses 5 and 6 the limitless nature of God's love, faithfulness, righteousness and justice is described by way of a series of metaphors reflecting the immensity of the created order. Such goodness is the source of hope for all creatures (v 6c).

In verses 7–10 God's vast and unfathomable love is expressed in more personal and intimate terms. This results in a deep trust and confidence in God (v 7), a sense of overflowing joy and delight in response to his generous provision (v 8) and the experience of both light and life (v 9). In verse 10 praise turns to prayer. Here is recognition that godly living is dependent upon the gracious gift of God's continual, loving presence in the midst of his people.

In John's Gospel we meet the one who has come to bring us life in all its fullness (10:10). The transformative impact of encountering Jesus is vividly illustrated in his changing of water into wine at the wedding feast at Cana (2:1–11). The mundane and ordinary can become infused by the power and glory of God (v 11) if we are prepared to respond in faith to the challenge to 'Do whatever he tells you' (v 5).

Beginning the service

With: a CD of the 'Wedding March' by Mendelssohn

After welcoming people either have the organist play, or play on a CD, part of Mendelssohn's 'Wedding March'. Ask what service in church they would expect to hear this played at. (People may not know!) Explain briefly that a wedding marks a big change. Two people become one. Since they love each other, each is willing to change to fit better with the other. But there's another relationship which changes the people involved in it through love – our relationship with God, and that's what we are going to explore and celebrate today.

Bible reading

Psalm 36:5–10 works well as a two-part reading. Divide the congregation into two, to read aloud. This version from the NIV is available as a PowerPoint download (YearC. Epiphany2_1).

> A   Your love, Lord, reaches to the heavens,
> B   your faithfulness to the skies.
> A   Your righteousness is like the highest mountains,
> B   your justice like the great deep.
> All You, Lord, preserve both people and animals.
> A   How priceless is your unfailing love, O God!
> B   People take refuge in the shadow of your wings.
> A   They feast in the abundance of your house;
> B   you give them drink from your river of delights.
> A   For with you is the fountain of life;
> B   in your light we see light.
> All Continue your love to those who know you,
>   your righteousness to the upright in heart.
>
> Psalm 36:5–10 (NIV)

Bible retelling

This story from John 2:1–11 should be told by a woman in conversational style.

There's nothing worse at a wedding than running out of food and wine. It reminds me of a time, years ago now, at a wedding of some friends of the family. In Cana in Galilee, it was. I don't know if the bride's dad had been a bit careful with the pennies or if there'd just been a mix-up, but long before the reception was over they had run out of wine. What a disaster!

I went and found my son. He was always good at knowing what to do in a crisis. 'They've run out of wine,' I said. He gave me one of his mysterious answers. 'What's it got to do with me; my time hasn't come.' But I knew he'd do something! So I went to the servants and told them, 'Just do whatever he tells you.'

He came over and told them to fill the big washing pots with water. These are the pots that we use to make ourselves pure when we come before God. They are huge, so the servants had quite a job because there were half a dozen pots and they hold around 100 litres each. They did moan a fair bit but they got on and did it.

Then my son said, 'Take some of the water out of one of the pots and give it to the man in charge of the ceremonies.' They looked extremely nervous and jumpy about doing that. They thought it was some kind of practical joke – water instead of wine – and they would end up looking foolish! But they did what my son told them.

When the man in charge tasted this water he was amazed. He called the bridegroom over and said, 'I'm puzzled. Most people serve the best wine first and keep the poorer wine for when people have had a few drinks and won't notice what it is they are drinking. But you've kept the best for last.'

So the wedding was saved: no embarrassment, no shame. But from then on, the people who knew what had gone on started looking differently at my boy, Jesus, because the person who could do a miracle like this must be someone very special.

Bible talk

With: a selection of wedding photos (preferably from people in the congregation, or use general ones from the Internet) on PowerPoint; a series of images as follows: high mountains, vast skies, deep underwater oceans, a crowd of people (as large as possible), herds of animals, diamonds and/ or gold, a hen with chicks, a colourful party, river, sunshine, the cross or crucifixion, available as a download (YearC.Epiphany2_2).

Someone begins by telling the story of the wedding at Cana (see **Bible retelling** above) or use another version by visiting *LightLive*; for example you could tell the story in song for under-5s by using the download (YearC. Epiphany2_3). Then show a selection of wedding photos on PowerPoint.

Ask for reasons why people might get married. *(Show the wedding photos.)* This should include the idea that people love each other so much that they want to spend their lives together. But how can we measure how much God loves us? Using the second set of images:

God's love is:
- as high as the mountains
- as deep as the ocean
- compassionate as he cares for people (like us)
- caring for animals too
- totally priceless
- as protective as a hen with her chicks
- like being invited to a fantastic party
- like swimming in a never-ending river
- like living in the sunshine.

All those images are in Psalm 36 which was read earlier. These images help us understand something about God's amazing love. But the New Testament gives us even more amazing evidence of God's love. Talk about the story of Jesus changing water into wine. Ask what that showed to the people at the wedding about who Jesus was and what was extraordinary about what he could do. If you used the previous service outline for the Baptism of Christ, refer to your exploration of Jesus' identity.

Ask for some more examples of what he did in his life that showed how he had come from God, to live as God among the people of this world. This showed us how God wanted us to live. That is evidence enough of God's love.

But there was even more. Show the image of the cross or the crucifixion. Ask someone in advance to read Isaiah 62:4,5 from the CEV. Explain that God, through the prophet Isaiah, was talking to his people, Israel. Although they had messed up and seemed a hopeless case, God went on loving them as much as a bridegroom loves his bride. God wanted them to be his people for ever.

God still loves us in a similar way. He still wants us to belong to him. We're messed up but Jesus died in our place (refer to the image again) so that we could be forgiven and make a fresh start with God. He will be with us for ever and show us, by his Spirit, how to live in a way that pleases him. Make whatever appeal for a response is appropriate in your situation. If you are asking children to respond to the love of God, make sure you have appropriate people available to talk and pray with them. In particular you may want to refer to *Top Tips on Helping a child respond to Jesus* (SU) – see page 221.

Prayers of intercession

With: wedding photo images from the **Bible talk**

Keep running on the screen the wedding photo images. Explain that you're going to ask people to pray silently.

- Ask each person to think of a happy family and ask God to go on blessing this family.
- Ask each person to think of an unhappy family and ask Jesus to be very close to this family, to make a difference, just as he showed his care at the wedding in Cana.
- Ask each person to think of a family who are finding life hard. Offer reasons such as finance, sickness, bereavement or broken relationships and ask God to strengthen and encourage them and help them to do the right thing.
- Ask each person to think of their own family and ask God for whatever they need the most.

Conclude by reading as a prayer (either from the front or together) Ephesians 3:14–21. (Use the NIV because some other translations lose the 'family' reference.)

Ending the service

Finish with a song/hymn of commitment such as 'O Jesus, I have promised' and then together say this prayer based on the marriage vows, also available as a PowerPoint download (YearC.Epiphany2_4).

Lord Jesus, we want to love you and live for you.
When things are good and when they're bad,
When we're well off and when we're hard up,
When we're sick and when we're healthy,
We want to love you, serve you and tell others about you,
For the rest of our lives.
Amen.

Helpful extras

Music and song ideas

Hymns/songs about the love of God include: 'Love divine, all loves excelling'; 'God's love is higher than the highest mountain'; 'Your love is amazing'; 'How deep the Father's love for us'; 'Oh the deep, deep love of Jesus'.

'God in my living' mirrors the theme of being really close to God, allowing him to be involved in every part of our lives.

Hymns/songs of response to God's love include: 'O Jesus, I have promised'; 'Be thou my vision'.

Game

With: a set of cards with the following images on them, also available as a download (YearC.Epiphany2_5) – a simple wedding invitation with the words 'Come to the family wedding in Cana', a chalice turned almost upside down with one drop falling (the cup is empty!), a face that is sad, six water jars (for purification), a chalice that is obviously full with a dark liquid, a symbolic face that is obviously happy

After telling the story of the miracle in John 2:1–11, give out the cards (if you have not already done so as people arrived for the service). The cards should be mixed up. Everyone is to get into groups with five other different card holders. Once in the group, put the cards in order of when they appeared in the story, then each person tells the part of the story which their card relates to. Then ask people in the groups to say how they would have felt if they had been there at the wedding, at each of the six points in the story. What might they have thought about Jesus?

Notes and comments

Briefly interview two married couples, if possible, making a contrast between a couple who have been married for a very long time and one more recently. Focus on the changes each has made in their lives as a result of being married.

Picking up the story of the wedding at Cana you could make the post-service refreshments more like a party with cake and chocolate biscuits.

Alternative online options

Visit www.lightlive.org for additional activities for children, young people and adults.

Easter Cracked
£11.99

This resource book is packed full of craft, drama, all-age service ideas and much more, to help you prepare for Easter!

For more details, visit www.scriptureunion.org.uk.

THIRD SUNDAY OF EPIPHANY

READINGS: **Nehemiah 8:1–3,5,6,8–10; Psalm 19**
1 Corinthians 12:12–31a; Luke 4:14–21

Bible foundations
Aim: to open ourselves up to hear and respond to God's Word

The God of the Bible is not silent. On the contrary, as Psalm 19 so eloquently proclaims, he is the God who continually speaks through both his works and his Word. While the natural order should act as a stimulus for our worship and praise (vs 1–6), we need to hear God's Word revealed in Scripture if we are to understand our own place within the created order and also God's will for our lives (vs 7–14). God's Word is depicted as dependable, pure and attractive; bringing life, wisdom, joy and enlightenment (vs 7–11). The psalmist's response is characterised by humility, reverence, trust and obedience. This psalm, beginning with the speech of heavens praising the Creator, ends with a prayer that the worshipper's own speech and thoughts are acceptable to the Saviour God (v 14).

In Nehemiah 8 we see the impact God's Word can have on his people, when they are eager and attentive to hear him speak (vs 2,3). On this occasion 'all the people' (vs 1,2,5,6,9) demonstrated a deep love for the Scriptures, which presumably included children (vs 2,3), reflecting the Bible's emphasis on the importance of the faith of younger people. A sense of reverent, worshipful anticipation (vs 5,6) was matched by a concern from the leaders that the Law of God should be heard and understood in an accessible way (vs 2,3,7,8). It should be noted that Israel's history had demonstrated the potentially serious consequences of a lack of understanding and knowledge – see Hosea 4:6.

Such understanding should have an impact on both our emotions and behaviour. God's Word by his Spirit can convict us of our neglect of God's ways (v 9) and also bring joy (v 10) as it cleanses and transforms. The Scriptures are given to enrich the lives of God's people, not to spoil them – they are a treasure and a delight (v 10).

Beginning the service

After welcoming people, ask them to form into small groups. For a couple of minutes talk about the following question: if your house were burning down and you could save just one thing (assuming all the people are safe) what would it be? Afterwards hear some suggestions. Explain that this question helps to sort out our priorities – what are the really important things in our lives. This service we are going to see how important the Bible is in our lives.

Alternatively, ask a few people in advance to come prepared with their answer to the question above. They could even bring their precious object to the service to show others.

Bible reading

If space permits, create a small raised platform and ask the congregation to stand around it. Arrange them in small groups. Make sure children are near the front where they can see. Explain that God had given Nehemiah the job of helping the people rebuild the walls of Jerusalem which had been broken down in the war, 70 or so years earlier. When the work was completed they gathered together – men, women and children (those old enough to understand) – to hear God's Word read to them. As we shall hear, they stood and listened all morning but we're just going to listen for a few minutes. As you all listen, imagine you're back in Jerusalem, at last. The walls have been rebuilt after a great effort on everyone's part and today you're going to hear the most important message you've ever heard.

In advance, ask someone to stand on the platform and read Nehemiah 8:1–3,5,6,8–10.

If possible use seven readers for Psalm 19. Reader 1 reads verses 1–6. Everyone reads verses 10 and 14, while the other verses are divided phrase by phrase between the other readers. Readers 2 to 7 should punch their lines out with a lot of energy, divided between the readers. A version of this psalm from the CEV is available as a download (YearC. Epiphany3_1).

Bible talk

With: paper plates (or circles of card) with sad/happy faces on each side, if possible, one for each person; three large card circles, red, amber and green; the words of Psalm 19:11 and then verses 12–14 in a format that can be displayed available as a download (YearC. Epiphany3_2)

Happy and sad faces

Either equip the whole congregation with happy/sad faces or ask a small group of volunteers to the front. Mention various situations which include the following and ask them to show the happy or sad face as appropriate.

- Someone is born.
- Someone has died.
- Someone is sick.
- Someone has won a prize.
- Someone has been naughty.
- Someone is having a birthday party.
- Someone is reading the Bible to us.

Most of the responses are obvious but the final one should cause some confusion. Remind people about the reading from Nehemiah and check that everyone knows the story. Read Nehemiah 8:9,10 again and ask the group/congregation to show the appropriate faces to indicate how the people were reacting.

What makes us sad as we read the Bible
Ask for ideas about what things in the Bible might make us sad to hear. For example, hearing what God wants and realising we don't do it. The people in Nehemiah's day were probably sad because they remembered how their parents and grandparents and great grandparents had been disobedient to God. As a result God had punished them by letting their enemies defeat them and take them into captivity.

What makes us happy as we read the Bible
Then talk about what things should make us happy. For example, hearing how God loves us, wants to forgive us when we fail and lets us start again. The people in Nehemiah's day could be happy because God had brought them back from captivity and enabled them to rebuild the wall.

Hold up the three large circles of coloured card. Ask what the colours mean (red = danger; amber = caution; green = safety). Although traffic lights hadn't been invented when King David was king, he knew how God's Word helps us to be aware of danger, warns us when to be cautious and shows us the things that are safe.

How obeying what we read in the Bible makes us happy or sad
Project the words of Psalm 19:11 with the words 'teachings', 'warned', 'obeying' and 'rewarded' highlighted in a different colour. If you don't have projection facilities read the verse emphasising the four words. Ask what happens if a car ignores a red traffic light and goes through on red. What happens when we ignore God's warnings? If we want to be safe and happy it's not enough to just read God's Word – we have to obey it. Refer back to the opening discussion about what things are most important to us. In the case of the Bible it's not whether we would carry it out of the house but whether we are willing to carry it out in our lives.

If appropriate, refer to the story of Jesus in Luke 4:14–41. Jesus was reading from his Bible, from the Old Testament book of Isaiah. He knew this was not just nice words written years ago but was God's commands that he (Jesus) was going to obey during his ministry. He would bring about change in people's lives and in society: for the poor – good news; for captives – freedom; for the blind – sight; for the sufferers – freedom from suffering.

Ask for suggestions of things we could do in the next week which we could see as obeying God's Word. Explain that it will be hard to do some of these things but God will help us by his Holy Spirit and we can help and encourage one another.

Project the words of Psalm 19:12–14. If you don't have projection facilities print them on your notice sheet. Explain that we are going to finish by using David's prayer to ask God to forgive us when we fail and help us to succeed. Suggest that everyone uses these words as their special prayer each day during the week. Finish the talk by reading the words together.

Prayer activity
With: two large happy/sad faces at the front and small happy/sad faces for each person or group; something to write with

If in the **Bible talk** everyone has had a happy/sad face, ask them to get into small groups and think about real situations they know where people are happy – for which we want to thank God, and sad situations – where people need God's help. After talking about these, each person should choose one person or situation and draw or write about it on the appropriate face. The group should try to split up roughly equally between happy and sad. When the prayers are drawn and written, the faces should be brought to the front and attached to the two large faces. In advance, ask two people to pray short general prayers of thanks and intercession.

If you don't want everyone to have a happy/sad face, give one happy face and one sad face to each group on which to record their group prayers.

Prayer of confession

God's people in Jerusalem became aware of their sin and the wrongdoing of those in their family, from generations back. Of course, we cannot do anything about their wrong, but we can be aware of our own ability to disobey God. But note that Nehemiah and Ezra urged the people to rejoice, 'for this is a special day for the Lord'. This confession is in two parts, following the pattern of God's people at the time of Ezra, with two different congregational responses.

Father God, we know that we do not read your Word as we should. We often choose to disobey you.

Father God, forgive us and help us.

Father God, we know that we do not always listen to what you say to us, when we read your Word or when we hear others explaining it to us.

Father God, forgive us and help us.

Father God, we know that as your people we sometimes do wrong, just as our parents, grandparents and great-grandparents did what was wrong in your eyes.

Father God, forgive us and help us.

Father God, we know that you long to forgive us so that we can be freed from our sins.

Father God, forgive us and help us to rejoice!

Father God, we know that you want us to be glad that we are your people and that we belong to you.

Father God, forgive us and help us to rejoice!

Ending the service

With: the following prayer to be displayed as appropriate

Together, say this prayer based on Psalm 19 and Luke 4 to conclude the service. It is available as a download (YearC.Epiphany3_3).

Lord, when we look at the sun and the stars, the skies and the world around us, help us to see you in them.
When we read your Word, the Bible, help us to discover you in it.
May your Law give us new life.
May your teachings give us wisdom.
May your instruction give us glad hearts.
May we value your Word more than the most precious things we own.
Forgive us when we don't live as we should.
Let our words and thoughts – the whole of our lives – be pleasing to you.
May others meet Jesus in us and be able to

hear your good news.
May others meet Jesus in us and find freedom.
May others meet Jesus in us and find sight.
Help us to help one another to live for you.
Hear our prayers, O Lord, our protector and redeemer.
Amen.

Helpful extras

Music and song ideas

Hymns and songs about the Bible include: 'Lord, thy word abideth'; 'God has given us a book full of stories'; 'Thy word is a lamp unto my feet'. Addison's hymn, 'The spacious firmament on high' is based on the first half of Psalm 19. It's quite a complex hymn but, with suitable explanation, could be used in an all-age service. 'How great thou art' also covers the theme of seeing God in nature.

Hymns and songs about obeying God's Word include: 'Don't build your house on the sandy land'; 'Lord, speak to me that I may speak'; 'Have you got an appetite?'; 'I want to walk with Jesus Christ'; 'Be the God of all my Sundays'; 'God of justice' ('we must go').

The theme of transformation is covered in 'O for a thousand tongues'.

Game

The puzzle below, and the answers, are available as a PowerPoint download (YearC. Epiphany3_4). Draw attention to the fact that each of the following words begins with a letter from the word 'Praised'. The clues are as follows:

1. Ezra stood on the _____ (PLATFORM)
2. The people listened _____ (INTENTLY)
3. The people shouted _____ (AMEN! AMEN!)
4. _____ was crying (EVERYONE)
5. Then the people _____ (REJOICED)
6. This day was _____ for God (SPECIAL)
7. The people were eating and _____ to celebrate (DRINKING)

1.	P						
5.	R						
3.	A			!			!
2.	I						
6.	S						■
4.	E						
7.	D						

Notes and comments

The imagery of Psalm 19 lends itself to all forms of creative art. Inspiration can be found from Internet images of galaxies, star systems, the sun – use a search engine.

In advance, ask anyone you know who has a story to tell about how what they've read in the Bible has changed them, to come prepared to briefly share their story at an appropriate point in the service.

Alternative online options

Visit www.lightlive.org for additional activities for children, young people and adults.

FOURTH SUNDAY OF EPIPHANY

READINGS: 1 Corinthians 13:1–13; Luke 2:22–40
Psalm 48; Ezekiel 43:27 – 44:4

Bible foundations

Aim: to explore how our understanding of God is limited, but that in time we will understand much better

Paul's magnificent hymn to love, found in 1 Corinthians 13, has a special place in the life of the church. It is often read, for example, at weddings or funeral services. We should not lose sight of the fact, however, that the original readers encountered this chapter as part of a sustained argument. It would appear that the Corinthian church thought they had already 'arrived' spiritually – see Paul's biting sarcasm in 4:8. They saw themselves as wise (see chapters 1–4) and assumed that their possession of spectacular spiritual gifts was a mark of advanced spirituality.

In 13:8–13 Paul stresses how the present existence of the church is characterised by imperfection and partial understanding. He explores this by using two images. First, we are currently childlike and limited in our speech, thinking and reasoning (v 11); and secondly, it is as if we see reality by way of a mirror, in an indirect and blurred fashion (v 12). (Corinth was famous for the manufacture of bronze mirrors.) Charismata, such as prophecies, tongues and God-given knowledge, have been provided to assist us to worship and serve God in the midst of our current limitations, but they are partial and temporary in nature (vs 9 and 10).

Realism about our present limited and fallible understanding should result in humility, both in our view of ourselves and also in our relationships. It will also lead us to place a priority on love, which belongs to both the present and the future (vs 8 and 13). We can rejoice that in this life we are fully known and accepted by God and that when Christ returns we will 'know fully' (v 12). This does not refer to a God-like omniscience – rather it speaks of an intimate and direct 'face-to-face' access to God (v 12) which will mark the future age (1 John 3:2).

Beginning the service

With: a carpenter's tool (eg a saw); a bride's bouquet; a baby doll

Prepare a couple of volunteers to come to retell the story of Mary and Joseph from Luke 2:22–40. This story should be fairly fresh in people's minds (since Christmas was only a few weeks ago) but the emphasis in this service is on what the characters knew as the story developed. Mention the season of Epiphany (which is about moments of revelation) and the story of the 'Presentation in the Temple' (often celebrated on 2 February – Candlemas).

Mary and Joseph knew a bit about each other at the start of the story but it was probably an arranged marriage between two local families. Mary knew that Joseph was a carpenter (give Joseph the tool) and Joseph knew that he wanted to marry Mary (give Mary the bouquet). Neither of them knew that God's own plan was that Mary was to be the mother of his Son, Jesus. (Give the baby doll to Mary as Joseph looks on in surprise or shock.) God's plan did cause Mary and Joseph some difficulties and their plans had to change several times. But they were to discover that God loved them and his plan is ultimately for the best.

When Jesus was still very young, Mary and Joseph took Jesus to the Temple to present him to the priests, as all Jewish families did. They were met by two very old people who told them more about what Jesus would become and what he would do (Joseph and Mary raise their hands in shock). This gave them even more to think about!

When Joseph and Mary agreed to be married, they had no idea what the future held. That can be said for anyone starting out in marriage but actually, it is true for all of us here. If possible, invite a newly married couple to comment on this fact! We don't know what the future holds and we don't know God's wider plans for us or for this world. That is what we will be exploring in this service.

Bible reading

An active retelling of Luke 2:22–40 is suggested for **Beginning the service**. The story could be read from the Bible with readers taking the various parts.

1 Corinthians 13 is often read at significant family events, particularly weddings. You could ask someone who had it read at their wedding to read it today – or ask a number of people to share the reading. This reading is also used at funerals, so be sensitive to those for whom this reading may stir up painful memories. 1 Corinthians 13 could also be used as a **Statement of faith**, available as a download (YearC.Epiphany4_1).

Bible talk

With: a set of children's books – a board book, a picture storybook, an information book and a fiction book; a large mirror, preferably with a slightly damaged glass so that the image is distorted

Today we listened to part of Paul's first letter to the Christians in Corinth. They thought they were pretty special and had seen God do some amazing things with them and among them. This had made them proud, as though they knew what they were doing and what God was thinking too. Paul wanted to remind them that they did not know very much at all. (Look back to the **Bible foundations**.)

Refer back to the story of Joseph and Mary. They did not know what the future held and what God's plan was for them or their son. Also comment on how at the start of a new term or the new year, although we all know some of the things that are planned for the year and we expect the seasons to happen as they always do, we have to admit that our knowledge is imperfect.

Paul gave these new Christians two pictures to help them see how we can begin to understand God's ways.

Understand like a child

Show the series of children's books, beginning with the picture book, the early reader, the information book and the text-heavy book. Ask what sort of books people of different ages in the congregation like to read, emphasising how a younger child will enjoy something which may be just as high quality (with beautiful illustrations and a well-written and presented story) as an adult book. But they could not tackle something more advanced because of their limited understanding and ability to read. In the same way, our understanding of God is very childlike and therefore limited.

Look into a mirror

Show the large mirror and ask someone to come to look sideways into the mirror. What can they see? What can they not see from the angle where they are standing? Explain that Corinth was known for producing mirrors made of bronze. A mirror only ever gives an imperfect image. Also, we often only see what we want to see. You could comment on the bent mirrors that are found in funfairs or child-friendly bookshops that intentionally distort.

Paul told these Christians that, at the moment, they looked at God as though looking at a poor image of him in a mirror. We have the promise that at the end of time we will see God and his ways much more clearly – with no distortions. Read how verse 12 is translated in *The Message*: 'We're squinting in a fog, peering through a mist. But it won't be long before the weather clears and the sun shines bright! We'll see it all then, see it all as clearly as God sees.'

Part of the reason for this lack of understanding is that God is far beyond what we can ever imagine! But the other reason why we cannot understand him is that we are imperfect ourselves. Our love is imperfect. How can we ever love as Paul suggests? This means that our understanding of God is imperfect, as Paul reminds the Corinthians. But we have the hope that we will meet with God; we will see him face to face!

We don't, however, know what the future holds, but right now we go on loving as best we can and we go on looking forward to the time when we will meet with God. We are grateful for the understanding that God has given us by his Spirit. We go on asking to see him more clearly. We know that he will be with us into the future and we can trust him. The **Prayer activity** would naturally follow on from this.

Prayer activity

With: one small mirror and baby's toy for each group

Split into small groups giving each a mirror and a baby's toy to place in the middle of the group. First of all, ask everyone to think of something about God that they find puzzling, something that he has said or done that is hard to understand. Invite people to share this in the group then say this prayer, holding up a baby's toy:

Lord God, we know that we only grasp a little of what you say and what you have done.

We are like small children in our understanding.

By your Spirit, help us to grow in our understanding.

Then ask everyone to think of one way they have failed to love other people as God wants them to. Assure them that they are not going to share this with anyone else. Pass the mirror around the group and as each person holds the mirror, they silently ask God to forgive them for the times when they have not loved as they should. Conclude with this prayer, holding up a mirror:

Lord God, we don't see things clearly because we are imperfect.
Forgive us for the times when we have deliberately done the wrong thing.
Forgive us for when we just have not loved someone as we ought.
Thank you that there will come a time when we will see you face to face!
Right now, may we see you more clearly,
love you more dearly,
and follow you more nearly,
day by day.

Amen.

Prayers of intercession

With: a Bible, a wedding photo; a map

This is a time to pray for those who are especially uncertain about the future. You could ask three people to prepare prayers on the following topics:

• We often give a Bible to a baby when they are baptised, blessed or dedicated – but babies can't read (although they can enjoy Bible stories from a very young age!). The Bible is something for the future and is there to help them as they grow and develop. However, a Bible is given to a child with the hope that the child will come to know and love God. Pray for all the children in church and ask God to help those who look after and nurture them.

• Wedding photos often capture a moment of joy or possibility, but reality soon catches up. If relevant, refer back to the reading of 1 Corinthians 13. Pray for newly married couples that they would continue to grow in love as they get to know each other and God better.

• There may be people in church who are facing challenging decisions about the future, as though they need a map to guide them – a change of job, facing unemployment, moving home, different family circumstances or bereavement. Pray for all those who need God to guide them in decision-making.

Ending the service

Rehearse and use the following action prayer. It is also available as a download (YearC. Epiphany4_2).

May God give us faith in him *(point up)*

and help us to trust one another. *(hold hands)*
May God show us the way he wants us to go *(point forward with both hands)*
and help us to travel together. *(walk on the spot)*
May God fill us with love *(hand on heart)*
and help us to love one another. *(point to everyone else with other hand)*
May God give us faith *(point up)*, hope *(both hands forward)* and love. *(hand on heart)*
Amen.

Helpful extras

Music and song ideas

The link between the reading and marriage may be worth exploring and you could use this as an opportunity to play hymns and songs that people may have had at their weddings. Alternatively, there are many hymns which pick up the theme of faith, hope and love, for example: 'Sing hosanna'; 'Overwhelmed by love'; 'Make me a channel of your peace'; 'Love divine'. The song 'Day by day' from the musical *Godspell* is appropriate and could be sung or listened to.

Statement of faith

The declaration of faith, based on the reading from 1 Corinthians 13 (CEV) which could be used as part of the **Bible talk**, is available as a download (YearC.Epiphany4_1). Divide the congregation into right and left for added impact.

Notes and comments

The activities explored in this session might provide an opportunity to connect with those who have been married in your church, or with the families of children who have been baptised, blessed or dedicated. Valentine's Day is only a couple of weeks away so you could make a link with this.

People who are particularly uncertain about the future, or those who may wonder where God is in their lives, may appreciate the opportunity to talk further with someone or to be prayed for.

Alternative online options

Visit www.lightlive.org for additional activities for children, young people and adults.

SECOND SUNDAY BEFORE LENT (COMMON WORSHIP)

READINGS: **Genesis 2:4–9,15–25; Psalm 65**
Revelation 4; Luke 8:22–25

Bible foundations
Aim: to wonder at the glory of God revealed in creation

Psalm 65 pictures God continually active and powerful in the Temple (vs 1–4), the whole earth (vs 5–8) and in the recurrent cycle of nature, culminating in harvest (vs 9–13). This is consistent with the biblical picture that God is both the creator of all things and also the one who saves, keeps and sustains. The psalm begins with the recognition that healthy relationships between God and humankind must be based on his forgiveness and acceptance and on our humble dependence on him (vs 1–4). God's majesty is evident in both the creation of the physically imposing mountain ranges and also in his domination of the powerful forces of nature (vs 6,7). This is paralleled by his control over political events (v 7c).

While God is always present, he is also seen as drawing near to care for his people (v 9). While a 'visitation' by a foreign conqueror might result in desolation and barrenness, when God comes, he waters the land, bringing fertility and a rich harvest (vs 9–13). For a farming community such as Israel, where a bountiful harvest might mean the difference between life and death, here is an evident sign of God's goodness and concern to meet human need.

The understanding that the created order proclaims the Lordship, character and glory of God is integral to the account of creation that we find in Genesis. Here we see God's power and sovereignty at work, while the focus of 2:4–25 is on his intimate and loving involvement with his creation, especially with human beings. Those who view the world through the eyes of faith and trust see in creation a revelation of God's glory and goodness, and joyfully join with creation in worshipping him (Psalm 65:12,13; Revelation 4). One day, this glory will be seen and acknowledged by all human beings (Habakkuk 2:14).

Beginning the service

With: magazine pictures; photographs or images on PowerPoint; video or music relating to creation; a large board or poster

Explain that in the service you will explore the theme of creation and our place in it. We are called to look after this world, but we are also called to wonder at the amazing things that God has created.

Produce a pile of pictures from magazines which show different aspects of God's creation. These should include a wide range of different locations or living things. Invite everyone to choose one each and say why they chose the image that they did. They could do this with their immediate neighbours or as a whole group.

Invite people to hold up their images for everyone to see. Appreciatively, point out the diversity of images. Then play some music or sing an appropriate song to help you think about God's creation. While this is happening invite everyone to come forward to stick their image on a board or poster which will be displayed throughout the service.

Bible reading

As Psalm 65 is read, display appropriate images on a screen. This psalm is very visual so a few well-chosen pictures could add extra meaning to the psalm. Alternatively, put the words of the psalm on PowerPoint and say it together.

Genesis 2 could be used as a dramatised reading. A version of this, from the CEV, is available as a download (YearC.2SunB4Lent_1).

Bible talk

With: a display board with the following shapes to be stuck on as the talk progresses – the simple outlines of two human beings, a cloud, a flower, an apple, two trees, a question mark (You could deliver this talk in the style of an artist wearing overalls, with a paint brush and palette and possibly an assistant or model.)

The story in Genesis 2 offers a wonderful picture of what the world was like, as God intended it. But it also identifies important things about what God has made and the purpose he has given for life.

People are all uniquely different
Start by sticking the rough shape of a human being on the board. It has no eyes, hands or other details and looks like a person made out of clay. The writer of Genesis talks about God forming the first man out of the earth but also says that human beings were made in the image of God (1:27). We are all different but all reflect part of God's character and creativity. Point out the rich variety of people in the congregation today with different shapes, sizes, gifts and personalities. We are all made in the image of God. Ask what you could add to the shape to make it more unique – such as eyes, hair, a beard or freckles.

People have been given life
Stick a cloud onto the chest of the person. This is breath. Genesis 2:7 says that God breathed life into the first human being. We are dependent on God for our continuing life and existence – and that is not just being able to breathe, but is also all about enjoyment and fulfilment. God wants us to live life to the

full. St Iranaeus in AD 170 said, 'The glory of God is a human being fully alive.' Ask what it might mean to be 'fully alive'.

Stick a flower on one side of the person and an apple on the other. God gave this human being all sorts of wonderful things in creation – good food to eat and beautiful things to look at (see Genesis 2:9). Human beings need both. Ask people to name their favourite food and to think of beautiful places or things. We need to recognise these aspects of our identity as human beings.

People have been given a purpose for living
Stick some trees around the figure. Human beings don't exist in isolation. God put the first person in a garden and gave him a job to do, which included looking after the garden and naming the animals. God has given all people a purpose for living.

Stick a question mark onto the head of the figure. God gave human beings the ability to be creative and to make choices. He expected the first person to name the animals. He also gave people the freedom to choose whether to obey his commands or not and was deeply saddened when they chose to go their own way. We need to recognise how powerful our creativity is but also how destructive it can be. Ask for examples of human creativity and also examples of bad decisions. When do we show how wonderful we are? When do we mess up?

People need each other
God knew that it wasn't good to have just one human being so he created two. Add a second shaped person who is different in some way, such as size or colour. He then had two human beings who were the same in some ways but different in others. They could be together, working together, enjoying the world together.

Step back to admire the illustration you have created. But what if we were to remove some of these things? What if there was no food, or no beauty, or purpose in living? What happens to people who have their freedom taken away?

As you remove the images from the display board, discuss how people's lives are affected if these elements of their existence are denied or reduced. Remind people of the first four verses of Psalm 65 – God knows about our sin and frailty but he forgives and blesses. We live in an imperfect world but it still belongs to God.

Finish by giving thanks for all the good things that God has given to us and pray for those who are not living life to the full because they just do not recognise God's awesome power and creativity.

Prayer activity

With: painting materials and clay; objects or images in creation that can be copied; measuring equipment; pens and paper

There are many different ways of looking at creation. Give people a choice to respond to creation in one of three ways. They could look at the world like an artist, picking out the beauty of what they see. They could look at the world like a scientist, attempting to understand how things work. They could look at the world like a poet expressing what things mean.

The artists – they paint, shape or draw images of beautiful things in creation, using their imaginations or painting something that they can see.

The scientists – they look at an object in the building and write down some facts about it. They could weigh it, measure it or examine it with any equipment you have available. What do the measurements tell them about the object? This could be, for example, the pulpit, font, PA system, a bicycle.

The poets – they write one sentence each which says something about creation, and includes at least one adjective. Join these sentences together to make a 'poem'.

Bring everyone back together to present their work to the whole congregation. Discuss the different ways people look at creation and how this affects the way they relate to the world. Emphasise that none of these perspectives are more important than the others. We need all viewpoints if we are in any way to see the world as God sees it.

Lead a time of open prayer in which you give thanks for artists, scientists and poets. Use the work produced by the groups as part of the prayer.

Prayer of confession

A prayer of confession that uses words and phrases from Psalm 65 (CEV) is available as a download (YearC.2SunB4Lent_2). Introduce the response: **Our terrible sins get us down, but you forgive us.**

Prayers of intercession

Ask a youth group or home group to lead a prayer of intercession, taking the theme of the environment and our impact on it. Alternatively, the following prayers could be used, based on the **Bible talk**. Appropriate images could be displayed as each section is read.

Thank you, Lord, for forming us in your image. You have made us all different but equally special, so we pray for those who are mistreated because other people can't see the work of God in them.

Thank you, God, for making us the way we are.
Thank you, Lord, for breathing your life into us. You want us to live life to the full, so we pray for those whose lives are limited because of illness, violence, hatred or fear.

Thank you, God, for the gift of hope.
Thank you, Lord, for the good things in creation. We thank you for works of beauty that nourish our senses and for the fruit of the earth which feeds our bodies. We pray for those who are denied beauty or a share in the riches of creation.

Thank you, God, for meeting our needs.
Thank you, Lord, for giving us minds with the ability to know, understand and decide. We pray for those whose decisions affect the lives of others and ask you to lead us from self-interest to love.

Thank you, God, for the gift of wisdom.
Thank you, Lord, for making us different and for giving us different gifts and viewpoints. We pray that you would help us to respect one another and to learn to work and think as one body.

Thank you, God, for the gift of community.
Lord God, you have created us and we are wonderfully made. Help us to acknowledge this gift by using our lives for the good of

others and fill our lives with the wonder and joy of creation as every moment becomes an act of worship and praise. **Amen.**

Ending the service

With: the poster or board of pictures that you produced for **Beginning the service**

You have reflected on the importance of different aspects of creation and the way their absence can affect us. Invite everyone to choose one thing in creation that they are going to pray for over the coming week. It could be a place, a person, an animal, a species, an issue or a situation. Who or what do they feel God is calling them to pray for?

Invite everyone to stand for a concluding prayer:
Thank you, God, for our bodies *(wiggle around)*
Thank you, God, for our breath *(hands on chest)*
Thank you, God, for our purpose *(hand in a determined fist)*
Thank you, God, for our bread *(fist turns into an open palm as if offering bread to another)*
Thank you, God, for our minds *(point to head)* which we use for both right and wrong *(hands stretched out right and left as if weighing the matter)*
Thank you, God, for each other *(hold hands with people on either side)*
Amen.

Helpful extras

Music and song ideas

Many hymns and songs pick up the theme of creation: 'All creatures of our God and King'; 'My Jesus, my Saviour'; 'All things bright and beautiful'; 'From the highest of heights'. Choose songs which mention our responsibility for creation or the need for justice: 'God in his love for us lent us this planet'; 'Touch the earth lightly'; 'The right hand of God'. Include at least one action song to celebrate creation: 'Who put the colours in the rainbow?'; 'If I were a butterfly'.

Game

Produce a short quiz based on scientific facts about the universe. Divide people into teams and see who knows most. The prize could be some fair trade chocolate. Point out that knowledge is only valuable if we use it wisely. We are stewards of creation and should use our knowledge for the good of others. Fair trade is an example of people using their knowledge and abilities for good. Invite people to think of some other examples.

Notes and comments

This service outline complements the outline for Proper 22, Year B, which explores marriage and family relationships. This is available in *All-Age Lectionary Services Year B* (SU)

An alternative RCL service for this Sunday is available in the next service outline, which uses different Bible passages.

Alternative online options

Visit www.lightlive.org for additional activities for children, young people and adults.

SECOND SUNDAY BEFORE LENT (REVISED COMMON LECTIONARY)

READINGS: **Isaiah 6:1–8; Luke 5:1–11**
Psalm 138; 1 Corinthians 15:1–11

Bible foundations
Aim: to hear and respond to God's call

The motif of God's call runs throughout the Bible. A helpful distinction can be made between a 'general' calling by God to a life of faith and obedience and a 'specific' call to serve him in a particular role or task. Within the New Testament such a general calling is depicted in terms of a summons to salvation and faith in Jesus Christ (1 Corinthians 1:9), while a specific calling may be either to a particular role or task in the life of the Church (1 Corinthians 12:28) or to a God-given vocation within wider society (1 Corinthians 7:17,20).

In Isaiah 6 we have recorded the dramatic call of Isaiah to undertake the role of prophet to God's faithless people. In Luke 5:1–11 Jesus summons his first disciples both to follow him as leader and Saviour (v 11) and to carry out the specific task of evangelism (v 10). There is a remarkable symmetry between these two call scenes. In both there is a readiness and sensitivity to hear the authoritative challenge, whether in the context of worship (Isaiah) or busy everyday activity (the disciples). There is also an overpowering recognition that such an experience involves an encounter with the Holy God, resulting in confession of sin and a deep sense of unworthiness (Isaiah 6:5; Luke 5:8). Such a response does not disqualify from service; rather it is the necessary first step to humble, dependent discipleship, reflected in a willingness to go where God leads (Isaiah 6:8; Luke 5:11).

If we respond to God's call upon our lives in such a manner we will also experience God's merciful forgiveness and gracious encouragement (Isaiah 6:7; Luke 5:10b), equipping us to be his servants. To obey such a call can be hard and costly (Isaiah 6:9–13; Luke 9:23–26), but there is no greater privilege than serving the Living God.

Beginning the service

With: paper fish shapes about 10 cm long, one for each member of the congregation

As people arrive, give them all a fish shape. These will be used in **Ending the service** so could be given out nearer the end if necessary.

Begin by ringing a bell, as in the school playground. Follow this by ringing a smoke or fire alarm, followed by a car horn or a bicycle bell. Talk about what effect these alarms have on people. What are they for?

Explain that during the service, you will be exploring what it means to hear from God and to respond.

Bible reading

Isaiah 6:1–8 is very evocative. Use several readers and sound effects as follows:

> Voice A: *(read in a confident male voice)* In the year that King Uzziah died, I had a vision of the Lord. He was on his throne high above, and his robe filled the temple.
> Voice B: *(with the sound of swishing wings as a wind, made with the mouth)* Flaming creatures with six wings each were flying over him. They covered their faces with two of their wings and their bodies with two more. They used the other two wings for flying, as they shouted
> A variety of voices: *(shouting and overlapping)* 'Holy, holy, holy, Lord All-Powerful! The earth is filled with your glory.'
> Voice B: *(a low rumbling sound, from a drum)* As they shouted, the doorposts of the temple shook, and the temple was filled with smoke.
> Voice A: *(trembling)* Then I cried out, 'I'm doomed! Everything I say is sinful, and so are the words of everyone around me. Yet I have seen the King, the Lord All-Powerful.' One of the flaming creatures flew over to me with a burning coal that it had taken from the altar with a pair of metal tongs. It touched my lips with the hot coal and said:
> Voice B: *(authoritatively)* 'This has touched your lips. Your sins are forgiven, and you are no longer guilty.'
> Voice A: After this, I heard the Lord ask,
> Voice B: 'Is there anyone I can send? Will someone go for us?' *(followed by a trumpet blast)*
> Voice A: 'I'll go,' I answered. 'Send me!'
>
> Isaiah 6:1–8 (CEV)

For a more visual presentation of Luke 5:1–11, one person could read the passage while others mime appropriately. Use as much of the worship space as possible. Emphasise: rowing, signalling for help, hauling in the net, Peter bowing at Jesus' feet, the disciples' decision to leave their nets and follow Jesus. Try to practise beforehand.

Bible talk

With: simple line drawings on large or small cards or as a PowerPoint, representing confession (kneeling), forgiveness (looking up and smiling) and willingness (walking), available as a download (YearC.2SunB4Lent_3)

In advance, either ask three volunteers to

stand up at the front throughout the talk to hold large cards displaying the artwork for 'confession', 'forgiveness' and 'willingness' or make enough copies of the cards for each person to have a set. Ask them to hold the pictures up when the words in bold below are mentioned.

Ask for suggestions for what is the most amazing thing anyone has seen, that makes them go, 'Wow! That's awesome!' In today's readings from Isaiah and Peter, two people both said 'Wow! That's awesome!' when they experienced God.

Isaiah encounters God
Think back to Isaiah. (You could give a Bible page reference for people to find the answers to questions.) Isaiah had an amazing vision. What did he see? What did he hear? It is hard to imagine and even harder to draw even though it was very visual! What Isaiah saw and heard led him to **confession**. *(Hold up pictures)* 'I'm doomed!' he cried. 'Everything I say is sinful!'

Peter encounters God
Then there was Peter who had been fishing all night. What had he caught? When Jesus told him to throw his net out on the other side, what happened? Peter's reaction was **confession**. He knelt in front of Jesus and said, 'Lord, don't come near me. I am a sinner.' Peter hadn't had an amazing vision, but he'd seen the awesomeness of God at work in a practical way.

We encounter God
What's our response when we become aware of the awesomeness of God at work? Saying 'Wow!' is great; it's a sign of our worship. But when we see God at work, does it also lead us to be aware of our own imperfection and sin which leads us to **confession**?

There was no way Peter and Isaiah could match up to God's holiness and glory. They were so aware of their own failing and sin. **Confession** was the obvious reaction. It was their response to the holiness of God.

Confession leads to forgiveness, followed by willingness
Can anyone remember what happened next to Isaiah? If necessary, prompt the congregation by reading Isaiah 6:6,7. Isaiah's **confession** led to God's **forgiveness**.

And what happened to Peter? Jesus told him not to be afraid. He didn't need to be afraid of the awesomeness of God because God had **forgiven** him.

Forgiveness makes us ready to do new things. We no longer feel all uncomfortable inside. We can start again, as if nothing has happened. We are encouraged to try again to do the right things.

What did Isaiah and Peter do once they had received God's forgiveness? They were **willing** to go wherever God sent them. They were **willing** to tell people what God wanted them to hear… 'I'll go. Send me!' said Isaiah. Peter and his friends left everything and went with Jesus.

When we see amazing things God has done, or amazing things he has created, are we **willing** to go and tell others who did them and who made them? When we see God's holiness, are we **willing** to respond in **confession**, by saying sorry that we don't match up to his greatness? And how do we respond when we are **forgiven**? Does it make us **willing** to go and do what God wants, like Isaiah and Peter?

Prayer activity

With: strips of paper about 10 cm high and 45 cm long (one for every group of 6–8 people) folded into a concertina shape with a man drawn on the front so that his hands and feet touch the edges (a gingerbread man cutter makes a good template for this); felt-tips; scissors

Organise everyone into groups of up to eight people and give each group a folded strip of paper, scissors and pens. Read out Luke 5:10b and ask each group to talk about different people to whom God is calling them to spread the good news. This could be individuals they know or groups in the community such as in school, the Scout troop, hospital or a place of work.

Someone in the group cuts round the template on the folded paper to make a string of people and each person decorates one figure with features or clothes that roughly resemble the person or group they have talked about. (Don't write names of individuals in the interests of privacy.) Lay the string of people in the middle of the group and at least one person can pray for the people who have been drawn, asking God to help group members to tell these people about Jesus. If possible, stick the strips around the worship space as a reminder to pray about spreading the good news.

Prayer of confession

With: a song that emphasises God's greatness

Sing a worship song that emphasises God's greatness and majesty (for suggestions see **Music and song ideas**). As the music dies away read out the following phrases with time between each for quiet reflection. Ideally these should be spoken by different people scattered about the worship space.

Lord, we are sorry that we are a people with unclean lips. We are sorry for words we say that hurt others. *(Pause)* For words we say that aren't true. *(Pause)*

For words we say which are rude. *(Pause)*

Lord, touch our lips with your holy fire and make them clean and ready to speak for you. *(Pause, then sing the song again)*

Lord, we are sorry that what we do does not match up to your holiness. We are sorry that we disobey others. *(Pause)*

We are sorry that we use violence instead of ways of peace. *(Pause)*

We are sorry that we sometimes go to places where we shouldn't go or are with people we shouldn't be with. *(Pause)*

Lord, we want to say, 'Don't come near us. We are sinners.' And yet we need you…

(A powerful voice, away from the others says): The Lord says: 'Your sins are forgiven. You are no longer guilty.'

Sing the worship song again as an act of commitment.

Ending the service

With: one fish shape for everyone; pens; baskets

Give out a fish to each person if you have not done this at **Beginning the service**. Remind the congregation that when God asked for someone to send his message Isaiah responded with the words: 'I'll go. Send me!' Peter and his friends left their nets at once and followed Jesus.

But the message isn't just for Isaiah and Peter. God calls us all to follow him and tell others about him. Invite anyone who wishes to, to respond by writing, 'I'll go. Send me!' on their fish and place it in a basket on the way out of church as an act of commitment. They could write their name on the fish or just put the fish in the basket if they want to follow Jesus. God will know they've put it there! You could all leave church singing a song of commitment such as 'Here I am, Lord'.

Helpful extras

Music and song ideas

There are three sections in this service reflected in the music options:

Songs to reflect holiness: 'Holy, holy, holy, Lord God almighty' (Jamie Owens); 'Holy, holy, holy'; 'I see the Lord' ('He is high and lifted up'); 'Majesty'; 'King of kings, majesty'; 'Be still, for the presence of the Lord'.

Our response to that holiness and majesty: 'I'm accepted, I'm forgiven'; 'Here I am to worship'.

Songs of commitment: 'I want to walk with Jesus Christ' ('Follow him'); 'Here I am, Lord' ('I, the Lord of sea and sky').

Statement of faith

The statement of faith and commitment is based on Isaiah's words, and is available as a download (YearC.2SunB4Lent_4).

Notes and comments

As an alternative **Beginning the service** ask someone who is wearing a fish badge or a cross to be prepared to explain why they wear it and what it means.

The theme for today's service is relevant for both baptism and Holy Communion. In baptism we are reminded that our sins need washing away and there is a sense of commitment that, by being baptised, we want to follow Jesus. As we take the bread and wine we are reminded of the forgiveness that Jesus gives us. Encourage everyone to say a prayer of commitment as they take the bread and wine.

Isaiah's vision of holiness reminds us of the 'otherness' of God, an aspect of God that is sometimes overlooked. This service gives an opportunity to focus on God's greatness and holiness. This is not to make people feel guilty, but is a reminder that God is not simply a comfortable friend!

An alternative CW service for this Sunday is available in the previous service outline using different Bible passages.

Alternative online options

For your convenience the following activities are available as downloads: YearC.2SunB4Lent_5 Isaiah 6 Rap; YearC.2SunB4Lent_6 Song for under-5s. Visit www.lightlive.org for additional activities for children, young people and adults.

SUNDAY BEFORE LENT

READINGS: **Exodus 34:29-35; Luke 9:28-36 [37-43]**
Psalm 99; 2 Corinthians 3:12 - 4:2

Aim: to explore the way God reveals his truth and glory

A bright aura of holiness surrounds Moses and then Jesus. Each time God is glorified and his truth is revealed. Both transfiguration stories are linked to 'mountain top' experiences. Throughout history, mountains or high places have been connected in some way with religion, even though we no longer believe we are physically closer to God on a mountain. Mountains represent revelation, worship and the presence of God in Israel's spiritual history – an awesome God who is worshipped on God's 'holy mountain' (Psalm 99). In the Gospels, similar meaning is found in high places, such as a sermon, Jesus' transfiguration, crucifixion and ascension.

Moses has just seen God's glory and received God's commandments on the mountain. The experience transfigures him. He radiates holiness, reflects God's glory, and reveals God's splendour. The people are afraid to come near until Moses puts on a veil (possibly a ritual mask designed to give priests and prophets anonymity, so emphasising their sacred role). This softened the glare from Moses' face so the people could concentrate on the words he brought from God. Paul (2 Corinthians 3:13,16) links the veil to the illusory and temporary glory of the law in comparison to the sure and lasting glory of Christ.

The disciples, as a result of the transfiguration, and seeing God's glory revealed in Jesus' face, made a connection between Moses and Elijah. As a cloud obscured the bright shining of Jesus' face, a voice confirmed what Peter had confessed a week earlier – Jesus was God's Chosen One. The terrified disciples connected the cloud with the very presence of God (Psalm 99:7). A shrine could not do justice to the experience, nor words describe it (Luke 9:36). But their new spiritual insight was not yet translated into spiritual confidence or power. God's truth and glory would only be fully revealed with Jesus' death in Jerusalem (v 31). (Note that verse 43 is the key to the optional verses in Luke.)

Beginning the service

With: a bridal veil or long material; different masks (plain and decorated); two or more mirrors placed so that they reflect out the light from a lamp or candle which is positioned between them – a disco ball hung above the light would be even better; projected pictures of inspiring mountain scenes, especially with light reflections

A visual display could be set up near the front of the church, using a long bridal veil (or material to suggest one) as a backdrop. The different masks could be placed on this. Being aware of safety issues, two or more mirrors are placed to reflect the light and the pictures of mountain scenes are projected before the service. Begin with the response below, based on Psalm 99, which is also available as a download (YearC.SunB4Lent_1).

Our Lord, you are King!
Only you are God!
You are praised in Zion,
Only you are God!
Your power alone is worthy of praise.
Only you are God!
We praise you and kneel down to worship you.
We praise you, Lord God.
Moses and Aaron were two of your priests.
You answered their prayers.
You spoke to your people from a thick cloud.
They obeyed your laws.
They worshipped you at your sacred mountain.
We praise you, Lord God.
We praise you, Lord God.
Only you are God!

Bible reading

Exodus 34:29–35 and Luke 9:28–36 could be accompanied by mime. The CEV provides the most suitable reading for this. Simple and recognisable props would emphasise the parts relating to God's glory and truth and link the two stories. For example, 'Moses' could carry the Ten Commandments tablets and wear a 'prayer shawl' on his head. Silver or gold face paint would make his face 'shine'. A plain mask (made from a paper plate) is used for the 'veil'. 'Elijah' could carry a stave. 'Jesus' could place and remove a large piece of gold or white material, such as net curtain, over himself at the appropriate moments.

The readings should be done slowly, allowing plenty of time for the mime actions such as telling the people the Commandments, showing their fear, the disciples praying, then falling asleep, which should be exaggerated enough to be seen, but not so as to be comical. 'Moses' should be the same actor in both stories. Using a different reader for each story will help listeners distinguish between them, while the one following the other shows the link.

Bible retelling

The sketch, available as a download (YearC.SunB4Lent_2), explores the effect of the transfiguration on the three disciples. The characters are Peter, James, John and two female disciples.

Bible talk

With: use the following from **Beginning the service** – picture(s) of mountains, a wedding veil, several mirrors, a variety of masks, including the plain one from the mime of

Exodus (Plain masks are available from craft stores/websites, or can be made from a paper plate.)

Meeting God

Begin by asking if anyone has ever been up a mountain (hold up a picture or show one on screen). What was best about the experience? What felt special? Someone might say they felt closer to God. If not, ask if anyone did feel closer. Explain briefly about the importance of mountains in the history of religion as places where people have felt especially close to God. Where else do people feel especially close to God?

Comment that we still talk about 'mountain top experiences' even though we may not have been up a mountain, and no longer believe God lives in the sky. Has anyone had a 'mountain top experience' which has changed their life? You could brief someone beforehand to share an appropriate personal testimony.

Both of today's Bible stories take place on mountains. Think about what Moses had been doing up God's holy mountain, what he saw, how special it was and what difference it made to him. Wonder what the people thought when they saw Moses' face shining and why they might have been afraid. If the person playing Moses in the mime wore gold face paint ask him to come forward. Ask the congregation whether, if this person were to talk to them, they might be distracted from listening by their fascination with the gold face.

Experiencing God's glory

Pick up the wedding veil. Explain that a wedding veil traditionally covered a bride's face until the priest declared the couple to be man and wife. The groom was thus not distracted from the serious business of the wedding vows by his bride's pretty face! You could demonstrate this with a girl/young woman volunteer. Maybe it was something like a wedding veil that Moses put on to cover his face so people could concentrate on the words that Moses had brought from God.

More likely it was something like a mask (pick up the mask). In many religions ritual masks were worn by priests and prophets so people didn't think, 'Oh, that's Jim, and that's Bob', but concentrated on the worship. Some masks were carved and decorated to honour the god *(show some if you have examples)*. You might consider whether Moses' mask was plain or decorated – it would probably have been made of beaten metal. Do your ministers wear anything which helps you think more about God and less about the minister's personality? If you are brave you could ask if anything he/she wears distracts people from worship! Does your church have anything decorated or carved that honours God?

Being in God's presence

Moses' story suggests humans can be changed by being in the presence of God. When we worship God we come into his presence. How does our worship change our appearance? Can people see the glow of God on us? Do we reflect God's glory like these mirrors reflect this light? What sort of face do people see when we leave church? A kind face? A gentle face? A loving face? Invite responses. Can other people see God in our lives?

We heard today that three of Jesus' disciples saw God's glory on a mountain too. It was very special for them, but the disciples' faces did not shine after seeing God's glory. Maybe this was why they did not say anything about the experience until much later, after the resurrection, when they realised what it all meant – like lifting the veil. Sometimes it takes a while for us too!

You could use the mirror facial expression activity available as a download (YearC.SunB4Lent_4) which will engage younger children and move on to the following **Prayer activity**.

Prayer activity

With: a paper plate cut as a mask, one for everyone; plenty of felt colouring pens (optional: flip chart, volunteer scribe and pens)

Invite people to call out things in the world, the church and our own lives that mask or hide the glory and truth of God – for example: injustice, spiritual blindness, anger or fear. These could be written on a flip chart. Invite everyone to use the colouring pens on one side of the mask to illustrate how we mask God's glory (writing, drawing or colouring). Then pray the following with everyone joining in the response, based on 2 Corinthians 3:12 – 4:2.

Leader	Something still keeps us from seeing the truth.
All	**The Lord's Spirit will set us free.**
Leader	Only Christ can take away the veil.
All	**The Lord's Spirit will set us free.**
Leader	Let us turn to the Lord.
All	**The Lord's Spirit will set us free**

Remind people of the kind of face we might have if we have seen God's glory in our worship, if we have God in our lives. Invite people to call out who might need to see our 'we've-been-with-God' faces and where we can make a difference. On the reverse of the mask invite people to colour it to reflect the glory of God and the truth of his love that we want to show the world. Then join in the following prayer and response.

Leader	The Lord's Spirit will set us free.
All	**Let us show his truth.**
Leader	The Spirit makes us more and more like our glorious Lord.
All	**Let us show his glory.**
Leader	God trusts us with his work.
All	**Let us show his love.**

Ending the service

With: gold, white and orange florists' ribbon cut into streamers so everyone can have two; the mirrors or disco ball from **Beginning the service**; the masks

Tell everyone we are going to finish by praising God for his glory and asking him to send us out to reflect his glory in the way we live our lives. So invite people to put on their masks if they want to, with the loving, glory, we've-been-with-God side facing the world. The mirrors or mirror ball will reflect the glory even more, if you are using one.

Celebrate by waving the streamers as you sing the song below to the tune 'Morning Hymn' or 'Doxology'. In 1674, Thomas Ken wrote these words as the last verse of the hymn 'Awake my soul and with the sun, my daily course of duty run'. He wanted to praise God in the mornings. It is appropriate to finish your worship with praise. Younger children could come to the front to dance.

If you are using the tune 'Doxology' by Jamie Owens, you could divide the congregation into four groups since this verse sounds best as a round/canon. (Number the groups 1 to 4 and explain that group 2 starts when group 1 has sung the first line, group 3 starts when group 2 have finished the first line and so on – you may want to sing it all together once as a reminder of the tune.)

Praise God from whom all blessings flow;
Praise him all creatures here below;
Praise him above ye heavenly host;
Praise Father, Son and Holy Ghost.

Invite everyone to turn to the door as you say the final prayer:

Lord God, thank you for revealing the glory and truth of your love to us in Jesus.

Bless us as we go out into your world and help us to reflect his love and glory. Amen.

Helpful extras

Music and song ideas

'Lord, the light of your love is shining'; 'Be still, for the presence of the Lord'; 'Glorious things of thee are spoken'; 'O Lord, my God' ('How great thou art'); 'My God is a great big God'; 'Holy, holy, holy, Lord God almighty'; 'Holy, holy, holy is his name'; 'Praise God from whom all blessings flow' (various versions).

Notes and comments

The masks can be threaded with elastic or wool to tie them on. Alternatively, they could be taped to a stick. This would have the effect of the masks worn by actors in Greek drama. You could also link the masks to Mardi Gras, especially the Venetian celebrations, which ties in very well with the imminence of Lent. The masks hide who people really are, a thread that could be developed further if the children are older.

Since this is near Valentine's Day you could comment on the fact that God's love is so great that we cannot grasp it. Like his glory we often cannot take it in or understand its implications. This would naturally lead on to commenting on God's love as shown in Jesus' death and resurrection.

Alternative online options

For your convenience the following activities are available as downloads: YearC.SunB4Lent_3 Mountain meditation for under-5s; YearC.SunB4Lent_4 Mirror Bible story for younger children. Visit www.lightlive.org for additional activities for children, young people and adults.

FIRST SUNDAY OF LENT

READINGS: **Psalm 91:1,2,9–16; Luke 4:1–13**
Deuteronomy 26:1–11; Romans 10:8b–13

Bible foundations
Aim: to explore how God protects his people, including his Son

Psalm 91 is a psalm of complete trust in God, an expression of confidence that God can, and will, protect those who believe and trust in him, in all danger and difficulty. The key to understanding this psalm comes in the testing of Jesus in the wilderness and how he responds to Satan's own use of verses 11 and 12 in the third temptation.

Following his baptism, Jesus is sent into the wilderness by the Spirit where he fasts and reflects upon his calling to fulfil God's purpose. Jesus becomes hungry and weak. Satan tempts Jesus to use his own power to meet his needs and to prove his divine Sonship, rather than believing and trusting in the words of his Father at his baptism (Luke 3:22), words cleverly used by Satan in two of the temptations (vs 3,9). Jesus, however, chooses to trust God and not his own powers. He refuses to take a moral shortcut to meet his hunger (v 4), knowing such 'cheating' eventually leads to the disastrous situation where wants become needs. In spite of the potential for good, Jesus declares power to be idolatrous (v 8), a rejection of God's protection and truth. He also rejects the temptation of invulnerability (v 10,11), aware that such a path would interfere with God's plan. Expecting God to set aside the way creation works is to test God. God's protection is not a divine guarantee that everything will be OK.

God makes us free. Temptation is part of his plan both for Jesus (verse 1) and for us. Testing is necessary as preparation for serious work. Testing is God's 'protection plan' for us. Through accepting vulnerability and resisting temptation Jesus builds his spiritual resources. He will continue to face temptation throughout his ministry, from his enemies, from his friends, from within, even on the cross – 'If you are truly the Son of God, come down!' The way Jesus deals with temptation has strong implications for his followers.

Beginning the service

With: a large sheet of cardboard covered in sandpaper on which are some large rocks (including one the shape of a small loaf); a table; a bread roll; water; a selection of items representing what we might put our trust in, or need, or think we need (such as a model of a house, toy car, bottle of wine, a vegetable, credit card, teddy bear, blanket, mobile phone, fashion/sports item, advert for a slimming club); signs saying 'I need…' and 'I trust…'

Place the bread roll, water and selected items on the table. Ensure the choice of items reflects the congregation's priorities and ages.

Introduce Lent as the six weeks we have to prepare for the festival of Easter. Easter is the most important Christian festival and it takes longer to prepare for than Christmas (Advent is only four weeks). Lent begins with the story of Jesus' temptations. Jesus' time in the wilderness gives us a clue as to how we can prepare for Easter. It also gives us a clue as to how we can expect God to look after us.

Some people give up something they like but don't need in Lent. (Pick up the 'I need…' sign.) There are a lot of things on the table which people often say they need. Pick up several and consider which ones are proper needs and which are not. What else might we really need rather than just like to have?

Some things on the table are things we rely on, things we trust. (Pick up the 'I trust…' sign.) Pick up and comment on things like the car (to get us to school or work), mobile phone (to keep us in touch with friends), credit card (when we're short of cash!). I wonder if they really are trustworthy? The Bible tells us there is something better.

Voice 1: The Lord is our strength and our refuge.
Voice 2: Our God in whom we trust.
Voice 1: Place your offerings before the Lord and worship him.
Voice 2: Rejoice in all the good things the Lord has given to us.

Bible reading

Psalm 91 is full of strong protective language. The following verses (1,2,9–16) contain commands, words that are said to God and words that God himself says. With three readers, read it as follows, from the CEV, but also display it on the screen. Everyone could join in as 'The rescued'. This is also available as a download (YearC.Lent1_1).

> **The commander:** Live under the protection of God Most High and stay in the shadow of God All-Powerful.
> Then you will say to the Lord:
> **The rescued:** You are my fortress, my place of safety; you are my God, and I trust you.
> **The commander:** The Lord Most High is your fortress. Run to him for safety, and no terrible disasters will strike you or your home. God will command his angels to protect you wherever you go. They will carry you in their arms, and you won't hurt your feet on the stones. You will overpower the strongest lions and the most deadly snakes.
> **The Lord:** If you love me and truly know who I am, I will rescue you and keep you safe. When you are in trouble, call out to me. I will answer and be there to protect

> and honour you. You will live a long life and see my saving power.
> **The rescued:** You are my fortress, my place of safety; you are my God, and I trust you.
>
> Psalm 91 (CEV)

Luke 4:1–13 lends itself to a dramatic reading with a narrator, Satan and Jesus. This is available as a download (YearC.Lent1_2).

Bible talk

With: flip chart/whiteboard or OHP and pens; items from **Beginning the service**

Invite people to call out the names and images of God in the reading of Psalm 91. Write them up. Which names best express who God is for them, and what he means for them at this particular time? Why? When have they experienced God's protection? Have there been times they've wanted his protection, but it didn't seem to be there? Christians get sick, injured and attacked. Has God chosen not to protect them?

Jesus' power to turn stones into food

We are going to explore what God's protection means, starting with the story about Jesus in the wilderness. He was there a long time with no food: 40 days in fact. For thousands of years people have used going without food for a while (fasting) as a way to get closer to God. How long could you go without food? (Pick up the loaf-shaped stone.) For really hungry people, even stones can look like food! After 40 days Jesus would soon need to eat, but there was no food. He had the power to turn rocks into food, but would that be the right way to use his power? He had more important things to think about. He wasn't going to die of hunger – he knew God would provide him with something to eat when the time was right.

What about us? In **Beginning the service**, we looked at the things that we really do need – though not as frequently as we claim! We also persuade ourselves we need other things when we don't, and miss the important things in life. What might they be? Jesus trusted God would give him what he needed. Will we trust God to give us all we really need?

The devil's offer of world power

The devil offered Jesus world power (a power that was not ultimately his to give). What would you do if you could be ruler of the world? Invite ideas and write them down on the flip chart – these could range from purely selfish ones to the altruistic. Make the point that power can be used for good, which is why power was such a tempting idea for Jesus. He knew that 'power corrupts, and absolute power corrupts absolutely'. Power means having what we want and controlling other people's lives. We are worshipping ourselves. Although there are some things we need to control, always wanting to be in control is thinking we know best. Do you know someone like that? Are you sometimes like that too? Jesus said 'No!' to power – worship God and he will protect you.

Jesus' power to reverse the laws of nature

Jesus trusted that God his Father really did know what was best. That leads to the devil's third challenge. 'Throw yourself off the top of the Temple! God's angels will catch you, just like it says in the Psalm.' What would happen if I jumped off the top of a really tall building? I'd fall! I might break some bones, maybe even kill myself. Why would I fall? God made gravity to hold the world together!

What if I catch a germ? I may get sick, but germs are needed in God's world. What if your boyfriend/girlfriend leaves you? Your heart will break but God has made us with the freedom to make choices and it's the way he made our hearts. So why do we think God should set aside the way his creation works just to suit us? Can you imagine the chaos if it was happening every time someone wanted God to go against his laws of creation?!

Jesus knew God's protection was not a divine guarantee that nothing bad would ever happen. He also knew God protects his followers by strengthening them to face bad things. Temptation is part of God's plan, for us as well as for Jesus. Jesus carried on being tempted, even on the cross. We will be tempted to test God's love all through our lives. Testing prepared Jesus for God's work. Testing prepares us for God's work – it is God's protection plan! During Lent everyone in church can aim to create extra time to spend with God, experiencing his protection in what may be a time of testing.

Prayer of confession

With: 5 cm rough wooden crosses (purchase cheaply at www.wooden-crosses.co.uk) ideally for each person or to be shared in a group; a small square of sandpaper

The cross is the symbol of God's love in Jesus. Jesus knew the path to the cross would not be easy, but God would be there. After each response everyone can rub a little of the roughness from their cross with sandpaper to remind them of God's strengthening protection. The emboldened response is:

And protect us in the time of temptation.

We think of the three temptations of Jesus as he prepared to fulfil God's purpose. We also think of how we fail to resist temptation: Jesus resisted the temptation to take a moral shortcut. We think of those times when we do the wrong thing to get what we need. We think of those things we think we need, but which are really luxuries. We think of how our environment and other people are harmed by our greed. Lord, forgive us…
And protect us in the time of temptation.

Jesus resisted the temptation to take power. We think of the times we have tried to control the lives of others, even times we have thought we were doing the right thing. We think of the times we have thought ourselves more important or better than other people. We think of how we have rejected God's protection and trusted in our own power and possessions. Lord, forgive us…
And protect us in the time of temptation.

Jesus resisted the temptation to test God. We think of the times we have tested God, when we have demanded proof of God's protection or when we have behaved like spoilt children and expected God to set aside the laws of nature, regardless of others. We think of how much spiritual growing up we still need to do. Lord, forgive us…
And protect us in the time of temptation.

Prayers of intercession

With: Taizé response reflecting Psalm 91.15: O Lord, hear my prayer. O Lord, hear my prayer. When I call, answer me.

Invite people to pray aloud (or in their heads

if they prefer) in three sections relating to the three temptations:

- those who have real needs
- those with the responsibilities of power, including in the church
- those who need reassurance of God's protection.

Alternatively one person/group could write and lead intercessions under these headings. After each section, sing the Taizé response.

Ending the service

Invite people to take home their crosses and over Lent think about their personal temptations, each time sanding their cross a little more, smoothing away the roughness, just as God does to our lives if we follow Jesus' way. When the cross becomes really smooth they could varnish or paint it and carry it with them to remind them of God's protection.

Holding the wooden crosses, close with this prayer and the emboldened response:

During Lent we are saying no to the things we do not need.
Lord, help us and protect us.
During Lent we are trusting in God and not ourselves.
Lord, help us and protect us.
During Lent we are learning to trust God and not test him.
Lord, help us and protect us.

Helpful extras

Music and song ideas

'Money, money, money' *(Fiddler on the Roof)* or 'Diamonds are a girl's best friend' *(Gentlemen Prefer Blondes)* could be used at **Beginning the service** to illustrate some of the points.

'All my hope on God is founded'; 'Be the centre of my life'; 'Be thou my guardian and my guide'; 'Cry "Freedom!" in the name of God'; 'Every minute of every day'; 'Father, hear the prayer we offer'; 'Forty days and forty nights'; 'God is our strength and refuge'; 'God the source and goal of being'; 'Jesus went away to the desert'; 'Lord of all hopefulness'; 'My God is so big'.

Notes and comments

The Grand Inquisitor's conversation with Christ in *The Brothers Karamazov* by Dostoevsky illustrates well the point about God's gift of freedom and might be used (perhaps as a dramatised dialogue) if the congregation consists of older children and adults.

The story of Dr Faust is a good illustration of the corrupting influence of power.

It might be appropriate for someone to give a personal testimony of a way in which God has protected them. Such stories can act as encouragement.

Alternative online options

For your convenience the following activity is available as a download: YearC.Lent1_3 Trust bracelet for children of all ages. Visit www.lightlive.org for additional activities for children, young people and adults.

SECOND SUNDAY OF LENT

READINGS: **Genesis 15:1–12,17,18; Psalm 27**
Philippians 3:17 – 4:1; Luke 13:31–35

Bible foundations
Aim: to recognise that God makes and keeps his promises

We can all feel compassion for a parent who is childless but longs for children. In Abram's culture having a son and heir was crucial. What was the point of prospering (see Genesis 13:2) if one had to leave it all to someone else (Genesis 15:3)? Who would remember you and tell the stories and carry on the family values? So when God speaks of rewarding Abram (v 1) it all rings a bit hollow. Similarly we may be conscious that God has blessed us in many ways but in the one thing that really matters it may seem he has withheld his blessing.

God makes Abram a promise which seemed impossible to fulfil – his own son would be his heir (v 4). Abram would soon be 99, and his wife Sarah, 90 (Genesis 17:1,17). So God helps him with a gigantic visual aid – the starry sky (v 5). Abram, having proved God's faithfulness up to this point, believes the stark word of God, and is therefore reckoned as righteous (see Romans 4:18–23). The promise of an heir comes with a promise of land, again of crucial importance in that culture. God generously gives Abram a guarantee of the truth of the covenant he is making with him, in terms of a practice common at the time. The significance of the blazing torch passing between the pieces of the animals (v 17) is that God is saying, 'I will be totally faithful to this promise – even if I have to die to keep it.' (One can't help thinking of Calvary.)

We too may say with the psalmist, 'I am still confident of this: I will see the goodness of the Lord in the land of the living' and be determined to 'be strong and take heart and wait for the Lord' (Psalm 27:13,14), knowing that 'the future is as bright as the promises of God', to quote Adoniram Judson, a pioneer missionary to Burma.

Beginning the service

Can you remember a promise you have made? Write out the words of a well-known promise, such as the Scout Promise, the oath taken before testifying in a court of law, or the traditional wedding vow. These three promises are available as a download (YearC.Lent2_1).

Cut the promise into sections or individual words, depending on length, and mix them up. Ask the congregation to reassemble the promise as quickly and accurately as possible. This could be done in small groups or altogether. Point out that it is not always easy to remember exactly word for word what we have promised.

Ask for a quick show of hands of those who have made one or more of these promises at some point in their lives. Each requires wholehearted, honest commitment, though different time frames are involved. Each is difficult to keep, in its own way. God's promises are not like our promises – because God is not like us in finding it difficult to keep his promises.

Bible reading

Genesis 15:1–12,17,18 begins and ends with Abram experiencing a vision and includes a night sky, the setting sun, thick darkness and a blazing fire. Emphasise these changes by the use of strategically placed lighting and two readers reading alternate verses, with plenty of dramatic pauses. This will need careful rehearsal with the lighting operator. The reading should end with muted red light, representing the blazing torch in verses 17 and 18.

For dramatic contrast, pause briefly at the end to allow the readers to leave and two new ones to take their places discreetly, then put all the lights up and move straight into Psalm 27, which should be read brightly and crisply, with the readers taking alternate paragraphs (verses 1–3, 4–6, 7–10, 11, 12 and 13, 14).

Bible talk

With: large stars strung on a thread (as with a Christmas decoration or make your own), fixed horizontally between two visible points before beginning the Bible talk; four clothes pegs in different colours to which are attached the following words: Abram, David, Paul, Us

Although he was a nomad, Abram was an extremely wealthy man. He was already wealthy when he left Ur, with his wife Sarai, his nephew Lot and all the possessions and people they had acquired in Haran (Genesis 12:5). He was showered with gifts by Pharaoh in Egypt (sheep, cattle, donkeys, servants and camels – 12:16) so that by the time he reached the Negev he had accumulated even more livestock, silver and gold. He and Lot had such huge flocks that they had to separate, because the land could not support all the herds. When Lot was abducted, Abram responded by sending the 318 trained men 'born in his household' (14:14) to rescue him. It's hard to guess just how big that household must have been! Abram insisted on being fully independent and would receive no gifts from the king of Sodom, so that he would never be able to say, 'I made Abram rich'.

But all this wealth would pass to a man who was not related to Abram, Eliezer, since Abram had no son. It was the biggest concern of his life. It was a personal matter. His wealth would not disappear, but it would not go to his own child.

God's promise to Abram
(Fix a clothes peg to the first star on the thread – far left as the congregation sees it.) The first promise God made to Abram was in response to the personal need Abram had expressed. (Note Abram's name did not change until Genesis 17:5. 'Abraham' sounds like 'father of many nations'.) God said he would have a son and many offspring, like the stars in the sky. It was a wonderful promise, yet simple, and Abram simply believed it. But God had not finished. He went on to promise Abram land, something he had never had before and not specifically asked for. This time, we do not read that Abram believed the promise immediately. This time, it was not a personal matter. Abram was now the representative of a future nation, rather than a childless, wealthy individual. He and God engaged in a complicated covenantal ritual involving animal sacrifice and it was in an altered state of consciousness, a deep sleep which is described as a 'thick and dreadful darkness', that Abram received God's promise about the land. The first promise, about a son, was one which Abram would see fulfilled in the flesh. The second, about the land, would be a much more complex issue, to be fulfilled many hundreds of years later, not immediately; a promise made to a people, not an individual.

David affected by the promise to Abram
Let's look at how some of Abram's descendants experienced the promises of God. One of them was King David, the psalmist. *(Fix the second clothes peg to a star about a quarter of the way along the thread.)* By the time he was born, Abraham's descendants had indeed taken possession of the land and David could look back over the entire history of God's dealings with his people – how he rescued them, conquered their enemies, met them in worship, showed them mercy and gave them strength. So David's confidence in the promises of God is great – 'Whom shall I fear?' 'The Lord will receive me.' 'I will see the goodness of the Lord in the land of the living'. This is confidence built not only on personal experience of God's goodness, but collective, national experience.

Paul affected by the promise to Abram
(Fix the third clothes peg to a star about halfway along the thread.) Then there was Paul, another direct descendant of Abraham. He too could look back over many centuries of history in which God had fulfilled his promises, from Abraham onwards, right past David and up to the first century AD. Therefore he was certain that the promises made by Jesus during his lifetime would be fulfilled. Through the power of Jesus' resurrection, Paul and all those living as Jesus' disciples (including us) can look forward to the coming of the Saviour, when we will experience 'citizenship in heaven', and 'transformed bodies'. Refer to the reading in Philippians 3:17 – 4:1, if you have read it.

We are affected by the promise to Abram
(Fix the fourth clothes peg to a star three-quarters of the way along the thread.) In many ways, we too are living in expectation of the same promises of which Paul writes. Some have not yet been fulfilled. But we belong to that same, unbroken chain of Abram's descendants, who can look back to see what God has done and like Abram (point to the

first peg) simply believe his promises. Like David *(point to the second peg)*, we can 'seek his face' in confidence and trust. Trusting in the promises of God will help us 'stand firm', as Paul says *(point to the third peg)*. It is not over yet… *(point to the remaining stars…)*

Bible talk

With: large piece of black paper on an easel or stand; silver and/or gold adhesive stars

Ask God to strengthen your faith in his promises and his reliability in keeping these promises by creating a prayer collage together. Display the large piece of black paper on an easel where everyone can see it. Place a container of small silver or gold adhesive stars beneath it. Explain that anyone who feels that the prayer you are about to read is what they want to say to God should come forward and stick a star on the black paper. This is not meant to be a sign of how much faith they have in God's promises, but of their desire to be strengthened in that faith. It would be appropriate to play quiet worship music in the background during this activity (such as 'Be still and know that I am God'), which should be limited to about 3 minutes to avoid any awkwardness. Prepare two or three people in advance to show what needs to be done. The following prayer is also available as a PowerPoint slide download (YearC.Lent2_2) and can be displayed on screen while it is being read. People can join in the emboldened responses.

Our wonderful Heavenly Father,
You made promises to Abraham and he believed you.
You kept your promises.
You made promises to David and he believed you.
You kept your promises.
You made promises to the disciples through Jesus and they believed him.
You kept your promises.
You made promises to the early Church, through the Holy Spirit.
You kept your promises.
Today we look forward to the fulfilment of your promises about the future.
We expect you to act in our lives today in fulfilment of other promises. Sometimes it is hard to wait and believe. Sometimes it takes years. Help us to put our faith in you, to know that you are our stronghold, our Saviour, the One who takes away our fears. We are confident that we will see the goodness of the Lord in the land of the living.
Help us to be strong and take heart while we wait on you.
Amen.

Prayers of intercession

These prayers are based on well-known Bible promises. Add your own ideas according to the current prayer needs of the congregation, the local community or world.

Lord, you promised that all who are weary and come to you will find rest. We pray for anyone who needs your rest…
Lord, in your mercy, hear our prayer.
Lord, you have promised to forgive those who are sorry for their wrongdoings. We pray for those who are burdened by guilt and need to know your forgiveness, and for those they have hurt or offended…
Lord, in your mercy, hear our prayer.
Lord, you have promised to instruct us and teach us in the way we should go. We pray for those who need guidance, help and counselling in problems and difficulties and for

those who try to help them…
Lord, in your mercy, hear our prayer.
Lord, you have promised us your peace,
not as the world gives, but as you give. Give
peace in those parts of the world which are in
conflict today…
Lord, in your mercy, hear our prayer.
Lord, you promised that when two or three
were gathered in your name, you would grant
their requests. We bring our prayers for
others to you.
Lord, in your mercy, hear our prayer.

Ending the service

Choose one of the hymns below or another song which affirms faith in God's promises. Place the container with silver and gold stars at the exit (see **Prayer activity**) and invite the congregation to take a star with them as they leave. They might want to stick it to an article of clothing, on their computer monitor, kitchen door, Bible or elsewhere, to remind them during the week that God keeps his promises.

Helpful extras

Music and song ideas

'Faithful One'; 'All my hope on God is founded'; 'God is working his purpose out'; 'Thy hand, O God, has guided', 'Our God is an awesome God'.

Game

With: adhesive stars

This requires advance preparation. Tell the children that there are stars all over the room – not in the sky, but on chairs, tables, the floor and other places. They will not have to move anything or climb on anything to find them. Ask them to collect as many as they can find. As they return with stars, spread them on the floor in front of you. When most of the stars have been found, gather the children again, sitting them around the stars. Ask whether anyone can count them. Some children may try, but quickly conclude that there are too many to count! Make the connection with God's promise to Abram.

Notes and comments

Corrie Ten Boom, the Dutch evangelist, said, 'Let God's promises shine on your problems.'

Dwight L. Moody, the American evangelist, said, 'God never made a promise that was too good to be true.'

It would be appropriate to invite one or two people to prepare ahead of time to speak briefly about how God has kept his promises in their lives. Ask them to focus on a specific Bible promise (they should read out the promise, not just paraphrase it) and how God acted to fulfil it. This might include long periods of waiting or doubt.

Alternative online options

For your convenience, the following activity is available as a download: YearC.Lent2_3 a rhyme for all ages to learn. Visit www.lightlive.org for additional activities for children, young people and adults.

THIRD SUNDAY OF LENT

READINGS: **Isaiah 55:1–9; Psalm 63:1–8**
1 Corinthians 10:1–13; Luke 13:1–9

Bible foundations
Aim: to find God's hope in adversity and hardship

In the context of Isaiah, the glorious invitations of chapter 55 come after the central account of the atoning work of the Servant of the Lord (52:13 – 53:12) and the celebration of the future glory of Zion (Isaiah 54). The promises in Isaiah chapters 40 to 55 presuppose God's people were living in exile in Babylon (see 40:1,2), experiencing adversity and hardship. In this context comes a universal invitation to anyone thirsty or poor to freely enjoy 'the richest of fare' (v 2). This is all tied up with Israel's messianic hope, the promise to David of an everlasting covenant (v 3 and also 2 Samuel 7:11b–16). From being bottom of the pile, Israel will be 'endowed with splendour' (v 5), and fulfil its mission to be a light to the nations (42:6; 49:6 and see Exodus 19:5,6).

If individuals are to enjoy this salvation, they must seek the Lord, and turn to him in repentance (verse 6). Similarly, Jesus reminds his hearers of the priority of repentance (Luke 13:3,5) to avoid coming judgement, and Paul warns his readers to avoid the idolatry and immorality of God's people in the wilderness (1 Corinthians 10:1–13). True repentance involves seeking God earnestly (see Psalm 63:1). As someone has said, it is not a casual 'sorry' any more than God's forgiveness is a casual 'not at all!' We need to recognise that God's ways and thoughts are far above ours (Isaiah 55:8,9) and what seems ordinary to us may offend a holy God. At the same time God's wonderful way of salvation is far greater than we could ever have conceived. His word (v 11) along with his promises in verses 3, 5 and 12 is sure and will bring transformation. Instead of desolation, symbolised by thorns and briars (signs of the curse in Genesis 3:18) will come joy and delight, symbolised by the pine and myrtle (verse 13).

Beginning the service

With: desert pictures or photos, particularly of the Desert of Judah

If anyone has been to the Desert of Judah they will recall the drive down from Jerusalem into the barren waste, stretching all the way down to the fertile fields around Jericho. Alternatively use the 'Desert quiz' available as a download (YearC.Lent3_1). Think for a few moments about living in an arid, inhospitable environment. In the Bible, this image is often used as a simile for spiritual dryness or adversity.

Bible reading

The reader of Isaiah 55:1–9 should be confident and address the congregation loudly as though speaking from a platform in a public place. Rehearse mimed reactions from members of the congregation, as follows:

Verses 1–3a: one or two people stand up and move out of their places to go towards the speaker. They do not look at each other, but give the speaker their full attention, holding out their hands to receive what the speaker is offering.

Verses 3b–5: another person gets up and moves forward, pen and paper in hand. He pretends to take notes on what the speaker is saying.

Verses 6,7: another person, after turning this way and that, catches sight of the speaker and moves towards him. He kneels down before the speaker.

Verses 8,9: all the participants kneel together in an attitude of humility. The speaker extends hands of blessing over them as he says the last words of the reading.

Bible retelling

Psalm 63 is told as a monologue with David as the speaker. He should pull a cloak around his shoulders, rub his hands together as though keeping warm, massage his back, grimace because of his stiff neck, and display similar indications of physical discomfort, while talking to God. Introduce King David.

'Dear God, I wish I could find you in this horrible place. I'm so worn out. I'm terribly hungry and thirsty, and it's so uncomfortable here. Just the bare rocks. Haven't seen a living thing for days, not even a rat. There's nothing here for them to eat, let alone me. And I really need a drink of water!

Dear God, it hurts me to think about how different it was, not so long ago, when I could meet you in the Temple, day by day. Such a lovely building! Such a feeling of your presence! Such magnificence! Your love was all around me and I just wanted to sing my heart out in praise to you. It was like being at a banquet, with the best food I could imagine. I'll think about that some more – it makes me feel much better, even less thirsty!

Dear God, it's almost morning and I can't wait for the night to end. It's been long and uncomfortable, lying here on the hard ground. I've been thinking and thinking – remembering all the times you helped me. And there's plenty to think about, because you've always helped me. Even though I'm out here in the wilderness, I know you haven't deserted me. I just need to imagine myself nestling in the shadow of your wing, or being supported by your strong hands. That helps. I'm going to hang on to that.

Dear God, dawn is breaking and I know

everything will be OK. It's funny, because although I feel so awful physically, inside I feel great! Those who want to harm me are in for a big surprise. They will have to eat their words. Because you will save me, I will shout out your praises. My God, dear God, how great you are! How great you are!'

Bible talk

With: the following two sets of three words 'Come – listen – seek (Isaiah 55)' and 'Seek – remember – rejoice (Psalm 63)' one set written around the edge of a 'pound coin' circle showing 'heads' and the other set on 'tails' (on screen or make an oversized cardboard version); three glasses or glass bottles, one containing water, one milk and one wine

Introduction (optional)
Every year, the Pharaoh's rally takes place across the desert in Egypt. It is a dramatic, demanding and yet luxurious event! Available as a download (YearC.Lent3_2) is a summary of what it is like, in sharp contrast to King David's desert experience. Read the summary (especially appealing to boys) or to find out more visit www.saudiaramcoworld.com/issue/199003/the.desert.game.htm

Give the dramatic likely background to David's stay in the Desert of Judah – persecuted by his own son, Absalom (see 2 Samuel 15–17). Contrast his life as king in Jerusalem, worshipping God in his temple on Mount Zion, with his life as a refugee, in fear of his life, humiliated, where God seemed far away. There were no twenty-first-century comforts for David, and he wasn't in it for the race money.

Psalm 63 and Isaiah 55 are like two sides of the same coin – in the first, David expresses his longing for God, which turns into the joy of expectation. In the second, the writer speaks of God's desire for his people to come to him and take the blessings he has prepared for them. It is likely that God's people at this time were in exile in Babylon, far away from Jerusalem, with little hope and living among those who did not know God.

Display the words on either side of the 'coin'. The concepts are taken from the two readings and provide the substance of the rest of the talk. Structure the talk around the instructions on what to do when we are in hard situations or adversity and how to respond. Expand on each point, using specific experiences you or others have had.

God invites us to come to him now
What God offers is free of charge (Isaiah 55:1) and better than any alternatives we might try to find for ourselves. (The other side of the coin is the psalmist, in trouble, but earnestly seeking God. He knows that God can meet his needs, however bleak the situation seems at the moment.)

We should remember the past
It is easy to assume that God does not speak to us when we are in difficulties. But he really does want to help us out in trouble because he has long-term plans for us (Isaiah 55:5) The psalmist points to remembering and taking note of God's past involvement in his life. Our past experiences with God will strengthen us in times of need and give us hope for the future.

We should look for new experiences of God in the future
We may not understand why things happen to

us, because we are so limited in comparison to God, whose thoughts and ways are higher than ours (Isaiah 55:8,9). The psalmist ended up exchanging despair for joy, rejoicing in him and singing his praises.

Revival – recreation – nourishment
Finish by displaying the three glasses or glass bottles of water, milk and wine. These are not only the material blessings which God promises to those who are going through a hard time. Yes, he will answer our physical needs. But these three liquids have a much more important symbolic meaning in the Bible. Which do you need most, right now? They are all free of charge.
Water – revival (refer also to John 4:13,14; Revelation 7:17)
Wine – recreation (refer also to John 2:1–10; Psalm 104:15)
Milk – nourishment (refer also to Joshua 5:6; 1 Peter 2:2)
Isaiah 55 was written in the context of the exiles summoned back to be restored as the people of God. If we feel like exiles, out in the cold, abandoned, in a dry, arid place, let's find hope from these wonderful Old Testament readings, which assure us that God satisfies needs, both material and spiritual, and is really there, waiting for us to seek him and call upon him. The desert experience is about to end.

(Children may find the idea of spiritual weariness and dryness hard to grasp. But boredom, tiredness, uncertainty or disappointment are very real emotions for them. They may not be able to understand why God has allowed things to happen or they wonder if he hears their prayers. Now that does make sense to them – and to adults too!)

Prayer activity
Ask the musicians to perform Graham Kendrick's song, 'O God, my Creator' while the congregation prays silently or in small groups, meditating on the words. Alternatively, simply read the song aloud, slowly and thoughtfully, as a prayer. The song can be found in *Songs of Fellowship* 414.

Prayers of intercession
With: the three glasses or bottles of water, wine and milk from the **Bible talk** to serve as visual reminders

You may wish to pray for people by name, if appropriate. Pause after each section.

Loving Father, you invite all who are thirsty to come to you, even if they have nothing to give you in return.

We pray for those who need reviving – for those whose spirits are flagging, who are exhausted or oppressed by difficult circumstances. Give them the water of your Holy Spirit, restore them, renew their strength and satisfy their needs.

We pray for those who need recreation – whose faith has become dulled or apathetic, for the cynical, the critical and all who think their lives boring or useless. Give them the new wine which cheers the soul and enlivens the heart and bring them the joy of new activities and friendships.

We pray for those who need nourishment – who are hungry and thirsty spiritually because they are not eating properly. Show them Jesus, the living bread, and build them up with the milk of your living Word. Help them grow and be strengthened.

We pray for those we know who are going though hard times, for whatever reason. Help us to share our hope and joy in you with them.

Amen.

Ending the service

Encourage everyone to remember what the water, wine and milk represent in spiritual terms – revival, recreation and nourishment. Invite them to accept these things from God, as they need them in the coming week. But also challenge them to be of help to others who are going through difficulties which have made their relationship with God dull and dry. Send them out with this blessing:

Bless us, heavenly Father, in the way that you have promised – by filling us with the good things you have prepared for us.

Strengthen our bodies, souls and spirits to face adversity and endure hardship. Because your love is better than life, we glorify you and praise you.

In your name, we lift up our hands and rejoice in you.

Make us channels of blessing to others in the coming week.

Amen.

Helpful extras

Music and song ideas

'Let your living water'; 'Awake, awake, fling off the night'; 'Father, I place into your hands'; 'O Love that wilt not let me go'; 'Blessed be the Lord' (Redman); 'Seek ye the Lord' ('Peace like a river'); 'Thy loving kindness is better than life'; 'Oh God, my creator'.

Notes and comments

The theme of weariness in the desert is very relevant for Lent.

If Communion is included in this service, it would be appropriate to comment that the blood of Jesus, as represented by the wine, has brought us new life.

Psalm 63 was appointed in the early Church as the Morning Psalm or Morning Hymn, prescribed as the introduction to liturgy by St Anathasius and Eusebius. It would have been one of the best-known psalms, as it was recited daily.

This service is based around the Old Testament readings. However, there is a link to the epistle, which speaks of temptation and withstanding it by God's help.

Alternative online options

For your convenience the following activity is available as a download: YearC.Lent3_3 Prayer idea. Visit www.lightlive.org for additional activities for children, young people and adults.

FOURTH SUNDAY OF LENT

READINGS: **2 Corinthians 5:16–21; Luke 15:1–3,11–32**
Joshua 5:9–12; Psalm 32

Bible foundations
Aim: to explore the depth of God's love and forgiveness

Helmut Thielicke renamed the parable of 'the Prodigal Son' as the parable of 'the Waiting Father', which helps us to see it in a new light. As Kenneth Bailey, an expert in Near East culture has pointed out, the father's behaviour at the time would have seemed astounding. His son, by asking for his inheritance (Luke 15:12), was in effect saying, 'I wish you were dead!' Jesus' hearers would have expected such gross disrespect to be severely punished, but instead the father agrees to his request.

When the son returns, smelly and ritually unclean from working with pigs (vs 15,16), he expects at best to be made a servant. Jesus' hearers would expect the father to be terribly angry and punish the son most severely. But his behaviour is extraordinary! Every day, he is watching for his son's return (v 20). On seeing him in the distance, he throws all dignity to the winds in a way quite inconceivable for a prosperous elderly man, and runs to embrace his smelly son. He interrupts his son's words of repentance (make connections with Psalm 32:5) and quickly instructs the servants to bring the best robe, a ring (probably a signet ring, giving the son authority) and sandals (the mark of a son, not a servant). He tells the servants to prepare for a huge party! John Wesley famously said that he exchanged the faith of a servant for the faith of a son – and so must we.

When we think of the cost of redemption we often think of Christ's love. But the depth of God's love includes the cost to God the Father when he 'did not spare his own Son' (Romans 8:32), but 'made him who had no sin to be sin for us' (2 Corinthians 5:21).

Beginning the service

Begin by welcoming everybody, commenting on how nice it is to be together with friends. We meet together, all part of Christ's church. Because of Jesus' life, death and resurrection, we are friends of God which makes us friends of each other.

Explain that in the service you'll be exploring how Jesus makes us God's friends.

Encourage everyone to welcome those around them, offering friendship by the simple gesture of shaking hands.

Bible reading

With: two readers

In advance, meet with two readers to practise the reading of 2 Corinthians 5:16–21 with appropriate actions. (If the readers lack confidence, divide the passage into smaller units and choose more readers.) Encourage the congregation to practise the following actions while shouting out the appropriate words (all key words from 2 Corinthians 5:16–21, GNB). You could also display it on PowerPoint, available as a download (YearC. Lent4_1). (Check if these are the right words if you are using another Bible version.) You may wish to explain the actions as you go through them:

'Christ':	Hold out both arms in a 'cross' shape.
'God':	Hold up one arm high and point finger upwards.
'Enemies':	Shake fist in front, as though threatening someone.
'Friends':	Hold both hands in the air and clasp them together.
'Sin':	Stab fist downwards in a 'thumbs down' gesture.
'Righteousness':	Hold both arms aloft as if in celebration.

> Reader A (verses 16–19): No longer, then, do we judge anyone by human standards. Even if at one time we judged **Christ** according to human standards, we no longer do so. Anyone who is joined to **Christ** is a new being; the old is gone, the new has come. All this is done by **God**, who through **Christ** changed us from **enemies** into his **friends** and gave us the task of making others his **friends** also. Our message is that **God** was making the whole human race his **friends** through **Christ**. **God** did not keep an account of their **sins**, and he has given us the message which tells how he makes them his **friends**.
>
> Reader B (verses 20,21): Here we are, then, speaking for **Christ**, as though **God** himself were making his appeal through us. We please on **Christ's** behalf: let **God** change you from **enemies** into his **friends**! **Christ** was without sin, but for our sake **God** made him share our sin in order that in union with him we might share the **righteousness** of **God**.
>
> 2 Corinthians 5:16–21 (GNB)

The story of the Prodigal Son or the Waiting Father (Luke 15:1–3,11b–32) could be read as a narrative script or you could read a retold version from *Must Know Stories* (SU) by Robert Harrison ('To trap a rabbi') or from *The 10 Must Know Stories* (SU) by Heather Butler ('The tale of two sons'). For more details see the SU website.

Bible talk

With: flip chart and paper; different coloured pens

In advance, draw and write out the two grids below onto two sheets of paper (one per sheet). Make sure the boxes are big enough for lots of writing as people may have plenty of suggestions to fill the boxes.

	Dad's 'enemy'	Dad's 'friend'
At the start of the story		
Looking after pigs		
The older son comes in		

	God's 'enemies'	God's 'friends'
What the Pharisees thought		
What Jesus' story says		
What Paul says		

After both Bible readings, refer quickly to the key ideas of each. Jesus' story is about a divided family, where one son leaves to spend his father's money and comes to regret it, while his brother stays at home. Paul writes to the church in Corinth about people being changed from being an enemy of God to become his friend. In the **Bible talk** you're going to explore how these two parts of the Bible are linked.

Ask for suggestions to fill in the first grid. At four points of the story, which son was a friend or an enemy of the father? Be open to creative suggestions at this point. Then look back at the answers to reflect on the changes. The younger son makes himself an 'enemy' of the father by demanding his money and going away, but when he returns, the father forgives him and makes him his 'friend' again.

Read Luke 15:1–3 again, since this tells us why Jesus told the story. Show the second grid and work out how to complete the first two lines – who are God's enemies? Refer to 2 Corinthians 5 before answering the final line on the grid. (The answers to the second grid will probably be more diverse and take more time.)

It should become clear that because of Jesus God is ready to love and welcome different and unexpected people as his friends. Summarise 2 Corinthians 5:21 by saying that Jesus came to share fully in the life and death of ordinary people so that ordinary people (like us, like the tax collectors and drunkards and the Pharisees if they would accept him!) can become God's friends by knowing and following Jesus.

Prayer activity

With: strips of paper like a luggage label, roughly 10–15 cm, each with the following text (with the highlighted word): There is **nothing** that will ever be able to separate us from the love of God which is ours through Christ Jesus our Lord (Romans 8:38,39) A download template is available (YearC. Lent4_2); a hole puncher; a piece of string long enough to tie around the wrist (one for each person); a toy pig or model pig

Photocopy enough luggage labels for everyone present. Punch a hole into one end of each label.

Show the toy pig or model pig. In Jesus' story the son had to feed pigs and eat what they ate which, to his audience at the time, made the son so dirty that it was impossible for his father to love him. Jesus showed that God's love is unstoppable, like the love of the father in the story. God sees us as his friends. Nothing can separate us from the love of God.

Give everyone a label with the Bible verse. Each person helps others to tie a label onto their wrist with the string. Read out the verse together. As God's friends nothing can separate us from God. Then thank God for the depth and vastness of his love.

Prayer of confession

Remind people of the handshakes you exchanged in **Beginning the service** and of the 'Friends' gesture used during the **Bible reading**. Chat about why clasped hands are a 'friendly' sign or how the handshake shows that two people accept or like each other.

Encourage everyone to get into small groups, maybe with someone they do not usually see as a 'friend'. Younger children should be accompanied by a parent or trusted adult. Guide the groups through the following way of praying for each other:

- Shake hands with each other, and tell each other their name if they do not know them.
- Give people time to think of something that God has done which shows that he loves them and forgives them, even though they may not deserve it – for example, he has given them something that pleases them, or they have spent time talking with God with the result that they feel close to him, or they have recently come to know God. Invite them to share this with others in the group.
- Join hands and then each person in turn prays for the others, asking God to forgive them for anything they have done wrong. This could be a general type of prayer.
- Conclude by asking God to bless everyone in the groups since God longs for all people to be his friend.

Prayers of intercession

Over the Easter period there are many opportunities to present the message of the cross and resurrection which makes it possible for people to change from being an enemy of God to being his friend. Pray for any plans the church has to communicate God's good news in the next few weeks, whether in schools, the community, or personally.

Ending the service

Use the following short prayer of response repeating the actions from the **Bible reading** if appropriate. The prayer is also available as a download (YearC.Lent4_3).

Leader: What does it mean to follow **Jesus**?
All: It means we are becoming **God's friends**!
(Repeat this)
Leader: Go out into the world, **friends** of **God**, and show his love to others!
All: We will! Amen!

Helpful extras

Music and song ideas

'And can it be'; 'Before the throne of God above'; 'Father God, I wonder'; 'Faithful one, so unchanging'; 'Father, your love is a faithful love'; 'God forgave my sin'; 'Here is love, vast as the ocean'; 'How deep the Father's love for us'; 'Lord, I come to you'; 'The love of God comes close'; 'There's a place where the streets shine'; 'To be in your presence' and 'Ubi caritas' (an English translation of this song from Taizé is also sung in many churches).

Notes and comments

The **Prayer of confession** idea may work as an **Ending the service** idea.

If you are looking for ideas to add to an all-age Communion service, the **Prayer of confession** could be used as a beginning to the prayers before Communion (in the place of the usual 'Peace').

Alternative online options

Visit www.lightlive.org for additional activities for children, young people and adults

All Age Service Annuals Volume 1-4

Each All-Age Service Annual includes 15 creative all-age service outlines to see you right through the year. The services cover all the major Christian festivals, along with other significant occasions that you'll want to celebrate together as an all-age congregation (for example: Mothering Sunday, Harvest and Remembrance Sunday).

Each annual also includes all-age service starters which are short activities, written to be used as service openers or closers when all ages are together.

For more details, visit www.scriptureunion.org.uk

MOTHERING SUNDAY

READINGS: **Exodus 2:1–10; Luke 2:33–35**
Psalm 34:11–20; 2 Corinthians 1:3–7

Bible foundations
Aim: to celebrate the role of women and mothers in God's plan of salvation

Can you imagine the heartache that Moses' mother (probably Jochebed – see Exodus 6:20) must have experienced? Pharaoh had commanded that all boys be thrown into the Nile (Exodus 1:22). She and her husband were powerless slaves, yet God had given them this fine boy. How could she give him up? So when it was no longer possible to hide him, she put him in a little boat on the Nile, trusting God to look after him. The natural curiosity and compassion of Pharaoh's daughter (2:5,6), combined with the quick-wittedness of Moses' sister, Miriam (see 2:7) saved the baby from certain death. The pain and sorrow in Jochebed's heart were short-lived (though probably to return with a vengeance years later, when Moses returned to the palace, and much later fled to Midian).

Mary, the mother of Jesus, may have been overwhelmed by a range of emotions, such as joy, happiness, loneliness or fear, after giving birth not just to an ordinary boy but to the Messiah, the promised Saviour. Very soon she was warned that though her son would be great, he would be rejected by many, and a sword would pierce Mary's own soul (Luke 2:33–35). She had doubtless already known rejection (as people accused her of illicit sex) and would continue to do so (see John 8:41), but this would be as nothing to the price she would later have to face. (A 'sword' would make her think of a Roman soldier.) Mary would continue to ponder over who this son of hers was – at a wedding (John 2:1–10) and as part of a crowd (Mark 3:20,21). She was there at the cross (John 19:25–27) experiencing such agony, and with Jesus' disciples waiting for the joyful coming of the Spirit.

Both Jochebed and Mary had a crucial place in God's plan of salvation, which we rightly celebrate in this service. These women were brave, prepared to take risks, did the right thing and cared deeply for their children, to their great cost. They and their faith are inspirational!

Beginning the service

With: flowers, volunteers

Many churches traditionally celebrate Mothering Sunday by distributing flowers to mothers. As an alternative, invite people to bring some flowers to the service in memory of, or to celebrate, a woman or mother who has been important to them in their life, including nurturing their faith in God. You will need to warn people in advance so that they can bring their flowers and, if they so choose, can say something brief about their chosen woman. The flowers can be given to those who would appreciate them, at the end of the service.

At the start of the service, invite those who have brought flowers to come forward to lay them on a central table or altar, with each person, if they wish, telling everyone one reason why they are thankful for the role of this woman in their life. Then thank God for these women and their role in these people's lives. Ask God to use this service to open your eyes to the women and mothers throughout history who have played a part in his plan for the world.

Bible reading

With: a volunteer, preferably a woman, to read Exodus 2:1–10; one or two large (clean) dustbins or similar containers holding a little water

Invite a few volunteers of mixed ages to come to the front to gently rock the bins to create the sound of lapping water. Other vocal sounds will be made by the volunteers and maybe everyone present – swishing reeds and a crying baby. (You may want to rehearse this!) During the reading of Exodus 2:1–10, people make the sound effects. You could include Exodus 1:15–21 to introduce the two other women who appear in the **Bible talk**, but make sure you explain what happened before the midwives come into the story.

Bible retelling

An alternative way of telling the story of Exodus 2 is to read the narrative poem for three women's voices – one slightly older, one younger and one child or teenager, which emphasises the theme of God's plan. It is presented as a lullaby. Appropriate sound effects would make this more effective. The script is available as a download (YearC. Mothers_1).

Bible talk

With: five women who are prepared to come to the front to read out one or two sentences, written out as follows on card (Ideally, in preparation they should read the Bible story from Exodus 1:11 – 2:10 and be able to ad lib answers to questions about their role. Then instead of telling the story, you could interview them.)

1. *(two women)* We will save the lives of all Hebrew baby boys!

2A. I must save the life of my baby son!

2B. I will bring up my baby son to hear the stories of God's faithfulness until he has to return to the palace.

3. I will give this baby boy a home, even though I know he is a Hebrew!

4. I will watch over my baby brother, to keep him safe! (The story of the early

weeks of Moses' life is packed with heroines: women who were brave, did the right thing and also cared deeply for their children. This was at great cost to themselves. All of them, in different ways, were faithful to God.)

Ask everyone what makes a great woman. After a few suggestions, explain that you are now going to meet five women who you think are all great – and so does the Bible. Ask the women to come forward. Then either tell their story or interview them.

The midwives, Shiphrah and Puah
Introduce the two women who together read card 1. Explain that these were midwives at the time when the people of Israel were slaves in Egypt. The Pharaoh wanted to reduce the power of the Israelites and decided to have all baby boys killed at birth. But the Hebrew midwives refused to do this. They gave the excuse that Hebrew boys were born too quickly, so could not be smothered in the process of being born. These were ordinary women going about their job, but they were very brave to stand up to the Pharaoh. The Bible says they were 'faithful to God' (Exodus 1:17,20,21).

Moses' mother, Jochebed
One woman then reads card 2A. Tell her angle on the story. She refused to allow her son to be killed and found a way to protect her child, at great danger to herself and her whole family. Hebrews 11:23 says that Moses' parents had faith in God and 'were not afraid to disobey the king's orders'.

Pharaoh's daughter
One woman reads card 3. She was very rich and privileged but to adopt a Hebrew baby may have been a challenge to the Pharaoh, whose intention was to punish the Hebrew slaves. What she did was brave and led to the survival of the man God had chosen to save his people.

Miriam, Moses' sister
One woman (younger) reads card 4. She is Moses' sister who watched over her brother and had the initiative to volunteer her mother as a nurse for him. Many years later she was to become a strong leader of God's people. She did the right thing, at the right time, in the right way – and she was very brave.

Jochebed again
The second woman reads card 2B. Moses' mother cared for her son and taught him the faith of his Israelite fathers. Hebrews 11:24 would suggest that he had a strong sense of his Jewish identity which he must have got from his parents. His mother did the right thing not only in caring for her son but in bringing him up to know God.

You assume that everyone would agree that these women:

- were all brave
- all did the right thing
- cared deeply for their son/newborn boys/ baby brother
- acted in a way that showed that they were faithful to God.

We might not talk about what makes a good mother in this way nowadays but such expectations are just as true today.

- Yes, women are to care deeply for their children, and it may be costly. If you have had the reading from Luke 2:33–35 you could refer to Mary's sorrow.

- Yes, women take brave decisions in doing the right thing – how might you, as a church, encourage people to be brave, for it is not just women who are called to be brave? How might you prepare children especially to be brave and do the right thing? (Pause at this point to pray for anyone who is struggling to be brave, which might include children who are being bullied or someone victimised at work, or in dispute with a neighbour.)
- Yes, women have their central part to play in caring for the faith of children, but that is not just mothers, but fathers too and also anyone within the church family. (Pause to pray for those who are seeking to build up the faith of children.)
- Yes, these women had a vital part to play in God's plan of salvation, each one of them, for Moses was so important.

Invite all the men and boys to stand up and silently pray for all the women and girls present, that they may be brave, do the right thing, nurture faith and be prepared to be used by God. Then ask the women and girls to stand up and pray in the same way for the men and the boys. If appropriate, you could make this more specific or participatory, or incorporated into the **Prayer activity**.

Prayer activity

With: various coloured photocopies of jigsaw pieces, enough for everyone to have two pieces each (they don't have to fit together); colouring pens or pencils; scissors

Distribute the pens or pencils and jigsaw pieces. Ask everyone to draw a picture of or write the name of a person (or group of people) on each jigsaw piece:

• someone they want to thank God for (possibly a woman or mother)

• someone they want to ask God to help, bless or protect in the future.

Then ask people to bring their jigsaw pieces forward. Explain that the five women in the Bible story were all fairly ordinary and getting on with life, but that they were part of God's plan and they did what was asked of them, being faithful to God. It was as though they were part of one giant jigsaw, which is God's plan since time began. It all came together when Jesus died on the cross and we have been part of what happened since.

Using as much floor space as you have available, arrange all the jigsaw pieces into the shape of a cross, just overlapping, not trying to fit the pieces together. Then ask the congregation to quietly think about the people they want to thank God for and the people they want to ask God's help for.

Ending the service

Use the following ending prayer, which takes up the theme from Exodus 2, to pray for everyone in the congregation as your service ends:

'I pray for you [or: 'Let us pray for each other']:
May God give you…
The determined courage of the midwives,
The strong love of Moses' mother,
The compassion of Pharaoh's daughter,
The insight of Moses' sister.
May God's extraordinary story break into every ordinary thing you do – this week, and for the rest of your life!'
Amen!

Helpful extras

Music and song ideas

Songs and hymns that focus on God's love: 'Over the mountains and the sea'; 'Our God is a great big God'; 'The love of God comes close'; 'And can it be'; 'How deep the Father's love for us'; 'God's love is higher than the highest mountain'.

Songs and hymns that explore courage and purpose: 'He who would valiant be'; 'Be bold, be strong'; 'Our God is an awesome God'.

Songs which focus on the idea of God's people or God's work stretching throughout history: 'Lord, for the years'; 'I will sing the wondrous story'.

A song that uses the words of Mary, Miriam or Hannah's songs from the Bible (such as 'Tell out, my soul'; 'Let it be to me') would also be appropriate.

Another way of integrating music would be to adapt the **Bible reading** or **Bible retelling** ideas to include a musical element, asking the music group to accompany the telling of the Bible story.

Notes and comments

Many people find Mothering Sunday a difficult day. While this service rejoices in the role that women have had in the Bible story, especially mothers, this is not the only theme that is explored. The challenge to be brave and stand up for what is right or to nurture the faith of children is relevant to all, young and old, male and female. You might decide to pray for families and those who nurture faith, including godparents and children's workers.

Additional ideas for Mothering Sunday can be found in the *All-Age Service Annual, Volumes 1–4*. See page 108 for details of family resources.

If there is a Communion service you could draw attention to the fact that Jesus exhibited all the characteristics that have featured in this service – he was brave, did the right thing, loved and cared for others and was very committed to nurturing the faith of all. This was very costly – he gave his life! All this was at the centre of God's plan of salvation which you remember as you take the bread and wine.

Some churches expect visitors to come to the church service on Mothering Sunday. If this is the case, adapt this material as necessary, not expecting them to know the story of Jochebed or Mary and not making them uncomfortable by asking them to say or do what they may not believe or understand.

Alternative online options

Visit www.lightlive.org for additional activities for children, young people and adults. There are many suggestions for the story of Moses in the bulrushes!

FIFTH SUNDAY OF LENT

READINGS: **Philippians 3:4–14; John 12:1–8**
Isaiah 43:16–21; Psalm 126

Bible foundations
Aim: to see what it means to be generous towards God

The whole-hearted devotion of Mary (John 12:1–8) is one of the highlights of John's Gospel. She and her sister Martha had been Jesus' friends for a long time. They had witnessed the amazing raising of their brother Lazarus from the grave when he'd been dead four days (John 11:39). Jesus' loving willingness to identify with her sorrow (John 11:33–35), combined with his awesome ability to bring new life to the dead, must have given her a great love for him.

She expresses this love by pouring fragrant nard (a very expensive perfume) onto Jesus' feet. It was probably her most precious possession, so it was as though she was giving away her savings and her security for the future. Jesus says that her act was pointing towards the day of his burial (when spices would be wrapped around a corpse, see John 19:40). Mary's act was very significant whether or not she understood this (compare Mark 14:8). She anoints Jesus (the term 'Messiah' meant 'Anointed One'), and recognises that he will soon die and be buried. Her understanding of the Messiah was not of a military saviour whom the Jews were expecting, but a suffering servant whom Isaiah said would bear the sins of his people and share the grave of a rich man (Isaiah 53:4–6,9).

Mary's action indicates that giving to God must flow from a love that is sacrificial and whole-hearted (see Philippians 3:7,13,14). We must not count the cost or whinge over alternatives as Judas does (John 12:4–6). Such love must also focus on who Jesus is – note the 'me' in John 12:8. Jesus doesn't just want our activity but the devotion of our hearts. Our generosity must also be intelligent, understanding the significance of the times and what such giving can mean. May people in this service be inspired as you spend time together in God's presence.

Beginning the service

With: a TV clip from the programme *Secret Millionaire* or a large box of chocolates or a small present for church members

Begin by singing a hymn or song of praise to God, one that everyone will know, such as: 'Praise him on the trumpet'; 'Shout to the Lord'; 'Praise God from whom all blessings flow'.

The theme of the service is 'generosity'. This means 'giving freely' and sometimes it means giving in a way that is sacrificial. To think what 'generosity' looks like in reality, show a clip, or retell a story from the TV programme *Secret Millionaire*. An Internet search would give you details. Alternatively, share a huge box of chocolates with the congregation, either by throwing the chocolates out or passing them round. Or you could give each member of church a wrapped up gift to reveal something of your own generosity.

The Bible tells us about God's acts of generosity to his people. He created a perfect world, he was active in the history of Israel and then in the life, death and resurrection of Jesus. Later, you will focus on how we might show generosity to others and to God in response to God's generosity to us.

Bible reading

Introduce the reading of Psalm 126 by explaining that the psalm was written in praise of God's generosity, when he allowed his people to return to their homeland, after being in exile in Babylon.

Either at this point, or as part of the **Prayer activity**, write a corporate psalm in praise of God's generosity, writing it up on a flip chart or typing into a PowerPoint slide. Think first of all about how you will address God. Encourage ideas from people of all ages. Ideas might include: praise for God's generosity in creation; praise for God's generosity in Jesus; praise for God's generosity towards us as a church family, praise for God's generosity towards us as individuals; praise for God's generosity in his work of salvation.

Philippians 3:4b–14 could be read by someone dressed in first-century clothes, speaking as though they are the apostle Paul telling his story.

John 12:1–8 is a wonderfully dramatic story that works well visually. As it is read, three 'actors' could interpret the story dramatically, speaking where necessary. Encourage the 'actors' to express the emotion of each character – Mary's expression of love for Jesus; Judas' critical spirit; Jesus' sense of fairness and acceptance of the generous act.

Bible retelling

As soon as the **Bible reading** of John 12:1–8 is completed, the 'actors' stay in role so they can retell the story, each from their point of view. A script is written below.

Mary

My name is Mary. I'm the woman who got into trouble with my sister Martha for not helping out when Jesus came to visit us. My brother Lazarus is the man Jesus brought back to life. Jesus is our friend and has been so generous to us.

I cannot put into words what Jesus' love, care and power mean to me. It's overwhelming, so I had to do something generous in return to show how much I love him. I took some of the perfume I have kept for the burial of my brother – mind you, we don't need it right now! – and poured it on Jesus' feet. I wiped his feet with my hair. It was expensive perfume and so the fragrance filled the whole room! Everyone could see what I had done! But I wanted Jesus to receive the best that I could give.

Judas
My name is Judas. I am one of Jesus' disciples. I could not believe what I saw (and smelt!). Mary wasted a whole jar of expensive perfume. Not just a little but a whole jar! But why? She says it was to show generous love to Jesus, but what a waste. She could have sold the perfume and given the money to the poor. It was worth three hundred silver coins you know – that's what I call generosity. I'm the keeper of the money bag, so it would have helped me out too. Why does Jesus always turn things upside down?

Jesus
Mary did the right thing. She showed her love and commitment to me by the way she lives and by the way she gives. What she did was a sign of extravagant love; worship that comes from the heart and from a life lived for God. The poor will always be around, but Mary was pointing to the fact that I won't be around for much longer. There will come a time when my dead body will be buried and it will need to be prepared. She does not understand but she will. Look at Mary for an example of how to live for me and to give to me. For the rest of history, she will be remembered for this.

Bible talk
With: a picture of an athlete about to burst over the finishing line (as contemporary or dramatic as possible); a rubbish bin with lots of rubbish inside; a clock (or a picture of one); chocolate coins with a sticky label on; baskets; pens

Living and giving
Begin by explaining that Mary showed her love for Jesus in generosity by the way she lived and the way she gave so freely. She knew that Jesus deserved the best. How can we show our love for Jesus in generosity, by the way we live and the way we give?

Show the congregation the four items above. Explain that each of these will help us to understand how we can be generous to God in our living and giving.

How we live
Race to the line – Paul in Philippians 3:13 encourages Christians to 'let go' of or forget what is behind, as though in a race, and press on to the goal or the finishing post. Talk about the picture of the athlete. Invite children to comment on any races they have been in or watched. It's easy to lose sight of what is important in our life with God, the finishing post, and get distracted. Mary was very focused on who Jesus was and her love for him. She did not let anything get in the way. Her generosity revealed her love for him.

A rubbish bin – Paul in Philippians 3:8 talks about giving up his old life and all it stood for, counting it as rubbish. Take out the bits or ask a volunteer to do so, perhaps giving them rubber gloves and making suitable 'Yuk!' sounds. For Paul, nothing was 'as wonderful as knowing Christ Jesus my Lord'. In pouring away her perfume, Mary was in one sense saying it was rubbish; it was not worth as much as showing how much she loved Jesus. This was true generosity.

How we give

A clock (or a picture of a clock) – it probably did not take Mary long to pour out the perfume and wipe Jesus' feet, although the smell would have hung in the air for a lot longer and her action would be remembered for much longer still. Generosity need not take a long time! (But note, Paul was very aware that his race towards spending eternity with God was going to take the rest of his earthly life!) We can be generous to God with our time. Acts of generosity, kindness and service done in Jesus' name reveal love for him.

In the year-long mission of Hope 2008, church members were encouraged to show love for God and community through 'a million minutes of kindness'. Some were involved in litter picking, cleaning, home help and even paying for people's car parking! Ask the congregation to talk in small groups about how they might show 'minutes of kindness' to people this week.

Chocolate coins – we can also be generous with our money. For Judas, it was the apparent waste of money that caused his outburst. But Mary gave freely and beyond expectation, in response to what Jesus had done for her.

Each person will have different levels of income and outgoings. In today's economic climate, it can be hard to be generous since meeting basic needs is a challenge. Pass the chocolate coins and pens around in a basket and invite people to quietly think about where they could be generous financially either this week or in the near future. For children it will be different to adults, but it might mean giving some pocket money away to 'Children in need' or for adults, a resolution to tithe or to give a one-off donation to a Christian relief organisation. Write the ideas on the coin's sticky label. You could play some quiet music while this is being done. The labels could be collected in a large jar as part of the suggested **Prayer of confession**.

What motivated Mary's living and giving was her love for Jesus. He has done so much for us, we can only respond in worship, not only singing, but in a life lived every day for God.

Prayer of confession

With: paper; pens; large jars or vases

This time of confession and commitment is based on Philippians 3:4b–14. Explain that this passage reveals Paul's response to Jesus' generosity.

Read verses 7 and 8a, then pray:
We are sorry, Lord, for the times when other things have been more important to us than knowing you – what we do, what we want, what we think or what we say. Help us to put you first as we live for you and give to you.

Read verses 8b and 9, then pray:
We are sorry, Lord, for what we have done that has let you down and for the times when we have been ashamed of you or put you to one side. Thank you that you love us for who we are. Help us to put you first as we live for you and give to you.

Read verses 12 and 13, then pray:

We are sorry, Lord, for the things that have got in the way of our relationship with you; for selfishness, for pride, for greed, for anger and lots of other things. We pray you will forgive us and help us to 'give you the controls of our lives'. Help us to live lives of compassion, kindness, humility, gentleness and patience and love. Amen.

Read verse 14, then pray:
Lord Jesus, we now recommit our lives to you. May we show generous love to you in the way we live and the way we give. Amen.

If at the end of the **Bible talk** people have written down ways they could be generous on the sticky label, they could place the labels into a large jar or vase placed at the front, or around the worship area.

Ending the service

End by singing a hymn or lively song of commitment to generous living and giving. An example is 'Over all the earth (Lord reign in me)'.

Helpful extras

Music and song ideas

Sing songs about God's generosity such as: 'How great thou art'; 'God who made the universe' (Spring Harvest Kids Praise); 'Oi oi we are gonna praise the Lord' (Doug Horley); 'Great is the Lord'; 'Great is your faithfulness, O God' ('Your grace is enough').

Game

Play this game after the **Bible talk**, as a brain break but also to consolidate the teaching points. This is a game of 'Simon says' substituting 'Generosity means' using the main points of the talk. The actions are as follows:

'Race to the line' – run on the spot with arms triumphantly in the air.

'Throw out the rubbish' – energetically empty a pretend rubbish bin.

'Give God your time' – arms make clock hands and tick one round in a circle.

'Give God your money' – pretend to give money as if paying for something.

'Show God your love' – hug yourself as if giving love.

When you say, for example: 'Generosity means – race to the line', then everyone does the action. When you omit 'Generosity means', no one should do the action and so on!

Notes and comments

Be sensitive to those who have low incomes, or are unemployed. Generosity is far more than giving financially. God has promised that he will provide for all our needs, and he seeks a generous heart.

Alternative online options

Visit www.lightlive.org for additional activities for children, young people and adults.

PALM SUNDAY

READINGS: Psalm 118; Luke 19:28–40

Bible foundations
Aim: to follow Christ on the road to Jerusalem

The joy that accompanies Jesus' entry into Jerusalem (Luke 19:28–40) says much about Jesus' identity and the purpose of his mission. So for example, Jesus shows authority over all possessions by taking 'ownership' of the donkey to ride into Jerusalem, justified by telling the owners, 'The Lord needs it' (vs 31,34). Jesus shows his mastery of the created world by riding a colt 'which no one has ever ridden' (v 30) – a colt would not normally be quiet for its very first rider! Jesus shows the nature of his Kingship by entering Jerusalem as Messiah not on a war-horse but in peace, sitting on a colt, fulfilling prophecy (see Zechariah 9:9). The exuberant praise of the crowd, largely comprised of his disciples (v 37) is 'for all the miracles they had seen' through Jesus. The healing of the blind, the deaf and the dumb had fulfilled prophecy about what would happen when God came to save his people (Isaiah 35:5,6).

Especially significant for the crowd were the words of Psalm 118:26 (quoted in Luke 19:38). This Messianic psalm is full of content relevant to the mission of Jesus. It celebrates the goodness and love of God (vs 1,2) seen in the victory won by his anointed king. This victory is celebrated in a great procession with the gates flung open not only for the king but also for the righteous (vs 19,20), who rejoice that their king has become their saviour (v 21). Though rejected by some, the king has become the capstone (literally 'head of the corner'), the stone on which the whole building depends. (Note the word play in the original Hebrew where the word for 'corner' can also mean 'chief ruler' – as in Isaiah 19:13.)

So the crowds shout 'Hosanna', the Hebrew word for 'save!' (Psalm 118:25). This king has come in God's name to save them, and they can't keep quiet about it!

Beginning the service

Ask everyone to think about who or what they have been following during the past week, and why. (Someone they respect or admire? A football team? A news story?)

Today is Palm Sunday and we are focusing on following Jesus as he enters Jerusalem and leads us on to the life-changing events of Good Friday and Easter.

Bible reading

With: a 'palm branch', one for each person, given out as people arrive (made out of newspaper or a green paper leaf)

Psalm 118 is a great psalm of celebration which looks forward to the future.

Invite everyone to follow the leader around the church while waving their palm branches. Either print out copies of the selected verses in a response form for people to hold or display the words on a screen. These are available as a download (YearC.Palm_1).

> This day belongs to God.
> **Let us celebrate and be glad in it!**
> Tell the Lord how thankful you are, because he is kind and always merciful.
> **The Lord is my God. I will praise him and tell him how thankful I am.**
> Open the gates of justice!
> **I will enter and tell the Lord how thankful I am.**
> We'll ask the Lord to save us.
> **I praise the Lord for answering my prayers and saving me.**
> March with palm branches all the way to the altar.
>
> Start the celebration!
> God bless the one who comes in the name of the Lord.
> **March with palm branches all the way to the altar.**
> The stone that the builders have tossed aside has now become the most important stone.
> **The Lord has done this and it is amazing to us!**
> The Lord is our God and he has given us light.
> **God bless the one who comes in the name of the Lord.**
> This day belongs to the Lord.
> **Let us celebrate and be glad today!**
>
> from Psalm 118

Luke 19:28–40 can be read with a narrator and other readers taking the different parts.

Bible talk

With: characters from Luke 19:28–40 (in Bible dress or headdresses) waiting to tell their story; four large card 'footprints' with 'confused', 'critical', 'curious' and 'certain' written on them

Jesus often called people by saying, 'Follow me.' We've heard that crowds of people followed Jesus to Jerusalem and we're going to meet a few of them now to find out why they were there and to help us to think about how we can follow Jesus more closely.

Confused disciples

(Show the 'confused' footprint.) The first group we meet are Jesus' disciples. They had all arrived in Jerusalem for the Passover feast. It was as though everything had been building

up to this moment. Jesus insisted on riding into the city on a young donkey which two of the disciples had gone to fetch earlier that morning. As Jesus rode on this donkey, crowds of people joined with the disciples, all shouting and throwing their coats down on the road. There had been plenty of crowds before, but not shouting and singing about Jesus being the King who comes in the name of the Lord. Jesus himself seemed quite solemn and serious. So what was going on?

The disciples had been following Jesus for quite some time. They went everywhere with him and couldn't imagine life without him now. There were still many things they didn't understand though, and the arrival in Jerusalem was very confusing for them. These disciples were very confused!

Critical Pharisees
The Pharisees had been watching Jesus with growing suspicion. *(Show the 'critical' footprint.)* They never knew what this 'teacher' would do next. He even had the audacity to ride into Jerusalem on the back of a young donkey. The prophet Zechariah had said that was what the Messiah, God's Chosen One, would do one day. They thought that Jesus had done this as a way of claiming he was the Messiah! Also, the Pharisees were worried that the crowds seemed to believe in Jesus. As Jesus came closer, some Pharisees asked him if he was going to tell his followers off for singing and shouting things which implied he was the Messiah. But all he said was, 'If they were quiet, the stones would cry out instead!' What on earth was that supposed to mean?

Wherever Jesus was, the Pharisees were never far behind. They wanted to see what he would do and say next. They weren't following him in the real sense of the word though. They were so busy trying to trick him or catch him out that they were blind and deaf to what he was really doing and saying and missed out on everything he came to offer them. All they could do that day in Jerusalem was criticise.

Curious donkey owner
(Show the 'curious' footprint.) We don't know if this man was in the crowd but the owner of the donkey must have been pretty shocked when two men came into his yard and untied his youngest donkey without asking permission or anything. When he asked them what they were doing, the two men simply said, 'The Lord needs it.' The man did not object as far as we can tell. Maybe he already knew Jesus or knew about him. In Jerusalem everyone must have known something about him. That's why the crowd gathered so quickly. And stories about Jesus must have spread, about how he fed a massive crowd of people and had even brought a dead man back to life. The donkey owner may have been really curious. There must have been others in that crowd like that, wondering what he would do next.

Show the three footprints again to remind everyone that there were people in this crowd who were: confused, like the disciples; critical like the Pharisees; simply curious, like the donkey owner.

Certain followers
But in general you would say that the crowd was joyful and certain that Jesus was the King who had come in the name of the Lord. *(Show the 'certain' footprint.)* But their certainty was not based on very much and soon it was to turn into quite the opposite emotion, as they

shouted for Jesus to be put to death. It was only after Jesus had died and come alive again in a new way that anyone could be certain who he was and what he had come to do.

There may be some people here today who are **confused** – they've been following Jesus for some time but there's much they don't understand, or they may just be puzzled. There may be some here today who have a **critical** attitude and have never quite let themselves respond to Jesus' invitation to follow him. There may be some here who are **curious** about Jesus and who he is and would like to respond to him. And there may be some here who know they have met Jesus personally, are **certain** who he is and want to follow him more closely. Talk briefly about the opportunities there are in your church for people to take their next step in following Jesus, followed by a short time of quiet while people make their own response.

Prayer activity

With: stones, one per person given out as people arrive – grey card 'stones' would be an alternative; three different prayer stations/areas with suitable materials

Ask everyone to pick up the stones they were given when they arrived. Stones have been mentioned in the **Bible readings**. Psalm 118 talks about the stone the builders tossed aside now becoming the most important stone which refers to Jesus. Luke records Jesus' remark that even if the crowds were quiet, the stones themselves would cry out in praise; and also, Jesus weeping for Jerusalem says, 'Your enemies will not leave a single stone in place, because you did not accept your opportunity for salvation.'

Praise stone area
This is an opportunity to praise God for who he is and what he has done. Provide 'wiggle eyes', glue, speech bubble-shaped pieces of paper and pencils so people can stick eyes on their stones and write an exclamation of praise on a speech bubble and then stick it to their stone.

Jesus the cornerstone area
This is an opportunity to think about Jesus as the most important stone holding everything together and to pray for our church family, our homes and our community with this picture in mind. Provide paints and fine brushes or markers so that people can decorate their stone beautifully with the name of Jesus.

Brokenness stone area
This is an opportunity to pray for any situation or person who needs to know the wholeness that Jesus the Saviour brings. Provide paints or markers so that people can paint a cross on their stone. Additionally these stones could be left at the foot of a cross or arranged in a cross shape.

Ending the service

Pray the following prayer with people joining in the refrain: May we follow in Jesus' footsteps.

Father God, as we step out into this Holy Week,
May we follow in Jesus' footsteps.
As he stands up for justice and truth,
May we follow in Jesus' footsteps.
As he washes the feet of his friends,
May we follow in Jesus' footsteps.
As he pours out his love on the cross,
May we follow in Jesus' footsteps.

As he rises with new life and hope,
May we follow in Jesus' footsteps.

Helpful extras

Music and song ideas

Traditional Palm Sunday hymns include 'Ride on, ride on in majesty'; 'All glory, laud and honour'. Suitable children's worship songs include 'Praise King Jesus riding into town' (D. Parsons in *Children's Praise*); 'Hosanna' (Helen and Mark Johnson in *Songs for Every Easter*). Other songs with a 'Palm Sunday' praise feel include 'Hosanna, hosanna, hosanna in the highest'; 'Lord, I lift your name on high'; 'Over all the earth, you reign on high'; 'Jesus is the name we honour'. Suitable songs with a more reflective feel include 'Will you come and follow me?' (John Bell); 'You chose the cross'; 'Who is there like you?'; 'All I once held dear'; 'All my days I will sing this song of gladness'; 'God is an awesome God' with the repeated final words 'Follow me!' *(Light for Everyone CD, SU)*.

Game

Who will you follow?
This would take place straight after **Beginning the service**.

Tell everyone that you're going to play a game of 'Follow the leader'. Ask two 'leaders' *(previously briefed)* to do actions for everyone to follow. Play some background music and ask the leaders to begin. They will then proceed to do completely different actions from each other. Ask everyone afterwards how they felt. How did they know who to follow? What would have helped them? Link this with the fact that Jesus had given many clues that he was God's Son, the leader to follow, by the time he arrived in Jerusalem.

Notes and comments

Where palm branches are mentioned, use whatever suits your church situation best. You could use flags or ribbons, paper palm leaves, real branches or palm crosses.

An alternative **Prayer activity** could be led from the front using the following: a picture of gates, praying for new openings in sharing Christ with our local communities; a picture of a donkey, praying for peace; coats (as placed on the road in the Luke passage), praying for those who serve in our church; palm branches, praying for those who need God's healing and transformation in their lives.

Alternative online options

Visit www.lightlive.org for additional activities for children, young people and adults.

GOOD FRIDAY

READINGS: **Psalm 130; John 18,19**
Genesis 22:1–18; Psalm 130

Bible foundations
Aim: to enter into the story of Jesus' passion

In the context of Good Friday, the story of God's instruction to Abraham to sacrifice his son Isaac in Genesis 22:1–18 is chilling. One question this incident provokes is: how could a father kill his son, even as an act of obedience to God? Of course, we can see it as the testing of Abraham's faith in God to be true to the covenant, his promise to provide an heir. Abraham passed that test with flying colours, and God did provide the sacrificial lamb. A second question might be: how could Isaac seem so passive and unresisting?

Those same questions arise when we encounter the passion narratives. How could God the Father allow his Son to die – the Son whom he loved, and who had been born to fulfil the covenant? We do not know the answer, except that this was the key act in God's plan of salvation. Again, we might ask how Jesus could remain seemingly passive when facing the horror of his tormentors and the agony that he knew awaited him. Unlike Abraham and Isaac, God the Father did watch his Son die; he also provided the required sacrificial victim – his Son! And Jesus, the Son, accepted all this. The psalmist in Psalm 130 writes of trusting the Lord in times of trouble. Might these have been Scriptures that flowed through Jesus' mind, as he waited to die, with soldiers watching his every move (vs 5,6)?

John's account in chapters 18 and 19 contains elements of the story not found in other Gospels. That is why it is profitable to concentrate on a single version of the story, to see which details one author included in his Gospel. The only verses not to be read from these two chapters (but you need not stick with these suggestions!) are those where Jesus is not, or no longer, present (that is 18:25–27; 19:31–42). In this service you will be waiting with Jesus in his last hours.

Beginning the service

With: three long strips of dark-coloured cloth, thick paper or crêpe

Ask three people to help you twist the three strips into one plait, the longer the better. Hang it up or lay it out where it can be seen during the service. Explain that so many key truths about God are woven together on Good Friday (as though in a plait) but still it is hard to make sense of them. Many of these things are very sad and bleak and even at the end of Good Friday, there is still no hope.

Explain that this service gives a chance to reflect on Jesus' trial and being with him as he prepares to die. There will be times for quiet reflection and some opportunities for active engagement. Everyone should do what they feel comfortable with. Much of the service will involve listening to the reading of the story, from John's Gospel.

Open with prayer by asking God to meet with each one of you. Use a Good Friday prayer from a prayer book or the following:

Lord God, this day is a dark day, a day when God the Father, God the Son and God the Holy Spirit experienced unimaginable loneliness and pain. We cannot begin to understand this mystery but we come to you now, asking that you will meet with us, by your Spirit and fill us with sorrow, awe and gratitude for what was achieved on this day. Amen.

Bible reading

Since there is so much reading from the Bible you will want to make sure that you have the best readers available and that they have practised so that they can help those listening to get involved in the story. Use an appropriate version of the Bible such as the NIV or CEV. There will not be a Bible talk, but comments and activities will be suggested throughout this outline. Introduce times of prayer at points you think best, although suggestions are included.

If possible, download the suggested works of art using an Internet search – there are just four. Display them during the reading of the Bible. There are so many images you could use that there is an almost limitless supply of alternative options you could choose to display.

Jesus' arrest

Read John 18:1–14, displaying an image of Judas betraying Jesus, such as Caravaggio's *Taking of Christ in the Garden* (in the National Gallery of Ireland in Dublin). This could be read with a narrator and people speaking the parts of Jesus and the soldiers. (If this style of **Bible reading** is to be repeated, use the same person to read the part of Jesus throughout the service.) You could add background sound effects such as stamping of marching feet, clashing of weapons, a night owl, a gasp of pain from Malchus, murmuring voices of the disciples. Younger people could be involved in creating these sounds. Allow them to use their imagination and practise to get the timing right.

Sing a song or listen to a recording of a hymn, a song or part of a classical piece of music from *The Messiah* or one of Bach's passions. Listening to music allows space for reflection.

Jesus' trial

Read John 18:19–24,28–39; 19:1–16 displaying an image of Jesus on trial such as Gerrit van Honthorst's *Christ before the High Priest* (which is in the National Gallery in London).

The lights could be dimmed since it was night-time.

As long as the PA system or acoustics in the building allow for this, it would be suitable to read this from different points in the building, to demonstrate that Jesus was taken from one place to another. (The exact positioning in the building is not significant.) The readers could walk from one place to the next. There is no rush. Verses 19–23 could be read in one place, verses 24,28 in another, verses 29–39 and 19:1–16 in a third.

This reading could again be read with a narrator and people taking the parts of Jesus, temple police, chief priests and Pilate. The crowd plays a large part in John's account of Jesus' trial and death. They could gather some distance away from the other readers and shout out raucously at the right time, or crowd members could be scattered in the seated congregation and stand up when it is the crowd's turn to speak or shout.

Pause for people to reflect on what this meant to Jesus – the insults, the rejection, the pain, the turning of the crowd against him – people who only a few days earlier had hailed him as their king. Children may find this too emotionally demanding but the image on the screen is not violent or gruesome. They can identify with suffering and injustice and both of those emotions are present in bucket loads in this story.

Ask the following rhetorical questions:
- How much was Jesus being bullied?
- How fair was it that Jesus should die instead of Barabbas?
- Why did the crowd turn against Jesus?
- What would you have done if you had been there?

Jesus is crucified
Read John 19:16b–24, displaying Bosch's *Christ Mocked – The Crowning with Thorns* (in the National Gallery in London). You could point out some of the characteristics of this painting:

- Only Jesus is wearing white garments of innocence and he looks so quiet against the anger and harshness of his tormentors. The tugging at Jesus' robe, the mocking touching of his hands and the pressing in of the tormentors has little effect on their victim.
- The spiky crown about to be forced onto his head looks like a strange halo.
- The four characters are arranged in a similar way to the four evangelists portrayed in other paintings of the time, but these are no friends of Jesus.
- The character top right is wearing a spiked dog collar, symbolic of the fact that Jesus' torturers were sometimes called 'savage dogs' and the oak leaf pinned to his hat may be symbolic of secular authority.
- The arrow through the headdress of the man top left with his armoured glove is symbolic of military force.
- The man bottom left has a crescent on his headdress, a sign that he is not a believer.
- The man bottom right is slipping out of the picture, as though Jesus is slipping from his grasp.

This reading could be followed by the **Prayer activity**.

Jesus dies
Comment that four of Jesus' recorded words from the cross are to be found in John's Gospel. Ask people to listen out for what he said as John 19:25–30 is read. The words

could be displayed on a screen or flip chart:

To Mary, his mother, "This man is now your son." (verse 26)
To his disciple, John, "She is now your mother." (verse 27)
"I am thirsty!" (verse 28)
"Everything is done!" (verse 30) (CEV)
As this is read, display an image which powerfully displays the cross such as a modern image on the Turn Back to God website (www.turnbacktogod.com/jesus-christ-wallpaper-sized-images-pic-set-22/).

Comment that Jesus cared for others, even as he hung on the cross in great agony and thirst. He knew that the purpose for his death had been achieved as he gave up his life and stopped fighting to live – strangely powerful words.

Follow this with **Prayers of intercession**.

Prayer activity

With: nails; small pieces of wood, two different lengths; string

In response to the third reading, invite everyone to come to a central point, maybe near a large wooden cross, to pick up a nail (be watchful of younger children). Ask people to picture the scene of Christ crucified as they finger the nail.

People can also take two pieces of wood and tie them together to make a rough cross. Again, ask people to picture the scene of Christ crucified as they make the cross.

Then lead in prayer, thanking Jesus for dying for us. You could conclude by reading Psalm 130:1–4.

Prayers of intercession

Good Friday, leading onto Holy Saturday, is the one time in the church's year when the mood encourages us to talk with God about how life often does not make sense (although we can of course talk with him about that at any time!). For the disciples, they had lost all hope. They had not expected Jesus to be killed like this, even though he had warned them. They were fearful that their own lives might also be in danger. As darkness fell on the Friday and the Sabbath began, life must have been utterly bleak.

It would therefore be appropriate to pray for all those who are without hope. Ask a few people to prepare prayers for those who are trapped by mental illness and depression, those who suffer from long-term sickness, those whose personal circumstances are full of trouble, those areas in the world where civil strife and unhappiness appear to be never-ending. Ask that God will be there, in those situations, making a difference and bringing his peace and order.

Don't forget that in two days' time, prayers and worship will be filled with hope and triumph. But don't dismiss this time of desolation.

Prayer activity

With: three strands of black wool and one of gold thread – long enough to make a wristband, one set for each person

To replicate the activity in **Beginning the service**, give out four pieces of wool/thread to each person. Ask them to tie the three black pieces in a knot and then plait together until the plait is long enough to be tied into a wristband or bracelet. People can put this on their wrist to wear for the next 36 hours, as a reminder that this is a day of mourning, but also a day when so many things came together in God's plan for the world. Refer back to the larger plait.

On Easter morning, suggest that people untie their plait and add in the gold thread and plait again. The wristband now speaks of hope and glory mixed in with grief and suffering. This idea could be developed in the Easter Day service.

Close with a suitably serious song.

Helpful extras

Music and song ideas

Traditional Good Friday hymns and songs have their place in this service, such as 'When I survey the wondrous cross'; 'There is a green hill'; 'Oh sacred head, surrounded'; 'Oh the deep, deep love of Jesus'; 'The head that once was crowned with thorns'; 'My song is love unknown'; 'Man of sorrows, what a name'. Listening to 'When I survey the wondrous cross' unaccompanied, to a tune in a minor key, can be extremely moving.

There are also newer songs with powerful words, such as 'When I think about the cross'; 'How deep the Father's love for us'; 'Oh to see the dawn' (Stuart Townend); 'Led like a lamb to the slaughter'; 'Lord, I lift your name on high'; 'From heav'n you came'; 'I'm special, because God has loved me'.

Notes and comments

If you do not have facilities to project the images on a screen, you could photocopy some small pictures and distribute at least one of them to focus the attention of the congregation.

Many powerful songs have been written about Jesus' death. A live performance of one of these would help people to reflect on his death without having to sing themselves. Alternatively, use recorded music for the same purpose.

There are a number of films which tell the story of Jesus' passion. Scripture Union has produced several retellings of the story which are available as DVDs – for example from the *Wastewatchers* or *Showstoppers* DVDs. Do not underestimate the solemnity of the occasion that should embrace everyone present. So long as there is plenty of variety and different learning preferences are recognised, with some interactivity, even young children will be able to be involved.

Providing hot cross buns with drinks after the service would make the service memorable, if you do not usually have much in the way of refreshments.

Alternative online options

Visit www.lightlive.org for additional activities for children, young people and adults.

EASTER DAY

READINGS: **Luke 24:1-12; 1 Corinthians 15:19-26**
Isaiah 65:17-25; Psalm 118:1,2,14-24

Bible foundations
Aim: to celebrate the wonder of Christ's resurrection

Jesus was well and truly dead. The women who witnessed his burial (Luke 23:55,56) now return with spices and ointments for the body. They thought they knew what they would find. They were not anticipating what had actually happened. The two men who greeted them needed to spell it out (Luke 24:6-8). Unsurprisingly, the people that they told did not believe them either (v 11). This is not just because they were female (and therefore not valued as witnesses) but that the claim of resurrection is almost beyond belief!

But no matter how outrageous, Christians have steadfastly maintained this claim throughout history. As Paul told the Corinthians (1 Corinthians 15:14), if Christ was not raised, then everything we believe is nonsense. Luke's cautious tone anticipates how shocking this claim is and how hard to take in. His account is notable for being so low-key: the women see two men (Luke 24:4), not angels (Luke 24:23), who tell them why Jesus is missing.

Christ's resurrection has smashed the ultimate enemy: death. He is the down payment (1 Corinthians 15:23), the assurance that all of us will experience the same thing. Christ now works to bring the whole of creation back under the rule and authority of the Father (vs 24,25), culminating in the general resurrection and the final destruction of death.

Isaiah gives us a picture of that redemption. He identifies a range of things that were distorted by the fall and imagines them all restored. The unfairness of early deaths (Isaiah 65:20), not reaping the fruits of your own labours (vs 21,22), and nature (v 25) will be returned into their opposites. Psalm 118:22 includes what was to become an extremely important text for the early church. In its context, verse 17 is probably a reference to continued life rather than resurrection. In the light of Christ, however, it becomes another pointer to the resurrection to come, both of Christ and for us.

Beginning the service

With: a picture of the cross; a copy of the Easter chant – 'Jesus Christ has been raised to life! (1 Corinthians 15:20)', on a screen or in the service sheet

The worship group should settle the congregation with a song to link together Good Friday and Easter Sunday (see **Music and song ideas**) while an image of the cross is displayed on a screen.

Introduce the Easter chant. Instead of shouting loudly, repeatedly chant the line quietly (see **Music and song ideas** for setting the rhythm). Explain that the wonderful news that Jesus was alive again was not initially shouted from rooftops. Rather, it was slowly and quietly revealed and spread.

If you wove the black plait on Good Friday (see previous service outline), you could weave in the golden thread, signifying the evidence of glory to be celebrated on Easter Day.

Bible reading

With: a large exclamation mark to display

The CEV or NIV are recommended for the readings of the Bible passages.

To emphasise the surprise and wonder of the resurrection, invite everyone to gasp or say 'Amazing!' at moments in the reading from Luke 24:1–12 when Jesus' followers would have been surprised. Arrange for a volunteer to hold up an exclamation mark, to indicate when to join in. Suggestions for when to respond are indicated below, based on the CEV.

> Very early on Sunday morning the women went to the tomb, carrying the spices that they had prepared. When they found the stone rolled away from the entrance (**amazing!**), they went in. But they did not find the body of the Lord Jesus (**amazing!**), and they did not know what to think. Suddenly two men in shining white clothes stood beside them (**amazing!**). The women were afraid and bowed to the ground. But the men said, "Why are you looking in the place of the dead for someone who is alive? Jesus isn't here! He has been raised from death (**amazing!**). Remember that while he was still in Galilee, he told you, 'The Son of Man will be handed over to sinners who will nail him to a cross. But three days later he will rise to life.'" Then they remembered what Jesus had said. Mary Magdalene, Joanna, Mary the mother of James, and some other women were the ones who had gone to the tomb. When they returned, they told the eleven apostles and the others what had happened. The apostles thought it was all nonsense, and they would not believe. But Peter ran to the tomb. And when he stooped down and looked in, he saw only the burial clothes (**amazing!**). Then he returned, wondering what had happened.
>
> Luke 24:1–12 (CEV)

Introduce 1 Corinthians 15:19–26 by pointing out that it contains the Easter chant. Paul is explaining the impact of Christ's death and resurrection, comparing it with the effect of Adam's actions. To emphasise this comparison ask people to stand up when 'life' is mentioned and sit down when 'death' or 'die' is said. Suggestions for when to respond are indicated below, using the CEV. Someone should show when to respond.

> If our hope in Christ is good only for this life (**stand up**), we are worse off than anyone else. But (Jesus) Christ has been raised to life (**stay standing**)! And he makes us certain that others will also be raised to life (**stay standing**). Just as we will die (**sit down**) because of Adam, we will be raised to life (**stand up**) because of Christ. Adam brought death (**sit down**) to all of us, and Christ will bring life (**stand up**) to all of us. But we must each wait our turn. Christ was the first to be raised to life (**stay standing**), and his people will be raised to life (**stay standing**) when he returns. Then after Christ has destroyed all powers and forces, the end will come, and he will give the kingdom to God the Father. Christ will rule until he puts all his enemies under his power, and the last enemy he destroys will be death (**sit down**).
>
> 1 Corinthians 15:19–26 (CEV)

Bible retelling

A 'Resurrection interview' script is available as a download (YearC.Easter_1).

Bible talk

With: a large image of the tomb painted on a sheet or flattened box with the label 'JESUS IS ALIVE' on the entrance; a large cardboard stone labelled 'JESUS IS DEAD' covering this entrance and the previous label; rolls of crêpe bandage cut into short strips and placed in front of the tomb; five surprise cards, either on their own or attached to Easter eggs, distributed around the church, with the following words on them: 'Surprise 1 – The Stone'; 'Surprise 2 – The Body'; 'Surprise 3 – The Angels'; 'Surprise 4 – The Message'; 'Surprise 5 – 'The Burial Clothes' (The five surprise phrases to project on a screen are available as a PowerPoint download (YearC. Easter_2).)

Ask if anyone has ever had a really good surprise. How did it make them feel? If you used the **Game**, refer back to the participants' reactions on discovering that the obstacles had gone. Link this to Luke 24 and talk about how Easter morning was full of surprises for Jesus' followers. Remind people that Jesus had been killed so his followers awoke on the Sunday with one subject dominating their thoughts: 'Jesus is dead!' Refer to the Bible retelling interview with Joanna and her explanation of why the women were going to the tomb. Point to the sign on the tomb, 'JESUS IS DEAD'.

Yet when the followers visited the tomb, there were various surprising things which pointed to something amazing. Invite a few people to look for the five surprise cards hidden around the building to bring to the front. Read out each surprise in sequence and expand on them. Each time you ask a question, you'll be expecting the answer 'Yes' or 'No'.

Surprise 1 – 'The Stone'
The stone should have been blocking the entrance to the cave. Ask, 'Was it?' and expect the answer, 'No'. Refer to Luke 24:2 and explain that the women would have been

really surprised at this. They thought it was going to be very hard for them to move the stone.

Surprise 2 – 'The Body'
Dead bodies stay where they have been put, inside a grave! They can't move on their own. Ask, 'Was the body still there?' and expect the answer, 'No'. Luke 24:3 says that the women could not find Jesus' body and were not sure what had happened to it.

Surprise 3 – 'The Angels'
Angels are not normally seen hanging around places. Ask, 'Were there any angels around?' and expect the answer, 'Yes'. (This will show whether people are following the plot and are not on autopilot responses!) The men in gleaming clothes who appeared were described by the women as being angels (Luke 24:23). Having been mystified by surprises 1 and 2, the women were now terrified.

Surprise 4 – 'The Message'
When an angel delivers a message, it's normally important. Ask, 'Was this message important?' and again expect the answer, 'Yes'. This message contained vital information about what had happened to Jesus; he had come back to life, just like he told them he would. Jesus had told his followers what was going to happen, but they could not understand, so this message was a big surprise. The message helped make sense of all the other surprises and convinced the women that Jesus had risen to life. These four surprises were enough to convince the women, but Luke 24:11 tells us that the disciples they told still needed more surprises.

Surprise 5 – 'The Burial Clothes'
Dead bodies don't take off the clothes they are buried in. Ask, 'Were any grave clothes left behind in the tomb?' expecting the answer, 'Yes'. Refer to Luke 24:12 and explain that Peter found the strips of burial clothes in the tomb. He saw this as a clue that something amazing had happened. If grave robbers had stolen a dead body they would not have wasted time removing the clothes.

Put the five cards in front of the picture of the tomb and remove the stone that says 'JESUS IS DEAD'. The sign saying 'JESUS IS ALIVE' should now be visible. This was an amazing surprise for the disciples and it is amazing news for us. Jesus keeps his promises. Jesus is powerful. One day his followers will all have new resurrection life as Jesus did – refer to 1 Corinthians 15:19–26. Death is not the end of Jesus' story, nor the end of our story.

Ask those who found the surprises to distribute the strips of bandage in front of the tomb. Each person should receive one as a reminder that Jesus came back to life and is able to give life to us.

Prayers of intercession

Christ's resurrection is the ultimate example of God bringing hope to a hopeless situation. Use news reports and local information to prepare short prayers on difficult or hopeless situations at a local, national and international level, asking for God's power to surprise you. Ask several people to each prepare a prayer for a specific topic. Conclude with a simple prayer asking for God's will to be done in these and other unnamed situations. If you used the suggestion for prayer on Good Friday, you could use the same topics but differently in the light of Easter Day.

Ending the service

With: the strips of bandage for each person (see **Bible talk**); a copy of the Easter chant (see **Beginning the service**)

As before, people whisper the Easter chant. Gradually build up the volume and encourage people to wave bandages in the air like celebratory flags. These can be taken home as a reminder of the resurrection.

Helpful extras

Music and song ideas

Percussion instruments should set the pace and volume of the Easter chant.

Use a drumstick on the rim of a drum or an egg shaker to accompany the whispered chant and as the volume increases beat out a rhythm on the drum skin using additional instruments.

Use a light-hearted tune such as 'Eye of the Tiger' by Survivor throughout the obstacle challenge (see **Game**).

Creative musical arrangements could set a mood of wonder. A solo voice singing 'Were you there when they crucified my Lord?' might settle everyone and build a link from Christ's death. 'Low in the grave he lay' captures the message of 1 Corinthians 15. The worship group could sing the verses, while the congregation joins in rowdily with the chorus, using shakers and whistles. Additional songs, apart from traditional ones, might include: 'You lived, you died'; 'You are mighty'; 'God's not dead'; 'We're so thankful to you'; 'Jesus, we celebrate your victory'; 'In the tomb so cold they laid him'; 'See what a morning'; 'Celebrate' ('Sing a song'); 'Living one' from *Bitesize Bible Songs 2* (SU) – a Learn and remember verse song – Revelation 1:18.

Game

A game suggestion is available as a download (YearC.Easter_3).

Notes and comments

The painting of the tomb, the Easter chant and further Resurrection interviews will feature in the next two services. The Easter chant is relevant to all the three services in the Easter series, and is at the heart of the reading from 1 Corinthians. But you might choose an alternative chant or call and response phrase such as the Learn and remember verse, Revelation 1:18, from the *Light* material, available as a song – see **Music and songs ideas**. Whichever chant or verse you use, adapt it to this service by whispering it at the start and repeating it three times at the end of the service, getting louder each time.

Be aware of health and safety issues during the **Game** and ensure obstacles are cleared away safely.

Alternative online options

For your convenience the following activities are available as downloads: YearC.Easter_4 Action rhyme for under-5s; YearC.Easter_5 Adult sermon. Visit www.lightlive.org for additional activities for children, young people and adults.

SECOND SUNDAY OF EASTER

READINGS: **Acts 5:27–32; John 20:19–31**
Psalm 150; Revelation 1:4–8

Bible foundations
Aim: to explore how God's people are changed by the fact that Jesus is alive

Knowing Christ is alive should be a source of peace to all Christians (John 20:19,21,26). Our sins have been forgiven (John 20:23; Revelation 1:5) and we have been given a ministry to fulfil for him (Revelation 1:6, see also Exodus 19:6; 1 Peter 2:9).

No matter how sceptical about the resurrection individuals might be, Christ still comes with loving assurance of his good intentions towards us. Jesus meets Thomas in his weakness and insecurity and offers him what he needs. Ultimately, along with Thomas, everyone is called to affirm that Jesus is our Lord and our God (John 20:28). In the twenty-first century we have no choice but to believe without seeing for ourselves (v 29) – Jesus blesses us for it.

Christ then sends his people out into the world, invigorating them boldly to share the news. Given the Spirit (John 20:22; Acts 2:1–4; 5:32), his disciples step out from the safety of a hiding place (John 20:19) to the public places (Acts 5:25). Since 'every eye will see him' (Revelation 1:7) at his coming, we should all ensure that before then all people have had the chance to hear.

Psalm 150 demonstrates one of the key elements of our response to the resurrection. We are called to praise God, in a variety of ways but especially with exuberance and full musical accompaniment!

NB Between Easter and Pentecost, the readings form three separate strands. We read in Acts about events in the years straight after the resurrection. Alongside this, a series of readings take us rapidly through Revelation. Finally, the Gospel readings take up various parts of Jesus' teaching from John. Genuine integration of these will not always be easy!

Beginning the service

With: a large painting of the empty tomb (see Easter Day); a bundle of ten balloons with question marks drawn on them, tied to a box; three helpers; two copies of the following questions, available as a download (YearC.Easter2_1). The questions are: Where is Jesus now? Are we going to get into trouble?; What should we do now? Will we see Jesus again? What will people think? What's going to happen to us? What does Jesus want us to do? Is Jesus really alive?

Ask if anyone remembers the chant from Easter Day (see previous service outline) and then ask if anyone remembers where we find it in the Bible. Gesture for people to chant it quietly, then get louder, before becoming silent. In the quiet that follows, two helpers read the series of questions into microphones while a third helper brings the balloons to the front and places them at the tomb. The questions should be read clearly but with a sense of urgency, and repeated three times.

Remind everyone that last week was a celebration of Jesus being alive again, having been killed on the cross. Point to the balloons and explain that although Jesus' followers were thrilled, they had lots of questions on receiving this news. The service explores how God's people were affected and changed by Jesus' resurrection, and how some of their questions were answered.

Bible reading

With: a large question mark on card

Use either the NIV or the Good News Bible.

Read John 20:19–31 with three voices: the narrator, Jesus and Thomas. The narrator also reads the words of the other disciples in verse 25. Encourage the readers to practise so that they can make eye contact with each other and the congregation, and sound appropriately excited.

Introduce Acts 5:27–32 by explaining that the disciples were in trouble because they were telling people that Jesus was not only alive but he could change lives. Interrupt the reading at verse 28 by holding up a large question mark and explain that Jesus' followers faced the question of what they were going to do now. They were in trouble. Were they going to apologise and get out of it, or were they going to stick up for Jesus? The reader then completes the reading. Ask what the disciples chose to do and see what answers you get.

Bible retelling

In this Resurrection interview, Thomas describes the impact the resurrection had on the disciples and then on himself. This can be live or recorded, using a digital camera. The script below is only a guideline for what to include.

Resurrection interview: Thomas

Interviewer: Thomas, you weren't with the other disciples when Jesus first appeared to them. Did they tell you what happened?
Thomas: They did, and I really didn't know what to make of it. They told me that they'd seen Jesus and his scars. They said they'd heard him speak, and he said some really important things. They were so excited, but I just couldn't believe them. I needed to see Jesus and his injuries for myself.
Interviewer: So, did you ever see him?
Thomas: Yes, but I had to wait a whole week. We were all together, and suddenly, there he

was, standing right in front of me. He spoke directly to me and invited me to touch his wounds.
Interviewer: Did this convince you he was alive?
Thomas: Absolutely! But more than that, I was convinced he was more than an extraordinary human being. I knew I was looking at God.

Bible talk

With: one bundle of question mark balloons (see **Beginning the service**); a box with ten balloons tied to it, with each of the following words written on two balloons: 'peace'; 'joy'; a mission'; 'the Holy Spirit'; 'belief'

Give examples of things that are hard to understand, such as how electricity works, how bees fly when their body appears too heavy for their wings or the answer to a difficult maths question. Some things puzzle us and make us ask questions. It might be appropriate to point out that many people have questions about God too, like how he can let bad things happen.

Distribute the question mark balloons to people across the whole church. Refer to the questions in **Beginning the service** and remind everyone that Jesus' followers had lots of questions once they had heard that Jesus had risen from the dead. John 20:19 describes the disciples as hiding behind locked doors, scared of the Jewish authorities. Repeat these four questions from **Beginning the service**: Where is Jesus now? Are we going to get into trouble? What should we do now? Will we see Jesus again?

Meeting Jesus changed them

Meeting the risen Jesus turned the disciples from a group of scared people hiding away in fear to become the bold and brave rebels described in Acts 5. If you can, mention contemporary television characters who change character for a short period of time. The difference between the disciples and these television characters is that the change in the disciples was permanent – something had happened to change them.

Meeting Jesus brought them peace and joy

Go to the second box of balloons and take the ones labelled 'Peace' and 'Joy'. Exchange these for some of the question mark balloons which you should hide away. Refer to John 20:19–21. The first words the risen Jesus spoke to the disciples were 'Peace be with you.' This was more than a traditional greeting. Jesus had brought them (and us) peace with God through his death. When the disciples heard his words and saw his wounds they were filled with joy because they had proof that he really was alive. Jesus' followers today can also have this joy and peace no matter how difficult life seems. By dying on the cross, Jesus has made it possible to be friends with him.

Meeting Jesus gave them a new mission and power

Exchange more of the question mark balloons for new balloons labelled 'A mission' and 'The Holy Spirit'. In John 20:21–23 Jesus gives the disciples the mission of carrying on the work he started. He said they were to be God's representatives to the world and would have his authority. To help his followers do this, Jesus gave them the Holy Spirit, God's presence in their lives. He also gave them, and us, a mission. Fulfilling God's mission is tough, so God's power is vital. Just like the disciples,

Jesus wants us to let people around us know about his love. However, we can't do it by ourselves – only in partnership with him.

Meeting Jesus convinced them that he really was God

Exchange the final question mark balloons for ones that say 'belief'. Only answer balloons should now be visible. Remind everyone of Thomas' meeting with Jesus, and refer to the fact he is often (unfairly) called Doubting Thomas. Once Thomas met Jesus he expressed the greatest faith of all the followers by saying, 'You are my Lord and my God.' Thomas, looking at the evidence of the resurrected Jesus, was persuaded that all Jesus had claimed to be and do was true – he really was God. The physical reality of the resurrection helped Thomas believe in him and can help us believe that Jesus was God. Expand on this, especially if you are aware of people present who are uncertain of whether Jesus is God.

All the new balloons should now be distributed among the congregation. Ask everyone who is holding one to pass it to someone sitting near them. Refer to John 20:29,31 where both Jesus and John, in writing his Gospel, make it clear that these blessings are not limited to the disciples. People living today can be affected by the fact that Jesus is alive. We who are his followers can also have peace, joy, a mission, the Holy Spirit and a reason to believe, even if we haven't met Jesus face to face. The disciples were changed into people who acted bravely and stood up for Jesus. So too, we can stand up for the One in whom we believe.

Prayer activity

With: the painting of the empty tomb; five prayer stations set up around the church each with a large empty bowl, a pile of plain paper and pens or pencils (Each station should be labelled with one of the following: peace; joy; a mission; Holy Spirit; belief, reflecting the themes from the **Bible talk**. With a large congregation set up as many prayer stations as you need)

Ask people still holding the answer balloons to take them to the relevant prayer station and tie them there. Explain that the blessings from the resurrection are still available to people today, so this activity focuses on asking God for these on behalf of ourselves and others.

Encourage people to visit one or more stations, write down the name of someone they know who is in need of a specific blessing (it could be themselves) and place the piece of paper in the bowl. They can repeat this as many times as they want with different names and needs. To show how it works, write out the names of specific people known to the whole church as being in need of prayer.

Ask for the five bowls to be placed before the picture of the tomb. Conclude with a prayer to focus on the fact that Jesus is alive, asking for God's blessings upon the people named.

Ending the service

With: the answer balloons (see **Bible talk**)

Through meeting the resurrected Jesus, the disciples' doubts and questions were transformed into joy and courage. Ask everyone to think for a moment if they still have a question that they would like answered. Encourage them to talk with someone about it, if they want an answer now. Sensitively indicate people who are willing to talk with them.

Remind everyone that Jesus gave his followers a mission to take his message of love to the world, and that includes us. Sing a song either of encouragement, such as 'Be bold, be strong' or one of commitment to mission, such as 'Here I am, wholly available'. You could process out of the church, carrying the answer balloons.

Helpful extras

Music and song ideas

Use percussion to support the Easter chant – see last Sunday's outline.

During the **Prayer activity** play pre-recorded instrumental music to allow the musicians to participate.

'Peace, I give to you' reflects the message of the **Bible talk**. Try increasing the tempo and encourage people to jump up and down in the verses, while moving their hands from side to side in the chorus (in the style of Hawaiian dancing).

The service moves from a place of doubt and questions to a place of hope and courage which could be reflected in the mood created by the music. Start with more reflective, slower songs and move to faster, more rousing tempos such as 'Alleluia, Alleluia'; 'Be bold, be strong'; 'All of me'; 'We're so thankful to you'; 'In Christ alone, my hope is found'; 'This love, this hope'.

Statement of faith

A statement of faith based on Peter's response to the Jewish leaders in Acts 5:30–32 is available as a download (YearC. Easter2_2). Before reading the statement together, display it and ask for suggestions for an action for each line. Practise the actions before saying the lines together.

Notes and comments

This is the second in a series of three Easter services exploring the impact of the resurrection on Jesus' followers both immediately after the resurrection and also in the present day. Common threads link the services together – the Easter chant, Resurrection interviews and painting of the tomb.

This theme lends itself to personal testimony, at **Beginning the service** or just after the **Bible talk**. Make sure that the focus is very specific, answering the question 'What difference does it make to you, that Jesus is alive?'

The **Bible talk** and **Prayer activity** provide opportunities to explore more fully the work of the Holy Spirit. If appropriate, have people at the Holy Spirit prayer station to lay hands on those requesting it, if this is something you are comfortable with in the all-age context.

Alternative online options

For your convenience the following activity is available as a download: YearC.Easter2_3 Alternative ending. Visit www.lightlive.org for additional activities for children, young people and adults.

THIRD SUNDAY OF EASTER

READINGS: **Psalm 30; John 21:1-19**
Acts 9:1-6 [7-20]; Revelation 5:11-14

Bible foundations
Aim: to receive forgiveness and a new beginning with Jesus

The disciples seem shy around Jesus. They recognise him (John 21:7) yet don't recognise him (vs 4,12), rush to be with him (verse 7) yet hang back from him (v 12). Notably, after the events surrounding the crucifixion, there is unfinished business – at least there is for Peter (vs 15-19). We must realise that nothing is hidden from God. But as with last week's reading when we saw Jesus' reaction to Thomas (John 20:24-29), Jesus does not rebuke or punish Peter. Jesus' questions draw him out. Peter loves Jesus: always has and always will. But he needs to have his confidence in his Lord restored, for he has indeed let Jesus down. He also needs to know that his Lord has confidence in him. Recent commentaries exhort us not to read too much into the changing verbs for 'love' in verses 15-17. The changes intensify the question without necessarily suggesting a change in the type of love that is being discussed.

Paul (like Peter), receives a new commission from Jesus (Acts 9:15). Jesus does expect an active response from those whom he has forgiven. Not that the task given to Paul is given to enable him to earn forgiveness. Christ constantly asks us to take up our cross and follow him. There could be no greater demonstration of God's total acceptance of Peter and Paul than can be seen in the trust he places in them to be his messengers and representatives here on earth.

Both Psalm 30 and the reading from Revelation stand apart from this message. Psalm 30:5 could be applied to Peter and Jesus' forgiveness of him, and verse 11, a possible description of how he might have felt after his conversation with Jesus.

Beginning the service

With: a grumpy helper with access to a microphone; the painting of the tomb; the Easter chant used on Easter Day

Welcome everyone and point to the image of the tomb as a reminder of the message of the past two services: It is wonderful news that Jesus is alive. His resurrection has made a great difference in people's lives. Invite everyone to join in with the Easter chant.

While this is going on, the helper should be clearly visible and, instead of joining in, looks grumpy and fed up. Once the chant is over, ask why they are not joining in and whether everything is OK. The helper dramatically makes the following points: they don't feel like it, they're having a bad day, everything's going wrong, and they have upset a friend and think Jesus is too busy to notice them. Invite them to pay attention to the service, as you explore the way Jesus turned a bad day into a brilliant one, as he expresses his love for his disciples, especially Peter.

Bible reading

Use the CEV or NIV for these readings.

John 21:1–19 is a long passage, so could be read in two sections, verses 1–14 and 15–19, with a song in between.

Use Psalm 30 as an expression of worship after the **Prayer of confession**. If you have someone gifted in dance, they could express the essence of the reading in dance. Alternatively invite a range of children to stand at the front and wave banners throughout the reading. Two readers could read the psalm antiphonally. Reader A reads verses 1,4,5b,7,11 while Reader B reads verses 2 and 3,5a,6,8 to 10, and verse 12 together.

Bible retelling

This Resurrection interview includes some background by making reference to Peter's earlier denial of knowing Jesus. It focuses on the different ways Jesus acted lovingly towards the disciples. The script only serves as a guideline. The interview can be live or pre-recorded.

Resurrection interview: Peter

Interviewer: After Jesus had risen from the dead, he gave instructions for you and the other disciples to meet him in Galilee. What happened there?

Peter: I suggested to some of the lads that we go fishing while waiting for Jesus to show up. We caught nothing. And then he appeared and told us to try fishing on the other side of the boat. That's when we caught loads. While we were bringing the catch to land, Jesus was cooking us breakfast. It was strange but brilliant to sit and eat with him. And it was after that meal, that he and I had this amazing conversation.

Interviewer: Can you tell us about this?

Peter: It was all about love and sheep! He asked me three times if I really loved him. I knew that he knew I did. So I told him this. Each time he told me I had to look after his sheep and lambs. He was the main shepherd, and was making me a little shepherd. It was a job I could do because I loved him.

Interviewer: Why do you think he asked you the same question three times?

Peter: Maybe because I'd messed up three times or maybe he just wanted to make the point! Just after Jesus was arrested, some people around the high priest's house where

Jesus was being tried saw me and asked if I was one of his friends. Three times I said I wasn't and that I didn't know who he was. When I realised what I had done, I was gutted. So by asking three times if I loved him, it was like he was giving me a new beginning.

Bible talk

With: enough food for everyone to have something to eat – biscuits or, if possible, something more sophisticated such as buttered toast, plus serviettes if it's going to be messy (Be sensitive to food allergies.)

Distribute the food to everyone. Explain that food was a key part in many of Jesus' meetings with his disciples. Often while people were eating with him, they grew in their understanding of God. Encourage people to eat the food as you speak.

A bad day, before breakfast
Ask people to make a 'thumbs down' gesture if they've had a bad day recently. If you used the helper at **Beginning the service**, refer to their bad day. Make the connection with John 21 and say that Peter was having a bad night and day and it wasn't even breakfast time. (*Everyone puts their thumbs down in sympathy with Peter's bad day.*) Peter had had a bad time at work; he and some of the other disciples had spent hours through the night fishing and had caught nothing, and now were tired and hungry.

A good day, before breakfast
Jesus appeared and helped Peter out and turned a bad day into a good day by breakfast time. (*Ask everyone to make a 'thumbs up' gesture.*) He showed the disciples where to find loads of big fish, and then when they got to land, he was cooking them a big breakfast. As an act of love, Jesus met Peter's needs, helping with his work, and providing rest and food.

A bad day, after breakfast
But it looked as though the day might turn bad again for Peter. (*Ask everyone to make a 'thumbs down' gesture.*) Give some examples of awkward questions that people might be asked such as 'How long have you actually been on the computer?' and 'Why did you lie to me?' Refer to verses 15–17 where Jesus asks Peter, 'Do you love me?' This was awkward because it touched a raw nerve. Peter had acted as though he didn't love Jesus when he said he wasn't his friend. Asking the questions three times would have brought memories of his failure back to him. Jesus could have given Peter a lecture on how he should have behaved, but he didn't.

A good day, after breakfast
Jesus didn't punish Peter or tell him off, and so everyone can give a 'thumbs up' gesture. Peter was right in saying that Jesus already knew that Peter loved him, but this was Peter's chance to say it out loud. Jesus was making the point! Jesus died on the cross so people could be forgiven. He put this into practice by forgiving Peter and giving him a new job to do, feeding sheep and lambs. Jesus was giving Peter this job not because Peter was perfect but because he loved Jesus.

You could develop the message further by saying that Jesus used this bad day to remind Peter of some important truths as he started building the church: obedience to Christ and partnership with him is the way to fruitfulness; fellowship and the sharing of food, particularly the bread and wine, is a vital foundation to build upon; love not perfection is the best basis for serving God.

As with Peter, our bad days are never too bad for Jesus to be involved in. He loves us and wants to help us. Give some practical examples of how people could allow Jesus into their bad days. These could include thinking about him at work, asking for his help, doing what you think he wants you to do, taking seriously his example to rest and be with friends. Also emphasise the need to ask Jesus to forgive them when they let him down. You could ask someone to share their personal testimony.

Conclude by drawing people's attention to the painting of the empty tomb. The day Jesus died was seen by some as an extremely bad day. (Ask everyone for a final time to put their thumbs down.) But two days' later, Jesus turned a bad day into the greatest day ever. (Ask everyone to put their thumbs up.)

Prayer activity

With: a very large sheet of plain paper; two thick marker pens; two helpers with clear writing; the Bad Day Prayer below; four people of differing ages to read the prayer out loud

What makes a bad day for the adults present? Children and young people should ask those sitting near them for examples of bad days, such as 'having too much to do', 'needing to pay bills', or 'a grumpy boss'. The two helpers record the children's answers on the large piece of paper.

Reverse the roles and adults ask the children and young people what makes a bad day. This information is similarly recorded. Everyone looks at the paper as the following Bad Day Prayer is read aloud by four people, each person reading one line.

A Bad Day Prayer

1: Dear Jesus, you know that we all have bad days.
2: When work is difficult, give us your help.
3: When we are tired and hungry, give us strength.
4: When we do or say the wrong thing, give us a second chance.
1–4: Thank you that you love us, even on our bad days. Amen.

Prayer of confession

With: a displayed copy of the response in the confession, also available as a PowerPoint download (YearC.Easter3_1)

The risen Jesus expressed his love for Peter by forgiving him. He continues to do that for us today, so a time for confession and forgiveness is a vital part of this service. Use background music to create a calm atmosphere and allow thinking time before the response is said.

Explain that four gestures will be used during the prayers and ask everyone to practise them – touching the head (representing thoughts), touching the mouth (representing words), wiggling fingers (representing actions) and making a heart shape using two thumbs and forefingers (representing love). As you read through the prayer, allow thinking time after each gesture is made and before saying 'Father God'.

In God's presence, let us think how we have not pleased him.

Point to your head
Leader: Father God,
Sometimes my thoughts have not been loving thoughts. Sorry.
Let us think what we have said that has not pleased God.

Put your hand on mouth
Leader: Father God,
Sometimes my words have not been loving words. Sorry.
Let us think what we have done that has not pleased God.

Wiggle your fingers
Leader: Father God,
Sometimes my actions have not been loving actions. Sorry.

Make a heart shape
Leader: Father God,
Thank you that you love me and forgive me. Amen.

Follow this prayer with the reading of Psalm 30 (see **Bible reading**).

Ending the service

With: the grumpy helper (see **Beginning the service**)

Ask the helper if they have found out anything to help with the bad day. The response summarises the key points of the service: Jesus loves us and can help us with our bad days; he helped Peter with his work, gave him food and rest, and forgave him when he had really let him down. So, Jesus can help us too. How great it is that Jesus is alive!

For the final time everyone does the Easter chant, starting as a whisper and building to a loud cheer using lots of instruments. This crescendo could lead into an upbeat worship song (see **Music and song ideas**).

Helpful extras

Music and song ideas

'I am a new creation'; 'God forgave my sins'; 'Oh happy day'; 'The cross has said it all' to focus on forgiveness, appropriate to use in the **Prayer of confession**.

Towards the end, as people offer themselves back to Christ, you could include: 'Lord, you have my heart'; 'I will offer up my life'.

Notes and comments

The Resurrection interviews, visual stimulus of the empty tomb and the Easter chant are common features in all three Easter services. This third service completes the exploration of the impact of the resurrection.

If this is a Communion service, remind everyone of Jesus' actions in John 21:13 as he broke the bread. This would have reminded the disciples when Jesus broke the bread at the Last Supper and his instruction for his followers to continue breaking bread and drinking wine to remember him. Jesus' death means that we can all be forgiven just as Peter was.

Alternative online options

For your convenience the following activity is available as a download: YearC.Easter3_2 Bible story with actions for under-5s. Visit www.lightlive.org for additional activities for children, young people and adults.

FOURTH SUNDAY OF EASTER

READINGS: **Psalm 23; Acts 9:36–43**
Revelation 7:9–17; John 10:22–30

Bible foundations
Aim: to see how God gives new life both spiritually and physically

The word 'shepherd' ties together three of today's readings. Being like his master, Jesus' disciple, Peter, was to discover that raising the dead was not just part of Jesus' ministry. Peter's healing of Tabitha/Dorcas might remind us of Easter Sunday. Christ's work has conquered death. So now, the gift of new life can (albeit very infrequently) be experienced as an extension of physical, earthly life.

The shepherd connection begins with Psalm 23. Undoubtedly the best known of all psalms, number 23 uses imagery familiar to the time of the psalmist. Secular rulers frequently styled themselves as shepherds. So while David's experience as a youth might have fuelled his use of the image, it was neither novel nor unique. God's spiritual care and new life is expressed through these pastoral scenes. The psalm is not purely about the spiritual life though; its imagery reminds us that everything we have, in the physical sense, comes from God.

The Gospel reading picks up the tale end of Jesus' 'Good shepherd' discourse in John 10. Its references to eternal life remind us that it is only those trusting in Christ who will experience new life. Jesus focuses attention onto himself: it is not God or the Father who gives eternal life (v 28) but Jesus.

We move a little further in the book of Revelation again. The great multitude (Revelation 7:9) has now received the ultimate gift from God: eternal life. This is because of the spiritual life and commitment they had to Jesus during their earthly life (v 14). The imagery in verses 16 and 17 is reminiscent of Psalm 23, especially in the references to the absence of hunger or thirst, springs of water and a shepherd.

Beginning the service

With: the illustrations to be used in the reading of Psalm 23, displayed in a random order, see **Bible reading**, available as a download (YearC.Easter4_1) (They could be on a rolling PowerPoint display, or fixed to a flip chart or large display board or wall.)

Invite everyone to see if they can work out which **Bible reading** the illustrations on show are connected with. Once the reading has been identified as Psalm 23, invite suggestions for the order in which the illustrations should appear.

Bible reading
Psalm 23

One person reads the psalm slowly as someone else illustrates it. This could be someone drawing the different elements onto a large sheet of paper, or by adding pre-cut illustrations to a background of fields, or with the different illustrations appearing in a PowerPoint presentation – see above. Ideally illustrations should be modern, rather than those of first century Palestine.

> You, Lord, are my shepherd. *(add shepherd)*
> I will never be in need.
> You let me rest in fields of green grass. *(add sleeping figure)*
> You lead me to streams of peaceful water, *(add stream)*
> and you refresh my life.
> You are true to your name, and you lead me
> along the right paths. *(add parent and child walking along path)*

> I may walk through valleys as dark as death,
> but I won't be afraid. *(add dark clouds)*
> You are with me, and your shepherd's rod makes me feel safe. *(add crook)*
> You treat me to a feast, while my enemies watch. *(add food)*
> You honour me as your guest, and you fill my cup
> until it overflows. *(add cup, and then froth that is overflowing)*
> Your kindness and love will always be with me
> each day of my life, *(add heart)*
> and I will live forever in your house, Lord. *(add rainbow over the picture)*
>
> Psalm 23 (CEV)

Bible retelling

Peter brings Dorcas back to life in the style of a news broadcast. The reporter and the bystander compete to tell the account.

Newsreader: Today's top story comes from Joppa where apparently a dead woman has come back to life. We go live to Joppa now to speak to our **Reporter**, Philip. What's been happening in Joppa today, Philip?

Reporter: It has been amazing here in Joppa. A well-known woman called Tabitha…

Bystander: *interrupting* But we also called her by her Greek name – Dorcas. Did you know that means 'deer'? Deer as in antelope, not dear as in nice, but she was really, really nice too.

Reporter: Er, thank you. Well, er, Dorcas, er, Tabitha, was well known locally for doing good things for people, giving lots of money to the poor. But she got sick and died.

Bystander: And her body was washed and placed in an upstairs room. That was it!

Reporter: As I was saying, Dorcas died…

Bystander: … and we thought we'd better do something really quick. Someone said that Peter, that forthright Christian leader, was at Lydda… and did we tell you Dorcas was a follower of Jesus?..

Reporter: … Joppa isn't far from Lydda…

Bystander: We'd heard that Peter was there. So we sent two men to say to him, 'Please come with us as quickly as you can!' And Peter came with them right away.

Reporter: As I was saying, as soon as these men arrived, they took Peter upstairs into the room. Many widows were there crying.

Bystander: Yeah, they showed him the coats and clothes that Dorcas had made while she was still alive. She was good at sewing.

Reporter: I understand that Peter sent everyone out of the room…

Bystander: That's right – I was there! He sent me out!

Reporter: Peter knelt down and prayed! Then he turned to the body of Dorcas…

Bystander: … though sometimes we called her Tabitha!

Reporter: And then Peter said, 'Tabitha, get up!'

Bystander: … but sometimes it was Dorcas!

Reporter: The woman, Dorcas or Tabitha, or whatever, opened her eyes, and sat up!

Bystander: Yeah, Peter just took her by the hand and helped her to her feet. And he called in all the widows and the others and showed them that Dorcas…

Reporter: … or Tabitha

Bystander: … had been raised from death.

Newsreader: And what is the latest in Joppa tonight?

Reporter: Well, everyone in Joppa has heard what happened, and many of them have put their faith in the Lord. It is incredible!

Bystander: And we've persuaded Peter to stay on for a while in Joppa. We've fixed him up to stay with Simon, the one who makes leather stuff.

Reporter: And now it is back to you all in the studio.

Bible talk

With: two large glasses and a large bottle of fizzy drink (at least 1.5 or 2 litres); a large plastic tray (to catch spills); kitchen roll or cloths (to mop up liquid) (The illustration will be easier to see if the drink is brightly coloured, such as blackcurrant or orange.)

Invite someone to pour themselves a drink, using one glass and the bottle. They are unlikely to pour out a full glass, so press them to take some more. If they decline, take back the bottle and pour in some more almost to the top. Invite them to take a mouthful or two. Immediately top up the glass. Invite them to take another mouthful, and again top it up. Point out that the glass is never going to be emptied, because no sooner does it empty slightly than it is filled up again. And not just filled up, but filled to overflowing. Pour in some more drink until it overflows the glass.

Remember the phrase from Psalm 23, used earlier: 'You fill my cup until it overflows.' David, who probably wrote this psalm, was reflecting on how God invites us to a grand feast where we are treated so well with sumptuous food and drink. That is how God wants to treat us. He fills our cup (and imagine we are like a cup or glass) with so much of his love and joy that it overflows. He keeps topping us up, not just a little bit (pour a little drink into the second glass), not even a generous amount (nearly fill the glass), but so freely that the glass overflows (fill the glass so it brims over). He does this by his Spirit. He wants to renew our lives all day, every day.

Remind everyone about the story of Peter bringing Dorcas (or Tabitha) back to life! Everyone was upset when she died. Peter prayed and God answered his prayer. God gave Dorcas new life. The sadness of her family and friends was turned to joy. They praised God and many came to put their trust in him. Their lives were filled to overflowing.

Remember what happened on the first Easter Day? Jesus had been killed, but God brought him back to life, a new life which he promised would be available to all who trusted in Jesus. God's power to bring about change and newness never ends. Point out that the bottle of drink would eventually run out if enough people had drinks, but God's supply of love and joy never runs dry. God's love is not limited to just a bottle-full.

Ask people to close their eyes and imagine themselves as a glass which is being filled with God's love and power and filled again and again. Allow a few moments for quiet reflection before saying this prayer:

Loving Lord, you lead me to streams of peaceful water, and you refresh my life. You fill my cup until it overflows. Help me to drink deeply of your kindness and love each day of my life, to know that I will live for ever in your house. Amen.

Prayers of intercession

With: props to be held by each person who leads in prayer – an outline of a dark cloud, an outline of a bright sun or a silver-lined cloud, a rainbow and an umbrella

Ask a family or a home group or members of the youth group to create some prayers based on varying weather to develop the ideas from Psalm 23. These could either be statements followed by silence or prayers that are read out. If the former, everyone could join in with a response: **Father God, you bless us and are with us at all times, whatever the weather.**

Fears (the dark cloud)
'I may walk through valleys as dark as death, but I won't be afraid.' Psalm 23:4.

Pray for those who are sad or fearful in any way, mentioning people by name as appropriate.

Blessings (the sun or silver-lined cloud)
'You treat me to a feast … you honour me as your guest, and you fill my cup until it overflows.' Psalm 23:5.

Give thanks for all those who are rejoicing at the moment – and mention specific people and situations, including anything to do with new life, physically or spiritually.

Promises (a rainbow)
'You are true to your name. Your kindness and love will always be with me.' Psalm 23:3,6.

Pray for those who have seen God's faithfulness in the past few days or weeks. You could invite people to think of examples of this at the start of the service and be ready to share evidence of God's faithfulness.

Decisions (umbrella)
'You lead me along the right paths.' Psalm 23:3.

Just as we have to decide whether or not to take an umbrella and/or trust the weather report, pray for any who have to make decisions, that they may be wise and actively trust God to guide them. Mention specific people as appropriate.

Gather up everyone's prayers by saying the Lord's Prayer together.

Prayer of confession

Based on Psalm 23, this is available as a download (YearC.Easter4_2).

Ending the service

Challenge everyone to look out for signs of God's love in the coming days. Particularly, ask them to think about God pouring out his love and joy every time they see a drinks container – whether that is a teapot, a can of cola, a water fountain or a carton of juice. Suggest that families might like to keep a running total of all the drinks containers they see in the week, particularly noting any unusual sources of drink they spot. They will be surprised by how many reminders they see of God's love and joy when they look.

Send people out with some words of God's power or his promise to bless and fill us ringing in their ears. These could be verses from Revelation 7, either verse 12 or verse 17. These could be put on a PowerPoint for everyone to say together.

Helpful extras

Music and song ideas

'The Lord's my shepherd, I'll not want' (Stuart Townend) or other versions of Psalm 23; 'Have you heard the raindrops'; 'To be in your presence'; 'Well, I hear they're singing in the streets' (Martin Smith).

Notes and comments

You may want to interview someone who has experienced the feeling of being constantly refilled with God's love. They could share this in the **Prayers of intercession**.

You could challenge the whole church to learn Psalm 23 together over the next few weeks. If learning from a new Bible translation, children may find this easier to do, since some adults may need to unlearn and then relearn the new version.

In a service of Communion, refer to how the God who feeds us (in Psalm 23) also feeds us as we participate in the bread and wine.

Alternative online options

Visit www.lightlive.org for additional activities for children, young people and adults.

FIFTH SUNDAY OF EASTER

READINGS: **Acts 11:1–18; Revelation 21:1–6**
Psalm 148; John 13:31–35

Bible foundations
Aim: to appreciate that the effects of the resurrection are far-reaching and eternal

Peter relates the events concerning Cornelius recorded in Acts 10 to the rest of the apostles and leaders in Jerusalem. The story is utterly unexpected, and yet they 'stopped arguing and started praising God' (Acts 11:18). The change in their thinking and practice is on a huge scale. Jews of this period frequently isolated themselves from non-Jews, and Peter's actions went against all of their cultural perceptions and values. The idea that Gentiles are not only clean but welcome to accept Christ and receive the Holy Spirit was a change of unprecedented dimensions.

After all the chaos of Revelation chapters 4–20, we read in chapter 21 of the restoration of creation. Everything will be put back the way it should be, as described in Genesis 1. The separation between God and the created world, which became reality from Genesis 3 through the whole Bible, is now done away with.

With the reading from John 13 we're back at Maundy Thursday. Jesus gives the commandment that will dominate John's first letter: love one another. As simple as this is, its implications are massive. Life with the resurrected Christ is one that demands connections and relationships with other Christians. Christ calls us not simply to put up with one another, but to actually love the other members of our church, and any other Christian we encounter. When Peter first heard Jesus give this command, he would never have anticipated that this would mean that he should love not just Jews but Gentiles!

As it reaches its close, the Psalter focuses increasingly on the praise genre. Psalm 148 relates to the reading from Revelation with its inclusion of wonderful creation imagery. In contrast to the brokenness (yet longing) of creation in Romans 8:19,20, the created order praises God.

Beginning the service

Begin by talking about what makes someone feel welcome. Expand this to reflect on what makes someone feel welcome in a home and then welcome in church. You could ask anyone who is relatively new how welcome they felt – and be prepared to respond to any negative comments!

This service is looking at how people feel welcomed into God's family and the barriers that may be erected to exclude or make people feel second class. Yet God welcomes all, and indeed makes his home with his people. It would be appropriate to learn Revelation 21:3 as a Learn and remember verse, by asking for signs that represent the meaning of this verse. Children will probably have several suggestions for how God might show he has made his home with his people. You could learn the verse at a later stage in the service if more appropriate.

Bible reading

With: a large sheet in which as many realistic (not cartoon-style) soft animals have been placed; a large picture or model of an angel; a wrapped gift parcel

One person reads Acts 11:1–18 while stage managers bring on the three props above where indicated. This is taken from the CEV. Explain that Peter is reporting to the church in Jerusalem about what had happened to him.

> The apostles and the followers in Judea heard that Gentiles had accepted God's message. So when Peter came to Jerusalem, some of the Jewish followers started arguing with him. They wanted Gentile followers to be circumcised, and they said, 'You stayed in the homes of Gentiles, and you even ate with them!' Then Peter told them exactly what had happened:
>
> I was in the town of Joppa and was praying when I fell sound asleep and had a vision. I saw heaven open, and something like a huge sheet held by its four corners came down to me. (*Bring in sheet carrying soft animals.*) When I looked in it, I saw animals, wild beasts, snakes, and birds. I heard a voice saying to me, 'Peter, get up! Kill these and eat them.' But I said, 'Lord, I can't do that! I've never taken a bite of anything that is unclean and not fit to eat.' The voice from heaven spoke to me again, 'When God says that something can be used for food, don't say it isn't fit to eat.' This happened three times before it was all taken back into heaven.
>
> Suddenly three men from Caesarea stood in front of the house where I was staying. The Holy Spirit told me to go with them and not to worry. Then six of the Lord's followers went with me to the home of a man who told us that an angel had appeared to him. (*Display the angel.*) The angel had ordered him to send to Joppa for someone named Simon Peter. Then Peter would tell him how he and everyone in his house could be saved.
>
> After I started speaking, the Holy Spirit was given to them, just as the Spirit had been given to us at the beginning. I remembered that the Lord had said, 'John baptized with water, but you will be

> baptized with the Holy Spirit.'" 'God gave those Gentiles the same gift (*Display the gift.*) that he gave us when we put our faith in the Lord Jesus Christ. So how could I have gone against God?
>
> When they heard Peter say this, they stopped arguing and started praising God. They said, 'God has now let Gentiles turn to him, and he has given life to them!'
>
> Acts 11:1–18 (CEV)

Someone introduces Revelation 21:1–6 saying that this is about a new heaven and a new earth, and indicate 'John', the author of it who stands at the front. Another person with a clear voice either speaks from behind the congregation, or out of sight but with their voice relayed over a sound system. Refer to verse 3 if you have learnt it earlier in the service.

> **John:**
> I saw a new heaven and a new earth. The first heaven and the first earth had disappeared, and so had the sea. Then I saw New Jerusalem, that holy city, coming down from God in heaven. It was like a bride dressed in her wedding gown and ready to meet her husband. I heard a loud voice shout from the throne:
>
> **Hidden voice:**
> God's home is now with his people. He will live with them, and they will be his own. Yes, God will make his home among his people. He will wipe all tears from their eyes, and there will be no more death, suffering, crying, or pain. These things of the past are gone forever.
>
> **John:**
> Then the one sitting on the throne said:
>
> **Hidden voice:**
> I am making everything new. Write down what I have said. My words are true and can be trusted. Everything is finished! I am Alpha and Omega, the beginning and the end. I will freely give water from the life-giving fountain to everyone who is thirsty.
>
> Revelation 21:1–6 (CEV)

Bible talk

With: three large signs, the sort that you might find over a doorway – 'Welcome for a meal', 'Welcome home' and 'All Gentiles welcome here!' (A PowerPoint version of these signs is available as a download (YearC. Easter5_1).)

Everyone has prejudices against at least one individual or group of people or a nationality which means that this person/these people are not welcome. Mention one example of racial, sexist or ageist discrimination which has been in the news recently. We may be shocked about it (or secretly agree with what we have seen).

The main reason why Jonah did not want to obey God and go to Nineveh was because he was afraid that the people of that city, who were not Jews, might repent and turn to the God of Israel. Jonah was behaving how the people of Israel had often responded to neighbouring nations. At the time of Jesus, Jews did not wish to be identified with those who were not Jews. They despised people like the Samaritans who lived in Judea but were not fully known as Jews.

You could mention the disciples' shock at seeing Jesus talk with a Samaritan woman or the powerful impact of the story of the Good Samaritan; he did the right thing for the injured Jewish man when the apparently good Jews did not. And of course, they were shocked when Jesus himself behaved as a servant in washing the disciples' feet – refer to the Gospel reading. Jesus had no time for social hierarchy or racial divisions.

This is the background to the story of Peter. Like all Jews of his time he did not wish to associate with non-Jews. But he was in for a shock.

God told Peter that he could eat what he had previously thought was unclean

God showed him in a dream that he could eat what would normally be forbidden to a Jew such as a pig or a rabbit (Deuteronomy 14:3–21). *(Show the sign 'Welcome for a meal'.)* These had been forbidden ever since God gave the food laws to his people over 1,500 years before. But Peter could now eat what Gentiles ate. Imagine 1,500 years of tradition being overthrown, just like that! And this was because God loved all people – not just Jews!

God told Peter that he was to go to the home of a Gentile

Peter's dream had prepared him for the invitation given him by three men who wanted him to go with them to a home of a Gentile (a man called Cornelius) in a seaside port (the same one that Jonah sailed from). Peter was willing to go with them. *(Show the sign saying 'Welcome home!')* At the home of this man, Peter was able to share the good news of Jesus and the man put his trust in him.

Peter told the church leaders that Gentiles could be Jesus' followers

Peter told his story to the Jewish leaders of the church in Jerusalem so that they would accept Gentiles as true believers and would not expect them to become Jews first (by circumcision). This was really shocking. *(Show the sign, 'All Gentiles welcome here'.)* What was just as shocking to them was that the Holy Spirit also came upon these Gentiles. There was nothing more to be said!

It is hard for us to imagine how it was for these Jewish Christians. They could only welcome Gentiles with their changed attitude because of the impact of the resurrection and the coming of the Holy Spirit. In the same way, in the church today, there is the challenge to welcome all people – those from different nations, people who are disabled or poor or rich or old or young or… just not like us or how we want to be! Only the power of the resurrection can change us so that we welcome others simply because we know that God loves them too.

Of course, the vision of what heaven will be like, a new creation, is of people of all nations coming together, where there will be no more crying, no more pain, no more suffering and no more prejudice! We have a taste of that now, but we will have to wait for heaven before we can fully experience life without prejudice. But until that time, the Holy Spirit enables us to love and serve those we do not naturally relate to.

Prayer activity

Ask people to get into groups where everyone has something in common which then makes them distinctly different from other groups. For example, split into age groups, or geographical groups, or gender groups, or if possible, nationality groups. Ask each group to identify what are the differences between them and other groups and what they may find difficult about other groups. Then pray for another group, either silently or out loud and ask for God's resurrection power to make a difference.

Prayers of intercession

With: images of current situations where there is hatred between different groups

Invite several people to prepare prayers for these situations, including prayers for Christian groups who are seeking to cross barriers in society and demonstrate the good news of Jesus. Show images to illustrate the prayers. For example, one group of immigrants recently suffered vandalism and were obviously not welcome. They had to leave their homes but local churches provided them with shelter and a welcome. Pray for such initiatives and also the resurrection power to change attitudes in society where 'tribal' hatred can flourish. Pray too that your church community will be welcoming and accepting of all.

Ending the service

Remind everyone that the effects of the resurrection are far-reaching. The good news of the resurrection is just as important in the twenty-first century as in the first century.

Ask everyone to think about one place they may pass on their way home where they do not imagine that God's name is ever used with respect or where they cannot imagine that people know God's love. This could be a wall of graffiti, a place which is overtly not Christian or a home where for some reason the people who live there are challenging. Suggest that people walk or drive past on their way home and pray that God's love and power will be evident there this week. Check next week to see what answer to prayer there has been – because we do need to expect God to answer prayer. Peter did not expect his prejudices to be shaken but they were, with eternal results! Send people out in the power of the Spirit to love and serve Christ.

Helpful extras

Music and song ideas

'There's a place where the streets shine' ('Because of you'); 'There is a hope that burns within my heart'; 'Great is the darkness' ('Come, Lord Jesus'); 'I will enter his gates' ('He has made me glad'); 'The trumpets sound' ('The feast is ready to begin'); 'Brother, sister, let me serve you'; 'There's a river of joy'; 'Come, now is the time to worship'; 'Come on and celebrate'.

Game

A suggested game where two teams share water is available as a download (YearC.Easter5_2).

Notes and comments

If this service includes Holy Communion, emphasise that all who love Jesus are welcome to share in it, although you will need to abide by your denominational practice.

The story of Peter and Cornelius is a very hard-hitting one so be sensitive to how people will respond but do not necessarily weaken the impact by watering down the message. It was deeply significant for the growth of the church which is why it is recorded more than once in the book of Acts.

Alternative online options

Visit www.lightlive.org for additional activities for children, young people and adults.

Scripture Union has three Bible reading guides for you to choose from:

Closer to God
For anyone who longs to hear God's voice in today's noisy world.

Daily Bread
A helpful, practical and inspiring guide that makes exploring the Bible enjoyable and relevant to every day life.

Encounter with God
A daily Bible guide designed for readers who want a thoughtful, in-depth approach to systematic Bible reading.

SIXTH SUNDAY OF EASTER

READINGS: **Psalm 67; Acts 16:9–15**
Revelation 21:10,22 – 22:5; John 5:1–9

Bible foundations
Aim: to see how the good news spreads

Psalm 67 reminds us that from very early times God's purpose was to bless his people in order that they may extend that blessing to all the nations of the earth. This psalm demonstrates parallelism, a literary technique often used to give a stronger emphasis on what is being said – for example verses 1 and 2 say the same thing using slightly different words to emphasise God's intention to spread the good news throughout the earth.

Examples of how the good news spreads increase in the New Testament. In John 5:1–9 Jesus brings good news in the form of healing to the man at the Pool of Bethesda. This healing provokes questions which lead to a proclamation about Jesus. In Acts 16:9–15 Paul receives a vision of a man in Macedonia who calls him to come and share the good news there. He responds and travels to the country going from place to place preaching the gospel. Paul's strategy as usual is to adapt to the environment he finds himself in. In Philippi, Paul waits until the Sabbath and then goes to a likely place, in this instance a place of prayer near the river, where many women gather. Here he speaks about the good news. Lydia, (who already acknowledged God) responds, is baptised along with her household and invites Paul and his companion to stay. This was the beginning of a church in this city. It is interesting to note the interaction in this event between human obedience (Paul responded to the vision and preached the gospel) and divine initiative (the giving of the vision and the sense of God opening her heart that Lydia experienced). It is good to remember that the good news often spreads through partnership.

Revelation 21:10,22 – 22:5 reminds us of the ultimate vision of the city of God which encompasses people from every tribe and nation, all who have responded to the good news.

Beginning the service

With: large sheets of paper displayed around the church; plenty of marker pens so people can write or draw a piece of good news on a sheet of paper before finding a seat; or balloons so everyone can take a balloon as they arrive, write a piece of good news on it, take it to their seat, and at a given signal, bat the balloon to someone else in the congregation

Both activities illustrate the fact that good news shouldn't be kept quiet and is definitely to be shared. Read out a few of the news items from the sheets of paper, or invite people to read the good news on the balloon they are holding. If all this news is worth sharing, God's good news is all the more worth sharing! Today we're particularly going to be looking at how his good news spreads.

Bible reading

If you have a play parachute (play canopy) available (often used for cooperative games but equally good for use in worship!) gather people around it, if the congregation is small enough, or have a pre-rehearsed group to stand around and hold it. As a reader slowly reads Acts 16:9–15, giving time to accommodate what's happening around the chute, the following actions could take place:

Verses 9,10: everyone holds the chute still and taut and echoes the words, 'Come over to Macedonia and help us.'

Verses 11,12: everyone round the chute makes waves with it.

Verse 13: the chute is lowered to the floor and everyone sits down around it.

Verse 14: someone who has already been asked to be Lydia (and maybe given a piece of purple cloth to put round her shoulders) stands up.

Verse 15: everyone lifts the chute so that Lydia (and her household) can stand under it to be baptised, and then, when the invitation to stay in Lydia's home is accepted, everyone can lift the chute over their heads and slide it down their backs as they sit down, now inside the chute.

Psalm 67, which is traditionally sung in services, has been set to music in a variety of ways. This psalm has been incorporated into the **Statement of faith**.

Bible talk

With: 'Lydia's Good News Stall' in the background – a table with a garden cane attached to each corner to make it look like a market stall and bunting tied round the top of the canes, with a sign which reads, 'Lydia's Good News Stall'; pieces of purple cloth on the stall with the headings from the **Bible talk** written on them

Ask the congregation to think about how they most like to hear good news. Many might say that it's directly from the person themselves. Say that's exactly how God chose to share his good news, by sending us his own Son, Jesus, the one who IS the good news. In today's Bible story, Paul, having received the good news for himself, can't help but take it to others. This makes us think how much the good news of who Jesus is and what he's done might so thrill us that we can't help but spread it. Let's see how the good news spreads in this story.

Listening to God
(Pick up the first piece of cloth from Lydia's stall.) Talk about how Paul doesn't rush around trying to share the good news in his own strength, in his own way. He does it in God's strength and in God's way. He takes time to listen to God. He hears God telling him to go to Macedonia. Do we need to spend more time listening to God, as well as talking to him, when we pray? Give a personal example.

Willing to go
(Pick up the next piece of cloth from Lydia's stall.) Talk about how Paul is willing to go, in this case by ship. He doesn't make excuses. He knows how important it is that these people should hear God's good news. We probably won't be called as far afield as Macedonia (or the equivalent) although a few of us might be. For most of us, sharing the good news will happen closer to home. There will be a group of people God puts on our hearts, maybe at school, work, the estate down the road, the young people who hang around in the churchyard. Are we willing to go to them? If you followed the suggested **Ending the service** from last week, it would be appropriate to ask for some feedback, at this point.

Knowing what to say
(Pick up the next piece of cloth.) Talk about how Paul knows what to say about Jesus to Lydia and the other women by the river. It's good to think through what we believe and to be able to put it clearly into words, however few. To do this, we need to spend time reading our Bibles, talking about it with others and being determined to explain as clearly as possible what our faith means to us. If the church has recently run an Alpha or discipleship course, make sure everyone knows how it went. You could pause to pray for all those involved.

With the Holy Spirit's help
(Pick up the next piece of cloth.) Talk about how the Holy Spirit is already at work in Lydia. She is ready to receive the good news about Jesus. She is excited to hear it and seems to respond at once. It's wonderful when this happens and we need to pray that God will enable us to meet people who are ready to respond, but we know that this isn't always the case. We sometimes need to be patient and continue to pray for the people we meet who are not yet quite as ready as Lydia.

Showing by actions
(Pick up the next piece of cloth.) Talk about how when Lydia receives Jesus she shows by her actions that she is different. She and her household are baptised, and she wants to welcome Paul and his team into her home. We know she is a business woman, selling expensive purple cloth. We're not told how receiving Jesus affects her business, but inevitably her customers would have noticed a difference. Maybe she told them that she'd discovered something much more precious than the expensive purple cloth she sold them!

Recap on the above points and pray that God will show you all how true they are to you as a church and as individuals.

Prayer activity
With: a piece of purple cloth; pens that can write on cloth; a large street map of your locality, either on screen or hard copies (one large or lots of small ones); coloured stickers; pieces of purple paper or card

This activity could be directed from the front, or people could go into groups, or prayer stations could be set up to give people a choice of what they do.

Display the map or give them out to individuals or to groups. Give out coloured dots and ask people to place a dot on the map in a place that they want to pray for. (This may be the same as the place they identified in **Ending the service** last week.) If you have Wi-Fi, use Google Earth to highlight significant places in your locality which you or a group of people had chosen before the service. Allow time for personal prayer.

Give out a small piece of purple cloth to each person for them to write on the name of someone they want to share the good news about Jesus with. Allow time for them to pray for that person.

Finally give out a piece of purple card or paper and ask everyone to think of one thing about Jesus that they most want to share with someone else. They can then either write or draw it on the paper/card. This should be fairly small because you don't want people to think that they have to write pages and pages!

Encourage everyone to take home their purple card and cloth.

Ending the service

With: these following words displayed or on the notice sheet – available as a download (YearC.Easter6_1)

Each phrase could be spoken by a different person:

God, our Father,
Yours is the good news which
Burst out of a tomb,
Broke prison chains,
Spread across continents,
Travelled through centuries,
Transforms people's lives,
Brings light in dark places,
Gives hope, peace and joy,
Puts love in our hearts,
And should never be hidden.

In the name of Jesus and in the power of the Holy Spirit,
Help us to share your good news this week, wherever we go.
Amen.

Helpful extras
Music and song ideas

'Tell out my soul'; 'How lovely on the mountains ('Our God reigns')'; 'There is a Redeemer'; 'Jesus is Lord'; 'Jesus, what a beautiful name'; 'Who is there like you?'; 'Thank you for saving me'; 'Lord, I lift your name on high'; 'Jesus is greater than the greatest heroes'; 'All I once held dear'; 'So amazing God', (*Light for Everyone* CD, SU); 'God's deep love', (*Light for Everyone* CD, SU) all proclaim God's good news, remind us how wonderful it is, or encourage us to share it.

Statement of faith

This statement of faith is based on Psalm 67, a psalm of good news. The leader reads the words of the psalm, in regular type, and the congregation respond with the words in bold. This IS the good news! It is also available as a PowerPoint download (YearC.Easter6_2).

Our God be kind and bless us! Be pleased and smile.

We believe in God who created us and loves us. Because of his great love he is kind to us and blesses us. His smile lights up our lives.

Then everyone on earth will learn to follow you, and all the nations will see your power to save us.

We believe that God wants everyone on earth to follow his ways and that he sent his own Son, Jesus, to save us and to show us his power, when he died on the cross and came alive again.

Let the nations celebrate with joyful songs because you judge fairly and guide all the nations.

We believe that God fills us with his Spirit. His joy and justice transform our lives and he guides us and shows us how to share his good news.

Our God has blessed the earth with a wonderful harvest.

We believe that God is faithful and fills the earth with good things, but that people have turned away from him and spoilt creation.

Pray for his blessings to continue and for everyone on earth to worship our God.

We believe that because of his great love, God forgives everyone who turns back to him and that as part of his new creation we can live with him, love him, worship him and enjoy the light of his smile forever.

Notes and comments

Make sure that at some point in the service you highlight what God's good news is. Using the **Statement of faith**, incorporating Psalm 67, would be an opportunity to do this, as would introducing some of the suggested songs before you sing them.

The **Bible talk** covers a number of points which give opportunity for prayer in your sharing of the good news and also in bringing people up to date with recent outreach into the community. If you are planning a holiday club in the summer, now would be a good opportunity to pray for it. You could intersperse the talk with prayer and interviews, involving as many people as possible.

Alternative online options

Visit www.lightlive.org for additional activities for children, young people and adults.

ASCENSION DAY

READINGS: **Acts 1:1–11; Luke 24:44–53**
Psalm 93; Ephesians 1:15–23

Bible foundations
Aim: to engage with the story of Jesus' ascension

It is no accident that the account of the ascension in Acts 1 is preceded by a summary of all that Jesus had done since rising from the dead. The disciples met with Jesus many times, as he was preparing them for the time when he would no longer be there for and with them. Gradually their confusion lifted as all that Jesus had shared with them about his life's purpose and the kingdom of God began to make sense to them. Then, when the time came, a few key things happened that were deeply significant for these first believers, and are just as relevant for us.

Jesus clearly stated that God's timing is entirely his, and there is little point in trying to 'second guess' what God has got planned. Instead the responsibility is on them (and on all of us too), to share the good news of Jesus in our own place, and further afield and at all times. This is done with the help and guidance of the Holy Spirit, whom they were instructed to wait for. It doesn't all rely on us!

The disciples watched Jesus leave which finally confirmed to them that he was in heaven with the Father, and they were now the ones who had to get on with bringing a taste of the kingdom to others. There is irony in them staring up into heaven in shocked amazement before being shaken from their awestruck state by what we can only assume were angels. If God can use them, with their failings and doubts, God can use all of us! Psalm 93 captures some of the majesty which surrounds Jesus, the Lord and King.

The ascension of Jesus reminds us of who Jesus is in all his majesty. It calls us to service, and it confirms that there's still much work to be done.

Beginning the service

Welcome everyone and explain that the service will be built around **Bible readings** and **Bible talk** with activities for individuals and groups. Sing a song which focuses upon who Jesus is.

Alternatively, place a large sheet of paper on the floor at the back or side of the room, with pens (or paints) available, and someone to supervise. Explain that you will be thinking about the time when Jesus went up to heaven to be with God the Father, but that we don't know what heaven is like. Invite everyone to go to the sheet of paper at any point during the service and briefly draw or paint what they think heaven may be like. This will be shared and displayed at the end of the service.

Bible reading

Acts 1:6–11 is best read using the CEV. A group of people say the questions in bold and an individual reads the rest. If possible, project the script for everyone to read out the emboldened sections. This is also available as a download (YearC.Ascension_1).

> While the apostles were still with Jesus, they asked him, **'Lord, are you now going to give Israel its own king again?'** Jesus said to them, 'You don't need to know the time of those events that only the Father controls. But the Holy Spirit will come upon you and give you power. Then you will tell everyone about me in Jerusalem, in all Judea, in Samaria, and everywhere in the world.'
>
> After Jesus had said this and while they were watching, he was taken up into a cloud. They could not see him, but as he went up, they kept looking up into the sky. Suddenly two men dressed in white clothes were standing there beside them. They said, **'Why are you men from Galilee standing here and looking up into the sky? Jesus has been taken to heaven. But he will come back in the same way that you have seen him go.'**
>
> Acts 1:6–11 (CEV)

A proclamation, based on Psalm 93, with a repetitive response is available as a download (YearC.Ascension_2). Different voices or groups of voices could say the alternate lines. You could use this in **Ending the service**.

Bible talk

This focuses on three aspects of the disciples' behaviour in the account of Jesus' ascension from Luke 24:44–53: they heard; they saw; they went. You may choose to intersperse with music and a number of activities which follow the three themes.

The disciples heard

Make sure you frequently say 'heard' and 'hear', encouraging everyone to cup their ears as you say it. The disciples had heard Jesus speak many times, and they thought they understood what he had been saying. But, now he was alive again, Jesus reminded them of some of the basic things about his life, and their faith. Their minds were opened as they began to hear and understand, really listening to Jesus' words.

- They heard that what happened was all part of the plan that God had at the beginning of time and which was made

known over 1,500 years before (Luke 24:44). God's big plan lasts for ever, and we are part of it, so we need to listen!
- They heard that Jesus had to die so that he could come alive again, to make forgiveness for all people possible. God has forgiven us through all that Jesus did.
- They heard that Jesus had a job for them. He told them to go and tell others in their own city first, then further and further away. No one here can avoid that – however young or old we are, God wants us to tell others about Jesus.

In our busy, noisy world there are plenty of things to hear, and plenty of noises that get in the way. The disciples finally heard and understood what Jesus wanted to say to them. How do we listen to Jesus?

Response to hearing

With: a range of items that make a noise, such as a recorder, percussion instruments, spoons, a short length of hosepipe, pieces of wood, a whistle, bells, a baby's rattle, water in a plastic bottle

Ask everyone to get into groups of around ten people. Talk through the following questions:

What do you hear when you wake up in the morning? What things do you hear that you don't like hearing? What do you hear at lunchtime? What can you hear right now? What sounds do you like to hear? Whose voice do you listen to? What stops you hearing?

Place the sound-making items around the building. Invite people to find these sound-producers and bring them back to the group. Then make the sounds in as many different ways as possible – such as loud and soft; fast and slow; banging against a chair, the floor or on the thigh.

Finally ask everyone to silently listen for one minute. What do you really tune in to in our noisy world? Do you take time to listen to Jesus? What might he be saying to you today?

If appropriate, someone can share how they listened to Jesus speaking to them and what helped them to hear (or not hear).

The disciples saw

Ask everyone to shade their eyes with their hands when they hear the words 'saw' and 'see'.

For some of the disciples it was a shock to see Jesus real and alive ... Some still doubted that Jesus had really come alive again. But as they saw him they knew that this was real, and on the hillside they had plenty to see!

- They saw Jesus raise his hands and bless them. This would have meant a lot to them, as they realised that Jesus wanted the best for them despite their doubt and fear. Jesus blesses us, and wants the best for us too.
- They saw Jesus taken up to heaven. We don't quite know how it happened, but as they watched, Jesus went! Now we can imagine/see Jesus in heaven with God, the Father – just where he should be!
- In Acts 1:10, they saw two men, like angels, who told them to stop staring into the sky because Jesus was in heaven and there was nothing more to see! We can wait around looking, instead of getting on with God's work!

The disciples saw Jesus ascend to heaven. We haven't seen Jesus go up to heaven, but we do see what Jesus does all the time! We have seen lives changed, we have seen and shared Jesus' love, and we have seen Jesus heal people. Let's not forget all that we see Jesus do!

Response to seeing

With: a sheet of paper and pencil

Invite everyone to explore the church or available room space in pairs, looking for things they've never really noticed before such as windows, carvings, doors, notices or photos on a notice board. Draw one of the things they have seen, helping each other as appropriate. In a room without many interesting features you may need to place extra interesting objects.

Bring everyone back together and discuss what was seen. It is amazing that when we are looking specifically for something, we are more likely to see it. The disciples did not know what to look for but gradually their eyes began to see what Jesus had been telling them all the time. If Jesus could come alive again, anything was possible!

If appropriate, ask someone to share how they have begun to see God doing all sorts of things because they are now expecting him to be active in their lives. It would be appropriate to sing 'Come see the Lord'.

The disciples went

Use the words 'go' and 'went'. The disciples were amazed by what they had seen on the hillside. But they didn't just stay there and keep it to themselves!

- They went back to Jerusalem, where Jesus had told them to start telling others about the good news of forgiveness and new life. They were waiting for something to happen (the Spirit to come), although they did not know what this would entail.
- They went back to pray and worship, remembering that it is important to praise and worship God. They were expecting God to do something!
- We know from the book of Acts that, after the Holy Spirit came on that first Pentecost, they went everywhere they could, to tell others about Jesus. The Spirit made them bold.

It was not enough to hear and see. Jesus told them to go and tell others, and they did! Here is the challenge to not only see and hear Jesus' words, but also to put them into action.

Response to going

It would be appropriate to pray for each person present to experience the boldness that the Holy Spirit brings in sharing the good news of Jesus with others. **The Prayer of confession** follows on from this.

Prayer of confession

With: a coloured square (8 cm squared) of material per person (you could recycle the purple pieces from last week); a pile of white pieces of material

Give out a piece of coloured material to each person and place the white pieces of material in the centre of your space, accessible for everyone, or place piles of white pieces around the church. Say the following and after each response (you may simply say it for people to repeat after you), allow time for reflection. This is also available as a download

(YearC.Ascension_3).

Jesus, Son of God, we are sorry for the times when we have not listened to you, and when we have not heard what you want to say to us.

Forgive us, and may your Spirit help us to listen.
Jesus, Son of God, we are sorry for the times when we have not seen all the good things you are doing in our lives and the lives of others.

Forgive us, and may your Spirit help us to look more carefully.
Jesus, Son of God, we are sorry for the times when we have not gone where you have sent us and when we have not told others about you.

Forgive us, and may your Spirit make us bold to go where you want us to.
Invite anyone who really wants to see the Spirit at work to place their piece of coloured material down, and pick up a white piece as a reminder of the men/angels in white who spoke to the disciples.

Ending the service

The proclamation of Psalm 93 could conclude this service on a positive note. The Lord is indeed King. Alternatively, the **Statement of faith** could be used.

Helpful extras

Music and songs ideas

'The Lord is King, lift up your voice'; 'Jesus is King, and I will extol him'; 'Come, see the Lord in his breathtaking splendour' (Martin Leckebusch); 'Hail the day that sees him rise'; 'Be still and know that I am God'.

Statement of faith

A proclamation of faith based on the ascension story could be used as a final prayer at the end of the service. It is available as a download (YearC.Ascension_4).

Notes and comments

Not many churches hold all-age services on Ascension Day but it is one of the great festivals of the Christian year and is extremely important for what it communicates about Jesus and the Trinity. There are many appropriate all-age activities that can be used to explore the ascension which will be meaningful for people of all ages. This service outline, of course, could be used on a Sunday close to ascension Day.

If this is a service of Holy Communion, you could comment on the fact that as you eat the bread which symbolises Jesus' body, you are also remembering that his resurrected body is now in heaven – his disciples saw him leave this earth. They heard him say that his Spirit would come in his place and they went to tell others. You celebrate Communion until he returns again, this time as King.

Alternative online options

Visit www.lightlive.org for additional activities for children, young people and adults.

SEVENTH SUNDAY OF EASTER

READINGS: **Acts 16:16-34; John 17:20-26**
Revelation 22:12-14,16,17,20,21

Bible foundations
Aim: to appreciate the significance of prayer for those who follow Jesus

For those who seek to follow Jesus, there is no greater example than Jesus himself and in John 17:20-26 we catch a glimpse of Jesus at prayer. At one of the most challenging times of his ministry we gain an insight into the relationship he had with his Father as we eavesdrop on the conversation. In this section of the prayer, having already prayed for himself and his disciples, Jesus prays for those who will follow him, that they may be united in the Father's love in order that the world would be able to know and experience that love. Such unity is an expression of the unity in the Godhead and a unity that Jesus is particularly conscious of in this prayer between himself and the Father.

In times of anxiety or difficulty we often turn to God in prayer – as did Paul and Silas after they'd been thrown into prison following the conversion of a fortune teller in Philippi, recorded in Acts 16:16-34. Prayer and worship was their instinctive response to their desperate situation. What an expression of faith both to focus on Jesus in the midst of the situation and to trust him for the outcome! They could have used a psalm such as Psalm 97 to remind them who God is and what he was able to do. In response to their prayerful worship there was an earthquake which shook the prison doors from their foundations. Paul and Silas however chose not to escape but through their willingness to risk their own lives were enabled to bring the jailer and his family to faith in Christ.

Revelation 22:12-14,16,17 remind us that one day we will see Jesus and be able to speak to him face to face for all eternity. This is the fulfilment of Jesus' prayer in John 17:24 – our communication with Jesus is significant for all time, not just the challenging times of this life.

Beginning the service

With: a selection of things designed to fit inside each other, such as a set of Russian nesting dolls, decorative boxes, toddlers' stacking cups, baking bowls, pastry cutters

'Hide' around the church all the individual items separate from the rest of their set, but not so they can't be easily found. Invite children (and adults too if you've hidden enough items) to find an item, bring it to the front and fit it with the rest of its set. Introduce today's theme which, although about prayer, is also about being one with God and one with each other. When we are 'one' with someone, that's when our communication will be at its best. When we are one with God, he is in us and we are in him. That's when prayer will be at its best. It would be good to read John 17:20–26 soon after this introduction.

If you are looking for other ways to explain the Trinity, read *Top Tips on Explaining the Trinity to young people* (SU) – see page 215 for details.

Bible reading

The reader could introduce John 17:20–26 by showing how a set of Russian dolls can be 'in' one another, a visual aid which may help some people to better understand the amazing concept of us being in God and him being in us. Explain that this is part of Jesus' final statement to his disciples.

Acts 16:16–34 can be read with the congregation responding each time they hear the following key words:

Paul: *they put their hands together as if in prayer.*
Silas: *they raise their arms as if in praise.*
Jail or jailer: *they say, 'Clink, clink', or jingle keys.*
Earthquake: *they stamp their feet loudly.*

Bible talk

With: strips of newspaper; strips of plastic; lengths of string; sticky tape and staplers; three sets of dark-coloured (negative) paper chains and one long set of shiny (positive) paper chains

Begin by running a Strongest Link contest. Invite three pairs of people to take part. Each pair is given one of the strips above to work with. Their task is to make the strongest chain they can with the materials given to them. Other volunteers come forward to test the links. This could be part of a **Game** early in the service.

Strong links have been described in both of the readings. To begin with, note that Jesus prayed that our links with him and with one another should be so strong that we are part of Jesus and he is in us. Also note that Jesus prayed for us and continues to do so (Hebrews 7:25). We are prayed-for people and we see God at work. We need to pray too of course since prayer (or conversation with God) is a strong and vital link with him. Communication is two-way. The story of Paul and Silas in prison gives some insights into the importance of prayer for all followers of Jesus, to maintain strong links with God.

Slave girl (Acts 16:16–18)
The slave girl's ability to tell the future did not come from God. Paul and Silas knew that the link she had with the evil spirit needed to be broken. (*Hold up one set of dark-coloured paper chains and break it.*) The link Paul and Silas had with Jesus was strong so they were able to

break the chains that bound her and she was freed from the control that the evil spirit had over her.

Paul and Silas (Acts 16:25,26)
As a result of Paul's actions, the men who owned the slave girl were so furious that they had lost their means of income and created so much trouble that Paul and Silas were put in prison. But they were not down-hearted! Even though they were now in chains they knew that their link to Jesus was much stronger than the links of the metal chains which bound them. *(Hold up a shiny set of paper chains, which are not broken.)* So they prayed and praised, not knowing what God might do in response. At midnight they found out! The chains which had been binding them in prison were broken as the earthquake struck! *(Hold up another set of dark-coloured chains and break them.)*

Jailer (Acts 16:27–31)
The jailer was frightened that he would get the blame for letting all the prisoners escape. He feared he might even be killed and prepared to kill himself. But Paul called out that no one had escaped. The jailer took a torch to check that Paul was telling the truth! He was so amazed that neither Paul nor anyone else had escaped that he asked for Paul to tell him about the Jesus who could save him. He realised that he was bound with chains of fear, chains that prevented him from knowing God. Paul and Silas told him about Jesus and the jailer believed. His chains were broken. *(Break another set of dark-coloured chains and then replace them with a shiny set of chains.)* The jailer was to learn what it means to pray and have a strong link with God.

Jailer's family (Acts 16:32–34)
Everyone who lived in the jailer's house also heard about Jesus and they put their trust in him. The Bible tells us that they were all very glad they had done so. They washed Paul's and Silas' cuts and bruises. Then, even though it was still night-time, the whole family were baptised. Only then were Paul and Silas given something to eat! This family was not only linked to Jesus, but also to Paul and Silas as fellow Christians. *(Hold up a shiny paper chain.)*

Lydia (Acts 16:40)
The story goes on with Paul and Silas being set free by the authorities who asked them to leave town. But instead they went straight to the home of Lydia (remind people of her from last Sunday) where Jesus' followers were meeting and no doubt praying for Paul and Silas. *(Hold up the shiny paper chains.)*

These Christians had discovered that they could not live without prayer, being linked to God – whether in prison, or facing other forms of opposition, or just as Christians meeting together with God. We too can meet with God, who is with us all the time, whether as we go about ordinary life, meet together or face particular challenges. If appropriate ask someone to share their own experience of being close to God, linked with him, as they talk with him.

Prayer activity

With: a shiny set of paper chains (if possible reuse the one from the **Bible talk**), long enough to wrap around the feet of four people who stand at the front in a square

Wrap the chain around the four people who, having been bound together, each pray for one of the following topics which could be written out on card. They are based upon part of Jesus' prayer in John 17.

Unity in the church
Read John 17:20,21. Pray that God will keep your church focused on the really important things of your faith and what it means to be a Christian community. Pray too for other churches in your area or any mission partners who may be facing situations where there is division.

Unity in families and community
Read John 17:22,23. Pray for families in your community and other related issues.

Unity in countries where there is war and political unrest
Read John 17:25,26 and pray for peace in the world with particular relevance to any conflict zone that is in the news.

Unity between us and God
Read John 17:24 and then reflect on what Jesus has done to make us one with God.

Prayer of confession

With: dark-coloured paper chains; something to write with; glue sticks or staplers; shiny coloured paper chain strips like the ones used in the **Prayer activity**

This builds on the idea of chains in the **Bible talk** and **Prayer activity**. Give a dark-coloured paper chain to small groups of people and invite them to write or draw something they are sorry for on their paper chain. ('Sorry God' will be enough for younger children.) Ask everyone to then stand up in a circle holding the paper chain and pray silently, asking God to forgive them. They then break the chain and are given a shiny paper chain strip in its place. As they receive this, speak words that reassure them that God forgives us.

Ending the service

Invite everyone to join hands with someone else to make a chain of strong links. Pray together using the following prayer, which is also available as a download (YearC. Easter7_1).

Father God, make us one with you.
Jesus, the Son, make us one with you and the Father.
Spirit, make us one with each other and with God – Father, Son and Spirit.
Amen.

Helpful extras
Music and song ideas

'There is a Redeemer'; 'What a friend we have in Jesus'; 'This is the air I breathe'; 'There is power in the name of Jesus'; 'Teach me to dance to the beat of your heart'; 'Purify my heart'; 'Our God is a great big God'; 'King of kings, majesty'; 'O Lord, hear my prayer' ('*Tcizé*'); 'Jesus, be the centre'; 'Before the throne of God above'; 'Christ, be beside me' ('*Iona Abbey worship book*'); 'Jesus put this song into our hearts'; 'Bind us together, Lord'; 'Call to me', (*Light for Everyone* CD, SU) are all suitable for a prayer on unity or the ascension theme.

Game

An activity to illustrate unity with God and with one another is a wool web. A ball of wool is thrown around the congregation. Anyone catching it winds it around their hand and throws it on. Eventually it forms a web, linking people together. If three balls of wool in different colours are used this also helps illustrate God as the Trinity. (This activity is great fun but be warned, with a large congregation it is very time-consuming! You may wish to break into smaller groups.)

Notes and comments

This is the Sunday after Ascension Day so you could put more emphasis on Jesus' ascension into heaven. The themes of unity and prayer can be closely linked with the ascension. The prayer link is crucial, now that Jesus has ascended. His prayer in John 17 is about the unity his followers can have in him and in the Father when he returns to heaven. Because of Jesus there can be unity between heaven and earth. John 17:24 gives a glimpse of Jesus welcoming his followers to heaven, being one with him for ever and seeing his true glory.

Alternatively, you could use the previous outline for Ascension Day. The story of Paul and Silas in prison lends itself to praying for those who are in prison for their faith or to pray for those who are imprisoned in their minds through mental illness. People do feel imprisoned in other ways too, but make sure that it is clear to children what you mean if you use the term 'imprisonment' in a way other than the literal sense. You might also like to pray for those in prison, including those who are Christians and are trying to build relationships with their own children. For more details, visit www.prisonfellowship.org.uk.

Alternative online options

For your convenience the following activity is available as a download: YearC.Easter7_2 Conga dance. Visit www.lightlive.org for additional activities for children, young people and adults.

PENTECOST

READINGS: **Acts 2:1-21; John 14:8-17,25-27**
Genesis 11:1-9; Psalm 104:24-34,35b

Bible foundations
Aim: to understand better the role of the Holy Spirit

Luke's account of the day of Pentecost in Acts 2:1-13 is very familiar. As Jesus returned to heaven he told his disciples to stay in Jerusalem (Acts 1:4) and wait for the Holy Spirit. When the Spirit came upon the disciples a few days later their transformation was immediate. And it was lasting. Jesus had promised them that the Spirit was coming (John 14:16) who, unlike Jesus, would always be with them. The Spirit's arrival had obvious outward effects as the disciples began to speak in other languages or were able to preach, with no preparation or sermon notes, an ability Peter suddenly acquired.

But the Spirit also brought the inward effects of helping, teaching, convicting of sin and peace-bringing. This outpouring was not just for the select few disciples. It was for all people of every language and race. Genesis 11:1-9 tells how the people of the world were scattered and confused after trying to become like God. At Pentecost we see people coming back together again in God's way and in God's time. The Spirit, who was involved in creation, now returns to renew the face of the earth (Psalm 104:30). In doing so he gives courage to Jesus' followers to 'declare the wonders of God' (Acts 2:11) for everyone to hear.

Jesus' work on earth was complete but the Spirit came, not as a replacement for Jesus, but to perform a parallel role as guide, comforter and counsellor so that all of us down the centuries could have the benefit of God's presence in our lives. The Spirit is given equally to everyone – all of them were filled. There are no half measures for 'lesser Christians'. The Holy Spirit is a gift of love to everyone who calls on the name of the Lord.

Beginning the service

With: anything to create a party atmosphere; a parcel, addressed by name to your church, containing the words 'Holy Spirit'

Create a party atmosphere as appropriate using streamers, balloons, joyful dance music, paper hats or even suggest that people come dressed for a party with birthday cake and candles. (Note that some children are nervous of balloons and party poppers. Handle with care!)

Ask everyone why they think the church is decorated like it is. Explain that Pentecost is often referred to as 'the birthday of the church'. Wish each other a Happy Birthday and sing 'Happy Birthday to you', inserting the name of your church.

Invite someone to open the parcel (since presents are given on birthdays) and reveal the words. At Pentecost God gave his people the gift of his Holy Spirit.

Bible reading

Acts 2:1–21 lends itself to a dramatic reading with congregational participation. Prepare some people in advance by supplying them with words in another language (see **Ending the service**) which they can read out at the end of verse 4. Prime other people to come to the front during verse 6 (they could encourage others to join them as they come) as if they are the crowd gathering to listen to Peter. Ask a confident man to read Peter's speech and prime some sons, daughters, young and old men and women to stand up and raise their arms with joy at appropriate points during Peter's speech.

John 14:8–17,25–27 works best if the CEV is used since this links in with the words used in the **Bible talk**. A download is available (YearC.Pentecost_1). This can also be displayed during the **Bible talk**.

Bible talk

With: a box labelled 'toolbox' containing: walking boots, a wedding ring, a map or compass, a picture of a heart, a textbook, a diary or pager, a globe or picture of the world; labels to stick on each item with the key phrases as given below; a small plastic bottle of fizzy pop and a shallow bowl or a picture of a winner with champagne

The key phrases in the CEV used in this talk from John 14 are: Do the things I am doing; helps you be strong; always be with you; shows you; lives in you; teaches you; reminds you. Write each of these on separate sticky labels.

Ask for a volunteer but don't tell them what you want them to do. Remind the volunteer that you didn't tell them what you wanted them to do! Then ask them to help you perform a simple, safe task such as measuring something, or doing an easy jigsaw. After completing the task say, 'There, that was easy. Now, can you also help me to be a good person and live like Jesus wants me to?'

Depending on the response, ask further questions such as, 'Can you teach me everything I need to know about God?' or 'Can you come with me wherever I go?'

As soon as you get a negative response, thank your volunteer and ask them to sit down.

Explain that what you really need is someone to help you to live life the way God wants and, despite your volunteer's best efforts, there really is only one person who can do that and that is the Holy Spirit. So, how does the Holy Spirit help?

Bring out the toolbox. Explain that it contains reminders of how the Holy Spirit helps us. Ask for another volunteer to take something out of the box. Challenge everyone to think about what each item represents before you stick on the label that explains what the Holy Spirit does. It doesn't matter in what order the items are removed from the box, but they are given below in the order of the words in John 14:16,17,25–27:

Walking boots (helps you be strong): strong walking boots help you walk boldly. The Holy Spirit is given to help us be strong to do whatever God wants us to do.

Wedding ring (always be with you): a wedding ring signifies a promise made to always be faithful to someone. Jesus promised that the Holy Spirit wouldn't just come and visit occasionally to see how we are getting on. Instead he promised that the Holy Spirit would always be with us.

Map or compass (shows you the way): like a map shows us the true path, the Holy Spirit shows us the right way to go and he helps us to know the truth about God.

Heart (lives in you): Jesus lived on earth as a human so it wasn't physically possible for him to be with everybody all the time. By the Spirit, Jesus is always inside us, prompting us to do things God's way and to follow the example of Jesus.

Textbook (teaches you everything): the Spirit teaches us everything we need to know to follow God. He helps us understand what we read in the Bible. He helps us to be obedient. Without the Spirit we would struggle to do things God's way, but he teaches us everything.

Diary or pager (reminds you of what Jesus said): the Spirit reminded the disciples of what Jesus taught them and he reminds us of things we've learnt. This could be a good moment to invite a member of the congregation to talk about when the Spirit has reminded them of something at a significant time. He also reminds us of God's love at times when life is tough and he encourages us to do the right thing when we're tempted to go wrong.

This is what the Spirit does for us. This is why God gives us his Spirit. But what effect should the Spirit have upon us? On the first day of Pentecost, the disciples couldn't help but talk about God. They told others of the wonderful things God had done. *(While you are saying this, bring out your bottle of pop and gently shake it in a casual manner!)* In fact, they couldn't keep all this amazing news inside them. *(Shake the bottle more vigorously and put the bowl on the table to catch the overflow.)* It was a case of it just bursting out of them… *(Remove the top from the bottle and catch the overflow! Or use the picture of a winner of the Grand Prix or similar event, with champagne.)*

The Spirit helps us respond excitedly to the wonderful things God has done. He will help us tell others the news, just like the first disciples.

Prayer activity

With: short strips of tissue or crêpe paper in three different flame colours – yellow, orange and red – enough for one set of colours per person

Give out the strips of paper. Explain that they represent the flames at Pentecost and you are going to use them to help you pray.

Leader 1: Jesus said, 'Do not let your hearts be troubled and do not be afraid.' Invite everyone to wave their yellow flame as, in silence, they bring to God anything that is worrying them or making them afraid. After a pause the leader says: Jesus said, 'My peace I give you.' Thank you for hearing us, Lord. Please help us to know your peace.

Leader 2: The prophet Joel reminds us that 'whoever calls out to the Lord for help will be saved' (GNB). Invite everyone to gently wave their orange strip as, in silence, they tell God about anyone they know who needs his help. After a pause the leader says: Lord, thank you that you care about each one of us.

Leader 1: Some of the people in Jerusalem asked, 'What does all this mean?' Invite everyone to think of somewhere they will go this week and someone they will meet there and to pray silently for this place or person as they wave their red strips. After a pause, the leader says: Lord, help us to bring your love to our friends and colleagues so they understand who you are.

Leader 2: 'The Holy Spirit took control of everyone.' Invite everyone to wave all three 'flames' as you pray: Lord, give us the joy of your presence and the courage to tell others about you wherever we go.

Amen.

Prayer of confession

This is a confession with two congregational phrases of response. Either display the responses or prepare people to repeat them as appropriate.

Jesus said, 'If you love me, you will obey what I command.'
Lord, we are sorry for the times we have disobeyed you.
Help us to love you and do what you say.
We are sorry for times when we think we know better than you.
Help us to love you and do what you say.
We are sorry that we are sometimes unkind, unloving and say untrue things and we do not do things you would want us to do.
Help us to love you and do what you say.
Thank you, Jesus, that you promised to send your Spirit to help us when we are tempted to do wrong.
Lord Jesus, send your Spirit to help us.
When we want to go our way instead of your way:
Lord Jesus, send your Spirit to help us.
When we are tempted to forget about you and be selfish:
Lord Jesus, send your Spirit to help us.
Lord, send your Spirit to help us this week in all we think, in all we say and all we do.
Amen.

Ending the service

With: words of praise in different languages

Display the words of 'Praise the Lord' in various languages (see below) around the church, enough for everyone to see a phrase. Invite everyone to turn to those behind them and greet each other using the different languages:

Praise the Lord:

Lob den Herrn (German); Il signore sia lodato (Italian); Louez le Signeur (French); El senor sea glorificado (Spanish); Looft den Here (Dutch), Hallelu jah (Hebrew).

Alternatively, an audio version of worldwide praise is available as a download (YearC. Pentecost_2) which includes 'Praise the Lord' in several more languages. Play the audio twice asking people to listen very carefully and then repeat at least one phrase to their neighbour, as best they can. Of course, if in the congregation there are people who speak other languages, ask them to join in pronouncing 'Praise the Lord' in their own language.

Send each other out with these greetings and a hymn of praise (see **Music and song ideas**).

Helpful extras

Music and song ideas

Traditional hymns for Pentecost include: 'Breathe on me, breath of God'; 'O thou who camest from above'; 'Come down, O love divine'.

More modern songs and choruses include: 'All over the world the Spirit is moving'; 'Be still for the presence of the Lord'; 'He that is in us'; 'O Holy Spirit, breathe on me'; 'For I'm building a people of power'; 'When the Holy Spirit comes upon you'.

A song that reflects the words of the prophet Joel quoted by Peter in his speech is Jarrod Cooper's 'Days of wonder'.

Hymns of praise to end the service include: 'Praise him on the trumpet, the psaltery and harp'; 'Alleluia, alleluia, give thanks to the risen Lord'.

Statement of faith

A simple creed based on the words from John's Gospel is available as a download (YearC.Pentecost_3). If possible, invite a group of children to create some actions beforehand so that they can lead everyone else.

Notes and comments

As today has been a celebration, share a celebratory cake or special biscuits after the service.

If your service takes place in the context of Holy Communion, put special emphasis on the Peace today, inviting everyone to greet each other with encouraging words such as: The Spirit of the Lord lives in you.

Alternative online options

For your convenience the following activities are available as downloads: YearC. Pentecost_4 Song for under-5s; YearC. Pentecost_5 Alternative prayer activity for all ages. Visit www.lightlive.org for additional activities for children, young people and adults.

TRINITY SUNDAY

READINGS: **Romans 5:1–5; John 16:12–15**
Psalm 8; Proverbs 8:1–4,22–31

Bible foundations

Aim: to understand that although God is far beyond our comprehension, we can see him at work

John 16:12–15 is a small section of what is known as Jesus' farewell discourse to his disciples. John records the conversations that Jesus had prior to his death where he spoke about particularly significant matters which his disciples needed to grasp. Part of this conversation was about the Holy Spirit, whom Jesus called the Counsellor or Advocate. The Holy Spirit is the third person of the Trinity – he convicts of sin and also guides into all truth. In verses 12–15, Jesus summarises something of the complexity of the Trinity – Father, Son and Spirit are separate beings and yet cooperate and serve one another; listening to each other and sharing from one another. God is beyond our understanding and all attempts to explain God fall down at some point, yet we see Father, Son and Spirit at work in different ways.

Proverbs 8:1–14,22–31 express something of the role of Father and Son at creation using the metaphor of wisdom to express the creative activity of God. In addition, David reflects on God's intricate creation in Psalm 8 as he wonders how this majestic God should have time or inclination to care for mere humans!

Paul seeks in Romans 5:1–5 to express something of the interaction of the Trinity in regard to our salvation. Because of faith in Jesus we are justified (made right) and therefore we can live at peace with God the Father. We are loved by the Father and the Son but we are able to experience that love because the Holy Spirit is within us, 'poured into our hearts' (verse 5). God's work within us is a complex process that we don't always immediately recognise. Paul challenges us to rejoice in our sufferings. Often, those who have learned to respond positively to God's ways seem to have developed the most Christ-like character and the deepest hope.

Beginning the service

With: a PowerPoint sound recording or video clips

Create a PowerPoint of images that show many ways in which God reveals himself, in creation and in the way that he acts. Play it as people enter, to music such as Chris Tomlin's 'Indescribable'. As a variation on this, film various members of the congregation over the week, talking about ways in which they feel that God has revealed himself to them, and play all the video clips on a loop as people enter the service.

A third option is to play a recording of Lockridge's famous 'My King' sermon, either along with images or by itself. (There is a choice of dozens of these on YouTube, both cut down and full-length, each set to different images or film clips, some to music.) This sermon builds in hundreds of different descriptions of Jesus, but then leads into the final section with the words, 'I wish I could describe him to you – but he's indescribable! He's indescribable! He's incomprehensible!' Wait until people are sitting down and ready to listen before playing the recording.

Alternatively, hold up pictures of creation and images of God's activity such as in the created world, of parental love, of someone helping another in obvious need (see **Prayer activity** for more specific suggestions) or just describe them, once you have welcomed everyone.

Explain that, throughout this service, we will be thinking about how indescribable and incomprehensible God is, but also about how he has chosen to reveal himself to us in so many ways, especially as we see him in Christ and the Holy Spirit.

Bible reading

Read John 16:12–15 with several readers, breaking up the passage into different statements about what the Spirit does. The CEV is a clear version of this.

Romans 5:1–5, again using the CEV (see below), could be accompanied by a mime while the passage is read clearly and slowly. The actions in brackets happen simultaneously with the verses, and should all be smooth movements between freeze-frames, rather than continuous acting. For clarity and convenience Actor 1 is referred to as 'he' and Actor 2 as 'she', but they could be of either gender.

> By faith we have been made acceptable to God. And now, because of our Lord Jesus Christ, we live at peace with God. *(Actor 1 stands with his arms out and head bowed, as if on a cross.)*
>
> Christ has also introduced us to God's undeserved kindness on which we take our stand. *(Actor 2 enters, looks at Actor 1, then approaches him and kneels as if at the foot of the cross in worship. Actor 1 bends to embrace her.)*
>
> So we are happy, as we look forward to sharing in the glory of God. *(Both actors stand and face the front, smiling, holding hands.)*
>
> But that's not all! We gladly suffer, because we know that suffering helps us to endure. *(Actor 2 turns away and covers her face as if crying.)*
>
> And endurance builds character, which gives us a hope that will never disappoint

us. *(Actor 1 reaches out and touches Actor 2 on the shoulder; she lifts her head but doesn't turn round until the next line.)*

All of this happens because God has given us the Holy Spirit, who fills our hearts with his love. *(Actor 2 slowly turns as Actor 1 mimes offering a gift in cupped hands. Actor 2 receives it and takes it to her heart in a single movement, finishing with hands over her heart.)*

Romans 5:1–5 (CEV)

Bible talk

With: a bag or box containing a set of objects that give clues about a person (someone well-known by people in church and who won't mind being 'analysed') – for example, something representing a hobby, a favourite food, a book, a piece of clothing

What clues tell us about a person

Produce the objects one by one, asking people to suggest what they reveal about their owner. See if anyone can guess which member of the congregation is represented! Then ask: how much do these clues really tell us about the person? What else might we want to know? What clues would there be if you were trying to describe yourself? At this point, people could split into small groups to talk about this.

What clues tell us about God

Explain that God has given us plenty of clues that show us something about himself. They are inevitably limited in what they reveal. Link back to the images shown at **Beginning the service**, or ask for ideas of the kind of clues these might be: for example, God can reveal himself to individuals through friendships, nature, experiences, verses of the Bible. Just like the clues in the bag (or box), we have to think carefully about what each of God's clues shows us about him.

What God tells us about himself

Now ask the person represented by the objects to join you and to comment on each object, correcting or expanding on what was said when everyone was just guessing. Thank them, and when they have sat down again, point out how much easier it is to understand the clues when the person is actually there to explain them! That is what Jesus and the Holy Spirit can do for us. Ask people to look up John 16:12–15, or show it on the screen, or print it on the notice sheet, and then call out what Jesus said the Spirit was going to do.

- He will come to show what is true.
- He will tell what he has heard from Jesus.
- He will let you know what is going to happen.
- He will bring glory to Jesus by taking Jesus' message and sharing it.
- Note too that the Father shares all he has with Jesus.

The disciples were gradually beginning to understand that when they looked at Jesus, they saw God himself. These points indicate just how the three persons in the Trinity are all bound up together.

Refer back to Romans 5:1–5. Paul mentioned three things in particular that Jesus has shown us about God's character: peace, grace (undeserved kindness) and glory.

So we understand some things, but not everything, about God – he is incomprehensible. But as Jesus said in the reading from John, the Spirit will come and lead us into 'all truth' so we will gradually understand more and more of God and come to understand just how much more there is to know. We can ask the Spirit to show us more of God.

Prayer activity

With: sets of small cards of pictures that show God revealing himself in the world, such as pictures of churches, people, mountains, a waterfall, space, a Bible, a newborn baby, Jesus as a child, Jesus as a man, Jesus on the cross; large thought bubble on a flipchart; pens

Give each person a card and ask them to get into groups of four or five, all with different cards. Ten suggestions are given above so you could ask people to get into groups of ten, (or more or less depending on the number of different cards you produce). Be sensitive to the group size so that it facilitates – rather than inhibits – group prayer.

Encourage everyone to look at each other's cards (or clues about God revealing himself) and then thank God that he has made himself known in such a wide variety of ways. This could be in silent prayer or one-sentence prayers going round the group. Remind people to ask the Holy Spirit to help explain God's character as they look prayerfully at the images.

When everyone has got back together (or this could be done in small groups) ask what else people wished they knew about God. Write their thoughts in the speech bubble on the flip chart. Reaffirm that, although we may never know answers to some of our questions until we get to heaven, there is more to God than he has revealed to us, and he does know the answers.

Prayer of confession

With: a picture or model of Jesus on the cross used in the **Prayer activity**; optional – stones

Show the picture of Jesus on the cross, then explain that in Romans 5, Paul tells the Christians to whom he was writing that God chose one particular way to communicate with us and show us what he is like – his Son Jesus – and it is the image of Jesus on the cross that does this most clearly. Because of the cross, we can live 'at peace' with God and have his 'undeserved kindness' or grace, even when we get things wrong.

Lead into a time of confession, either using your usual confession or, making this into a **Prayer activity**, encourage people to bring the things they have done wrong – in the form of stones or other representative objects – to the picture of the cross in an easily accessible place. Afterwards, read the Absolution or Romans 5:1 again.

Ending the service

Read John 16:12,13a again, encouraging people to be on the lookout for the Spirit's guidance in the everyday incidents and situations that come up during the week! These verses could be printed on the service sheet, or on a wallet-shaped card to take away if they wish.

Helpful extras

Music and song ideas

'Immortal, Invisible'; 'Ye watchers and ye holy ones'; 'Come, Holy Ghost, our souls inspire'; 'Holy, holy, holy' (various versions); 'From the highest of heights to the depths of the sea' (Chris Tomlin *Indescribable*); 'What can I do' (Graham Kendrick – *When I see the beauty of the sunset's glory*). Taizé (sheet music and MP3s for these and more can be found at www.taize.fr) 'Dominus Spiritus Est'; 'Vieni, Spirito Creatore'.

Statement of faith

Emphasise that despite God's incomprehensibility, there are things that he has revealed to us through Jesus that we know and can be sure of. These are the things that are listed in your usual statement of faith or creed. In that context, say the creed together.

To continue the theme of 'clues' from the **Bible talk**, ask members of the congregation to hold up objects or pictures at appropriate points during the statement of faith: for example, a globe to represent creation, a picture or statue of Mary, a cross, an image of a tomb, the resurrected Jesus, a cloud for the ascension and a flame for the Holy Spirit.

Notes and comments

The suggestions in this service centre around images, but you may wish to consider the accessibility of this for people who respond to God in non-visual ways: for example, the groups in the **Prayer activity** could gather around a scented candle, a bowl of herbs or flowers; or sounds, music, recorded birdsong, songs or psalms based on biblical texts – all evidence of God in creation.

To give the service even more focus, choose the same collection of images to show for **Beginning the service**, **Prayer activity**,

Prayer of confession and/or **Statement of faith**.

The suggestion to ask the Holy Spirit to help reveal God's character in the **Prayer activity** could be taken in many ways, from a simple prayer led from the front, to a time put aside afterwards for people to share what they feel they have seen or learnt about God. A prayer team being available during the activity or after the service will help people to continue praying as a result of their encounter with God.

You are strongly recommended to read *Top Tips on Explaining the Trinity to young people* (SU) which is a clear explanation of the mystery of the Trinity and full of suggestions for how to attempt to explain the Godhead. This is relevant to people of all ages. For more details see page 215.

Alternative online options

Visit www.lightlive.org for additional activities for children, young people and adults.

PROPER 4

READINGS: **1 Kings 18:20,21,30–39; Luke 7:1–10**
Psalm 96; Galatians 1:1–12

Bible foundations

Aim: to recognise that faith grows when we see God do something extraordinary and when we simply trust Jesus

The story of Elijah on Mount Carmel is a well-known piece of drama. Elijah was caught in a battle with Queen Jezebel and her weaker husband, King Ahab of Israel, along with all the false prophets of Baal. Whose God is the greatest? Elijah cuts an isolated figure 'I only am left' (v 22) as he challenges God's people to stop sitting on the fence, wobbling between two opinions. The immensely powerful demonstration of God's power convinced them to believe in Elijah's God. This resonates with the wavering nature of many people's 'faith' in our culture today, with the proliferation of faith options and a longing for authenticity, proven to be true.

The apostle Paul similarly challenged the Galatians to remain faithful to the gospel of Christ, a gospel which was not a figment of human imagination but came from Christ himself.

The faith response of the centurion in Luke 7 is in stark contrast to the Elijah story. He came from another culture, a wealthy man who had respect for the Jewish traditions. Yet having heard of Jesus he does not use his position to curry favour and does not even go himself in search of the itinerant miracle-worker. He just needed Jesus to speak the word from a distance and he believed his slave would be healed. His faith was rewarded and he has been held up for posterity as someone who was not Jewish yet whose faith Jesus saw as exemplary.

Psalm 96 makes a clear statement about the Lord's supremacy over all other gods and the responsibility of God's people to declare this to others. People through this service can discover that their faith will grow as they put their trust in God, listening to what is said about him, observing his actions with their own eyes and by telling others of his greatness.

Beginning the service

With: examples of extraordinary things people have said or done or extraordinary events

Show an image or explain your example of an extraordinary feat that someone has just done (broken a world record, swam a long distance in shark-infested water and survived etc) or an extraordinary event which is hard to believe (raised £20,000 at a school fete) and then ask if you believe it. You could state several such facts and turn this into a quiz deciding which are actually true and which are false. At the end of this, ascertain that sometimes we need evidence that something is true, but sometimes we accept that it is true, as an act of faith.

In this week's Bible story, we will hear how the prophet Elijah was involved when God did something amazing, after which people were convinced that what Elijah had been saying about God was true. But another man simply accepted that what Jesus said was true without personally seeing any evidence. He had heard about what Jesus had done and that was enough for him to put his faith in Jesus.

Bible reading

The reading from 2 Kings 18:20–39 in *Common Worship* misses out verses 22–29 to keep the emphasis on the choice facing the people rather than the actions of the false prophets. You could point this out to the congregation.

2 Kings 18:20,21,30–39 lends itself to a dramatic reading with a narrator, Elijah and the people acting out suitable movements (and speaking their parts) with appropriate sound effects – such as swooshing water, crackling fire, piling stones on top of each other. These sounds could be pre-recorded or the whole congregation could make a stab at creating the sounds with body percussion – thumping the chest for the stones (12 times) (v 32), rushing water sounds with the mouth (v 33 – 12 times!) and silence (v 21). There are also a lot of numbers – 12 stones, 1 bull, 4 jars of water 3 times, and a crowd of people. Children could be asked to listen out for the numbers in the story.

Luke 7:1–10 could be read from two parts of the building with the centurion being invisible as he makes his declaration of faith in verses 6 to 8.

Bible talk

With: candle and lighter/match or indoors firework; simple illustrations of an eye, an ear and a mouth, large enough to be seen at the back of the worship area, available as a download (YearC.Proper4_1) – these could also be used for the **Prayer activity** and introduced by the **Game**.

Miraculous fire

Light a large candle. If possible and safe, you could light an indoors sparkler or firework – which would be more memorable. Point out that the only way you could light this was by striking a match/using a lighter. You did not even have to think about it. It was a bit different for Elijah.

Briefly tell the story of Elijah, who had set the false prophets an impossible task: to call down fire upon an altar and a sacrificed bull as a way of proving that their god existed. They failed. He then set about building his altar but made it extra hard for God by drenching the altar and his bull with water. Extraordinarily, when he called on his God to send fire to set it all alight, God did just that. The people looking on then knew who the true God was. They had needed convincing.

Ask people in small groups to work out why Elijah had made it more difficult. What was the point? What did he want to show the people about God? Ask for the answers that people can give.

Elijah was angry that the false prophets had such an influence over the king and queen and the people. He was angry that they were not following God. He was utterly convinced that the true God could prove that he was not only true but was all-powerful. But such dramatic action is not our normal experience of God at work in the world, although he does still cause extraordinary things to happen.

Miraculous healing
In advance prepare someone to come to the front who has been injured or ill and is comfortable for everyone to know about this. Ask about their condition and then say that this person (and maybe the whole church) has been praying to get better. Christians have faith that God can and does heal. But we also know that he does not always do that because sometimes that is not going to be the best thing for us or for his wider purposes. (You do not need to spend a long time exploring Christian healing but establish that God does heal.)

This was like the man in the second story from Luke's Gospel. Briefly tell how the centurion had sent a message to ask Jesus to come to heal his sick servant. He had so much faith in Jesus' power that when he heard that Jesus was on the way, he asked Jesus not to bother to come to his house, but just heal the servant from far away. Unlike the people with Elijah, he did not need a dramatic sign. Jesus was amazed that the man had such simple faith in him. The servant was healed!

Refer back to **Beginning the service** and the discussion you had about whether you need to see something to believe it is true. Thomas, one of Jesus' disciples, saw Jesus alive after the resurrection and then he believed. But then Jesus praised those who had not seen and yet they still believed. The centurion had heard about Jesus but the Gospel writer does not say that he himself has ever seen Jesus perform a miracle. In that sense, he is like us. He believed what he had heard and he expected Jesus to do something which he may have thought was impossible.

What stops us from believing that God is able to do amazing things in our lives and in the world around us? What stops us having faith like the centurion? Show the following symbols and give the explanation.

An ear: we don't listen to what people tell us about what God has done. The people of God at the time of Elijah were not prepared to listen to what Elijah said about God, but the centurion had listened and acted on it.

An eye: we don't look around to see what God is doing and we do not read the Bible to discover more about what God has done in the past. The people of God at the time of Elijah were not looking around for evidence of God's goodness or power.

A mouth: we don't speak about God's great deeds to others, for it is often in telling others that we become convinced ourselves. (Refer to Psalm 96, if you are using all the readings in the lectionary, where the psalmist encourages people to sing to the Lord and declare his salvation and wonders to the world.) The centurion told lots of people why he could have such deep faith in Jesus.

Show the symbols again.

An ear: if we listen to what others tell us about Jesus, then our faith can grow.
An eye: if we look around us, we can see evidence of God at work in our world and so our faith can grow.
A mouth: if we tell others about Jesus, then we can see how they too respond to him and our faith can grow.

Prayer activity

With: small copies of the three symbols, enough for each person to have one, available as a download (YearC.Proper4_1); pens or pencils

Distribute the small copies of the symbols, or let people choose once you have explained what is required. You may want to play the **Game** at this point to familiarise yourselves with the three symbols. Explain that each person is to choose which of the three symbols/prayers they want to use to talk with God. The three options are available as a PowerPoint download (YearC.Proper4_2).

1. **Ear** – To ask God to help us to listen – in church, in a small group, in conversation – to what others tell them about Jesus' goodness.
2. **Eye** – To ask God to help us see what he is doing in the world eg changing tough situations, making things new, helping people grow in faith.
3. **Mouth** – To ask God to help us tell others about Jesus.

Each person takes one of the symbols, writes their name on it and any details they want to tell God. In a short silence, ask each person to speak with God. Encourage everyone to take their symbol home. Conclude with the following prayer:

All-powerful God, help our faith to grow in you as we listen to what others tell us about you, as we read the Bible and see what you are doing in the world and as we tell others about you. Thank you that you always hear and watch over us. Amen.

Prayers of intercession

It would be most appropriate to thank God for answers to prayers spoken to God in recent services and to thank him for where there is evidence of his power. This could be followed by members of the congregation identifying where in the world they long to see God making a difference. Do you have the faith to ask? Ensure that you do bring your requests to God, acting in faith, and follow this up in subsequent services.

Ending the service

The song 'You shall go out with joy' is an old song but one which can therefore be sung with confidence and it picks up the theme of Psalm 96. Use percussion instruments, if that is your practice, and encourage everyone to leave church singing and dancing, to tell others of the greatness of God.

Helpful extras

Music and song ideas

'Over all the earth'; 'Our God is so big'; 'God is an awesome God' (*Light for Everyone* CD (SU)); 'You shall go out with joy'; 'Great is thy faithfulness'; 'Faithful one, so unchanging'; 'Jesus is Lord, the cry that echoes over all creation…'

Game

With: a grid of 12 squares (see below), available as a download (YearC.Proper4_3) or create your own

This is a game with 12 squares on a grid with six sets of two symbols as follows: 2 red ears, 2 blue ears, 2 red eyes, 2 blue eyes, 2 red mouths, 2 blue mouths. Create two teams and each team has to find, in turn, the position of the identical pairs of symbols. If they find one set, they get a point. The purpose of this is to familiarise everyone with the symbols used in the **Bible talk** and would serve to introduce the **Prayer activity**.

Notes and comments

The **Game** is a useful introduction to the **Prayer activity** but you could also use it for **Beginning the service** if you did not want to have something a bit more light-hearted between the **Bible talk** and the **Prayer activity**.

The suggestion to use indoor fireworks may be too much of a health and safety risk, but using them would be a memorable way to introduce the story of Elijah on Mount Carmel. An Internet search will give you the full price range of indoor fireworks. They are not necessarily expensive.

The story of Elijah on Mount Carmel is told with puppets and in song as an episode in the video of the SU holiday club programme *Groundbreakers*. It is only available as a VHS, not a DVD.

Alternative online options

For your convenience the following activity is available as a download: YearC.Proper4_4 is a rhyme to learn for younger children. Visit www.lightlive.org for additional activities for children, young people and adults.

PROPER 5

READINGS: **1 Kings 17:17–24; Luke 7:11–17**
Psalm 30; Galatians 1:11–24

Bible foundations
Aim: to rejoice in the way God brings life from death

Here are two powerful stories in which God literally brings life from death. In 1 Kings 17:17–24 we read of the widow of Zarepheth's son who has died and is raised to life by Elijah's prayer. Then in Luke 7:11–17 we have a similar experience with a widow's dead son, though this time it is Jesus who speaks life to him.

Elijah was a prophet of God in the time of Ahab, King of Israel. He was required to speak God's truth even when it was unpopular. He experienced miracles of God's provision and intervention in response to his obedience and faithfulness to God. He had been staying at the widow's house for some time. They had all experienced the miraculous provision of God in giving them flour and oil which did not run out, yet the miracle of restored life was beyond the widow's comprehension. She responded with joy and recognition that Elijah was a man of God and spoke God's truth. Elijah is seen by some as a type of Christ and so, as Jesus carried out a similar miracle, it may have been that those around would have been reminded of the story of Elijah and been challenged to recognise that here also was a man of God who spoke God's truth. Luke reminds us that as a result of the healing, people were filled with awe; they recognised that God was at work and spread the word about Jesus.

In Psalm 30 David gives testimony to the powerful intervention of God in healing and sustaining; giving joy in place of grieving and dancing instead of wailing. If God can bring life from death, there is nothing that is too difficult for him! In Galatians 1:11–24 Paul the apostle adds his testimony, focusing on the way that God brought him 'new life', that is, spiritual life from death, turning his life around from a zealous persecutor to a preacher of hope in Christ.

Beginning the service

With: a PowerPoint of 'before and after' images

Show a presentation of 'before and after' photos or film clips from various products, adverts or television programmes (using an Internet search), for example, face creams, kitchen cleaners, slimming products, room or garden makeovers and so on. Ask everyone what they think about when you mention Jesus 'before and after' his death, and to talk with each other about it. Ask for suggestions from all ages.

Finish with a photo of a gravestone (or of the cross) and one of someone looking alive and happy (or of the empty tomb). God's 'before and after' is to bring life from death and that is the focus of this service.

Bible reading

Either the reading from 1 Kings 17:17–24 or Luke 7:11–17 could be accompanied by a mime or performed as a sketch using the Bible text with a narrator reading the action and actors taking their parts. A scripted example for Luke 7:11–17 from the NIV is given below. Display the words either on screen or printed in the notice sheet. It is also available as a download (YearC.Proper5_1).

Psalm 30 would be very effectively read with a music background – see **Music and song ideas**.

> **Reader:** Soon afterwards, Jesus went to a town called Nain, and his disciples and a large crowd went along with him. As he approached the town gate, a dead person was being carried out, the only son of his mother, and she was a widow. And a large crowd from the town was with her. When the Lord saw her, his heart went out to her and he said,
> **Jesus:** Don't cry.
> **Reader:** Then he went up and touched the coffin, and those carrying it stood still. He said,
> **Jesus:** Young man, I say to you, get up!
> **Reader:** The dead man sat up and began to talk, and Jesus gave him back to his mother. They were all filled with awe and praised God.
> **Congregation:** A great prophet has appeared among us. God has come to help his people.
> **Reader:** This news about Jesus spread throughout Judea and the surrounding country.
> Luke 7:11–17 (NIV)

Bible talk

With: a flip chart or board divided into two columns: 'before' and 'after'; two coloured marker pens

Refer to the 'before and after' images from **Beginning the service**, and point out that for each of the readings, there is a 'before and after'.

Elijah, before and after the son came alive
In 1 Kings 17:17–24, Elijah has been staying with a widow during a famine. Ask if anyone can tell you what happened in this story leading up to and including the death of this widow's son. Write down the key words from the story in the 'before' column. Write down any words that specifically relate to God in a different colour. You will get answers such as:

- Elijah met the widow at a time of famine (this is in the first part of chapter 17).
- She was preparing to cook a last meal for her son before they both died.
- God helped Elijah to give her a never-ending supply of oil and flour.
- The widow's son fell ill and died.

Then ask for key words for what happened afterwards and record those in the 'after' column, making sure that everyone is clear about the storyline in this event.

- Elijah carried the boy upstairs.
- Elijah prayed.
- God was able to bring the boy back to life.

Comment on what Elijah and the woman would have discovered about God. Refer briefly to Psalm 30 where the psalmist rejoices that God has brought him 'out of the pit'. He has been in a hopeless situation, but God has put it right. The psalmist says that God has 'turned his mourning into dancing' and 'weeping remains for a night, but joy comes in the morning'.

Jesus, before and after the son came alive
The Gospel story in Luke 7:11–17 is about Jesus raising another widow's son to life. As before, ask for words to write down in the 'before' column and write the words about Jesus in the colour used to indicate God in the previous story.

- The boy was already dead, in a coffin, on his way to be buried.
- His mother was a widow and probably dependent upon him, as he was her only son.
- Jesus stopped the funeral in its tracks.

Do the same for the 'after' column.
- Jesus spoke to the dead boy in his coffin.
- Jesus gave the living son back to his mother.

Ask what similarities there are between these two stories.

Before and after Jesus came alive
Comment that with the life of Jesus there is a very definite 'before and after' – before his death on the cross and after he came alive again. But there is also a 'before and after' in the life of all followers of Jesus.

Before and after the followers of Jesus come alive in Christ
In his letter to the Galatian church, Paul writes about his own 'before and after', in 1:23: 'The man who formerly persecuted us is now preaching the message.' He met Jesus and his life was never the same. Summarise Galatians 1:11–24. It would be very appropriate for someone to talk about how their life has been transformed with a 'before and after' experience. You will probably also want to reassure people that a dramatic encounter with God, the sort that Paul experienced, is not the usual pattern that we see in the Bible or in our lives. What matters is that we know that we have been transformed and are being transformed.

Summarise by saying that:
- God transforms our own hopeless situations.
- God transforms who we are and makes us like Christ.

All this is possible because God himself, in the person of Jesus, was prepared to go through a hopeless situation and to transform it into the most hopeful day in history. The Easter story, God's biggest 'before and after' moment, means that we can bring our own 'before' life to him, and ask that we too may be transformed.

Prayer activity

With: two large billboards fixed at the front of the room, with the words BEFORE and AFTER

Ask a group of people (a family, home group or youth group) to identify situations which have a 'before' and an 'after', such as someone was well and has now fallen ill, a country was at peace and is now at war, a couple did not have a child but now the new baby has come/ is due to arrive. The 'after' situation need not always be better.

The group prepares prayers in two parts: the first part is to describe the situation, either thanking God for it or saying where God's action is needed; the second part either thanks God for his intervention and answer to prayer or intercedes for him to take action. The person reading each prayer moves from the BEFORE billboard to AFTER just before reading the second part of the prayer.

This way of praying could be opened up to allow spontaneous contributions from the congregation, as others see where God has answered prayer or where God is needed to transform a situation. People could come to stand by the BEFORE billboard and move to AFTER.

Prayer of confession

With: two large billboards fixed at the front of the room, with the words BEFORE and AFTER, as used in the **Prayer activity**

Remind people that before we followed Jesus we were not able to communicate with God, we did not love him, and we let him down in more ways than we can ever imagine.

Stand under the BEFORE billboard and acknowledge that we are all sinners in God's eyes. Ask people to think of ways in which they have let God down this week.

Stand under the AFTER billboard and invite people silently to ask God to forgive them. Then assure everyone that God forgives all those who ask him for forgiveness and he gives us new life by his Spirit. We are indeed alive in Christ.

With a small congregation, you could invite everyone to stand under the BEFORE billboard and then move to AFTER as the time of confession proceeds. (Note that in this instance, the AFTER is much better than BEFORE, unlike in the **Prayer activity** where this need not be the case.)

Ending the service

Ask everyone to remember something they were thinking about before they came to church, then to notice one thing that they have thought about or learnt during the service. Invite people to share that one thought or thing they have learnt with someone sitting near them. (Children will be used to doing this at the end of a lesson in school – it is an important way of learning.)

Challenge everyone to think how what they have learnt or discovered in the service has had an effect on what they thought about before coming to church. Has there been a 'before' and 'after'?

Helpful extras

Music and song ideas

Songs with themes of 'before' and 'after' such as 'When I call on your name you answer (I've found a love)' Ben Cantelon; 'I am a new creation'; 'Amazing grace'; 'In Christ alone'; 'Lord, I lift your name on high'; 'The greatest day in history'.

Suggestions of music to accompany the **Bible reading** of Psalm 30 such as a song that includes words from the psalm, or wordless music that could be used as background, such as 'Mourning into dancing' Tommy Walker or 'Morning Mood' from *Peer Gynt Suite No 1* by Edvard Grieg which builds gradually, evoking a sunrise, and would sound very effective timed carefully to reach a climax as the reading finishes.

Notes and comments

The theme of this service provides an ideal opportunity to invite testimonies from members of the congregation or visiting speakers of their 'before' and 'after' experiences. This does not have to be just when they first put their trust in Christ. What they say should be fairly brief, in language that is accessible to all ages and free from jargon. Give some warning, although some churches will be more comfortable about asking for a spontaneous response. Such a response could be especially helpful in the **Prayer of confession**.

Coming to faith in Jesus is unique to each person. For some it is a dramatic encounter with Christ with a clear 'before' and 'after', for others a more gradual process or a whole series of commitments. This is explored in *Top Tips on Helping a child respond to Jesus* (SU) – see page 221 for details. It is relevant in exploring the response of people of all ages.

The theme of this service also suits baptisms particularly well. If a baptism is part of this service, it may be an idea to ask for a testimony from the candidate (if a teenager or adult) or, if the candidate is an infant, to include the child in the **Bible talk** by inviting their family and godparents to consider their hopes for the child's 'after' picture, and how God may use them to be a part of that.

Alternative online options

Visit www.lightlive.org for additional activities for children, young people and adults.

PROPER 6

READINGS: 2 Samuel 11:26 – 12:10,13-15; Luke 7:36 – 8:3
Psalm 32; Galatians 2:15-21

Bible foundations
Aim: to accept the forgiveness that God offers

2 Samuel 11 and 12 records the story of King David's adultery with Uriah the Hittite's wife, Bathsheba. Unfortunately, Bathsheba becomes pregnant and in order to cover his tracks David engages in a series of deceptions, ultimately creating the opportunity for Uriah's death in battle. He is an adulterer and a murderer and hoping to get away with both. However, God knows and sends his prophet Nathan to confront David by means of a clever parable. He draws David into the story until David speaks out words that turn out to be his own condemnation (2 Samuel 12:5,6). Nathan tells him very clearly that, 'he is the man who has sinned'. David acknowledges his sin – and acknowledges that primarily it is against God (v 13). Nathan reassures David that God will forgive him but that there will be consequences to his actions – in this case the baby will die. David accepts both God's forgiveness and the consequences, and his relationship with God is restored. Some of the psalms he writes reflect that experience and his own testimony of confession and forgiveness (see Psalms 32 and 51).

Luke 7:36 – 8:3 records the gratitude and worship felt by a sinful woman who had been able to accept the forgiveness that Jesus offered her and to respond extravagantly. Everyone else had judged her but Jesus allowed the possibility of cleansing and change. Luke sets up the contrast between the self-righteous Pharisee who senses he has no particular need of forgiveness and the woman, acutely aware of her failure. Again a parable in verses 41-43 emphasises that the person who is more aware of how much they have been forgiven is much more grateful and loves the person who has forgiven them even more. In Galatians 2:15-21 Paul emphasises that forgiveness is not something earned or deserved but a gift of grace that we can receive as a result of Christ's death on the cross. May everyone in this all-age service experience God's forgiveness and respond appropriately.

Beginning the service

With: Praise response from Psalm 32 on display – available as a download (YearC.Proper6_1)

Welcome everyone then join in the following Praise response from the CEV.

> Our God, you bless everyone,
>
> **Everyone whose sins you forgive and wipe away.**
>
> Our God, you bless everyone by saying:
>
> **You told me your sins, without trying to hide them.**
>
> And now God forgives us.
>
> We worship you, Lord
>
> And we should always pray
>
> **whenever we find out that we have sinned.**
>
> from Psalm 32 (CEV)

Bible reading

For the reading of Luke 7:36 – 8:3 choose a narrator and two others to speak the words of Jesus and Simon the Pharisee. Rehearse the line in 7:49b where the other guests start to say to one another what the whole congregation can join in to say – 'Who is this who dares to forgive sins?' (CEV). The readers can stand at the front or, for further interest, they could be posed with Jesus seated, Simon standing leaning over him and the narrator somewhat apart. Someone quietly kneeling at Jesus' feet could suggest the woman's part.

Bible retelling
2 Samuel 11:26 – 12:10,13–15

With: silk or real flowers, ideally roses, planted in a large trough; a single flower planted in a pot

This version of the story of David's adultery does not mention that he had sex with her and she became pregnant before the murder of Uriah. This is because the emphasis is on the fact that David took what was not his to take, snatching what was precious to someone else. He did not even realise his wrongdoing. Nathan's parable is also reworked. (The storyteller could mime the plucking of the single rose.) If you are uncomfortable with this version, read the story from 2 Samuel 11 and 12.

In the springtime, while his army was off fighting a war, King David stayed at home. He was very rich and lived in a wonderful palace. From the roof of his palace he saw a beautiful woman bathing and he fancied her. Her name was Bathsheba, but she was married – married to Uriah the Hittite who was off fighting with David's army. It was wrong for David to act on his attraction to her but, because he was king, he could do anything! He arranged something very terrible. He arranged for her husband to be left undefended on the battlefield, making sure he would be killed. And that was exactly what happened.

(*Pause.*)

Later, when David received the news of Uriah's death, he made Bathsheba his wife. God saw all this and he sent Nathan, the prophet, to tell David a story, like this:

There was once a gardener who had a garden full of roses – red ones, yellow ones, pink ones, purple ones and white ones – loads and loads of beautiful flowers, with deep, strong scents.

Next door lived a poor man who didn't have a garden but he did have a window box and in that window box he grew the most beautiful rose of all – just one. The poor man would sit for hours and look at his rose. He took photos of it, he painted pictures of it; he even made a video of it. He loved that rose. It brought him so much pleasure.

One day the queen came to visit the gardener. He was very honoured and wanted to give her a gift – a rose. He didn't give her one of his red roses; he didn't give her a yellow one; he didn't give her a pink one or a purple one or even a white one. No, he leaned over the fence and stretched out his arm towards the poor man's window box where the single rose stood tall and beautiful. He plucked that rose with one sharp snap – and he gave it to the queen!

King David listened to the story and was furious with the gardener. 'He must pay for that four times over,' he shouted fiercely.

Nathan looked at King David for a long time and then quietly said, 'But you are that man! You are the richest man in the kingdom and yet you struck down Uriah the Hittite and took his wife to be your own.' (Pause)

Then David said, 'I have sinned against the Lord.'

Nathan replied, 'The Lord has taken away your sin. You are not going to die. Bathsheba is pregnant, but the son she is carrying, he will die.'

Bible talk

With: a pot with a single rose – see **Bible retelling**; a large bottle of expensive perfume; words to display Psalm 32:1–5, available as a download (YearC.Proper6_2)

(Show the single rose.) All ages should be aware of the sin portrayed in David's story on one or both levels, after the **Bible retelling**. Ask how David reacted when he realised his sin. Would you have expected that? How else might he have responded? (You should note that Nathan's parable was about a favoured lamb rather than a rose but the special rose illustrates the same point.)

Then ask how God responded. Comment that although there was forgiveness, there were also consequences to bear.

(Show the perfume.) Refresh everyone's memory of the story in Luke 7. Split people into small groups with half discussing how the woman reacted and why they think she did what she did and the other half doing the same for Simon the Pharisee. Ask for feedback. There will be mention of her contrition, faith, gratitude, humility and generosity in giving such expensive perfume. Simon showed none of these.

Ask a very challenging question and build it up as such. It can either be answered in the small groups or all together. The question is: Was David more like Simon the Pharisee or more like the woman? Encourage some discussion, since David was not self-aware until Nathan visited and he was wealthy and powerful – like Simon. The woman was quite the opposite but both she and David realised how much they needed forgiveness. We don't know the consequences of her actions.

David wrote about this experience in his psalms. Psalm 32 shows the joy that he found in forgiveness. Display Psalm 32:1–5 and allow people time to respond quietly. You could move directly into the **Prayer of confession**.

Prayer activity

With: a sand tray; or strips of card, pens and pencils; or a flip chart and marker pens

Psalm 32 uses metaphorical language to describe how David felt, when he knew he had sinned against God ('bones wasted away', 'groaning all day long', 'sapped strength as in the heat of summer') and how he felt when he was forgiven ('surely the rising of the mighty waters will not reach me', 'You are my hiding place'). Explain this to everyone then ask people to use picture language to describe how they feel when they have done something wrong. Give examples such as feeling sick in the stomach, trembling, wanting to dig a hole in the ground and bury yourself, cover your face with a big hat or hide in the dark!

Then ask how people feel, again using picture language, when relationship difficulties have been sorted and there has been forgiveness, or when, after being forgiven, they realise exactly what the implications of something they have done wrong are (but sense it is going to be OK). Examples might be feeling relieved and relaxed, wanting to bounce up and down, wanting to hug everyone and feeling safe.

There are many other metaphorical words used in the Bible which you could also read out. For example:

Isaiah 64:6a and 61:10: All of us have become like one who is unclean, and all our righteous acts are like filthy rags. The Lord God has clothed me with garments of salvation and arrayed me in a robe of his righteousness.

Isaiah 1:18: 'Come now, let us reason together,' says the Lord. 'Though your sins are like scarlet, they shall be as white as snow; though they are red as crimson, they shall be like wool.' See also Psalm 51:7.

Give out the pieces of card and suggest people draw two pictures: one to represent how they feel when they've done something wrong and the other how they feel when they've been forgiven, one on either side of the card, or invite people to come to a sand tray to draw the first picture in the sand with their finger and then rub it out. That is how God deals with our sin. Alternatively, ask for an artist to draw the suggestions as they are made on a flip chart.

Bring the prayer time to a close using this prayer:

We pray for those who mourn, that they will be comforted.
We pray for those who are broken-hearted, that they will know your peace.
We pray for those who are imprisoned for Christ's sake, that they will be released.
Thank you, Lord God, that you loved us so much that you sent your only Son to die for our sins so that all who believe in him will be saved.
Increase our faith, we pray, that we may live life to the full, knowing our sins are forgiven. Amen.

Prayer of confession

Read or display Psalm 32:1–5 (from CEV), available as a download (YearC.Proper6_2).

Allow time for personal silent response and then use the prayer, available as a download (YearC.Proper6_3), as a collective response. Either two people can read it alternately, or display the words of the prayer for people to join in as appropriate.

Ending the service

Conclude by affirming the truth that if we confess our sins God is faithful and just and will forgive.

Use the words from Psalm 51:10–12 as a blessing, words that David may have written when he realised what he had done.

Helpful extras

Music and song ideas

Follow the Praise response at **Beginning the service** with an uplifting song such as 'Praise him you heavens' ('Great in power'); 'Rejoice, rejoice'; 'My lips shall praise you'; 'Praise my soul the King of heaven'.

Songs of confession and forgiveness such as 'All I once held dear'; 'O Lord, your tenderness'; 'Majesty' ('Here I am'); 'For the joys and for the sorrows'; 'Dear Lord and Father of mankind'.

During the **Prayer activity** a recording of Samuel Barber's 'Adagio for strings' might be played or your musician/s could play a selection of quiet music.

Notes and comments

If possible find a pot similar to the alabaster one used by the woman in Luke 7 to use in the **Bible reading** and for the **Bible talk**. If it is inexpensive, smash it to illustrate how they got the perfume out of it!

A tableau or freeze-frames during the **Bible reading** would be preferable to any attempt at drama as anything dramatic might detract from the message.

Feel free to act out Nathan's (revised) story in the **Bible retelling** as this will help the understanding of the younger ones in the service. You may wish to explain that Nathan's actual story was about a precious lamb kept as a pet in the family, but that this version makes the same point.

Some people may ask for private prayer or counselling about forgiveness in their lives, so make sure that people are available at the close of the service to pray with others.

Alternative online options

For your convenience the following activities are available as downloads: YearC.Proper6_4 Extra storytelling idea; YearC.Proper6_5 Creative prayer for older children; YearC.Proper6_6 Play dough sorry prayer for under-5s. Visit www.lightlive.org for additional activities for children, young people and adults.

PROPER 7

READINGS: **Psalm 22:19–29; Luke 8:26–39**
Isaiah 65:1–9; Galatians 3:23–29

Bible foundations
Aim: to celebrate the freedom that Christ brings

While the first part of Psalm 22 is particularly well known, less familiar perhaps is the astonishing transformation of mood that comes in verse 21. The verses set for today begin with a cry for help from someone who feels himself to be at the point of death (vs 19–21). Declaring that God has rescued him, the psalmist responds with praise. Whereas verses 1–18 depict individual desolation, this second part offers a far-reaching vision of communal worship. Starting with the gathered congregation of the nation (vs 22–26), the psalm envisages a global turning to God in worship (vs 27,28) which extends even to the dead (v 29).

Having just depicted Jesus' authority over the natural world, Luke emphasises (8:26–39) the extent of that power in human life, and its effect. This is not just that the unnamed man is free of the demons that tormented him. It is a story that speaks of restoration and wholeness. Luke stresses significant boundaries evident in human life: geographical, religious, and social. Jesus has crossed the sea into Gentile territory, and encounters things which make a Jew ritually unclean – demons, tombs, and pigs – what a list! The man in this passage is completely isolated by his condition, unable to enjoy normal social interaction.

In the power struggle that takes place we see the importance of being able to name the opponent. This can help to put the things that threaten us into perspective. In Jesus we see the compassion of the Most High God on the demons as well as on their victim. Yet freedom can be scary. Adapting to a new way of being was hard for all those concerned. Jesus was not welcome in Gerasa.

Beginning the service

The theme of this service is praise in response to what God has done. Read Psalm 22:22,23a to set this theme, following it with a strong hymn of praise (see **Music and song ideas**). Alternatively give a few words of introduction and use the reading of Psalm 22 suggested below to open the service.

Bible reading

Psalm 22:19–28 could be read together by splitting the congregation in two groups for alternate verses. Reading the Bible to each other like this can be a powerful way of sharing in the life of the psalms. A PowerPoint which sets the text out for this purpose is available as a download (YearC.Proper7_1).

To add pace to the storytelling of Luke 8:26–39, two narrators could read alternate verses. This gives the effect of two witnesses both keen to share what they've seen. You will need additional voices for Jesus and the demons/cleansed man. The Good News Bible lends itself to this approach.

Bible retelling

There is a sketch, 'Gossip in Gerasa', which retells the Gospel story, available as a download (YearC.Proper7_2). It lasts approximately 7 minutes. If used it would replace the need to spend time exploring the story at the beginning of the **Bible talk**.

Bible talk

With: projection facilities for displaying the portrait of Picasso by Juan Gris (which is in the public domain, copyright having expired), available at: http://upload.wikimedia.org/wikipedia/commons/8/81/JuanGris.Portrait_of_Picasso.jpg; children's large floor jigsaws of well-known scenes or characters

The purpose of the talk is:
- to explore all the ways in which the man with the unclean spirits is unable to function normally
- to understand that the freedom he later experiences is the freedom to be the person God made him to be, which comes when he is restored to wholeness by Jesus.

The man was recognisable as a human being but could not function normally
Display the portrait of Picasso by Gris, and ask the congregation what they see. The image is recognisable as a man, but as seen you could not, for example, go up and shake his hand – the image is fragmented. Alternatively, select a single piece of a large-piece jigsaw. Even in its broken state, children are likely to recognise a favourite character, such as Thomas the Tank Engine, from a part of the whole. What they see in one or two pieces however, is not an engine that could function. Whichever illustration you use, point out that this is a bit like the man in the story. (Check that people have grasped the details of the story, referring to the retelling in 'Gossip in Gerasa'.) The man was unable to function normally. All the things that make life meaningful have been broken up by the presence of the unclean spirits: his sense of self, his ability to live with other people, to feed and clothe himself, to act responsibly and contribute to the life of the local community.

Talk through the story, inviting people to contribute their thoughts and observations about what happened and how the various characters felt.

It was spiritual power that distorted who the man really was

Point out that there was an evil power that gripped the man. Other things can 'tie us up' too. People might like to suggest things that stop us from being true to what God wants for us. It might be things like misuse of power we have over other people, or the distorting effect money can have (whether we have it or not). People might feel constrained in some way by their circumstances. It might also be things like self-loathing or lack of self-worth. Children might mention the power of the bully or fear of failure. (Of course, some of the things mentioned may not necessarily find their source in what is evil, but the result of them could well be described as evil and not of God.)

After Jesus restored him, the man experienced freedom in several ways

Ask in what ways the man could be seen as free. You may get suggestions such as: he was freed from whatever was binding and destroying him as a person; he was free from fear; he was free to respond to Jesus; he was free to be the person God made him to be; he was free to return to his community. (A word of warning: freedom can be quite scary! Jesus would not let this man go with him; he had to stay with the people who knew him as a madman. They all had to get used to the huge change that had come about in their community. They were scared enough to send Jesus away, but they couldn't deny the man and his testimony.)

Comment on the fact that Jesus came to set people free from the effects of sin and being bound by the Law. If appropriate you could read the epistle reading, Galatians 3:23–29, which is full of promises for those who are in Christ, which includes being equal with each other.

At a suitable point, younger children could be invited to complete the floor jigsaws during the rest of the talk. At the end of the talk, see how they have got on, and comment that now the picture is whole, we can see what it's meant to be. Thomas (or whatever jigsaw piece you used at the start) is now ready to get on his way (or similar).

Prayer activity

With: copies of a jigsaw person template and empty person template, available as a download (YearC.Proper7_3); pens/pencils; OHP and pens if required; large free-standing cross

This activity could incorporate confession and intercession. It could be used as an individual activity or as a corporate one.

Individual

Give everyone a copy of the template of a human outline divided by jigsaw shapes. Invite them to think about themselves. Is there anything that they are aware of that prevents them from being true to themselves as a person loved by God? Or anything that causes conflict inside them, which they need to talk about with God? It may be a memory which haunts them, or an envy or admiration of someone who seems to be so good at something or someone who possesses what they would like. Are they hanging on to something because they are scared of change?

Encourage people to write down or draw on the jigsaw on the template whatever it is they have thought of. Invite each person to place their jigsaw at the foot of the cross, as a reminder that there are no boundaries to God's love. They should then pick up an 'empty' person sheet before returning to their seat. Encourage each person to write on their new sheet something like 'whole', 'restored', 'forgiven' or whatever best sums up the effect for them of laying these things at the foot of the cross. You could use the following prayer:

Lord God, we have laid before you
the things that damage your image in us.
Help us to receive your love,
that we will be restored to wholeness in its light,
and be able to tell others what you have done for us.
Amen.

This activity should work for all ages. Young children will obviously need help from an adult, but can be asked to think about things that go wrong, for example, at home, nursery or school. They might think of children being unkind in some way, or things that are not fair. These can be written or drawn onto their jigsaw person.

Altogether

Use a copy of the jigsaw template on a screen or flipchart, and focus on the 'body' representing the local church or community, as appropriate. Invite people to suggest ways in which this 'body' is fragmented or fractured such that it cannot function well. Write these things in the jigsaw shapes and lead a time of intercession for the things represented. The prayer above might provide a suitable conclusion.

Be aware that for a very few people, the power that grips them may actually be a power that is not of God. Talk about how you will respond if such a situation should arise and a time of specific ministry is called for. Of course, in the course of the service, the Holy Spirit may have been active in people's lives in a deep way so provide an opportunity for listening and prayer ministry.

Prayer of confession

Sin itself cuts us off from God and prevents us from being the people God wants us to be. It would therefore be appropriate to spend some time asking God's forgiveness for anything people are aware they have done that they need to tell God about. It would not be right to mix this up with the things people have written down on the person jigsaw template that prevent them from being free, since there is no suggestion in the story that the man's condition was a result of personal sin. We don't know why he was as he was.

A simple time to talk with God and ask for his forgiveness, followed by an assurance that he has forgiven us, would be quite sufficient in this context.

Ending the service

Read again Jesus' words to the cleansed man in Luke 8:39: 'Return to your home, and declare how much God has done for you.' Suggest a brief moment of quiet for everyone to think about where they are going next. How might they 'declare how much God has done' in that context? If appropriate, suggest that everyone has a go at sharing what God has done by talking with their neighbour.

Finish with a strong hymn or song of praise.

Helpful extras

Music and song ideas

Hymns of praise particularly appropriate for today's theme: 'And can it be'; 'Jesus, the name high over all'; 'Jesus, we celebrate your victory'; 'God, the source and ground of being' (verse three specifically refers to the idea of being the person God made us to be); 'O for a thousand tongues to sing'; 'In the presence of your people' is taken directly from Psalm 22:22. The Taizé chant 'Laudate Dominum' (translation 'praise the Lord all nations') expresses the sentiment of verses 27 and 28.

More reflective music on the theme of healing, inner peace and self-offering: 'Be still and know that I am God', 'Calm me, Lord as you calmed the storm', 'I give you all the honour'; 'Just as I am, without one plea'.

Notes and comments

The story of the demon-possessed man in Luke 8:26–39 could be seen as rather alarming for children, especially for those who love animals or those who find the idea of demon possession a challenge (a quite likely response). With younger children you could describe the man as someone who had a troubled mind which meant that he was unable to be part of a normal community and was not able to respond to Jesus. Jesus was able to change all that!

If the service is a Communion service, the 'jigsaw people' could be brought to the cross at the point of receiving Communion. In this act, we are most vulnerable to God, receiving the gift of his love in receiving bread and wine. This makes most sense in a context where people get up from their seats for Communion. They could pass the cross on their way to receive, and collect the 'empty' person on their way back to their seat.

If something more is needed for young children, the jigsaw illustration could be adapted. The leader doing the **Bible talk** should keep back one or two pieces for use at the beginning of the talk, but the others could be hidden around the church so that they have to be found before being put together. This could happen while the talk is going on.

Alternative online options

Visit www.lightlive.org for additional activities for children, young people and adults.

PROPER 8

READINGS: **1 Kings 19:15,16,19–21; Luke 9:51–62**
Psalm 16; Galatians 5:1,13–25

Bible foundations
Aim: to recognise that serving God comes at a cost

1 Kings 19:15,16,19–21 pinpoints a small but highly significant event in a big story. The corruption and idolatry within Israel reaches new depths during the reign of Ahab and his cruel wife Jezebel. Having demonstrated the presence of the true God, Elijah is completely exhausted. Elisha is part of God's answer to Elijah's need, as are the two kings Elijah is instructed to anoint (vs 15,16). This provision is a reminder that God holds the bigger picture. The perspective shifts from Elijah's understandable despair, to the continuing relationship between God and his people.

The partnership between Elijah and Elisha may not look too promising. Elijah passes by and throws his cloak over Elisha, but we are given the impression that he doesn't stop. When Elisha runs up to him, Elijah's response almost suggests indifference. By contrast, Elisha is clear and decisive. He takes the tools of his livelihood and destroys them in a farewell gesture to his community. There is no going back for him.

Everything about the two events recorded in Luke 9:51–62 is stark – the unbelief of the village, the desire of James and John for retribution, Jesus' rebuke, and his response to the would-be followers. Having read 1 Kings 19:20,21, verse 62 seems particularly harsh. Whereas Elijah permitted Elisha to go back and say goodbye, Jesus does not. Is this a picture of Christian life? In simple terms the answer is no. We have God-given family responsibilities which we must not simply abandon. The key here is in verse 51. Jesus has 'set his face' towards Jerusalem. The time is near when he will 'be taken up' (see **Notes and comments**). It all points to Jesus' determination to face the particular events that await him in Jerusalem. At this moment there is no time to go back.

Beginning the service

Start with a few moments of quiet to draw people into an awareness of God's presence. We usually come to church with a lot of things on our minds. Encourage people to be aware of what these things are, and, in the silence, to offer them to God.

The first ten verses of Psalm 139 introduce the idea of a journey with God, so that wherever we are and whatever we do, God is with us. These verses could be read by one person or as an affirmation by the whole congregation, perhaps alternating verses with the leader. A PowerPoint version of Psalm 139:1–10 is available as a download (YearC.Proper8_1). The prayer below could be used to conclude this time of quiet, followed by an appropriate hymn or song.

God of glory, we give you thanks
for the world which you have given us.
God of compassion, we give you thanks
that you walk with us in it.
By your Spirit, open our hearts and minds to hear your call
as we come to worship you today.
Amen.

Bible reading

Introduce 1 Kings 19:15,16,19–21 to help those unfamiliar with the wider story to understand what is going on. Elijah has been God's prophet to the people of Israel for some years which has been at considerable personal cost. His life and ministry are coming to a close. So God tells Elijah how to find Elisha, who will be his helper.

Luke 9:51–62 lends itself to a dramatic reading. A version of this, from the Good News Bible, is available as a download (YearC.Proper8_2) with the use of different voices indicated.

Bible talk

With: a rucksack; holdall; lots of camping equipment (or similar); three large labels (to be attached to a guy rope with three tent pegs) on which are written: 'Commitment', 'Courage' and 'Clear call'

The theme of the talk is that we are all on a journey with God, where it is likely we will encounter surprises and challenges.

Journeys we have taken

Everyone has been on a journey today – to get to church. Use these questions to open out the idea of journeys: How did people travel – on foot, in the car, bus, bicycle or even by train? Did they say goodbye to anyone at home when they came out? What did they bring with them? Encourage people to show things that they have brought to church, such as a favourite toy – parents of small children may have all sorts of necessities or there may be handbags and pockets full of 'useful things'. Share some examples of your own.

What do people expect to do when they leave church? Most people will expect to be going back home. Some may be doing something different, but almost everyone will have something planned.

What about bigger journeys – holidays for example? You could catch up on people's holiday or school journey plans as the holiday season in the northern hemisphere is approaching. What would people take with them? Who would they go with?

Move on to adventurous journeys. Show the camping equipment you have brought (or mountaineering or canoeing equipment if that is what you have available), such as a large rucksack, a tent, sleeping bag, camping stove, plate, bowl and cup, cutlery, small kettle, suitable food, spare clothes. Children could be involved in packing the things into the rucksack. If there is not enough room, use a holdall as well.

Elisha's surprising journey
Briefly mention Elisha. He was called to a surprising journey in a very unusual way: Elijah threw his cloak over Elisha. The striking thing about Elisha is his utterly trusting response. He burns the source of his livelihood.
Both Elijah and Elisha had to do extremely unexpected things.

The expectations of people who travelled with Jesus
Explore what people expected if travelling with Jesus, such as:
- James and John may well have thought that everything would be great and wonderful things would happen. They could not accept that some people would not receive Jesus, and wanted a display of divine power to destroy the people of the village – a sort of divine, 'I told you so'.
- There would always be at least the basic necessities of life – a shelter at night for example.
- Following Jesus would still enable family responsibilities to be maintained and carried out.
- Setting out on a journey with Jesus can happen after saying goodbye at home.
- But look at the comments Jesus makes in Luke 9:51–62. What does Jesus suggest a life would be like to those who follow him?
- Possibly living with the discomfort of knowing that some people don't want Jesus.
- Possibly being homeless, or at best dependent on the hospitality of others for basic needs.
- Allowing the call to proclaim the kingdom of God priority over important social and family responsibilities.
- No looking back – not even to say goodbye to loved ones.

(Observe that Jesus might not have let Elisha do what he did!)

Look again at the rucksack of things prepared for an adventurous journey. Those who helped you pack might help you take things out again one by one – decide which of the objects are absolutely necessary for following Jesus – probably none of them although you might want to share the use of them with others!

So what should we take with us, if it is not that sort of thing? (Take out the three labels and as you explain the following, attach them to a guy rope or tent or stick them on a board with three tent pegs.)

Commitment – be really committed and not half-hearted.
Courage – be brave when things go wrong.
Clear call – be clear what it is God has called us to be and do, whatever that might mean for our family and social responsibilities.

All these are things which are counter-cultural:
Commitment – many people are reluctant to commit themselves to someone or to a project, unsure if they can stick with it/the

person and suspecting that something better may turn up. That's why it is important to be part of a church family, to be committed to God and to one another, involved together in following him.

Courage – many people are afraid of failure or looking stupid in the eyes of others. God's love for us and his acceptance is so great. He gives courage to those who make mistakes or who suffer for being Christians. He gives us courage to face what may seem impossible.

Clear call – there are so many choices that people can make about life that it is hard to know what is the right thing to do, what it is that God is calling us to. We need to learn to listen hard as we read the Bible, pray and talk with others who know God. Our families are important here too in advising us!

Perhaps the most important thing is the attitude we carry with us. Following Jesus, for most of us, means staying where we are and doing what we do to the very best of our ability, for God. That is the journey he calls us to go on. It does mean living without the kind of clutter that gets in the way of his call to proclaim the kingdom of God. (And for some of us, it does mean literally going on a journey for God.)

Prayer activity

With: paper and pens

The focus for this activity is to think about what gets in the way of us responding to Jesus' call. What do we need to do to hear him and make him welcome?

Ask people to be quiet and picture Jesus in their mind, as he spoke with the disciples in the Gospel story. They found it hard to accept that Jesus was not welcome and they found it hard to take in what Jesus was saying. Lead in prayer, asking Jesus to help you listen and take in what he says to you.

Then ask everyone to draw an outline of something that symbolises how we welcome someone, such as a tea cup, a toy to play with, a pint glass, a coat peg. Inside the outline everyone can write down one thing that prevents them from serving God wholeheartedly at the moment. It could be a circumstance, a fear, or an attitude. Ask God to give you all the willingness to commit, to have courage and to hear a clear call. The outlines can be held up in a prayer time, and also be taken home as a reminder to pray during the coming week.

Ending the service

End on a joyful note. Serving God is costly, and letting go of things that get in the way can be scary, but ultimately trusting in God for everything can be liberating.

The Lord's Prayer offers an appropriate summing up of the themes, and could be said together before one of the 'travelling' or final hymn suggestions below.

Helpful extras

Music and song ideas

Hymns which relate to the readings: 'Thou didst leave thy throne and thy kingly crown'; 'Dear Lord and Father of mankind'.

On the theme of following Jesus: 'Will you come and follow me?'; 'Follow me, follow me'.

On walking/travelling with Jesus: 'Step by step, on and on'; 'The Spirit lives to set us free'; 'The journey of life'; 'I heard the voice of

Jesus say'; 'In heavenly love abiding'.

Two possible final hymns might be 'Take my life, and let it be' (everything being at the service of God); 'Tell out my soul' (proclamation of the kingdom).

Game

A variation of the memory game, 'My grandmother went shopping and she bought…' could effectively be incorporated into the service. In the original the first person makes the statement above and adds an item of shopping. The next person repeats what has been said and adds another item. The game continues in this way, each player taking it in turns to memorise everything that has gone before and add another item. Here, the initial statement could be something like 'I went on a journey and I took…', or perhaps something that specifies the kind of journey – 'I went on holiday and I took…' This could be used in a variety of ways:

- near the opening of the service to introduce the theme;
- at the very beginning of the **Bible talk**; if used here the suitcase/rucksack idea would probably not be needed;
- with a small group of volunteers who come out to join the leader at the front;
- in small groups of three or four where people are sitting.

The most important point is that if this is used, it should be picked up again towards the end of the **Bible talk**, and the opening statement changed to: 'I/we went on a journey with Jesus and I/we took…'

Notes and comments

A significant number of modern translations of the Bible add the words 'to heaven' after 'taken up' in Luke 9:51. This is not present in the Greek. Luke knows that what Jesus faces in Jerusalem is betrayal, arrest, sentencing and crucifixion. The danger of over-translating is that in seeing the 'happy ending', we too easily lose sight of the enormous cost of getting there. In these verses, the link with Elijah is significant. He also is 'taken up' (2 Kings 2:1–12), at which point Elisha inherits his spirit. In Acts (also written by Luke) it is at Jesus' ascension that his Spirit is given to his followers.

The first part of the **Bible talk** is obviously adaptable. If you don't have access to camping equipment, think about an exotic holiday with a large suitcase containing sun lotion, sunglasses, bathing suit, guide books, airline tickets, mosquito net and insect repellent. Or alternatively a family seaside holiday in Britain: buckets and spades, beach ball, beach towels, umbrella, waterproofs, woolly jumper, deckchair, cool bag/box for picnics, picnic plates.

It doesn't matter too much what you choose; the point is to draw a contrast with the kind of journey that following Jesus is, and the fact that the people in the Gospel reading had no opportunity to prepare. Whatever 'adventure' you feature, ensure that the three words beginning with C that are on labels are appropriate, such as three buckets, or towels or umbrellas.

Alternative online options

Visit www.lightlive.org for additional activities for children, young people and adults.

PROPER 9

READINGS: **Galatians 6: [1–6] 7–16; Luke 10:1–11,16–20**
Isaiah 66:10–14; Psalm 66:1–9

Bible foundations
Aim: to consider the challenge of sharing the good news of Jesus

To be a follower of Jesus means more than just enjoying his presence. It may also involve being sent out by the 'Lord of the harvest' (Luke 10:1–3) in order to share his good news and introduce others to him. This is not just the responsibility of those who are 'full-time' evangelists or those who are exceptionally gifted; from Luke's Gospel we see that the special mission of the 12 disciples, who were especially close to Jesus (Luke 9:1–11), was followed by the mission of the 70 (Luke 10:1–20).

In commissioning these 70, Jesus pulled no punches. He made clear that sharing his good news would be a challenging task. Significant ongoing effort is required (v 2) and sacrifices would be necessary (v 4). The end result may sometimes be hostility and a rejection of the message (vs 3,10). In this the experience of the servant follows that of the master, for there is a close identification between the messenger and the one who stands at the very heart of the message (v 16).

Given the difficulties involved, we, like the apostle Paul, need a strong conviction of the importance of the message of Christ and the cross (Galatians 6:14). In addition, the sharing of the good news is best carried out in the context of mutual support and encouragement (Luke 10:1), prayer (v 2) and a spirit of humble dependence and confidence in Jesus (vs 4,19). For those who are faithful, the challenges are overshadowed by the joy of sharing the good news and by the evidence of the power of Jesus to liberate and transform lives and situations (Luke 10:17; Psalm 66:1–9). Ultimately, both the challenges and the joys of this God-given task need to be seen in the context of his saving love and our possession of eternal life (Luke 10:20).

Beginning the service

With: a picture of harvest fields

Talk about the evidence that indicates that harvest-time is approaching. The challenge is to gather the wheat or hay when it is ripe and the weather is good. What pieces of equipment are needed for that harvest? (Suggestions include combine harvesters, tractors and balers.)

In today's Gospel reading, Jesus refers to another harvest and gives us another challenge. This harvest is a harvest of people; people coming to know him, people coming home to him. During the service we will be thinking about what equipment we need for this task.

Bible reading

In reading Psalm 66:1–9, use three voices placed in different parts of the worship space so they can echo praise. This version is from the NIV.

> Voice 1 Shout for joy to God, all the earth!
> Voice 2 Sing the glory of his name;
> Voice 3 make his praise glorious.
> Voice 1 Say to God, 'How awesome are your deeds!
> Voice 2 So great is your power
> Voice 3 that your enemies cringe before you.
> Voice 1 All the earth bows down to you;
> Voice 2 they sing praise to you,
> Voice 3 they sing the praises of your name.'
> Voice 1 Come and see what God has done, his awesome deeds for mankind!
> Voice 2 He turned the sea into dry land, they passed through the waters on foot –
> come, let us rejoice in him.
> Voice 3 He rules for ever by his power, his eyes watch the nations – let not the rebellious rise up against him.
> All 3 Praise our God, all peoples, let the sound of his praise be heard; he has preserved our lives and kept our feet from slipping.
> Psalm 66:1–9 (NIV)

Luke 10:1–11 could be read by one voice with pictures to illustrate key points. For example:

Verse 1: Two people moving out together
Verse 2: A ripe harvest
Verse 5: A person giving a greeting of peace
Verse 9: An act of healing
Verse 18: Lightning

Galatians 6:(1–6),7–16 can be read by someone sitting at a high desk with a quill in hand, as if writing the original letter. The reading can therefore be musing in tone but it allows for deliberate emphasis with a slow delivery.

Bible talk

With: a suitcase containing a T-shirt to express individuality such as a loud Caribbean-style shirt, or shirt with a slogan such as 'I do all of my own stunts'; a map with some areas crossed out; a purse or wallet with credit cards and money; a pair of sandals; two cards cut in two shapes (praying hands and a dove of peace); apron/overalls

When we go on adventures and expeditions we need to pack our suitcase. We often take far more with us than we could ever use. If you have travelled with a budget airline you are only allowed to take a certain weight of luggage. Probably many of us have been in the position where we have packed too much and then had to repack, reducing the number of clothes we take with us. Ask for any experiences people have had of discarding items at the airport because of excess baggage!

Jesus challenges his disciples to reduce their possessions even further. In this way they too will be able to travel light and be flexible to serve Jesus.

(As you talk, show the emboldened items as appropriate and ask for personal anecdotes if suitable.) Here is our **suitcase** and on our adventure with Jesus we will want to take clothes, for example, a **T-shirt**. This one suggests a person full of their own importance (or whatever message is on the T-shirt). Jesus advises against such individuality. It is dangerous. Work in pairs and learn to support and encourage one another. If you are not careful you can become too proud of your own achievements. Such teamwork is a challenge and also a 'safety net'.

We would not want to get lost, so we would probably take a **map**. The danger is we might only want a map of the pleasant 'tourist' areas. Look at this one with certain areas crossed out as unsuitable. Jesus says, 'Face the challenge. Go to every town and place where I am going.'

We would certainly want to take a **purse** or **wallet** and cheque cards, money in various currencies, health cards, insurance details, lip salve, passport, driving licence… and that is the trouble. The list goes on and on. We can put our trust in things we have arranged and think we need and we shut out God. Jesus says, 'I challenge you to trust entirely in God.'

It is always difficult to decide which shoes to take… wellingtons for when it rains, **sandals for the heat**, slippers for relaxation, shoes for normal walking, running shoes for exercise. Jesus says, 'Travel light. Make it easy. Take just one pair of sandals. You won't be worrying where you've put all the other shoes.'

Our case is empty. What does Jesus challenge us to rely on? He tells us to rely on things which should be part of us and our relationship with him. What do we do for guidance and help?

Jesus tells us to ask and pray to the Lord of the Harvest. Here is the outline of a **dove of peace**. What is it Jesus' disciples are to do, when they arrive in each house? They are to say, 'Peace to this house'. We are to be carriers and heralds of God's peace.

When Paul writes to the Galatian Christians he stresses something that is present throughout Jesus' ministry. He encourages them to carry each other's burdens, to help and serve one another. If you were helping someone in a messy job what would you wear? Paul encourages Christians to wear love. Love is our **apron/overall** to enable us to deal with the difficulties of life. Paul tells us not to grow weary in doing good. At first we might think that our case should have room for an apron or pair of overalls. On the other hand we should be wearing them all the time. Being a Christian does not mean that we just switch into 'helping mode' every now and then. It is an attitude for 24/7.

This is Jesus' challenge to us. Go out and tell others of our enthusiasm and love for Jesus and of how he has changed our lives. But in the process do not get weighed down with lots of unnecessary clutter. Travel light and trust in him.

Prayer activity

With: photos and information about holiday activities and missions connected with the church (For specific ideas about Scripture Union missions and holidays, visit www.scriptureunion.org.uk/holidays.)

As the summer season is approaching in the northern hemisphere, when there will be many opportunities to share the good news with holiday-makers, children and young people in the school holidays or older people's holiday-at-home events, it is important to pray for opportunities available to those in church.

Create different groups, each with a picture or information about one activity that will be taking place. Invite people to choose which group to go to and after sharing information, encourage prayer within that group. If any people are involved in the leadership of an activity, invite them to the front to be prayed for specifically, as they make their preparations. To tie in with the **Bible talk** you could ask what they are taking with them and what they are not taking with them.

Prayers of intercession

With: the visual aids from the **Bible talk**; the congregational responses (in bold), available as a download (YearC.Proper9_1)

The prayer is threefold: a request, a congregational response and a confirming verse from Galatians (CEV).

Lord, we bring before you our individuality, our different talents and interests. *(Someone holds up the shirt and places it before the table)*

Each of us is different. May we work together for you.

> Paul wrote: But I will never boast about anything except the cross of our Lord Jesus Christ. Because of his cross, the world is dead as far as I am concerned, and I am dead as far as the world is concerned.
> (Galatians 6:14)

Lord, we lay before you our possessions. *(Hold up the pair of sandals)*

Lord, you have given us everything. Help us to use what you have given us in your service.

> Paul wrote: Don't get tired of helping others. (Galatians 6:9a)

Lord, we carry money and bankcards around with us everywhere. We now offer you our money. *(Hold up the purse or wallet)*

You are our true wealth and treasure.

> Paul wrote: You obey the law of Christ when you offer each other a helping hand. (Galatians 6:2)

Lord, the whole world is yours. *(Hold up the map with areas blocked off)*

May we go wherever you send us.

> Paul wrote: We should help people whenever we can, especially if they are followers of the Lord. (Galatians 6:10)

Lord, we step out as people of prayer, as people of peace wearing the apron of love to serve your creation. *(Hold up the apron or overall)*

May our words not be empty but may they be matched by deeds and action – to honour the name of Jesus.

May peace and mercy and the grace of our Lord Jesus Christ be with us.

Amen.

Ending the service

Jesus' mission instructions were 'not to greet anyone on the road'. To us this probably seems impolite. Yet Jesus was making a point. He was stressing the urgency of the task before the disciples. He was saying, 'Just get on with it. Don't be sidetracked.' We are left with that same challenge.

Be focused and get on with the task of taking the good news of Jesus to everyone. We go in peace to love and serve the Lord and to spread his word.

Helpful extras

Music and song ideas

'Here I am' refers to the fields being white unto harvest and the need for labourers; 'I, the Lord of sea and sky' celebrates our readiness to serve in mission; 'Send me out from here' is based on the Gospel reading and would be effective as a solo for meditation; 'We want to see Jesus lifted high' focuses on prayer and mission and the tumbling down of evil; 'All I once held dear' speaks of putting Jesus as our number one priority.

Statement of faith

This is based on Psalm 66:1–9, available as a download (YearC.Proper9_2).

Notes and comments

If there is a person who has served God overseas or is a mission partner, they can give a pertinent witness and testimony. They could especially describe how they packed and made themselves ready for departure. They can highlight how their trust in Christ was not misplaced. The worship leader can highlight these points by interviewing the person. Alternatively someone from the mission team can share news about a link missionary.

Alternative online options

For your convenience the following activity is available as a download (YearC.Proper9_3). Make a 'Thank you' card for those who are sharing the good news of Jesus – for younger children. Visit www.lightlive.org for additional activities for children, young people and adults.

PROPER 10

READINGS: **Psalm 25:1–10; Luke 10:25–37**
Deuteronomy 30:9–14; Colossians 1:1–14

Bible foundations
Aim: to explore what it means to love your neighbour

Whatever his motives, the first question posed by the expert in the Jewish law (or lawyer) concerning eternal life is of vital importance (Luke 10:25). Jesus' answer to this question highlights how an authentic faith will overflow in acts of love towards both God and our neighbour (v 27). A life characterised by such behaviour is an appropriately grateful response to the God of grace and mercy (Psalm 25:1–10).

Jesus' vivid storytelling acts to subvert and refocus the lawyer's second question, 'Who is my neighbour?' (v 29). Such a question presupposes that there are limits to loving one's neighbours, which can be expressed in ethnic, religious, economic or educational terms. Jesus' reply challenges the validity of such a premise by, in effect, answering the different question as to what it means to be a good neighbour. He does so by making the hero of the story a Samaritan, a member of a despised race (also, for example, see John 4:9; 8:48), rather than a pious Jew.

The Samaritan represents a fine example to be followed, for in him we see: a response of compassion and mercy towards someone in need; a reflection of the very character of our God (Psalm 25:6–10); a willingness to get involved, whatever the personal cost and inconvenience (in contrast to the priest and the Levite, both of whom sought to put space between themselves and the wounded man); a love which knows no human boundaries; sacrificial and wise use of personal possessions (oil, wine, money, donkey).

The lawyer had come to Jesus anticipating an interesting abstract theological debate, but he left reflecting on a personal challenge: 'Go and do likewise' (v 37). This call to be a good neighbour echoes down the centuries to you and me, likewise, to challenge us to Christ-like acts of love towards others (see Luke 7:13).

Beginning the service

With: a poster saying, 'There are no strangers here, only friends you haven't yet met' and another poster saying, 'There are no strangers here, only neighbours we have yet to learn to love' – an artist in the congregation could illustrate these

Talk about the posters above, which were displayed in a hotel in India, and discuss the effect they may have had on guests. Then compare this with the world we all share. Here we have to learn to know and love one another as neighbours. The rest of the service will explore what it means to love our neighbour.

Bible reading

The reading of Luke 10:25–37 can be presented in a number of ways. Either the whole passage can be read by one person while five people mime appropriate actions after pauses in the following places: in verse 30a a traveller; verse 30b a robber who mugs him; verse 31 a minister in cassock and surplice or with clerical collar walking pompously by; verse 32 a chorister/church official in choir robes lost in a hymn book/ rule book; verse 33–36 a foreigner miming the actions of help – putting an arm round a victim, bandaging/plastering wounds, giving a drink from a flask, placing down two silver coins. Later during the talk these actors can be visual aids.

Alternatively, the reading can be dramatised. Three voices are needed, one for the narrator, one for the 'expert' and one for Jesus. This version from the NIV (YearC. Proper10_3) is also available as a download.

Narrator: On one occasion an expert in the law stood up to test Jesus.

Expert: Teacher, what must I do to inherit eternal life?

Jesus: What is written in the Law? How do you read it?

Expert: 'Love the Lord your God with all your heart and with all your soul and with all your strength and with all your mind'; and, 'Love your neighbour as yourself.'

Jesus: You have answered correctly. Do this and you will live.

Expert: *(after a pause and spoken smugly)* And who is my neighbour?

Jesus: A man was going down from Jerusalem to Jericho, when he was attacked by robbers. They stripped him of his clothes, beat him and went away, leaving him half-dead. A priest happened to be going down the same road, and when he saw the man, he passed by on the other side. So too, a Levite, when he came to the place and saw him, passed by on the other side. But a Samaritan, as he travelled, came where the man was; and when he saw him, he took pity on him. He went to him and bandaged his wounds, pouring on oil and wine. Then he put the man on his own donkey, brought him to an inn and took care of him. The next day he took out two denarii and gave them to the innkeeper. 'Look after him,' he said, 'and when I return, I will reimburse you for any extra expense you may have.'

Which of these three do you think was a neighbour to the man who fell into the hands of robbers?

Expert: The one who had mercy on him.
Jesus: Go and do likewise.

Luke 10:25–37 (NIV)

For another alternative *The Street Bible* by Rob Lacey presents a vigorous and modern version of the parable of the Good Samaritan.

Bible retelling

The parable can be retold with the aid of smileys projected on a screen. Some people might need to be given the clue that smileys are text symbols which need to be rotated 90 per cent to the right. With the basic smiley :-) the colon for the eyes is then at the top with the hyphen for the nose and the bracket for the mouth underneath.

There was a man who travelled :-I (neutral face)
He was mugged by robbers. (:)t (robber with hat and gun)
The man was hurt. ;'-C (man crying)
A high-ranking religious person <>:) (bishop) walked by and said nothing. <>: x (x = says nothing) (Note not :-X = person with bow tie)
Then a church official +:) (priest) who went by whistling a hymn. +: "
But a stranger helped him. Either @:) (Sikh with turban) or O:) (angel at heart) and compassion produced joy. (:-) (smiley big face)
He had a heart of love. <3 (heart – rotate to left)

Bible talk

With: the five actors who mimed the reading of the parable

Some people are held up as examples. They might be examples of behaviour to imitate. They might be examples of behaviour we should avoid. Jesus told a number of example stories. The parable of the good Samaritan is one such example story. In this parable Jesus introduces a number of people who are bad examples and he gives us one person who is a good example.

What does love in action mean?
(Enter the traveller and the robber who again mime the mugging.)
If we live in a trouble spot where there is mugging, robbery and violence, then we can become afraid. We want to protect ourselves. But we may also want to help. (The traveller lies wounded.)

It is from the religious officials that we might expect love and care.
(Enter the minister who walks by.) Is that what we would call love in action? In fact the priest whom Jesus refers to had a kind of excuse. For all he knew, the traveller was dead and if he, as a priest, touched a dead person, the Old Testament Law (Leviticus 21:1) said he was not in a fit state to lead worship to God. On the other hand the priest was going down that road, away from Jerusalem having carried out his duties. He was not on his way up to

Jerusalem. So actually there was no excuse.

(Enter the choir member singing a hymn and walking by.) Is that what we call love in action? You could make excuses and say this person was worried that robbers were still in the area and that it would be his turn next. He was, however, lost in the words of worship rather than the actions that should characterise a person who worships God.

(Enter the foreigner who stops and starts to help the traveller.) Does he show love to his neighbour? He acted like a caring neighbour and showed what it means to love your neighbour. What did he do? He came; he saw; he conquered with compassion. Compassion is the key idea. The original Greek says his heart was churned up with compassion. The shocking aspect to this story, which would have really shaken Jesus' audience, was that this foreigner was a member of a hated minority group, yet he was doing the right thing, in contrast to the religious men who were respected and admired.

Loving your neighbour means this

- Knowing who your neighbour is. 'Anyone near you' is the original meaning of neighbour. In Jesus' story Jews and Samaritans were not known to be good neighbours. They were considered ancient enemies. Your neighbour includes those whom you have not even considered friends or countrymen. Your neighbour is any person in need. In our world it is like an Iranian helping a Jew; a Taliban fighter helping an American; a Somali pirate helping a European merchant sailor.
- Giving love and showing compassion. What did the foreigner do to show his care? He treated the wounds and bandaged them, took the traveller to a place of safety, took personal care of him for some time, paid for extra care when he had to leave. (The money he paid the innkeeper was enough to cover the next 24 nights.) Loving your neighbour is costly in time, in money, in emotions.

We can all behave like the first two people in the story and pass by on the other side. Recently one clergyman dressed up as a tramp and begged for money from his congregation as they went into church. He was seeing how compassionate they were. He then went inside to take the service (www.dailymail.co.uk/news/article-1033988/Priestdisguises-tramp-teach-churchgoers-lesson.html). We need to show our neighbourly love by meeting needs around us.

Prayers of intercession

With: for each person a sheet with two columns, each with five cells entitled 'Neighbourhood' – in the five cells of the left column are a map/picture of a road, a map of your own village or town, the outline of the country, a picture of the world, the silhouette of a face; a copy of the related emboldened prayer responses (YearC.Proper10_1), also available as a download

Invite people to name or draw specific 'neighbours' in each category in the right-hand column, remembering that these people might not be the people we usually think of as neighbours. Help younger children as appropriate. Alternatively this chart can be completed altogether on an OHP or flip chart. The emboldened sentence is a corporate response.

Lord God, you ask us to love our neighbour.

You ask us to break through barriers to treat everyone as our neighbour.

We remember those people in our own road or street. May we be ready to show love.

A true neighbour is one who shows mercy and compassion.

We remember those in our own wider neighbourhood, in our town/village. Give us eyes to see need and hands that help. May we not pass by.

A true neighbour is one who shows mercy and compassion.

We think of our country. We pray for those people of other cultures. May our arms reach out to all people.

A true neighbour is one who shows mercy and compassion.

We share one world. Help us to show neighbourly love to those who live in poverty.

A true neighbour is one who shows mercy and compassion.

Each person is made in God's image. We pray for those we find difficult to love.

A true neighbour is one who shows mercy and compassion.

Lord, you showed compassion to us. Help us to show compassion to others and so honour the name of Jesus. Amen.

Ending the service

We have celebrated the peace with our immediate neighbours. We then celebrated it with a wider group and then with the whole church community. Christ challenges us to take that peace, that love and compassion into our wider neighbourhoods beyond this church.

The religious expert knew the two great commandments. He also knew they were interlinked. We must love the Lord our God but not leave it there. We must also love our neighbour. The first commandment to love God cannot be fulfilled independently of the second command to love our neighbour.

We go to meet Christ in our neighbourhood outside and in the world. God is our loving and compassionate Saviour. Our hope is in him all day long.

Helpful extras

Music and song ideas

'Brother, sister, let me serve you' is a song which pictures people as fellow travellers on a road helping one another; 'When I needed a neighbour' ends with a personal promise of our availability to serve; 'Hark my soul, it is the Lord' celebrates good Samaritan-type actions of love and compassion in verse two; 'Beauty for brokenness' asks for compassion towards the poor; 'Give me a heart of compassion' asks for compassion, a hope for the lost and a passion for the broken and down.

Statement of faith

Based on Psalm 25, this statement (YearC. Proper10_2) is available as a download.

Notes and comments

'The peace' can be celebrated in stages. Invite people to share 'the peace' with their immediate neighbours in front and behind them. Then invite them to share 'the peace' with those in a wider area. Finally invite them to extend that peace throughout the worshipping community, to enact the ripple effect of Christian neighbourliness.

This service provides the opportunity to feature the work of the Samaritan's Purse charity: www.samaritanspurse.uk.com/ 'meeting critical needs of victims of war, poverty, famine, disease, and natural disaster while sharing the good news of Jesus Christ.'

Alternative online options

Visit www.lightlive.org for additional activities for children, young people and adults. There are many to choose from.

Top Tips on Explaining the Trinity to young people
978 1 84427 396 6

What does the Bible say about God in all his fullness? How has the church wrestled with making sense of the Trinity? This book helps children's and youth workers enrich an understanding of God by what they teach and model in worship, mission, ministry in a multi-faith context, the language they use and the message they communicate!

This book is a must-have for anyone working with people of all ages! For more details visit www.scriptureunion.org.uk

PROPER 11

READINGS: **Genesis 18:1–10a; Luke 10:38–42**
Psalm 15; Colossians 1:15–28

Bible foundations

Aim: to see that hospitality can be offered in many different ways and places

Genesis 18 and 19 focus on the destruction of Sodom, but the account begins on a less solemn note, with the intriguing account of Abraham's hospitality to three strangers. They turn out to be very special guests! The reader is let into the secret from the start (Genesis 18:1), but Abraham only realises the divine character of his chief visitor after a courteous and generous display of hospitality, which includes feet-washing (v 4) and a lavish meal (vs 6–8). He discovers in an unusually direct way that an openness and warm-hearted kindness to others acts as a service to the Lord himself (Matthew 25:40).

The New Testament contains many references to hospitality. It formed the setting for much of Jesus' ministry (see Luke 19:1–10). Also its importance for the early church in a variety of circumstances is found in passages such as Acts 2:46; 10:6; 16:15; Romans 12:13; 1 Timothy 3:2 and Hebrews 13:2. Hospitality is seen as the means by which unity among God's people can be built up, practical needs met and the ministry of itinerant workers aided.

Perhaps the best known incident of hospitality in the New Testament involved Jesus' visit to the home of Mary and Martha (Luke 10:38–42), in Bethany (John 11:1). While Jesus clearly valued the kindness shown to him and recognised the importance of domestic hospitality (vs 7,8), he used Martha's 'distractedness' (v 40) to underline the need for his followers to get their priorities right (v 42). It is also all too easy for busyness and a preoccupation with practical tasks, perhaps performed in the context of church life, to become all-consuming. Appropriate 'hospitality' towards Jesus should combine hands-on service with an overriding concern to develop our relationship with him and learn from him.

Beginning the service

With: at least one person, key to running the service, is at the door to personally welcome every person who arrives – children and adults, newcomers and regulars – before the service begins (Use the regular team to give out hymn books, notice sheets etc.)

Ask if anyone noticed anything different about church today. Ask how it made people feel to be personally welcomed. Ask people to share their different experiences of offering hospitality (you may need to prime people beforehand). This might include putting up relatives or friends, working at a night shelter or on a soup run, or giving a beggar money for a coffee. Also ask people to share experiences of receiving hospitality, such as going to a friend's house for a meal. If you have international experiences of hospitality in different cultures include these.

Explain that God is welcoming and hospitable and invites us to reflect him in that behaviour. Our culture has tended to weaken the role of regular hospitality in our society but God clearly places a very high value on it. Today we will explore what it means that God is hospitable and how we might respond to the challenge to be hospitable too.

Bible reading

With: Genesis 18:1–10 printed or on a screen (The version below (Year C.Proper11_1) adapted from the CEV is also available as a download.)

Split the congregation into three parts: narrator, Abraham, the Lord.

Narrator: One hot summer afternoon Abraham was sitting by the entrance to his tent near the sacred trees of Mamre, when the Lord appeared to him. Abraham looked up and saw three men standing nearby. He quickly ran to meet them, bowed with his face to the ground, and said...

Abraham: Please come to my home where I can serve you. I'll have some water brought, so you can wash your feet, then you can rest under the tree. Let me get you some food to give you strength before you leave. I would be honoured to serve you.

Lord: Thank you very much, we accept your offer.

Narrator: Abraham quickly went to his tent and said to Sarah.

Abraham: Hurry! Get a large sack of flour and make some bread.

Narrator: After saying this, he rushed off to his herd of cattle and picked out one of the best calves, which his servant quickly prepared. He then served his guests some yogurt and milk together with the meat. While they were eating, he stood near them under the trees, and they asked...

Lord: Where is your wife Sarah?

Abraham: She is right there in the tent.

Narrator: One of the guests was the

> Lord, and he said....
> **Lord:** I'll come back about this time next year, and when I do, Sarah will already have had a son.
>
> Genesis 18:1–10 (CEV)

Bible retelling

With: a script for two women, fairly close to each other in age

Martha: It was so exciting. Jesus was coming to visit us! We only had a few hours' notice – he sent one of the disciples on ahead. Dinner for an extra 20 people and only three hours' warning! There was so much to do…

Mary: It was so exciting. Jesus was coming to visit us! We only had a few hours' notice – he sent one of the disciples on ahead. What would he teach us? Would there be room for another woman to join his group to listen? I really needed to pray…

Martha: And then he arrived with the others. I welcomed them and got water. One of the servants washed their feet, while I personally made sure there was plenty of cool watered wine for all the guests. You get so dry and dusty out walking…

Mary: And then he arrived with the others. I welcomed them and invited them to sit with me in the family room. They were in the middle of a discussion so I waited until I really knew what they were debating and then I asked Jesus a question…

Martha: I was so focused – making sure the servants were using the best tableware, checking that the salad was properly washed, testing the sauce to go on the roasted meat. There were so many things to do and I realised Mary was just sitting joining the discussion with Jesus…

Mary: I was so focused – listening carefully to everyone's comments, trying to remember all that I knew of the Psalms and Torah, mentally rearranging things in my head to see how Jesus' teaching fits in. There were so many things to think about and I realised Martha was missing out on it all, rushing around…

Martha: So, I went in and said to Jesus, 'Don't you care that my sister isn't helping? Tell her to come and do her share.' His reply blew me away.

Mary: So, Martha burst in and said to Jesus, 'Don't you care that my sister isn't helping? Tell her to come and do her share.' His reply blew me away.

M and M: He said the conversation was more important than the food and that was what we should focus on!

Bible talk

With: pictures or props related to hospitality such as a welcome mat, tea and biscuits, dustpan and brush, kiss, hug, ear for listening

Offering care and compassion to all

Explain that 'hospitality' and 'hospital' come from the same root word, 'hospes', which is Latin for 'guest'. Both words convey care of and compassion for guests. They may be people we know or strangers. Hospitality is about the care we show. This includes the practical provision we make *(show the tea and biscuits)*, which of course depends on our circumstances; someone may be able to foster a child or young person long term, another may have to offer hospitality away from home – at a cafe, night shelter or church. Hospitality may come anywhere on that scale and at all points in between.

Hospitality reflects the provision God makes for us. Paul reminds us in Colossians that 'in him all things hold together'. God is on a mission to restore all that was damaged by the fall, at the beginning of time. It is God who makes the sun shine, the rain fall, the crops grow. He provides us with family, friends, shelter and comfort.

Preparing to offer hospitality

Integral to provision is preparation. *(Show the dustpan and brush.)* If someone is coming to stay, we will get a room and food ready.

God too is preparing a place for us. He has already invited us to come to his banquet and Jesus has gone to the Father to get everything ready. He offers us hospitality. But there is more to it than that.

One of the commonest comments from retired nurses is that things have become so medically focused that there is no time to spend with patients as people. This is the other side of hospitality. Hospitality is not just about being ready and providing; it is about caring enough to build relationships, to share ourselves. Hospitality is about attitude as well as action. *(Show the welcome mat.)*

Building relationships

Relationship is central to understanding who God is – the three in one God. God is a loving Father who seeks to build his relationship with us and give us what will do us most good.

Abraham practised hospitality by welcoming guests who were strangers, providing for every material need he could. His attitude was of open friendliness and willing service. Was the hospitality reciprocal? Culturally, Abraham and Sarah were impoverished by their lack of a son. The Lord saw this and provided them with a son.

Similarly, Mary and Martha both offered and received hospitality. Later in the Gospels, we hear how Jesus restored Lazarus to them.

What about us? God has prepared a place for us and provided the way for us to be reconciled to himself through the work of Jesus. He longs for us to develop a relationship with him.

Challenge 1

Have we prepared a place for the Spirit to live in us? Have we provided open access for God to renew our minds and replace our hearts of stone with ones of flesh? Have we spent time building relationship?

Challenge 2

Are we prepared to be hospitable? Have we looked at the best ways we can provide for others? Have we opened our hearts to 'love the ones that God loves' and build relationships with others?

Prayer of confession

This confession (YearC.Proper11_2) is available as a download.

Prayers of intercession

With: newspapers; sugar paper; glue sticks; scissors

Give each group of people a few newspapers and ask them to find stories that show people who need hospitality – shelter, food, comfort, care, healing and friendship. Talk about what they need as you cut out the pictures and stick them on sugar paper to make a 'care collage'. Once the collage is made, one or two people in the group ask God to provide directly or through his people for those who need care. Pictures of those who are providing care could also be added and prayers of thanks to God for them could be said.

Ending the service

Ask the congregation to remind you what Abraham gave to the Lord. What did the Lord give? What did Martha and Mary give? What did they gain? What are the three aspects of care you want them to remember? *(Preparation, provision and relationship.)*

Ask them to think how they can build relationships this week that will enable them to develop the gift of practising hospitality.

Conclude by challenging people to shake hands (or hug) at least five people before they leave, including one person they do not usually speak with. As they do so, ask them to think if there is any way they could offer hospitality to each of these people.

Helpful extras

Music and song ideas

There are many songs you could sing: 'Brother, sister, let me serve you'; 'How lovely is thy dwelling place' (or other songs based on Psalm 84); 'Jesus Christ is waiting'; 'Come on in and taste the new wine'; 'Forth in thy name, O Lord, I go'.

If the congregation is used to reflection, project images of those 'in need' with a worship song like 'All who are thirsty' or 'The Lord is gracious and compassionate' played at the same time.

Statement of faith

This statement (Year C.Proper11_3) is available as a download.

Notes and comments

You do not want anyone to leave the service despairing that they cannot entertain a large family to lunch or offer an open home. Sensitively point out that hospitality has many expressions!

For uniformed organisations at church parade, find out if they have taken or plan to take badges related to hospitality, such as home maker or cooking.

You may wish to expand talking about Mary and Martha to explain Mary had a hospitable, relational attitude and Martha demonstrated her hospitality in her actions. We need to balance hospitable actions with the time to build relationships – which Martha missed.

Where Holy Communion is integral to your service, you could outline that the original context for the sharing of bread and wine at the Last Supper and as celebrated in the early church was in the context of a hospitable meal of celebration and remembrance.

Alternative online options

For your convenience the following activity is available as a download: Year C.Proper11_4 Being still – for under-5s. Visit www.lightlive.org for additional activities for children, young people and adults.

Top Tips on Helping a child respond to Jesus
978 1 84427 387 4

- Gives wise advice to help you guide a child on their journey with God
- Explores the varied ways that Bible characters responded to Jesus
- Looks at practical issues such as rites of passage, family influence and the importance of listening.

For more details, visit www.scriptureunion.org.uk

PROPER 12

READINGS: **Genesis 18:20–32; Luke 11:1–13**
Psalm 138; Colossians 2:6–15 [16–19]

Bible foundations

Aim: to explore some of the things that the Bible says about talking with God

Luke underlines the importance of prayer by his depiction of both the practice and teaching of Jesus (see Luke 5:16; 6:12; 18:1–14). In Luke 11:1–4 we have Luke's version of what we now refer to as 'the Lord's Prayer', given in direct response to the disciple's request for guidance on how to pray (v 1). Justifiably, Jesus' response has been understood by Christians down through the centuries as a 'model' of how we should talk with God.

For Jesus, prayer needs to be based on a right understanding of the relationship between God and his people. He is our Father (v 2) and we are his beloved children. This highlights the intimacy and directness of Christian prayer; which needs to be accompanied by appropriate respect ('Hallowed be your name', v 2). The prayer is also marked by humble submission and a strong sense of dependence upon God, reflecting the truth that both our physical and spiritual well-being is a gift from him (vs 3,4).

The parable and teaching which follows (vs 5–13) are set within a culture where both the supply of food and opportunities for its storage were significantly more limited than today. If a grudging neighbour will respond to a request for food in an emergency (v 8), how much more willing is a gracious God to hear and answer our prayers in the best possible way (though this doesn't guarantee a 'Yes'). In this passage Jesus stresses the need for persistence, boldness and expectancy when we speak to God. These characteristics were certainly evident when Abraham interceded for the city of Sodom (Genesis 18:20–33)! This extraordinary incident demonstrates that God will hear our heartfelt and tough questions, though these need to be expressed in a spirit of humbleness and reverence (vs 27,30), accompanied by an openness to God's answer (vs 32,33).

Beginning the service

With: PowerPoint or hard copy images of people communicating

After watching, ask what the images had in common and then invite people to suggest their favourite ways of communicating.

Alternatively you could prepare several mimes of people communicating and ask what all the mimes have in common, such as: someone writing a letter, putting it in an envelope and posting it; typing an email on a keyboard; two people shouting to each other through cupped hands; someone in the pulpit telling someone below that they love them, in Romeo and Juliet style; using a mobile to phone and text. Explain that during this service you will be looking at some of the things that the Bible says about talking with God.

Alternatively, watch the clip from *Bruce Almighty* (towards the end) where Bruce and God talk and God asks Bruce to pray. Bruce gives an unhelpful and then a helpful example. Ask the congregation what ideas come into their heads when you say 'prayer' and whether they are realistic!

Bible reading

Split everyone into four groups and project the words (or print them) from Luke 11:1–13 so that everyone can join in reading it, in the four groups in turn. A CEV version (YearC.Proper12_1) is available as a download.

Bible retelling

With: old man; TV chat show host

Host: Tonight's guest is a born survivor! He has lived through many adventures and even survived arguing with God! A special welcome for… Abraham!

Abraham: Thank you, it's lovely to be here…

H: Indeed – almost a miracle we might say. Tell me, what is God like to meet in person?

A: Well, I always found him to be very warm and welcoming. Then again, he did have special plans for my family.

H: Yes, not everyone has found him to be so warm. Can you tell us about what happened at Sodom and Gomorrah?

A: You have to realise those cities were full of people who were blatantly denying God's way of living – selfish, inhospitable, unkind…

H: *(interrupting)* But God did wipe them all out.

A: Yes, it's the biggest regret of my life that I didn't press God on that.

H: Ah, yes – the famous 'argument'!

A: Well, I don't know about argument… I just reminded God about who he was and what he was like…

H: Tell us more…

A: God came to warn me that he was going to deal with those towns. They'd ignored all the warnings he sent. But I said, what about the good people there?

H: How did God take that?

A: He was very amenable – each time I lowered the number by saying, 'But what if there were 40…or

H: 30… or 20', he agreed to save the whole city. It wasn't really an argument, because God kept agreeing with me.
H: So why do you regret it then?
A: Well, you know what happened there. The cities were destroyed. And I wonder if I just didn't go far enough.
H: What do you mean?
A: Well, I stopped asking when we got down to ten good people. God said he would save the city if he found ten good people, but there obviously weren't even ten people. It shows what dreadful places Sodom and Gomorrah were. And I just wonder – what would God have said if I had asked, 'What if you only find one good person'? You see my nephew and his family lived there… my nephew, Lot.
H: Well, I guess we'll never know – so folks, there's the story of the man who argued with God, AND SURVIVED!

Bible talk

With: megaphone, placard, trumpet or klaxon and people to use them; copy of the sentences of the prayer message in the **Prayer activity**, also available as a download (YearC.Proper12_2)

Ask the people with the equipment to jump up and make a noise to get everyone's attention. Once they have been quietened and have sat down again, ask if the congregation thinks God needs us to make that kind of fuss to get his attention.

When the disciples asked Jesus about prayer, he made things very simple and gave them a pattern to use when they wanted to pray and talk with God. Display the prayer message and fill it in together as you go through the **Bible talk**, making it as personal as possible to the whole congregation. Everyone will be encouraged to complete their own prayer message in the **Prayer activity**.

Getting started

Ask people, including the children, how they address a variety of people – head teachers, the doctor, church leader, neighbour, friends and family. How might you address someone differently if you wanted them to do something for you? Using the title 'Our Father' at the start of this prayer reminds us that we are part of one family together – our prayers are not just for ourselves, but others too. It also reminds us that a perfect dad delights in hearing his children and talking back – it raises expectation of conversation rather than a monologue! Note that some versions include 'in heaven' which also reminds us to give God due respect as well as love.

Fill in: Hello, God, Father God, it's _____ speaking.

Places of need

God has invited us to be his co-workers and by asking for the kingdom to be visible on earth, we can bring to God the people, places and situations where we know there to be darkness, pain or sin and wrongdoing. These prayers for others may be offered with tears, in silence or with angry shouts. God understands when we are angry about injustice or oppression or abuse.

Fill in: You know just how bad things are in _____. Please set up your kingdom there.

What we need

As a good father, God delights in giving good things to us, providing for all our needs, including the food we eat. We can go to him with concerns great or small – good weather for an outdoor event, enough food to feed the family, a secure place to live, healing for our pet. Ask for suggestions for what people need.

Fill in: You know that I need _____. Please provide for me what I need.

Sorry

At the same time, God wants us to strengthen our relationship with him. That means being honest about when we fail. When we admit our failures, mistakes and wrongdoing, God does forgive us and starts again with us. However, his desire is to help us stand firm when we are tempted to do wrong. So we can ask for him to help us as we try to move on.

Fill in: I am sorry, God, for the time this week when I did something wrong or failed to do something such as_____. Please forgive me.

The prayer Jesus used was a good model, but it isn't the only sort of prayer! There are other kinds of prayer too. Abraham offered hospitality to the three men and then realised that God was present. God confided his plans to Abraham, who felt a need to butt in on God's business. He held the mirror back up to God and reminded God of who he was – a God of justice, for sure, but also a God of mercy and compassion. We can butt in too to ask God to show who and what he is!

The Psalmist poured out his heart in the psalms; he shared his love of God, his praise of God but also his confusion with God and even his anger and disappointment with God. God can take it. The world can be a cruel and harsh place. When our emotions are stirred, God prefers us to let them out rather than bottle them up. He understands us and does not get irritated or annoyed by us being honest.

Challenge the congregation to think of times during the week when they could easily put aside time to be with God – to share their minds and hearts with him and even to hear his still, small voice speak back.

Prayer activity

With: a prayer message, also available as a download (YearC.Proper12_2) for everyone to complete; pens and pencils

These can be completed either in a group or in pairs or individually. The messages could then be collected and brought to the front to physically represent offering up our prayers. Anyone who is not keen or able to write could draw themselves, a place in difficulty, their last meal (or what they need) and write the words 'Sorry, God' inside the boxes, as appropriate. Make sure everyone has the help they need to complete this.

My prayer message to God

Hello, God, Father God, it's _____ speaking.

You know just how bad things are in _____. Please set up your kingdom there.

You know what I need _____

> ------------------------------.
>
> Please provide for me what I need.
>
> I am sorry, God, for the time when I did something wrong or failed to do something such as
>
> ------------------------------.
>
> Please forgive me.

Prayer of confession

This prayer, available as a download, (YearC.Proper12_4) could be read by two halves of the congregation.

Ending the service

Remind everyone that we can speak with God in many different ways; we can whisper our love, we can weep our sorrows, we can shout our anger, we can bargain on behalf of others, we can chat over our day, we can plead for help, we can ask for mercy. God does not limit our communications, though we often do. He is keen to 'incline his ear' and listen.

Together say the following two phrases, first in a whisper, then by shouting, then speaking slowly and deliberately, and finally with enthusiasm: Dear God, thank you for being with us today. Thank you for listening.

Helpful extras

Music and song ideas

An interesting song to play at **Beginning the service** might be 'Hungry I come to you' by Kathryn Scott.

During the **Prayer activity**, fill the silence with an appropriate song such as 'Father in Heaven, grant to your children' by Niles and Maquiso or Brian Doerkson's 'Our Father, in heaven, holy be your name'.

Other songs might include 'My lips shall praise you'; 'Father God, I wonder'; 'Guide me, O thou great Redeemer'; 'Seek ye first the kingdom of God'; 'We have sung our songs of victory' or others to reflect the focus on prayer.

Statement of faith

This statement (YearC.Proper12_3) is available as a download.

Notes and comments

If you have a parade service, quiz the children about special ways of communicating that the group use; for example, the Guides use a raised right hand to mean 'stand still and stop talking'.

If there is a baptism, explain that prayer will be a crucial part of the life of faith and encourage everyone present to be serious in the time they spend praying for the baptised person – and the relationship of love and support they build too.

You may wish to include in the **Bible talk** other forms of prayer that fit with your church tradition.

Alternative online options

For your convenience the following activity is available as a download: YearC.Proper12_5 Action prayer for under-5s. Visit www.lightlive.org for additional activities for children, young people and adults.

PROPER 13

READINGS: **Ecclesiastes 1:2,12–14; 2:18–23; Luke 12:13–21**
Psalm 49:1,2; Colossians 3:1–11

Bible foundations
Aim: to explore what the Bible says about possessions

The parable of the rich fool in Luke 12:13–21 comes in the context of Jesus' warning about the hypocrisy of the Pharisees and his encouragement to the disciples to live as those who trust in God and who therefore don't need to fear judgement, either by God or people. To start with, a man asked Jesus to rule in a dispute with his brother over their inheritance. The man is concerned about having an equal part of the possessions to be divided. Jesus calls this what it is: greed. He warns against being so preoccupied with possessions that God is forgotten.

The parable of the rich fool illustrates this perfectly. He has a bumper harvest and barns which are too small to hold all his crops. Rather than thanking God and giving the surplus away, the fool comes up with the idea of tearing down his existing barns and building bigger ones in order to keep all of his harvest for himself. God speaks to the rich fool, pointing out to him that when he dies his crops will do him no good. He will have the benefits neither of his crops nor of God's love, having ignored God during his life on earth.

Jesus tells the crowd listening to him that the same will happen to anyone who keeps their possessions to themselves, and doesn't thank God or use their possessions for the good of others. The writer of Ecclesiastes makes a similar point in 2:18–23. Why work to simply gain possessions to leave to someone else?

This message still has a huge challenge for us. We face the same temptations that the rich man faced: to keep all our possessions for ourselves. We are faced with the same choice as the rich fool: will we keep what we have to ourselves, or will we thank God for what he gives us and use what we have to help others?

Beginning the service

With: a suitcase overflowing with clothes; a drawer overflowing with toys; a briefcase overflowing with papers

Show the three objects one at a time and with each one, ask, 'What's the problem here?' then, 'What can be done about it?' You're looking for answers that draw out that the object is overflowing and that the solution is to get a bigger suitcase/drawer/briefcase. You may get answers along the lines of 'Take fewer clothes', 'Don't have as many toys', 'Take less papers', but direct the conversation so that you get the solution of 'Get a bigger one'.

The theme of the service is to think about how we use what we already have, rather than trying to get more and more things.

Bible reading

Ecclesiastes 1:2,12–14; 2:18–23 could be read thoughtfully, with regret. Introduce this by saying that the king's son (probably Solomon) was pondering what would happen to all his wealth and possessions when he died. He speaks of working hard only to have to hand on the results of this work to the next generation who haven't worked for it, not knowing whether they will use the inheritance wisely. How might you have advised him?

Luke 12:13–21 could be read using the following script based on the CEV, also available as a download (YearC.Proper13_1). The congregation's parts should be displayed either on paper or on the screen, with a board on which is the word 'ALL' to display when everyone needs to join in. Readers (narrator, man, Jesus, a rich man, God) could wear appropriate costumes. As props, use a cardboard model of a small barn, which, at the appropriate point in the story, the rich fool throws away to replace with a model of a bigger barn. The final response has been inserted to bring home the point of the parable. Although non-readers cannot speak the words there is the acting to watch.

Narrator: A man in a crowd said to **Jesus:**
Man: Teacher, tell my brother to give me my share of what our father left us when he died.
All: **Tell his brother to give him his share.**
Jesus: Who gave me the right to settle arguments between you and your brother? Don't be greedy! Owning a lot of things won't make your life safe.
All: **No – owning a lot of things won't make your life safe.**
Narrator: So Jesus told them this story:
Jesus: A rich man's farm produced a big crop, and he said to himself,
Rich man: What can I do? I don't have a place large enough to store everything.
All: **He doesn't have a place large enough to store everything!**
Rich man: I know what I'll do. I'll tear down my barns and build bigger ones, where I can store **All** my grain and other goods.
All: **He'll tear down his barns and build bigger ones!**
Rich man: Then I'll say to myself, 'You have stored up enough good things to last for years to come. Live it up! Eat, drink, and enjoy yourself.'
Narrator: But God said to him:
God: You fool! Tonight you will die. Then who will get what you have

	stored up?
All:	**Who will get what he's stored up when he's dead?**
Jesus:	This is what happens to people who store up everything for themselves, but are poor in the sight of God.
All:	**This is what happens when we store up everything for ourselves, but are poor in the sight of God.**

Bible talk

With: memory verse used in the **Game**, Luke 12:15

Recap the story, asking a series of questions. To make sure that everyone feels involved, target a particular question at a specific age group. For example:

11–14s: What did Jesus say to the man who asked him to settle an argument with his brother

8–10s? How did Jesus describe the man in the story who had a lot of crops?

6–8s: Where did the man put his crops?

Under-5s: What did the man do to his barns?

All: What happened when the rich fool died? What was Jesus teaching through this story? Then learn the memory verse, using the jigsaw of the barn as a **Game**.

The story starts with a man in the crowd asking Jesus to settle an argument between him and his brother about what belonged to each of them. Jesus told the man off. He said, 'Don't be greedy. Owning a lot of things won't make your life safe.'

Tell the following true story or one similar known to you: Shadrach was a vicar and a farmer in Kenya. One year he was given a pile of rich manure to use on his fields. As a result his harvest that year was astounding. It was the talk of the town. He cut it down and brought one-tenth of his crop into the church because he wanted to thank God. It took up so much space. Just imagine! This was the talk of the town! And then he shared the harvest with others. Ask how this man's attitude and behaviour was different from the rich man in Jesus' story.

At the very end of the story God asked the rich fool who would get his crops when he died. In other words, God was telling him that all the crops in the world wouldn't do the rich fool any good when he died. When he'd finished telling the story Jesus told the crowd that the same thing would happen to anyone who stored up things for themselves but ignored God.

In pairs or small groups ask people to make a list of the good things that they have been given or that they have worked hard to make or earn. Then ask them to think about which of these they would be reluctant to share with others or which they pride themselves on possessing. (This should only take a short time.)

Sometimes we're tempted to take what we have for granted and to keep it for ourselves. Like the rich fool, we're tempted to ignore God and do everything in our own strength. But we know that if we say sorry to God he will forgive us and make us like new because he loves us. According to the story from Luke 12:13–21, everything we have comes from God. If we want to avoid being like the rich fool we need to give thanks to God for all that he gives us and then use what we have to help others.

Prayer of confession

This prayer is also available as a download (YearC.Proper13_2). The congregation join in the emboldened words.

Heavenly Father,
We are sorry for the times when we are greedy.
Please forgive us.
We are sorry when we take for granted all that you give us.
Please forgive us.
We are sorry for clinging on to all that you give us as if it is ours alone.
Please forgive us.
We are sorry for when we rely on our own strength and not yours.
Please forgive us.
Wash us and make us clean again, for Jesus' sake. **Amen.**

Prayer activity

With: a square sheet of paper and a pencil for each group; a timer

This **Prayer activity** should follow the **Prayer of confession**. Divide into small groups. If unaccompanied children are present make sure that there is an adult with each small group of children.

The mistake of the rich man was to hold on to the bumper harvest with which God had blessed him, without giving thanks to God for it. Saying 'thank you' to God for all he gives us helps us not to fall into the same trap. Using the timer, give the small groups 2 minutes to write down as many things as they can think of to thank God for.

When the 2 minutes are up, ask people to fold their sheet of paper into the shape of a flower or something simple you might be thankful for. An Internet search will give you instructions on how to fold a paper square into a flower. (Is there anyone in church who is an expert in origami?) When complete, each group passes their folded prayers of thanks to a neighbouring group who then open up the paper to read out and share in the list of thanks. If appropriate, someone in the group should lead a short prayer of thanks to God.

Prayers of intercession

Ask for people to prepare intercessions for people in our country and in our world who are living in hunger and poverty or where the harvest has failed or is predicted to fail.

Ending the service

Collect in the paper 'flowers' and read out loud some of the things which people wanted to thank God for. Remind everyone that God has blessed us with all sorts of good things. The point of the Bible story is not to cling on to everything we have, but to use it to help others.

Conclude by praying as follows:

Heavenly Father, thank you for the many ways you bless us:
For warmth, homes, food, friends and family.
Thank you for loving us as your precious children.
Help us never to take these things for granted.
Help us always to be grateful and thankful to you.

Lord Jesus, give us the courage to use what we have to help others.
Amen.

You could use the final prayer on its own to end the service.

Helpful extras

Music and song ideas

'All to Jesus I surrender' ('I surrender all'); 'Blessed be your name in the land that is plentiful'; 'For the fruits of his creation'; 'God of grace and God of glory'; 'Give thanks to the Lord' ('Forever'); 'I count as nothing every earthly blessing'; 'I give you all the honour' ('I will worship you'); 'I will enter his gates with thanksgiving in my heart'; 'Kyrie Eleison' ('Lord, have compassion') Taizé chant; 'Praise God from whom all blessings flow'; 'Seek ye first the kingdom of God'; 'Take my life and let it be consecrated, Lord, to thee'; 'Thank you, Lord, you love us'; 'Yes, I thank you, O Lord'.

Game

With: a large piece of card, on which is the outline of a barn, divided into four segments so that when cut up, it makes a jigsaw puzzle – each segment contains the following, to be read consecutively: Don't be greedy!/Owning a lot of things/won't make your life/safe. Luke 12:15

Make up the barn jigsaw with the words displayed outwards, so that they can be seen by everyone. Read through the whole verse a couple of times altogether. Then turn over one of the sections, blanking out one phrase at a time. With no words left on view, everyone should be saying it together from memory.

Notes and comments

The reading from Ecclesiastes 1:2,12–14; 2:18–23 sets the scene very well for the Gospel reading from Luke 12:13–21. If you use this reading do give a brief explanation of it before it is read.

If there is a baptism, dedication or thanksgiving for a child as part of this service you could include a challenge to the child's parents to thank God for their child and to dedicate their child to God.

Alternative online options

Visit www.lightlive.org for additional activities for children, young people and adults.

PROPER 14

READINGS: **Genesis 15:1–6; Luke 12:32–40**
Psalm 33:12–22; Hebrews 11:1–3,8–16

Bible foundations

Aim: to learn not to hang on to what we have, so that we can be ready to serve Jesus

In Luke 12:32–34 Jesus challenges the disciples about their attitude to possessions. He tells them not to be afraid because God wants to give them the kingdom. Their response should be to sell their possessions and use the income to help the poor. Their hearts will then be in the right place, focused on God and not themselves. As a result, their treasure will be in heaven, with God. Nothing (for them the danger came from moths and rust), not even an economic crisis, will be able to destroy that treasure. This attitude towards God was exactly what Abraham showed, in Genesis 15:6. God gave him a promise and Abraham trusted him to keep his word.

The parable of the master and the servants in Luke 12:35–40 continues the theme of serving Jesus, with the focus on being ready. The servants were to be ready for their master's return. The one verse parable about the thief speaks of being constantly ready to protect your house, because you never know when the thief will come.

These parables challenge the disciples to be ready for the Son of Man (Jesus himself) to come. Luke is referring both to the first coming of Jesus to Israel and his second coming as Lord of the universe. This is a complicated concept to explore in all-age worship, so it's being expressed throughout as a readiness to follow Jesus and to do what he wants us to do.

In order to follow where God wants us to go and to do what he wants, we need to hold on lightly to what we have. If we cling on to our possessions our focus will be on our own lives and not on Jesus. Being ready to use our possessions for the good of others, keeping our attention firmly on Jesus and serving him, our hearts will be in the right place. We'll be storing up treasure in heaven.

Beginning the service

With: a blank PowerPoint slide which someone can type into; or an OHP with a blank acetate; or a flip chart; suitable pens

Ask everyone to imagine that someone very important has sent a letter to the church saying that they are coming to visit. Ask what you would need to do to get the church ready and everyone present, to welcome them. Make a list on the PowerPoint slide, the acetate or the flipchart. Explain that the theme of the service is to explore what we need to do with our possessions, in order to be ready to serve Jesus.

Divide the congregation into groups A, B and C and then say the following response based on Luke 12:33,34,40, also available as a download (YearC.Proper14_1).

Group A: Make sure your treasure is safe in heaven.
Group B: Where thieves cannot steal it and moths cannot destroy it.
Group C: Your heart will always be where your treasure is.
All: **Always be ready! You don't know when the Son of Man will come.**

Sing a suitable opening song such as 'Make way, make way!'

Bible reading

Genesis 15:1–6 could be read with a narrator, Abram and the Lord. Explain that Abram was Abraham's name when God first called him. The name 'Abraham' sounds like 'Father of many nations'.

Bible retelling

The following script from Luke 12:32–40 (CEV) is an action reading. During the reading everyone listens for the words in bold. Whenever they hear one they need to do the action that goes with it. Ask for volunteers to do the actions at the front, during the reading. The key to doing this effectively is to read at a reasonable pace, not allowing long pauses for people to do the actions.

Money: pretend to be counting money
Treasure: pretend to be hugging a pot of treasure to protect it
Ready: sit up really straight, look bright and alert
Servant: pretend to be dusting or polishing
Master: still sitting down, pretend to have a nose in the air, looking superior

> My little group of disciples, don't be afraid! Your Father wants to give you the kingdom. Sell what you have and give the money to the poor. Make yourselves money bags that never wear out. Make sure your treasure is safe in heaven, where thieves cannot steal it and moths cannot destroy it. Your heart will always be where your treasure is.
>
> Be **ready** and keep your lamps burning just like those servants who wait up for their **master** to return from a wedding feast. As soon as he comes and knocks, they open the door for him. Servants are fortunate if their **master** finds them awake and **ready** when he comes! I promise you that he will get **ready** and have his servants sit down so he can serve them. Those servants are really fortunate if their **master** finds them

> **ready**, even though he comes late at night or early in the morning. You would surely not let a thief break into your home, if you knew when the thief was coming. So always be **ready**! You don't know when the Son of Man will come.
>
> Luke 12:32–40 (CEV)

Bible talk

With: the text of the story 'Ready, Steady, Pack!' available as a download (YearC. Proper14_2); a storyteller's armchair visible by all

Ask the children to sit down on the floor around you, so that they can listen to the story, 'Ready, Steady, Pack!' Read it out loud with expression. (It is a story about three brothers who needed to be ready when their father came to take them home from holiday.) A different person could read the story, to make it clear when the story finishes and the **Bible talk** begins. It will take about 4 minutes to read.

After the story, be careful to make the links between it, the Bible story and the theme of the service. If you have used the charades as a **Game** you should also refer to those to make further links. This can be done by asking questions to explore the story. See examples below but think of others.

- Which brother was the only one ready to go home with their dad?
- What happened to Harry? Why?
- What mistake did David make?
- What was the result of that mistake?
- What was the similarity between John in the 'Ready, Steady, Pack!' story and the servants in the story Jesus told? (The answer is that they were all ready.)
- At the start of the **Bible reading**, what did Jesus tell his disciples to do?
- (In 'Ready, Steady, Pack!' Harry and David got left behind because they weren't ready. Harry's mistake was to unpack his suitcase after he'd packed it. David's was to have too many possessions which he couldn't get in his suitcase. He couldn't bear to leave anything behind at Aunt Edie's.)
- Which of the three brothers do you think Jesus would want us to be like?
- Why? (You're looking for the answer of John, because he was ready to go, not necessarily because he was tidy – this is not a challenge to untidy people to be tidy. Nowhere in the Bible is that said!)

We should be ready to follow Jesus wherever he wants us to go, and ready to do whatever he wants us to do. But we can't do that if we're like Harry who unpacked his case and wasn't ready, or like David, who loved everything he had so much that he couldn't bear to leave anything behind and so wasn't ready either!

Jesus does not want us to cling on to what we have. As he said to the disciples, we need to make sure that what is important to us is our friendship with him, and not our toys, or what we own, or how much money we have in the bank. When we make our friendship with Jesus more important than all that belongs to us, we're doing what Jesus told the disciples to do: we're storing up treasure in heaven with God. Then we will always be ready to follow Jesus and to do what he wants us to do.

Prayer of confession

This prayer is available as a download (YearC.Proper14_3). Either use the prayer on PowerPoint, in a written order of service, or by telling the congregation what the response is.

Prayers of intercession

With: copies of pictures on card of a poor person, a heart, treasure and a man ready to race; pens or pencils; display board; something to stick prayers on the board

Give one picture to each person. (You could give these out as people arrive.) Make sure that there are roughly equal numbers of each picture. Also give out pencils or pens.

Ask people to pray according to the picture they have. They could write or draw their prayer on the back of their card.

The poor person: pray for the poor of the world.
Heart: focus on telling God you love him.
Treasure: ask God to help you share your possessions to help others.
Man racing: ask God to help you to be ready to follow him.

When people have finished, they should take their card to the display board and stick it up. While people are writing or drawing their prayers and sticking them to the board, you could play the song, 'Father, I place into your hands'.

Ending the service

With: a brief summary of what has been learned in the service; a set of 'Treasure Prayer Cards' (A6), one for each person (on one side is the picture from the **Prayers of intercession** and on the other the following words: Make sure your treasure is safe in heaven … Your heart will always be where your treasure is. Luke 12:33,34)

Ask everyone to turn to their neighbour and share what one thing they will tell their friend or family member about the service. What have they learned? (Children will be very used to doing this at school.) Then give everyone a card, giving people time to read it. Pray as follows and encourage people this week to put the card somewhere they can see it, as an encouragement to be ready to serve Jesus.

Heavenly Father,
Thank you for all that you give us.
Help us not to guard what we have as if it only belongs to us.
Help us to use all that we have to help others.
Give us strength to be always ready to serve you.
We ask this in Jesus' name. Amen.

Helpful extras

Music and song ideas

'All my hope on God is founded'; 'Be thou my vision'; 'Blessed be your name, O Lord, in the land that is plentiful'; 'Christ is the King'; 'O friends rejoice'; 'Father, I place into your hands'; 'Fix your eyes upon Jesus'; 'Glorious things of you are spoken'; 'He is Lord'; 'I give my heart to what I treasure' (Treasure); 'I love you more each day'; 'In Christ alone'; 'In heavenly love abiding'; 'Make way, make way for Christ the King'; 'My God, how wonderful thou art'; 'O Lord of heaven and earth and sea'; 'Open my eyes, Lord, I want to see Jesus'; 'Praise God from whom all blessings flow'; 'We look to you, Almighty God'; 'You servants of the Lord'.

Game

If you are using this game of charades, it will be most effective if it comes before the **Bible talk**, as the theme of 'getting ready' will be touched on then.

Divide the congregation into teams. Before the service starts, ask someone who is good at miming to mime at the front a series of tasks. Give them the tasks in advance so that they can prepare their mime. In the service, ask for another volunteer to spot which team puts their hand up first and to keep the score. You might like to use PowerPoint, an OHP or a flip chart to keep track of the score.

The person mimes a number of scenes of 'getting ready', such as packing for a holiday, getting ready for bed, getting ready for a visitor, getting ready for work, getting ready to go out in the rain. Add your own ideas. When all the teams have had an equal number of turns, announce the winning team.

Notes and comments

The other set readings from Psalm 33:12–22, Genesis 15:1–6 and Hebrews 11:1–3,8–16 all explore the idea of trusting in God. For Abraham the challenge was not to look at the impossibility of him and Sarah having children, but to trust God to be faithful to his promise. This is explored both in Genesis 15 and Hebrews 11:1–3,8–16. The Psalmist speaks of depending on God and not on horses or people's strength. These all link with Jesus' teaching on being ready to welcome him by holding on lightly to possessions. All involve depending on God and not on things that the world values. If you use these passages in addition to Luke 12:32–40 you will need to establish those links clearly for people.

If your service includes a baptism or thanksgiving for a child, speak in terms of helping the child to learn what it means to be ready to follow Jesus. You could include the child and family in the intercessions, praying that the family will be ready themselves and will teach the child to be ready to follow Jesus.

If the service includes Holy Communion speak of how sharing in bread and wine helps us to keep our focus on Jesus.

Alternative online options

Visit www.lightlive.org for additional activities for children, young people and adults.

PROPER 15

READINGS: **Hebrews 11:29 – 12:2; Luke 12:49–56**
Jeremiah 23:23–29; Psalm 82

Bible foundations
Aim: to put our trust in God in the face of opposition or difficulty

Opposition and difficulty have always been part of living God's way. That was true for people of Old Testament times and for Christians following Jesus up to the present day. And, of course, this was illustrated ultimately in the life and death of God's Son, Jesus.

The letter of the Hebrews was probably written to Jewish Christians. It's obvious that they were having a hard time. Experts can't be sure who the author is, but it's clear he wants to encourage his readers to keep going. He sets about explaining how Jesus – prophet, priest and king – is greater than all that has gone before. Jesus is now the one and only way to God the Father.

Chapter 11 is a catalogue covering thousands of years of God's people who trusted in him and endured unimaginable suffering for his sake. (Jeremiah was one such sufferer – Jeremiah 23:23–29.) Yet, these men and women of faith didn't have the privilege of knowing Jesus as their Saviour, as we do. Therefore, says the writer at the beginning of chapter 12, shouldn't we, who do have the knowledge of what Jesus has done for us, be ready and willing to persevere in whatever difficulties we face for his sake?

Hebrews 12:1,2 invites us to imagine a great stadium full of supporters – perhaps the believers who've gone before us – cheering us on. We need to throw off anything which gets in the way of our performance. At the finishing line stands Jesus, urging us on, wanting us to finish the course he has set for us. Luke 12:49–53 underlines the reality and difficulty of our call to live for him. But we know what Jesus has done for us and we can trust in his promises. So, let's get ready to run the race. Let's fix our eyes on Jesus.

Beginning the service

With: simple fitness training equipment (eg weights, skipping ropes, fitballs, small trampoline, exercise bike); cumbersome clothing (see later); large, lightweight boxes

Encourage children or young people to use the fitness training equipment as people gather for worship, ensuring supervision at all times. Then start the service by welcoming everyone.

Invite two or three young people to take part in an 'obstacle race' set out around the meeting area or up and down the aisle, with a finishing tape to mark the end. Ask each competitor to put on cumbersome clothing such as wellington boots, heavy overcoats, hats and gloves and give each of them a large lightweight box to carry. This is a walking race which will give time for the rest of the congregation to cheer the competitors on.

Congratulate the winner. Did any of them throw off their awkward clothing en route or get rid of their large box (see Hebrews 12:1)?

The race you've just witnessed wasn't made easy. For some Christians going God's way is often difficult. The Bible makes it clear that it won't always be easy to live for God and we have to train ourselves for when things are tough. That might mean letting go of some things in our lives so that we can focus on Jesus more clearly. The Bible compares the Christian life to a race which is the theme of this service.

Bible reading

With: banner or sign to hold up which says in large, clear letters: 'faith'

Explain that Hebrews 11 is about the difficulties God's people have faced over centuries of time and about their faith and trust in God which enabled them to cope with the suffering. The reading of Hebrews 11:29 – 12:2 aims to bring out the importance of faith or trust in God in the face of difficulties and opposition.

Two readers prepare the reading in advance and a volunteer will hold up the 'faith' sign at points agreed with the readers. At these points everyone will be invited to say the word 'faith'. For example: 'By faith the people passed through…' etc.

The congregation can say the word 'faith' at other appropriate points, not just where the word occurs in the text. For example: I do not have time to tell about Gideon (everyone says: 'faith'), Barak (everyone says: 'faith')… etc.

The readers need to be aware when the congregation is going to speak. End with everyone saying together, 'faith'.

Bible retelling

With: a prepared and well-rehearsed sketch involving two volunteers to read or speak the words from memory; a group of at least five 'actors'; simple props to suggest the different characters

This is a suggestion for a dramatised reading of Hebrews 11:29 – 12:2. The general idea is that while the readers are reading alternate parts or words from Hebrews 11:29–39, individual or groups of actors walk across the front of the 'stage' area acting out the role of the characters in the reading. Actors will need to keep moving and turn around quickly and cross the 'stage' again as a different character, or acting out whatever is being described. The overall impression should be of a large number of people who down through the ages have lived faithfully for God.

The group should use their imaginations in preparation, using humour wherever appropriate. For example in the list of characters in verse 32, the actors could deliberately look increasingly tired as they hurry to keep up with the reading, while doing something different each time to suggest the different characters.

Conclude the Bible retelling/sketch as follows: as the readers come to the end of Hebrews 11:40, the actors look exhausted from rushing backwards and forwards. They then come to the two readers and, as a group, they put their arms around one another's shoulders. Addressing the congregation they say together (breathlessly, but with emphasis to encourage everyone) the words of Hebrews 12:1,2.

Bible talk

With: two or three prepared interviewees to talk about how following Jesus has sometimes been difficult or examples of how they've coped with opposition to their faith (include adults and young people); an image of Jesus on the cross

It's not easy living for God

Comment that it wasn't easy for Jesus to follow God's way and he made it clear that following him wouldn't be easy for us either. Listen to what he said. Read Luke 12:49–56 with a solemn voice, which could have a threatening thudding drum beat in the background.

Explain that, like the Old Testament heroes you heard about in the earlier reading from Hebrews, following Jesus is sometimes costly for us too. You could give brief examples. Then say that you're going to hear from people in your congregation about difficulties they have faced because of their faith in Jesus – and how they had to trust God through those times.

Trust in God

Introduce your interviewees, encouraging them to tell the congregation their story:

- A time when it has been difficult to be a Christian or they've faced opposition.
- How faith and trust in God played an important part in that experience.

If your church has a mission partner serving God in a difficult situation, you could include a phone or Skype interview with them.

End this section of the talk by emphasising the important role of faith and trust in our living for God. Point out that although the Old Testament heroes were ready to suffer for their faith, they didn't have the special privilege of knowing… who? (Hebrews 11:39,40). Ask the children/young people if they know who you are talking about – the answer is 'Jesus'!

Look to Jesus

(At this point show the image of Jesus on the cross.) When it's hard living God's way, what should we do? Say that the writer of the book of Hebrews gives us some clues. Read Hebrews 12:1,2 again. Then bring out the following points:

- We're not alone. There are many others who have lived faithfully for God in the

past. Then, there are all the Christians we know and those in church here today. Imagine them all standing around you, as if you're in a race, cheering you on (a bit like in the race earlier) to the finishing line, where Jesus stands ready to welcome you.
- We'll need to persevere. It's not easy running a race – or living for God. We need to be determined and get rid of all the things that get in the way. Ask for some suggestions of things that might 'hinder' (v 1).
- Fix our eyes on Jesus. He's run the race, even though it was more costly than we can imagine – and he has made it possible for us to 'win' the race too, because of his death and resurrection (v 2). Keep our eyes on him.

Encourage people to support one another in the difficulties they face and always to stay focused on Jesus, trusting in him.

Prayer of confession

With: the image of Jesus on the cross from the Bible talk or a large wooden cross; a raised area at the foot of the cross, eg a table covered with a cloth; three or four large rocks (set up a pile of these on the table) and stones (enough for one for each person)

Say these words from Hebrews 12:1: Such a large crowd of witnesses is all around us. So we must get rid of everything that slows us down, especially the sin that just won't let go. (CEV)

In a time of quiet, ask people to consider if there are any things which are getting in the way of their living for God, such as sin to confess or obstacles in their lives that stop them following Jesus. Encourage everyone to talk with God about these things (or, if people are comfortable to do so in your church, they could ask someone else to pray with them).

Remind everyone that we need to persevere in living for God. As a sign of wanting to persevere and deliberately 'throwing off' things that get in the way, invite people to quietly come forward to reverently place a stone (given to them as they entered church) on the pile at the foot of the cross. Alternatively, if you wanted to remind people of the 'race' theme, you could set up a finishing line and urge people to come forward with energy.

Prayers of intercession

With: images as PowerPoint slides, or printed on the service sheet, of Christians living in difficult situations, in your area, known to the church or found through an Internet search; quiet reflective music

Introduce the images, encouraging people to pray for the people and situations. Play quiet music so that people can pray aloud or in silence.

Encourage everyone to join in the following words at the end: Let us fix our eyes on Jesus (Hebrews 12:2).

Ending the service

With: small crosses (could be simple wooden ones, palm crosses, or cut out from card), one for each person; the words of Jude 24,25 displayed on PowerPoint available as a download (YearC.Proper15_1)

Ask volunteers to give out the crosses. Encourage people to take their cross home and put it somewhere they will see it often as a reminder of Jesus and what he went through for us, and as an encouragement to persevere when things make it difficult to keep trusting in God.

Close by praying for one another using the words of the doxology from Jude 24,25 (NIV):

'To him who is able to keep you from stumbling and to present you before his glorious presence without fault and with great joy – to the only God our Saviour be glory, majesty, power and authority, through Jesus Christ our Lord, before all ages, now and for evermore! Amen.'

Helpful extras

Music and song ideas

Facing opposition and difficulty: 'Fight the good fight'; 'Be bold, be strong'; 'O Jesus, I have promised'; 'He who would true valour be'. Trust in God; looking to Jesus: 'Father, I place into your hands'; 'Turn your eyes upon Jesus'; 'Be still and know'; 'Led like a lamb'; 'In Christ alone'.

Notes and comments

In the race in **Beginning the service**, encourage enthusiastic participation and support. This game introduces some of the ideas from Hebrews 12:1,2 which are picked up later in the **Bible talk**.

Both the **Bible reading** and the **Bible retelling** will need some preparation. Find confident volunteers. The **Bible retelling** should be fast-moving and the performance amusing.

You'll need volunteers to tell their stories in the **Bible talk**. You may need to interview them to help them be brief and succinct. Choose people carefully and include children, young people and adults. This is a good way to encourage people to grow in faith as they share their story and also helps to build up the sense of Christian community.

For the **Prayer of confession**, set up the pile of rocks on a table (visible to the congregation) beneath the cross (image or actual). This could be in place from the beginning. You will also need to give out stones to everyone as they arrive at the beginning of the service.

Alternative online options

Visit www.lightlive.org for additional activities for children, young people and adults.

PROPER 16

READINGS: **Hebrews 12:18–29; Luke 13:10–17**
Isaiah 58:9b–14; Psalm 103:1–8

Bible foundations
Aim: to understand that Jesus brings healing and peace rather than legalism

The reading from Hebrews 12 develops some of the themes from last week's service. Hebrews 11 reminded us of God's people who had lived faithfully for God, even though they would not see God's promises of eternal hope fulfilled in Jesus (vs 39,40). Unlike them, we are privileged to know Jesus and all the blessings he has brought, so let's respond with determination and perseverance to live for him.

In 12:18–29 the writer to Hebrews expands this theme. The coming of Jesus means things have changed from the old legalism and concerns about rule-keeping. Now we can come close to God through Jesus. He uses the ideas of 'Mount Sinai' (vs 18–21) and 'Mount Zion' to help his readers think about the old and new covenants. Moses received the Ten Commandments from God on the physical 'Mount Sinai'; it was a terrifying time (see Exodus 19). The spiritual 'Mount Zion' however (see also Revelation 21:1,2; 22:1–5) depicts the situation after Jesus' death and resurrection (v 24). No longer do God's people need to fear the outcome of his judgement for their sin.

The story of the healing of the woman with the bent back (Luke 13:10–17) shows Jesus' disapproval of empty rule-keeping (typically practised by the Jewish leaders of Jesus' time). Jesus, instead, shows a new way, acting powerfully out of love to bring peace and healing.

The book of Hebrews makes it clear what enormous privileges God's people have because of Jesus. We share in his worship with the angels (v 22). The writer encourages us to respond to God's loving invitation and come near to him, not forgetting what a holy and awesome God he is (vs 28,29).

Beginning the service

With: images of an erupting volcano, either stills or on video; a large pile of boxes or a grey blanket to cover the pulpit to suggest a 'mountain'; a large sign saying: 'Mount Sinai – Do not touch!'

Before the service erect the mountain shape at the front of your meeting area. Place the large sign on this: 'Mount Sinai – Do not touch!' Keep empty the first couple of rows of seating at the front. Those leading the service should have bare feet (pick up on this to emphasise the holiness of God – and the need to approach him with reverence).

Once you've welcomed people to your service, invite children or young people to come and sit in the front rows. But then tell them that they must take off their shoes before they come anywhere near the 'mountain'. If anyone comes close to touching the 'mountain', emphasise that it's very important not to do so. Suggest that there will be severe consequences if they do. At the same time draw attention to the drama of an erupting volcano.

You could then sing together the hymn 'Holy, holy, holy' or another hymn or song which emphasises the holiness of God.

Bible reading

With: a large sign saying: 'Mount Zion – Welcome' hanging off the 'mountain' at the front, but begin with the back of the sign facing the audience; images of an active volcano – see **Beginning the service**

Explain briefly that the Ten Commandments were given by God to Moses on Mount Sinai. This event was so special and God is so holy, that the people (except for Moses) were told not to come near the mountain (Exodus 19:10–13). If they did, the punishment was death. Here is what the writer of Hebrews said about that time.

Someone reads Hebrews 12:18–21, dramatically and with emphasis. As the words are being read show again the images of the active volcano. At the end of the reading, turn around the sign on the 'mountain' to: 'Mount Zion – Welcome!' Explain that Zion was another name for Jerusalem, God's holy city.

Explain briefly that things changed when Jesus came. Because of him we can come, without fear, to God. Then read Hebrews 12:22–29. You could sing another hymn, expressing thankfulness for what Jesus has done for us, for example, 'Alleluia, alleluia'.

Bible retelling

With: volunteers for this drama, a retelling of Luke 13:10–17, rehearsed in advance; actors wearing contemporary clothing

Introduce this drama, explaining that it is a story from Luke's Gospel which makes it clear that Jesus doesn't want people to live under the old legalism. He has come to bring peace and healing.

Characters: an old lady who hobbles, walking with difficulty; two or three 'synagogue' leaders; two or three 'onlookers'

The scene: an old lady with walking frame (or sticks) hobbles across the front area. Two or three synagogue leaders are standing nearby on one side. Two or three 'ordinary' people (the onlookers) stand on the other side, listening to Jesus who is teaching.

Jesus: *(Looks up, sees the woman and goes over to her.)* Woman – be well! (Jesus lays his hands on her. Immediately she begins to straighten up, then cautiously to walk unaided. She gleefully throws aside her walking aids and praises God.)

Old woman: Thank you, Jesus! Praise God! Look what he has done for me! (She walks away, continuing to praise God.)

(Meanwhile, the synagogue leaders have started to look indignant and are muttering. They rebuke Jesus.)

Synagogue leader 1: What do you think you are doing?! Call yourself a teacher – yet here you are disobeying our law. Surely you know that you're not allowed to work on the Sabbath.

Synagogue leader 2: Yes, there are six days when you can work – so let the woman come on one of those days if she wants to be healed, not on the Sabbath!

Jesus: You are such hypocrites! You even look after your animals' physical needs on the Sabbath. How much more should I bring healing (and God's peace and rest) to this woman who has been suffering for years?

Onlookers *(Among themselves)*: Yeah! That told them – the leaders are just jealous. Jesus is doing great things! Praise God!

Bible talk

You could start with the 'limbo game' (**Game**) to make the point that rule-keeping is difficult, failure has consequences, and to introduce the following ideas.

Then and now

Until Jesus came God had given rules that had to be kept if people were to come close to him. That's because he is perfect and holy. But we are not, and breaking his laws brings death – as the story of Moses on Mount Sinai shows (Exodus 19). God gave his laws to teach people that he is perfect and to help them live in a way which pleased him. Over time, the Jewish religious leaders got more bothered about rule-keeping for its own sake rather than doing what was right.

When Jesus came he pointed out their empty legalism. The Jewish leaders found it hard to accept. They were proud of their knowledge and law-keeping and were missing the point of God's law (Luke 13:10–17).

Jesus' death and resurrection changed the old ways of getting to God by keeping rules. Now God welcomes his people to come close to him because Jesus has taken all the punishment for the ways in which we have 'sinned' or broken the rules (Hebrews 12:24). Now, God speaks with us directly, rather than through someone else. Now, everyone can have peace with God through Jesus.

How should we respond?

- With praise and worship. We are part of God's people together with the angels. In spite of our inability to keep God's perfect law, we have been 'made perfect' through the sacrifice of Jesus (v 24).
- With trust and obedience. Forgiveness through Jesus shouldn't be taken lightly. We need to say 'Yes' to him, and trust and obey him (v 25).
- With reverence and awe. We no longer need to be bound by empty rule-keeping – that's not what the Christian life is about. Jesus came to bring us into relationship with his Father, God – and we must never forget what a privilege that is (v 28). Yet

that relationship brings to our lives his peace and healing (see also Luke 13:12,13).

Prayer activity

With: sticky notes given out as people arrive; pens and pencils; words of Hebrews 12:23a displayed on a PowerPoint slide, available as a download (YearC.Proper16_1)

Ask everyone to write their name on the sticky note they received as they came into the service. Then read out Hebrews 12:23a. Remind everyone that as God's people, their names are written in heaven. Ask everyone to come forward and stick their sticky note on the model of 'Mount Zion' – to show that they are one of God's people. As they do so, encourage them to think about what God has done for them through Jesus and thank him.

Prayers of intercession

With: PowerPoint slide with the words of Luke 13:12b,13 available as a download (YearC.Proper16_2)

Comment that because of what Jesus has done, we do not need to be crippled by guilt about our sin and failings, or by anxiety or health problems. Encourage everyone, in silence, to speak with God about areas of their lives where they are troubled. Ask them to imagine Jesus, seeing their need, coming over to them, laying his hands on them and saying, 'You are set free.'

If you like, instead of making this personal, encourage people to pray for someone else in the congregation who they know especially needs Jesus' help and healing at the moment.

Depending on what the congregation is used to and comfortable with, suggest that people exchange 'the peace', praying for the other person as they do so.

Conclude with a song about love and peace in Jesus, for example 'Here is love' or 'Be still, for the presence of the Lord'.

Ending the service

With: verses from Psalm 103 displayed via PowerPoint (suggested verses:1–5; 6,8; 10–18; 20–22) available as a download (YearC.Proper_3), with different sections highlighted, to make it clear how these are to be read alternately by the congregation

Divide the congregation into two parts to read alternate 'sections'. Encourage everyone to read confidently and to imagine themselves addressing God as they do so. You're aiming for a great sense of enthusiastic praise to God in response to what he has done for us and what you've heard during the service. End with a hymn of praise, for example, 'O for a thousand tongues to sing' or 'And can it be'.

Helpful extras

Music and song ideas

'Holy, holy, holy'; 'Our God is an awesome God'; 'Alleluia, alleluia, give thanks to the risen Lord'; 'Praise him, praise him! Jesus our blessed Redeemer'; 'Here is love, vast as the ocean'; 'Be still, for the presence of the Lord'; 'O for a thousand tongues'; 'And can it be'.

Game

With: equipment to play the limbo game; small prizes for the winning team

Set up the limbo game over a gym mat, foam or other soft floor covering. The aim is to illustrate, in a light-hearted way, the idea of rules, the importance of keeping them and the penalty which is imposed if they are broken. The game could be used at **Beginning the service**, in a pause during the **Bible reading** from Hebrews after verse 21, or to introduce the **Bible talk**.

Play the limbo game with two teams of no more than five people in each team. Set up the game with, for example, a long garden cane balanced on two upright supports. There will need to be as many settings for the cross-bar as people in the team. Don't make the lowest setting too low!

The teams should have alternate goes at getting under the limbo pole without dislodging it. As you explain the game, emphasise that what's really important is that they DON'T TOUCH the pole. If they do, their team will lose the game and won't be getting any prizes! It's very important to keep this rule. The aim is for your whole team to succeed in getting under the pole without dislodging it or falling over.

Play the game, encouraging onlookers to cheer, clap and boo as appropriate. Reward the winners with a small prize.

Statement of faith

If appropriate, use your usual statement of faith as a confident declaration of what you believe.

Notes and comments

The 'mountain' of boxes or the grey blanket need to be set up carefully before the service begins. It should be big enough to make an immediate visual impact as people enter the building. The two signs 'Mount Sinai' and 'Mount Zion' pick up the themes in Hebrews 12:18–28, suggesting the time of rules and legalism in the Old Testament era and then the freedom we have to approach God after Jesus has come.

Remember to organise a volunteer to give out sticky notes to everyone as they arrive for the activity in **Prayer activity**.

Look through the outline to make sure you have everything you need for the service. Some things need to be prepared in advance: for example, the signs for 'Mount Sinai' and 'Mount Zion'; the equipment for the limbo game (if using) and volunteers to prepare and rehearse the **Bible reading** and the drama for the **Bible retelling**.

Alternative online options

Visit www.lightlive.org for additional activities for children, young people and adults.

PROPER 17

READINGS: **Proverbs 25:6,7; Luke 14:1,7–14**
Psalm 112; Hebrews 13:1–8,15,16

Bible foundations

Aim: to hear the challenge to act with humility in embracing the values of the kingdom

Well-known teachers were customarily invited to meals after the Sabbath synagogue service. Such occasions were more than gastronomic experiences as they often took the form of a discussion on religious themes. The meal in the house of a leader of the Pharisees (as recorded in Luke 14:1–14) had an additional dark dimension, given that the Pharisees in attendance were seeking to find grounds to criticise Jesus.

Jesus used what was going on around him to identify issues which go far beyond right behaviour at meals. His parable in verses 7–11 (which echoes Proverbs 25:6,7) highlights how conventions about status would have been clearly reflected in the seating arrangements. The embarrassment experienced by the demoted individual in the story warns us against an exaggerated sense of our own importance. Rather, those who submit to God's reign (or 'kingdom') should be characterised by humility in relation to both God and others.

The second incident in verses 12–14 elaborates on this theme of humility. In ancient cultures there was a strong expectation that invitations to meals would be reciprocated (and this is not unknown today!). Such invitations would have a strong element of self-interest, particularly with high status guests. In the upside-down kingdom of Jesus, however, our service should be motivated by a concern for others based on disinterested goodness rather than calculated self-seeking. This will result in generous care for the vulnerable and poor (Psalm 112:4–9; Hebrews 13:16). We will not be repaid in material terms, but humble service on behalf of Jesus and others, not seeking our own status and material well-being, will not go unnoticed by God (Luke 14:11,14).

Beginning the service

With: child-friendly musical instruments (optional)

Sing together an opening hymn which acknowledges who Jesus is. If you have any instruments, pass them around so that children and adults have a chance to play. As a congregation, read out loud the words of Psalm 112:1. Repeat this a few times, increasing in volume, and encourage those with instruments to play loudly after the words: 'Shout praises to the Lord!'

Explain that in this service, there will be the opportunity, as directed by the psalm, to worship the Lord and to obey his teachings. You will discover that the values of God's kingdom turn everything upside down. Play the **Game** if appropriate.

Sing a couple of 'child-friendly' worship songs encouraging the playing of instruments. See **Music and song ideas**.

Bible reading

With: as many people as possible to mime this reading (at least seven)

As Luke 14:1,7–14, people can mime the movements involved. They will need to practise this. The reading below comes from the CEV.

> **Verse 1**: One Sabbath, Jesus was having dinner in the home of an important Pharisee, and everyone was carefully watching Jesus. *(At least four people sit down but probably not in a lying position, as was the custom. There is a lot of hustling to ensure that people are sitting in the 'right' place. The most 'pompous/arrogant' sits at one end, decreasing in pomposity going down the line.)*
> **Verse 7:** Jesus saw how the guests had tried to take the best seats. So he told them: When you are invited to a wedding feast, don't sit in the best place. Someone more important may have been invited. Then the one who invited you will come and say, 'Give your place to this other guest!' You will be embarrassed and will have to sit in the worst place. *(A master of ceremonies stands next to the most pompous and waves to the two people at the bottom of the line to come to the top, nearest him. There is more shuffling and embarrassment as the most pompous two go to the other end.)*
> When you are invited to be a guest, go and sit in the worst place. Then the one who invited you may come and say, 'My friend, take a better seat!' You will then be honoured in front of all the other guests. If you put yourself above others, you will be put down. But if you humble yourself, you will be honoured.
> Then Jesus said to the man who had invited him: 'When you give a dinner or a banquet, don't invite your friends and family and relatives and rich neighbours. If you do, they will invite you in return, and you will be paid back. When you give a feast, invite the poor, the crippled, the lame, and the blind. They cannot pay you back. But God will bless you and reward you when his people rise from death.' *(The master signals for two or three people in dishevelled dress, sitting in the congregation, to come to the front to sit near him. They amble up to the front.)*
> Luke 14:1,7–14 (CEV)

Bible retelling

With: slides or cards of mirror images of words in Luke 14:11b: If you humble yourself, you will be honoured

This retelling focuses on Luke 14:11b. Take each word of the verse and write it out in mirror writing, (or if you use the 'Paint' computer program, use the 'image – flip/rotate' horizontal tab) either on slides to be projected, or on sheets of paper or card to pass around to small groups. In groups, or altogether, work out what each word says, then put them together to form the sentence. Recite the verse a number of times together until it is learnt off by heart.
eg humble becomes *(humble upside down)*

Bible talk

With: readers to read Hebrews 13:1–8,15,16; information about the persecuted church; strips of coloured paper, pens and staplers; postcards or A6-sized pieces of card

Notes and comments will help to set the scene for this talk. Luke's Gospel is full of instances where Jesus tells stories or heals people in order to reveal the nature of the kingdom of God. In this particular parable, he wants his followers to embrace the values of his kingdom – not with pride like the Pharisees (who considered their place in the religious order to be important) but with humility – coming to serve more than to be served.

Jesus put these values into practice: he chose to spend his time with people who were low in status (eg the Samaritan woman at the well); he went to places where his life was at risk (eg Jerusalem, at a time when he knew he would be arrested); he chose to serve others (eg washing the disciples' feet and healing men with leprosy).

Embracing the values of God's kingdom with humility is challenging but also rewarding. Hebrews 13 encourages Christians to live this out. Read Hebrews 13:1–8,15,16. Each command could be read by a different person, scattered around the congregation.

(For the rest of the **Bible talk**, people can get involved in activities and discussions to consider the kingdom values as outlined in this passage from Hebrews. Some activities can take place in groups, some led from the front. Through each activity also consider the place of humility in your response to God's Word.)

Keep being concerned about each other. Turn to the person next to you or behind you and ask how you can pray for them this coming week. Remember to actually pray!

Be sure to welcome strangers into your home. Talk to your family or neighbour about who you could invite for a meal, or welcome them in some way, sometime soon – preferably someone you don't know very well. Not everyone is part of a family and so this might be an opportunity to invite or be invited! (You could refer back to the service for Proper 11.)

Remember the Lord's people who are in jail… and those who are suffering. Look at information about those who are suffering in other countries, or at home, because of their faith. You can download prayer information to inform this part of the service from www.opendoorsuk.org/pray/prayer_resources.php) as well as information provided by

Christian Aid, Barnabas Fund and other such organisations.

Have respect for marriage. Interview a married couple (maybe a couple not well known in church) to talk about what marriage means to them as well as the place of humility and the values of God's kingdom.

Don't fall in love with money. Be satisfied with what you have. On paper chain strips, write something that you have that you value. We are materially blessed and it is good to give thanks to God for these things. In a group, or along a row in the church, link the strips together using a stapler to form a long paper chain. At the end of the service, the chains can be linked to form one very long chain representing the things we have been given.

Don't forget your leaders who gave you God's message. Try to have faith like theirs. On a postcard, write or draw the name of the person (or people) who told you about Jesus. Children who go to a Sunday group might want to write the name of a leader or a parent. Older people can write down which of the values of God's kingdom this person's life reflected.

Humility is an underlying value in all the commands in Hebrews 13: thinking about others and looking out for their well-being as well as our own. Humility is also about being the people God made us and not trying to be something or someone else. God's kingdom is not for the important – it is for those who humbly recognise their faults and come before God as they are.

In conclusion, pray that God will give humility for the events of the coming week.

Prayer activity

Read out Hebrews 13:15: Our sacrifice is to keep offering praise to God in the name of Jesus. In smaller groups or altogether, ask for suggestions for what people want to praise God for. Give some fresh ideas. Then invite everyone to choose one of the suggestions and, after a song of praise, everyone all at the same time speaks out loud to God. Remind people that we can only come into God's presence to speak with him because of Jesus.

Prayer of confession

Read Hebrews 13:16a: Don't forget to help others and share. Ask people to think of times in the past week when humility and the needs of others have not been a priority. Recognise these situations before God, and collectively join in the words of a prayer of confession.

Prayers of intercession

With: newspapers; local magazines; church newsletter

Create a PowerPoint collage of local and national prayer needs. Alternatively, create a paper copy of such needs. For a heading, print the words of Hebrews 13:16b: This too is like offering a sacrifice that pleases God. This prayer time is offering a sacrifice that pleases God.

Give people the option of praying on their own or in groups for the prayer needs, or you may choose to lead everything from the front. During the prayer time, a reflective song such as 'This is the air I breathe' can be played.

Ending the service

End the service with this final prayer:

You are the Servant King, Jesus. You gave your life in humility for us so that we might know God. Help us this week to act in humility among our families, our friends, at work and school and in our times with you. Amen.

Conclude with a final hymn of praise.

Helpful extras

Music and song ideas

'Love divine, all loves excelling'; 'Jesus shall take the highest honour'; 'O Lord my God' ('How great thou art'); 'This is the air I breathe'; 'Praise him on the trumpet'; 'Be bold, be strong!'; 'God is our father'; 'From heaven you came'.

Alternative songs from CDs are: 'Great Big God' (from the Vineyard *Great Big God* CD); 'One way, Jesus' (from the Hillsongs *Kids Worship* CD).

Game

Put together a series of pictures where the image colours are 'upside down' or the image itself is at a peculiar angle. You could choose pictures of famous people, or household items such as a hand whisk held by a green hand, or a purple postbox or upside-down writing. Use the people in the church who are computer-competent. You do this with a computer by pasting an image into the Paint program using the 'image' tab, clicking on 'invert colours' and the picture will look more like a photograph negative. This new image can be copied and pasted into a PowerPoint presentation or printed off and laminated for use with a smaller congregation.

What is different/not quite right/'upside down' about the images? Comment on how, in God's kingdom, values sometimes seem upside down.

Notes and comments

In the Gospel of Luke, Jesus is revealed as a political figure who, in introducing the kingdom of God, turns the beliefs and practices of the religious people of the day upside down. In the parable told earlier, he points out to the religious leaders that their place in the religious order was no longer important because the kingdom of God also belongs to those from outside the church structures – including Gentiles, the poor, lame and needy. He also talks about being humble – in God's kingdom there is no place for those who think they are better than others. As Jesus says in the beatitudes, 'Blessed are the poor in spirit.' His life was the perfect model of a life lived in humility.

Alternative online options

Visit www.lightlive.org for additional activities for children, young people and adults.

PROPER 18

READINGS: **Philemon 1–21; Luke 14:25–33**
Deuteronomy 30:15–20; Psalm 1

Bible foundations
Aim: to consider what it means to follow Jesus

The attractiveness of Jesus – his warm and generous personality and his teaching, among many other things – can lure the unsuspecting into thinking they are in for an armchair ride, with a best friend whose main purpose is to meet all needs, solve all problems and make them happy. Luke 18:18–30 tells the story of a rich ruler who was obedient, earnest and wanted to be a disciple. Jesus sets a test to measure his commitment. As in Luke 14:25–33, the man is urged to think about it very carefully. Verse 26 concerns family, a very pertinent issue in the ancient world. Verses 28–32 take examples from ordinary life to show that people generally plan carefully before undertaking a building project or waging war. How much more so when considering making a lifelong commitment to follow the Messiah? With a chilling glance towards his own future, Jesus likens it to carrying a cross (v 27). As this normally led to crucifixion, his listeners could know this meant shame, suffering and ultimate death. No room for half measures (v 33)! But as Paul points out (Romans 6:1–14; Galatians 2:20), the death which all true followers of Christ experience is followed by resurrection to new life, new perspectives and new motivations.

When writing to Philemon, Paul applies the Gospel command in a real situation. Philemon is asked to view Onesimus, his runaway slave, through a completely new lens. The gospel has engendered a transformation for Onesimus and now the social and cultural challenge of the cross is laid at Philemon's feet. Paul urges him to receive Onesimus back for a completely new start. Philemon must decide for himself what he will do. Similarly for us today, the words of Jesus make extreme demands upon our life and we must respond if we wish to follow him as his disciple.

Beginning the service

Either:
Begin by interviewing someone who has made a choice to do the right thing for God, as an act of obedience, even though it may have been costly or difficult.

Or:
Offer a series of five factual either/or choices or preferences. People have to make what will be a limited choice. Ask everyone to hold out both hands and then count the As on their hand on one side of the church and the Bs on their other hand. (Not all children know left from right.) Who has scored more on the left than the right is irrelevant. For example: You can choose/prefer to:

A – wear red or **B** – wear blue
A – travel on the bus every day or **B** – don't travel on the bus every day
A – pay for phone calls on a contract or **B** – pay for phone calls as pay-as-you-go
A – drink orange or **B** – drink water
A – support X team or **B** – support Y team

Some people will have chosen more left-hand choices than right-hand ones, but actually none of these choices really mattered. However some choices really do matter, eg letting down a friend, whether we spend time with God or care for others. Explain that in this service you will be looking at doing the wise thing, obeying God, even though it may be costly.

Bible reading

Deuteronomy 30:15–20 introduces the idea of making a deliberate choice to follow and obey God.

Luke 14:25–33 contains a series of questions (vs 28 and 31), followed by answers. Verse 26 could be introduced with the words:

How can someone be a disciple of Jesus? One reader could read the questions while another reads the answers.

Bible retelling

Below is a dramatic monologue reading of Philemon 1–22, based on the NIV.

(Philemon wears vaguely New Testament clothing and enters holding a scroll.)
Apphia, I'm home! Just met the postman in the street. Here's a letter all the way from Rome, from Paul. I hope he's OK. That prison is no place for such a good friend. Let me read it to you: *(He reads from a scroll and adds asides as he goes along.)*

Paul, a prisoner of Christ Jesus, and Timothy our brother. (Well, at least he's got company.)

To Philemon our dear friend and fellow worker – also to Apphia our sister, to Archippus our fellow soldier – and to the church that meets in your home. (Remind me, Apphia, to read this letter to them this evening.)

Grace to you and peace from God our Father and the Lord Jesus Christ. I always thank my God as I remember you in my prayers, because I hear about your love for all his people and your faith in the Lord Jesus. I pray that your partnership with us in the faith may be effective in deepening your understanding of every good thing we share for the sake of Christ. Your love has given me great joy and encouragement, because you, brother, have refreshed the hearts of the Lord's people. (Did you hear that? Good old Paul, he always begins his letters on a positive note.)

Therefore, although in Christ I could be bold and order you to do what you ought to do, yet I prefer to appeal to you on the basis of love. (I wonder what's coming now.) It is as none other than Paul – an old man and now also a prisoner of Christ Jesus – that I appeal to you for my son Onesimus – (What? That useless creature! That wretched runaway slave! Let me get my hands on him! I'll beat him senseless! In fact, I could have him put to death! Yes, yes, I'll keep my voice down…) I appeal to you for my son Onesimus, who became my son while I was in chains. (What on earth does he mean? Onesimus isn't his son.) Formerly he was useless to you (you can say that again) but now he has become useful both to you and to me. (Useful? Him? You must be joking… sorry, I'll read you the next part.)

I am sending him – who is my very heart – back to you. (Ah, so that's what this is all about. Paul wants to suggest a suitable punishment for our runaway slave. It'd better be painful.) I would have liked to keep him with me so that he could take your place in helping me while I am in chains for the gospel. But I did not want to do anything without your consent, so that any favour you do would not seem forced but would be voluntary... (I'm not sure I like where this is going.) Perhaps the reason he was separated from you for a while was that you might have him back for ever – no longer as a slave, but better than a slave, as a dear brother. (What? Yes, that's what it says. I think I'd better sit down.) He is very dear to me but even dearer to you, both as a fellow-man and as a brother in the Lord. (A brother in the Lord? Well, there's a turn up for the books!)

So if you consider me a partner, welcome him as you would welcome me. If he has done you any wrong or owes you anything, charge it to me. I, Paul, am writing this with my own hand. I will pay it back – not to mention that you owe me your very self.

I do wish, brother, that I may have some benefit from you in the Lord; refresh my heart in Christ. Confident of your obedience, I write to you, knowing that you will do even more than I ask. (Well, since you put it like that, Paul…)

And one thing more: prepare a guest room for me, because I hope to be restored to you in answer to your prayers. (Apphia, did you hear that? Wonderful!)

Epaphras, my fellow prisoner in Christ Jesus, sends you greetings. And so do Mark, Aristarchus, Demas and Luke, my fellow workers. The grace of the Lord Jesus Christ be with your spirit. (That's the end. I'm amazed. Just give me a minute. Who's that knocking at the door? It couldn't be… could it? *(Peeps through the window.)* Onesimus! *(Freeze – to leave the question of what happens next completely open.)*

Bible talk

With: two signs on card: A: Calculate, can you afford this?; B: Take the prize

Remind the congregation of the Mastercard slogan: 'There are some things money can't buy. For everything else, there's Mastercard!' We may not agree with the second part, but it is certainly true that there are some things money can't buy.

Today's readings lead us from thinking about the cost of following God to the reward that he gives. How do we get from A to B?

In Deuteronomy 30:15–20, the cost of obeying God's commands is high – *love* the Lord your God, *walk* in his ways, *keep* his commands. None of this is easy. Being a Christian can seem like following a whole load of rules, never having any time off and giving up a lot too. Talk about some common misconceptions such as: if you're a Christian you have to go to church every Sunday; or, you should only listen to worship CDs. Jesus makes it sound even harder. Refer to the reading in Luke 14. Hate is a strong word; perhaps Jesus meant that our love for others should be pale in comparison with our love for him. Can we do this? Jesus then uses two illustrations.

A: Calculate, can you afford this?
(*Show sign A. A child could hold it up.*) You might work out exactly how much it will cost you to insure your car for your 18-year-old son to drive or how much it would cost to buy the latest game. In some cases, counting the cost may mean you are able to do what you want to do, such as buy the latest game. In other cases, it may not be possible so you have to delay doing something because you don't have the resources for the task. Philemon, the Christian slave owner, faced a decision. Should he take back Onesimus as a brother/fellow Christian, which would affect his household finances and maybe his pride or reputation, or should he reject him, handing him over to the authorities for punishment for running away? We do not know what he decided. Either choice had a cost attached.

A king with a small army threatened by 20,000 enemy soldiers cannot do his calculations and then decline to fight. He will be attacked anyway. He has to find an answer to the challenge. Either he decides to fight with an inadequate army, or asks for terms of peace. Jesus asks his disciples to find a way of doing that, rather than politely declining. It will not be easy. He asks us to love him more than any of our possessions but to think hard before we choose to love him.

B: Take the prize
(*Show sign B.*) What we gain as followers of Jesus is priceless. His love for us is more than we can ever imagine. That is the prize that we receive in return: life, rather than death; a blessing, rather than a curse; increase, rather than destruction. God says, 'Choose life', in Deuteronomy 30:19.

Prayer of confession

Allow individuals time to respond silently.

Lord Jesus, although we want to follow you, we are often put off. We do the sums and count the cost and it seems too high. So we think we can continue being your disciples, without any further cost to ourselves. It is hard and we need your help.
We confess that we love our families more than we love you…
We confess that we love earning money more than loving you…
We confess that we find keeping your commandments hard…
We confess that we prefer to do things our way not your way…
We confess that we find it easy to turn away, to be distracted, to lose our focus…
Strengthen us in our weakness and help us see that the life you bring is priceless in comparison to any cost. Amen.

Prayers of intercession

Pray for those known to the church who have counted the cost of following Jesus such as mission partners, people who have chosen a change in career direction in order to serve God, carers who have put their own needs and desires in second place, young people who are making a stand for Jesus in their school, university or place of work etc.

Ending the service

Use Philippians 2:5–11 as an affirmation. The congregation could join in saying verses 10 and 11 together.

Helpful extras

Music and song ideas

'Jesus, holy and anointed one'; 'Blessed is the man' (Psalm 1), instead of reading the Psalm; 'O Jesus, I have promised'; 'Dear Lord and Father of mankind'; 'Father, I place into your hands'; 'Forth in thy name, O Lord, I go'.

Game

Arrange for someone to talk briefly about what it has meant for them to count the cost of following Jesus in practical terms (perhaps involving a move, selling property, changing lifestyle or habits) and what the (unexpected?) benefits have been. Alternatively read Jovin's testimony available as a download (YearC.Proper18_1).

There are many examples of real and spoof Mastercard adverts on the Internet. You could encourage youth groups or house groups to create their own during the week, using them and the Gospel passage as a basis for discussion about values in life.

In a service of Holy Communion remind people what Jesus' death cost him as you eat bread and drink wine.

Alternative online options

Visit www.lightlive.org for additional activities for children, young people and adults.

PROPER 19

READINGS: 1 Timothy 1:12–17; Luke 15:1–10
Exodus 32:7–14; Psalm 51:1–10

Bible foundations
Aim: to rejoice that God looks for us when we are lost

It has always outraged religious people that God doesn't share their sense of good taste. He seems to have one set of expectations of behaviour and devotion for them with another for those who either ignore him or have never known him. In Luke 15:1–10 the Pharisees and teachers of the Law look on in disbelief and contempt as Jesus not only tolerates the presence of 'sinners' but even accords them the honour of eating with them. For them this was inconceivable. Jesus speaks of a God who loves the sinner passionately – almost to distraction, since he, the shepherd, abandons the best part of his flock to hike across the hills in search of a stupid sheep which has failed to stay close to the shepherd. His emphasis is upon joy (vs 5–7,9,10) – the thrilling, overwhelming, almost hilarious sense of happiness because this one sheep has been saved or, in his second illustration, a coin has been found. This is what God is like. Compare the miserable muttering of the religious people in verse 2.

Paul points out this joyful mercy and grace of God (1 Timothy 1:14) when speaking of his own rescue by God. He considers himself the worst of sinners (v 15) owing to his record of blasphemy, persecution and violence (v 13, see also Acts 8:1–3; Galatians 1:13,14). God has not changed. Paul describes him in majestic terms which the Pharisees and other religious zealots would recognise: 'the King eternal, immortal, invisible, the only God …', glory, honour (v 17). Paul could have added characteristics like mighty, just, powerful, frightening. He understands that God has sent Christ precisely to save sinners (v 15), to rescue the lost (Luke 15:6) and to spare no effort to find what belongs to him (Luke 15:9). Good taste and religious scruples are of less interest to God than the exhilarating joy of seeing 'sinners' turned round.

Beginning the service

Ask if anyone has lost anything in the previous week. In advance, prepare some people to make suggestions. Then ask who has found anything they have lost. Lots of things turn up but not everything does. Ask who has given up looking for something they have lost.

That's logical. That's human. That's so unlike God.

Briefly tell the story of the lost sheep or the lost coin. You could do this by hiding one coin or sheep in the building, asking the children to go in search of it, and when they eventually find it, ideally after some difficulties, explain how Jesus used an example of finding something lost and precious, to say how much God searches for us. Another suggestion for telling this story is available as a download (YearC.Proper19_1). You are going to find out more about lost things in the service.

Begin with the hymn, 'I will sing the wondrous story of the Christ who died for me'.

Bible reading

Exodus 32:7–14 may be read by two readers, as follows: first reader (verses 7–10); second reader (verses 11–13); first reader (verse 14).

Psalm 51:1–10 could be read with the congregational response: 'Have mercy on me, O God', after every second verse (see below from the NIV) which could be used in the **Prayer of confession**.

> Have mercy on me, O God, according to your unfailing love;
> according to your great compassion blot out my transgressions.

> **Have mercy on me, O God.**
> Wash away all my iniquity and cleanse me from my sin.
> For I know my transgressions, and my sin is always before me.
> **Have mercy on me, O God.**
> Against you, you only, have I sinned and done what is evil in your sight;
> so you are right in your verdict and justified when you judge.
> **Have mercy on me, O God.**
> Surely I was sinful at birth, sinful from the time my mother conceived me.
> Yet you desired faithfulness even in the womb;
> you taught me wisdom in that secret place.
> **Have mercy on me, O God.**
> Cleanse me with hyssop, and I shall be clean;
> wash me, and I shall be whiter than snow.
> Let me hear joy and gladness;
> let the bones you have crushed rejoice.
> **Have mercy on me, O God.**
> Hide your face from my sins and blot out all my iniquity.
> Create in me a pure heart, O God, and renew a steadfast spirit within me.
> **Have mercy on me, O God.**
>
> Psalm 51:1–10 (TNIV)

Bible retelling

1 Timothy 1:12–17 is presented with this monologue:

Paul's CV

(A smartly dressed man or woman sits behind a desk, sifting through a bundle of papers. He/she pulls one out and examines it.)

Hmm, now, here's an interesting CV.

Name: Paul of Tarsus

Former name: Saul of Tarsus

Religion: Jewish

Denomination: Pharisee

Education: University of Gamaliel – Well, the qualifications are good.

Work history: Persecutor

Recommendation from former employer: Saul is a great persecutor. He enjoys applying violence and mindless thuggery. He is particularly motivated to persecute Christians. There are many examples in his service record of persecutions carried out showing great attention to detail. Well, we are looking for someone who is interested in close detail.

Current employment: Servant of Jesus Christ – There seems to be a discrepancy here – let me see – ah yes – Footnote 1. Even though I was once a blasphemer and a persecutor and a violent man, I acted in ignorance and unbelief. Hmm, OK. If you say so.

Personal attributes: Strength (given to me by Christ Jesus), faithfulness (in serving Jesus), grace (poured out on me abundantly), faith and love. Interesting.

Personal statement: Here is a trustworthy saying that deserves full acceptance: Christ Jesus came into the world to save sinners, of whom I am the worst.

Any other information: Now to the King, eternal, immortal, invisible, the only God, be honour and glory for ever and ever.

(Presses buzzer) Is that my new assistant? Could you please call this person, Paul, and invite him for an interview? He is? Oh, well, perhaps when he comes back he could give us a call. How long will he be away? I see. What's he doing? Travelling around the entire Mediterranean? We may have to wait a long time.

Bible talk

With: visit www.professorsolomon.com for details of finding lost things; either PowerPoint slides or a set of cards with the following options written on them:
- a young offender who never thinks about God
- a teenager who goes to church but doesn't believe in God
- a youth leader who has fallen for other youth leaders
- a 31-year-old man who plans to turn to God when he starts a family
- an 11-year-old girl who thinks God is for old people
- a member of the Secular Society
- a pensioner who has been a Sunday School teacher, but complains that God lets her suffer too much
- a 40-year-old who thinks all religions lead to God
- a crowd of good people
- one of the people who wrote part of the Bible.

What do you mean by 'lost'?

Would people agree that some things are more lost than others? Are some people more lost than others? What do we mean by 'being lost'?

(A Professor Solomon, a 'findologist', would say that some things are less worth searching for (eg easily replaceable items or low-value items. See www.professorsolomon.com or an Internet search will give you more information on his book *How to Find Lost Objects* and his 12 principles. You could use these to introduce the idea of being lost.)

Ask people to sort the set of cards into order, according to who they think is the most lost. 'The whole bunch of good people' and 'the Bible writer' may end up near the bottom of the list as the least lost, if not actually at the bottom! In fact, some may say they should not be on the list at all.

Can we say that people are replaceable or are of differing values? What if God were to shrug his shoulders and give up the search for one of us? The Bible tells us that this is exactly what he will *not* do.

Lost people in the Bible
In Exodus 32:7–14, the majority of God's people had been rescued from Egypt, led across the Red Sea and promised a wonderful future. But they decided to pool their earrings and make a golden calf to worship in place of God. God was angry. He decided that this wilful turning away, their deliberate choice of the wrong path leading to being utterly lost, was their own fault and should be punished. Yet God relented and did not destroy them.

Or take the apostle Paul in the Bible retelling. He was a religious man who honestly believed he was the avenging hand of God against Christians. But then he encountered Jesus Christ and became his servant. His ignorance caused him to be lost. He initially didn't know God through Christ. He went on to become one of the most important figures in the Early Church and wrote a lot of the New Testament, but he was extremely hard on himself. He calls himself the 'worst of sinners', worse than… (refer to the 'most lost' person on the board). He would have put himself at the top of the list.

The writer of Psalm 51, who was probably King David, knew that his wrong actions were worthy of terrible punishment. He knew God's law and deliberately broke it. Yet his knowledge of the God of Exodus led him to hope that God would be merciful, would forgive him and change him. He was truly sorry. He asked for a pure heart, a steadfast spirit, and the joy of salvation.

The message of the lost sheep and coin
There are two keywords in Jesus' conclusion to the stories of the lost sheep and the lost coin. One is **rejoicing**. God rejoices, and all heaven with him, when one lost person is found by God. The second keyword is **repentance**. The reason the lost person has been found is because he is a sinner who repents. Jesus even goes on to say that righteous people who do not repent are actually more lost than this one person. (Where did the 'whole bunch of good people' end up on the list? According to Jesus, they should be at the top.)

None of the people on our list, or the people in the Bible whose lives we have looked at today, could have saved themselves or found themselves. Let's rejoice because God searches for us, keeps us in sight, and never gives up on us when we are lost.

Prayer of confession

Use Psalm 51 as a basis for confession. If you did not use the responsive version as a **Bible reading**, use it now. Alternatively, here is a paraphrase.

Have mercy on us, O God, because you love us so much. Blot out all the bad things we have done and make us clean.

We know just how bad we are. We can't pretend to be perfect. Even if we think nobody has been hurt by our actions, we have still sinned against you.

We are all in the same boat, because we are human. But that's no excuse, because you have taught us what we should do.

You don't want us to make huge donations or sacrifices to show how sorry we are. You want us to show we are sorry in our hearts.

So give us pure hearts, Lord, and help us to be strong when we feel like sinning. Give us your Holy Spirit. Let us be joyful and happy because you have saved us and you love us.

Prayers of intercession

Lord, we pray for those we know who are lost (in various ways) and need you to find them. We bring them to you now. (Invite the congregation to mention people by name, or remember them in silence, as appropriate.)

- Those who have turned their backs on parents or family
- Those who have never known that Jesus loves them
- Those who have drifted into bad company
- Those who have stopped believing in God
- Those who have dropped out of work and social obligations
- Those who are successful and think they are managing fine without God
- Those who find life one long struggle.

Ending the service

Use Hebrew 13:20,21 as a blessing.

Helpful extras

Music and song ideas

'O let the Son of God enfold you'; 'Amazing grace'; 'The King of love my shepherd is'; 'When I feel the touch'; 'I will sing the wondrous story'; 'Oh I was lost but Jesus found me'.

Play a recording of the Gospel song 'Love lifted me' (such as the version by the London Community Gospel Choir).

Notes and comments

If you want to talk about Professor Solomon, the 'findologist', include him at **Beginning the service** or at the start of the **Bible talk**, exploring his 12 principles.

Although the stories of the lost sheep and the lost coin are well known, it is a good idea to read them from the Bible, to ensure that everyone knows that these are Bible stories. God speaks afresh even through what is familiar.

Alternative online options

Visit www.lightlive.org for additional activities for children, young people and adults.

PROPER 20

READINGS: **Amos 8:4–7; 1 Timothy 2:1–7**
Psalm 113; Luke 16:1–13

Bible foundations
Aim: to see how God wants his people to act justly

God cares about justice for the poor, the marginalised, the downtrodden, the hungry and the disadvantaged. Consequently he has very strong things to say through his prophets about those who cause such injustice or do nothing to put it right. Amos calls Israel back to the righteous expectations of God, made crystal clear in his Law. The fact is that the oppressors are spiritually bankrupt. They don't care for religious celebrations like the New Moon festival or even the Sabbath (Amos 8:5). Such festivals get in the way of the trade they want to get on with. They trade unfairly with short measures, price fixing, and mixing dust with wheat, caring so little about the poor and needy that they would make them slaves for a pair of sandals (v 6). God's indignation and outrage are clear as he swears that this injustice will never be forgotten (v 7).

The parable in Luke 16 is difficult so it is important to keep a few guidelines in mind when working out what Jesus was saying. First, passages like Amos 8 are in the background. God always hates deception and usury. Secondly, the context is of absolute urgency: the master's judgement is imminent and the debts are huge. Jesus' parable is a call to action. Thirdly, Jesus is not endorsing the manager's dishonesty, but commending his sense of priorities. Money is only of temporary value and far more important things are in view for the people of God. Verses 10–13 pick up key terms from verses 8,9 to explain that how they handle money now has eternal consequences – honesty even in small worldly things is crucial; there can be no divided loyalties (v 13). In this sense Jesus is correcting one possible misconception of the parable: dishonesty is never acceptable in the kingdom of God but a radical review of priorities most certainly is. This spirit is to be found in Paul's words to Timothy.

Beginning the service

With: small stickers; enough wrapped sweets for everyone

Before people arrive, mark a quarter of the seats in the room with a sticker. Announce that people who are sitting in a place with a sticker can have a prize. Produce your sweets and hand them personally to the privileged few. Tell them not to eat the sweet yet and try to insist that the sweet isn't handed to someone else, for example from a parent to a child, as this will defeat the object of the exercise.

When the people with stickers all have a sweet, acknowledge that you still have a lot of sweets left. Share them out so the sticker people have about four each.

Ask, 'Don't you think I did that well?' Hopefully someone will suggest that it would have been better to share them equally between everyone. Suggest that those who have sweets give their spare ones away until everyone has a sweet.

Point out that your way of sharing sweets was very unfair. Some people were going to have more than they needed but most were going to have nothing. God himself is always just. Explain that 'just' means fair. He wants us to be just too. Today's service will help us think about this further.

Bible reading

Amos 8:4–7 could be read by three voices, one saying the words of God (verses 4, 5a and 7) and the others reading alternate phrases spoken by the greedy people.

1 Timothy 2:1–7 forms the basis of the **Prayers of intercession**.

Bible talk

With: a mobile phone; a Bible with the relevant verses marked (see below); a large pizza box with a delivery boy (in a uniform if you wish); a display board; four volunteers, of any age; a 'pizza' made as below

(Make a circular pizza in four separate quarters using bumpy packing box card to give the idea of chunkiness. Each quarter just fits into the box so that the complete pizza is as large as possible. The top of the pizza could be painted to look realistic but with the wording, shown below, written clearly and horizontal when displayed.

- Mark the first quarter with 'everyday needs'; on the back write 'Amos 8:4,5'.
- Mark the second quarter with 'freedom'; on the back 'Amos 8:6'.
- Mark the third quarter with 'prayer'; on the back '1 Timothy 2:1,2'.
- Mark the fourth quarter with 'God's Son'; on the back 1 Timothy 2:4,5'.

Store the quarters on top of each other, so that the one you need first is on top and the rest are in the correct order.)

Say that you are feeling hungry so you will just order a pizza. You had better make it a large one as there are several people to share it with. Make a pretend phone call, 'Hello, is that the Almighty Pizza Parlour? Can I order one of your extra large giant-sized pizzas, please? Oh, we'll just take pot luck with a selection of toppings. Thank you!'

As soon as you start to talk again a loud cry of 'Pizza delivery!' should interrupt you. Be amazed at the speed of delivery and ask the price. The delivery boy should reply, 'Oh, this is from Almighty's. He doesn't charge.'

You will now need four volunteers but only one at a time. Say that you are going to share out the pizza.

Everyday needs

Ask for your first volunteer. Open the box and give them the first quarter. Question what topping it has and decide together it must be 'Everyday needs' such as food, clothing, shelter. Display the quarter on the board and talk about how good and generous God is with the everyday provisions.

Freedom

Ask for your second volunteer. Give them the second quarter and decide together its 'topping' is 'freedom'. Display this quarter beside the first and talk about the freedom this volunteer enjoys in his life: freedom of speech, freedom to choose a lifestyle and to worship how he wishes.

Prayer

Give your third volunteer the quarter saying 'prayer'. Display it on the board and remind the volunteer what a privilege he has to be able to talk to God at any time.

God's Son

Give your fourth volunteer the last quarter saying 'God's Son'. Finish the pizza circle as you talk about how privileged this volunteer is to know Jesus and his forgiveness through his death on the cross.

Make as if to look in the box for another piece of pizza. Realise that there isn't any more and point out that although these four people have some great food there doesn't seem to be any more. Suggest that keeping all that pizza just between the four people might not be the fairest way of sharing it out.

Take down the first section, reading it out again. We all enjoy plenty of good food, clothing and shelter, our everyday needs, but what does God have to say about it? Turn the quarter over to show 'Amos 8:4,5' and ask someone to read out these verses. God wants us to share our material goods with the poor and needy. There really is enough for everyone. Display this quarter again, with the Bible reference showing.

Take down the second section and read 'freedom'. Although we enjoy freedom, there are many people in the world who don't. Turn the quarter over and reveal the Bible reference which is read out. Ask if people have ever bought a pair of sandals. Amos said that some people were being sold for the price of a pair of sandals. Some shoes in the world are not made in a fair trade way. God does not want people to be slaves but to be able to live in freedom and work for a fair wage.

Take down the third section saying 'prayer'. Wonder how this can be shared out; turn it over so that the verses from 1 Timothy can be read. We are not told to pray for ourselves but for others. Prayer is a wonderful gift from God but we should not be selfish with it.

Take down the last piece of pizza, 'God's Son'. What does God have to say about this? Turn it over and the verses are read. The way we can share this 'topping' is to tell everyone the good news about Jesus.

Finish by reminding everyone that God has given us so much. He also wants us to be just and to share his good things fairly with others.

Prayers of intercession

These prayers are based on 1 Timothy 2:1–7 so it would be helpful to have a second voice to read the appropriate verses between each section.

Reader: Verse 1: 'First of all, I ask you to pray for everyone. Ask God to help and bless them all, and tell God how thankful you are for each of them.'

Leader: Think of the people sitting around you… the person on your right… on your left… in front of you… and behind you. Think of your family and friends. Thank God for them and pray that they may know his love in their lives, his will for them, and that they may be fair in all their dealings. *(Pause)*

Reader: Verses 2 and 3: 'Pray for kings and others in power, so that we may live quiet and peaceful lives as we worship and honour God. This kind of prayer is good, and it pleases God our Saviour.'

Leader: Pray for world leaders… those who govern our country… those in local government… that they may act wisely and make decisions for the good of everyone. Think of someone who has authority over you, your boss… your teacher… your parents. Pray for them in their responsibilities and that any decisions they have to make will be fair ones. *(Pause)*

Reader: Verses 4 and 5: 'God wants everyone to be saved and to know the whole truth, which is, 'There is only one God, and Christ Jesus is the only one who can bring us to God. Jesus was truly human, and he gave himself to rescue all of us.'

Leader: Remember how privileged we are to have heard the good news about Jesus. Think about the people you know who need to know it too… members of our families… work colleagues… neighbours… those we meet every day in shops or on transport. Pray now for one particular person who does not yet know Jesus, that the good news may be shared with them too. *(Pause)*

Ending the service

With: card circles (tea plate size); scissors; pens

Split into small groups and give a circle to each group, asking them to cut it as fairly as they can so that each person has an equal slice. Suggest that everybody writes on theirs something they can do to be more just in their lives, eg buy fair trade products, or treat their friends more fairly. Pray that together you will help fulfil God's will to be just people. The slices should be taken home to use as bookmarks or similar.

Helpful extras

Music and song ideas

Well-known songs and hymns that fit the theme include: 'Brother, sister, let me serve you'; 'Hark the glad sound'; 'When I needed a neighbour'; 'Make me a channel of your peace'; 'We'll walk the land'; 'God of grace and God of glory'; 'Hail to the Lord's Anointed'.

Game

To demonstrate unfairness run a quiz which is scored using noughts and crosses: one side has really easy questions while the other has really difficult ones.

Statement of faith

Divide the congregation into two groups. Group A should say the beginning of each statement and Group B the ending. The words are also available as a download (YearC.Proper20_1).

We believe that God has a heart for justice…
… because Jesus gave himself as the sacrifice to pay for our sins.

We believe God has a heart for freedom…
… because Jesus died to set us free from the power of sin.

We believe that God has a heart for the poor…
… because in his words and actions he speaks out for them.

We believe God has a heart for the unloved…
… because although none of us deserve it, he has poured out his love upon us.

Notes and comments

To make the **Bible reading** more visual, a small group (two or three at most) could mime the actions in Amos 8:5 and 6.

Make a point of serving fair trade refreshments at church events.

Psalm 113 shows how God sees everything that happens on earth and is free from partiality. Show a picture of the statue of Justice from the Old Bailey to demonstrate how justice should be free of prejudice. You could ask a local magistrate to explain how just decisions are made in a court case. If possible, arrange a church visit to a court.

As an alternative **Beginning the service**, you could hold your own court case! Someone was caught eating a jam tart when supposed to be watching their waistline. Should they be found guilty or not guilty, and what might be a just punishment?

If you wished to think specifically about how we value money and honesty from Luke 16, use the ideas that are included in the **Bible foundation**. 'Honesty even in small worldly things is crucial; there can be no divided loyalties' (v 13). Is this something that adults can talk about after the service?

Alternative online options

Visit www.lightlive.org for additional activities for children, young people and adults.

PROPER 21

READINGS: **1 Timothy 6:6–19; Luke 16:19–31**
Amos 6:1a,4–7; Psalm 146

Bible foundations
Aim: to understand the importance of putting God first, before our wealth

Christians find it difficult to place eternal spiritual values above the prevailing wisdom. In Jesus' parable, both the rich man (often called Dives) and the poor man (Lazarus) are 'sons of Abraham'. Yet the rich man enjoys his wealth and luxuries and ignores the plight of poor Lazarus whose death cannot come too soon. Death is the great leveller for everyone – the ultimate statistic. Biblically speaking, God's judgement awaits everyone. The irony is that all human beings know about the inevitability of death. Both the rich man and Lazarus knew about the ensuing judgement which some might seek to deny. In the parable, judgement is both a triumphant and a bitter reality – bitter for the rich man who finds himself in hell, all the more bitter as he realises what he should have known. The Law and the Prophets were clear enough (Luke 16:29). He begs for someone to be raised from the dead to tell his descendants (vs 27–31). Jesus' teaching simply reinforces what has been perfectly clear all along: spiritual values from the mouth of God take precedence over material well-being and comfort.

Paul continues Jesus' emphasis. Priorities are again central as food and clothing are to be enough to make us content (1 Timothy 6:8). Again, the eternal perspective is paramount. In fact riches, while not despised, can be a real snare (vs 9,10). They can be well used but all too often bring temptations and distractions from what really matters. In verses 17–19 Paul encourages Timothy to speak to the rich people in his church about not putting their faith in their wealth. The way to handle wealth is to take the long view, seeing it in the light of their hope of eternal life. Interestingly Paul is not advocating getting rid of wealth but rather using it responsibly. This is a battle to be fought for the sake of our all-powerful and all-glorious Lord (vs 12–16).

Beginning the service

Ask people to put up their hands if they would be willing to do something horrible, scary or embarrassing, like eat a live worm, do a bungee jump or sing a silly song in front of thousands of people. Come up with your own examples.

Now see if more people would be willing to do these things if they were to be paid money. How much would you have to offer them before they changed their mind?

The examples you've used so far have been merely horrible, scary or embarrassing. What if they had been asked to do something illegal or immoral? Would people be willing to break the law for money?

Point out that rules of right or wrong are constantly being broken (or bent) by people all over the world. Sometimes it is clear that a crime has been committed. There are always stories in the news about fraud, bribery or corruption. Mention some recent cases.

More often people make more subtle choices. What they do isn't necessarily illegal, but it may not be exactly right either. Talk about some of the 'little white lies' or 'half truths' that get told in the pursuit of profit.

Is it OK to bend the rules for personal gain? What happens when we do? Explain that the readings today are a warning that there are consequences to our choices and actions. We often need to choose between our way and God's way. If we act out of self-interest we may find we lose more than we gain.

Bible reading

Psalm 146 is a **Statement of faith** which could be used in **Ending the service**.

Luke 16:19–31 could be mimed or acted out with different people taking the roles of the rich man, Lazarus, Abraham, the angels and the five brothers.

1 Timothy 6:6–19 could be split into 'what it is like to live as someone belonging to God' (verses 7,8,11–14,17–19) and 'what it is like for those who do not' (verses 6,9,10). Verses 15 and 16 could be put on a screen or printed on the notice sheet for everyone to join in together at the appropriate time.

Bible talk

With: three large cardboard coins with writing on both sides as follows: 'Discontented/Put your trust in God'; 'Blind to the needs of others/Help everyone… share what you have'; 'Not interested in God's way/Live to be like God'; three volunteers

There is nothing wrong with money in itself, but both Jesus and Paul had things to say about the way people used, desired or hoarded wealth. Paul was writing to his great friend and disciple, telling him to urge others to live in a way that pleased God. Timothy was a church leader.

Ask the volunteers to the front and give each of them one of the large coins. There are two sides to every coin and these three coins show that personal gain can have a flip side. We often make choices which we think will be good for us, but they can have negative consequences.

Discontented

(Show the first coin.) The rich man was very rich and lived in luxury. People who put their

trust in their wealth can never be satisfied because there is always more that they can have: more clothes, more possessions, things that are bigger and better than what they have at the moment. Note that this is a result of 'putting their trust' in these things, not just possessing them. Paul pointed out to Timothy that we should be satisfied with the food and clothes that we have. *(Turn the coin over.)* This is what Paul told Timothy to tell others, especially the rich – see verse 17. God himself is rich and richly blesses us with everything we need to enjoy life.

Blind to the needs of others

(Show the second coin.) The rich man lived his life of luxury and although he must have known that Lazarus existed, he did nothing to help him. The story says that he thought about his five brothers after he was dead but he did not think of anyone else apart from his family. He was blind to the needs of others. Paul urged Timothy to tell those who belong to God to 'do as many good deeds as they can and help everyone' (verse 18). *(Turn over the coin.)*

Not interested in God's way

(Show the third coin.) The rich man had lived his life without reference to God's law. After dying he wished he had read what Moses and the prophets had said. But it was too late. He had not wanted to live a life that pleased God. *(Show the first side of the coin.)* Paul on the other hand urged Timothy to 'Try your best to please God and to be like him' (verse 11). *(Turn over the coin.)* If we seek to live like God, then we will handle our money in the right way. Our wealth will not stop us being aware of the needs of others and sharing with them. This is the way that points to heaven, to be with God for ever.

Read 1 Timothy 6:19 as a summary. You could put it up on the screen and ask people to think about it.

Living like this 'will lay a solid foundation for the future, so that (you) will know what true life is like. 1 Timothy 6:19.

Prayer activity

With: coins

Make sure that everyone has a coin. Invite them to look at the side with the 'head'. Money is useful when it is used to help people or meet our needs. We need money to live. Ask people to think of things that they want to be thankful for – or for ways that money has been used wisely. Thank God for the gift of money.

Now invite people to flip over their coins to the 'tails'. The same coin can be used for good and for evil. Ask people to think of ways that money – or the love of money – has caused trouble. Give them some current examples of dishonesty, misuse of money or the failure to support those in need. Ask people to think of ways that money has been an issue for them – or for other ways that they have been motivated by self-interest. Ask for God's mercy, forgiveness and help.

Turn the coins back to the 'heads' side. God is always willing to turn our lives over from darkness to light – from bad to good. Invite people to use coins as a way of meditating on God's forgiveness.

Prayers of intercession

With: images of a fundraising project that the church is involved in, whether locally or overseas

Remind people of the project and the need for money and, if appropriate, the giving of time and other non-monetary gifts. Show the images as you do so. In advance ask a group of informed people to pray for this project and to pray for everyone in church to give generously, in the spirit of generosity that Paul urged upon Timothy.

Ending the service

With: cards with ideas for random acts of kindness printed on them

Remind people that simple acts of kindness or generosity can have a big effect. These acts are particularly meaningful if we can expect no reward. For example, you could pay for someone else's bus ticket, leave a coin in a trolley, hold a door open for a stranger, make someone a cup of tea – or just smile.

Explain that you have a pile of cards which all have suggestions for 'random acts of kindness' on them. Invite people to take one and make it their challenge for the week ahead. If they don't like the first one they draw, they could always put it back and take another one – this should be positive and fun, rather than difficult or challenging.

Finish the service by praying for each other, and ask God to help you make positive choices, live generously and follow Christ.

Psalm 146 is a celebration of God's generosity and concern for justice. This could be read as a final statement of faith. See below.

Helpful extras
Music and song ideas

Many popular songs or show tunes pick up on the theme of money, wealth or greed. You could use some of these during the service, particularly at the beginning.

Appropriate hymns and songs may include 'All I once held dear'; 'Beauty for brokenness'; 'Overwhelmed by love'; 'Lord, I lift your name on high'; 'You laid aside your majesty'; 'Who is there like you?'

Statement of faith

Based on Psalm 146, this statement of faith is also available as a download (YearC.Proper21_1). Divide into three groups and the sound builds up as the second and third groups join in. Children who cannot read can practise shouting out the first and final refrain.

All: Shout praises to the LORD!

1:	With all that I am, I will shout his praises.
1,2:	I will sing and praise the Lord God
1,2,3:	for as long as I live.
1:	You can't depend on anyone, not even a great leader.
1,2:	Once they die and are buried,
1,2,3:	that will be the end of all their plans.
1:	The Lord God of Jacob blesses everyone
1,2:	who trusts him
1,2,3:	and depends on him.
1:	God made heaven and earth;
1,2:	he created the sea
1,2,3:	and everything else.
1:	God always keeps his word.
1,2:	He gives justice to the poor
1,2,3:	and food to the hungry.
1:	The Lord sets prisoners free
1,2:	and heals blind eyes.
1,2,3:	He gives a helping hand to everyone who falls.

1: The Lord loves good people and looks after strangers.
1,2: He defends the rights of orphans and widows,
1,2,3: but destroys the wicked.
All: **The Lord God of Zion will rule for ever!**
Shout praises to the Lord!

Game

Use the format of the well-known TV show *Who Wants to be a Millionaire?* which could be renamed, 'Who wants to be rich and selfish?' As the cash prizes build up they should be accompanied with forfeits. For example, when a contestant receives 1,000 pounds, they are also told that they will lose their best friend.

When they finally get an answer wrong they are given a choice. They could either keep the money – and all the forfeits – or give it all away. Whatever they decide, you should then point out that money doesn't last for ever but God's blessings are given freely – plus you haven't got any real money to give them. If they made the wise choice you could give them an undeserved prize. Suggestions for forfeits are available as a download (YearC.Proper21_2).

Notes and comments

Danny Wallace wrote *Join Me* which was about the way he accidentally set up a 'cult'. It's very funny but makes some serious points. Advised by a couple of Christian ministers, and inspired by some quirky experiences, he ended up with a group of people who followed one simple rule – Do one random act of kindness every Friday. He demonstrates how simple kindness can have a big effect.

There are a number of quotable passages. The film *Evan Almighty* makes a similar point.

Look at the Generous campaign (www.generous.org.uk). This is an imaginative website which enables people to share simple ideas and actions which can have a life-changing impact.

The Church of England has created a resource called 'Love Life Live Lent' (www.livelent.net) which encourages generous living for children, young people and adults. Think about using this next year.

Alternative online options

Visit www.lightlive.org for additional activities for children, young people and adults.

HARVEST (COMMON WORSHIP)

READINGS: **Deuteronomy 26:1–11; Psalm 100**
Philippians 4:4–9; John 6:25–35

Bible foundations
Aim: to explore what it means to come to God overflowing with gratitude

God's people were always encouraged to thank God for the way he blessed them, especially in the gift of the land. The word 'gift' crops up six times in Deuteronomy 26:1–11, which also includes a liturgical declaration in verse 3 – 'I have come into the land'. God also cared for their ancestor, 'the wandering Aramean', believed to be Jacob, as he set off to Egypt (Deuteronomy 26:5). This verse is followed by a series of statements of faith (vs 5–9), quite possibly used by the people once they got into the land. Gratitude at God's provision is central, both individually and corporately. Sadly most of the instructions found in Deuteronomy were not kept and God's people time and again chose not to live as God intended – see 28:1–14 for the blessings, and verses 15–68 for the curses resulting from disobedience.

The apostle Paul urged the followers of Jesus in Philippi to be constantly grateful. They did not need to worry (Philippians 4:6) but they did need to be thankful. Thanks and prayerful requests are bound together. God's blessing would result. Paul himself had set them an example in being grateful that he was not forgotten in prison (v 10). This characteristic of God, as one who cares and feeds the hungry, is at the heart of what Jesus himself told the crowds in John 6:35. Jesus sets this reminder in the context of the desert wanderings of God's people, which connects to the instructions from today's Deuteronomy reading.

Psalm 100 embraces an attitude of gratitude for who God is, the Lord, good, loving and faithful for ever (Psalm 100:3,5) and for what he has done, in creation, in caring for and making his people his own (v 3). How else can anyone respond to this God, other than with gratitude? May that be true of your congregation in this all-age harvest service!

Beginning the service

Either begin the service with the **Bible reading** based on Psalm 100; or sing a song of thankfulness to God as people bring their harvest gifts to the front. Make sure that the collecting of the gifts is done smoothly and that each person is thanked for their gift, an example of genuine gratitude – the theme of the service.

Bible reading

Print out sections of Psalm 100 on long strips of paper and lay them out at the front. Ask adults and children together to put them in the right order. (Begin by identifying all the phrases which begin a sentence, with a capital letter.) You could have the following 14 phrases, using the CEV: Shout praises to the Lord, /everyone on this earth. /Be joyful and sing /as you come in to worship the Lord! / You know the Lord is God! /He created us, / and we belong to him; /we are his people, / the sheep in his pasture. /Be thankful and praise the Lord /as you enter his temple. /The Lord is good! /His love and faithfulness /will last for ever.

Everyone involved can say the psalm together for the benefit of everyone else.

The reading of Deuteronomy 26:1–11 would benefit from people miming the actions described in the reading. For example: someone walks to the front clasping a basket filled with produce from the land and gives it to an official-looking person; this person receives and takes it to a place which is associated with God's presence in your building, which could be close to a Bible, or the altar, or pulpit; someone reads from the pulpit or in a loud voice about the deeds that God himself has done, from verses 7–9.

Bible talk

With: objects to illustrate your gratitude to someone, such as a 'thank you' card, a mobile phone, a CD/book, a pair of brand new shoes or piece of clothing (you need to imitate someone else's fashion sense – see below); a cross; bread and wine which you use in Holy Communion

Symbols of gratitude

Talk about how you might show gratitude towards someone who has taken you out for a really great day's treat. Imagine what this day out would be like, where you might go, what would make it so special etc. Show the symbols as you talk about showing gratitude. You might:

- write to thank them or send them a card
- because you enjoy their company, phone them up to suggest doing something with them
- because you respect their opinion, go to visit somewhere or read a book or play some music that they have recommended
- because you want to look like them, buy a pair of shoes or clothing that is like what they were wearing that day (an extreme example!).

All these actions have become symbols of your gratitude.

Gratitude for the crops God had given them

Remind people of the reading from Deuteronomy 26. These were the instructions of how God's people were to show their thanks to God once they had settled into the land that he was leading them

273

to. What prompted them to be thankful was an abundant harvest. They were to take the first fruits of the crop and give them back to God. Read verses 10 and 11 again. These gifts were symbols of their gratitude to God, thanking him for the food and crops he had given them. Remind everyone of your thanks for the great day out that you were given. Look at the harvest gifts that people have brought. We are indeed grateful for food to eat. These gifts are symbols of our gratitude.

Gratitude for what God has done
But this present attitude of gratitude prompted God's people to remember all that he had done for them in the past.

- God blessed Jacob, 'the wandering Aramean', as he went down to Egypt, and became the father of a great nation.
- God heard his people's misery in Egypt as they cried out to him for help.
- God protected his people as they wandered around in the desert and finally brought them to a new and fertile land.

Thinking about all this should have made them grateful to God.

Ask what one practical thing people want to thank God for that he has done for them in this past week? (You may need to ask people to come prepared with a suggestion. Try to keep answers practical and immediate. The final part of this **Bible talk** focuses on what God has done in history.)

God did more than just provide food and care for his people, as important as that is. He did more than just look after his people and guide them. He actually rescued them from Egypt. He did this very dramatically. Read verses 8 and 9. God is a God who rescues, or saves, his people.

God's people were given the Passover as a meal to help them remember, year after year, what God had done for them. Among other things, this meal was a symbol of their gratitude.

Of course, Jesus did even more than that. In dying on the cross he made it possible for people to come back to God. He made it possible for our damaged relationship with God to be restored. He rescued us. He saved us. (Hold up the cross for everyone to see, the symbol that is central to the Christian faith.)

In a service of Holy Communion or the Last Supper we have a symbol of gratitude, as we remember and are thankful for all that Jesus did for us on the cross. (Hold up the bread and wine.) Bearing in mind the church's policy on children partaking in Communion, expand on this.

In conclusion, you could teach everyone the Scripture Union chorus, 'I see the love of my Father' – see **Music and song ideas**.

Follow the **Bible talk** with the **Prayer activity**.

Prayer activity

With: one or several (enough for each group) pre-prepared cubes – see below, or a number of dice

Some people may be familiar with a dice to use when saying grace before a meal. If possible show an example of this. The dice has six short prayers of thanks on it. It is rolled and the grace that ends up on top is the one that is prayed. Use such a dice at this point, or use the following adaptations, which encourage spontaneity.

Make either one large or several small cubes out of strong card (enough for the number of small groups you could break into). On three sides draw three simple purple symbols that represent who God is, such as a shepherd's crook, a crown and a strong tower. On the other sides draw three simple symbols in red for what God has done, such as a heart, pictures of things in creation (mountain, tree) and a manger or cross. When the cube is rolled and the purple symbols are on top, one-sentence prayers of thanks are said for who God is, and for the red symbols, thanks for what God has done, in the past and present. The prayers do not have to be just connected to the symbols on the cube.

A simpler option would be to throw an ordinary dice. Numbers 1–3 give thanks for who God is and 4–6 for what he has done.

Prayers of intercession

If harvest gifts have been given for a specific charity or good cause, it would be appropriate to pray for the work that is being done and to pray for the effectiveness of the gifts. Introduce this prayer-time by reading Philippians 4:4–7.

Ending the service

With: two large baskets, one filled with grapes or some small fruit; apple or pear-shaped pieces of card; pens or pencils

Give out the cards and ask everyone to write or draw on them one thing for which they want to thank God. Remind people of the personal examples that were given during the **Bible talk**. (This is especially important if you have visitors in the service.) As people leave or during the final song, invite them to bring their card to place in the empty basket as a symbol of thanking God. They then take a piece of fruit, to remind them that God not only wants to receive our thanks but also wants to bless us.

Conclude with this final blessing from Philippians 4:7 (CEV):

Always be glad because of the Lord! And then, because you belong to Jesus Christ, God will bless you with peace that no one can completely understand. And this peace will control the way you think and feel.

Helpful extras

Music and song ideas

The old Scripture Union chorus 'I see the love of my Father' is particularly appropriate to this service. The words and music are available as a download (YearC.Harvest_1). The words are:

I see the love of my Father,
In the earth, the sky and the sea;
But I see it best in the gift of his Son,
Who died on the cross for me.

'Praise God from whom all blessings flow'; 'Praise him, you heavens'; 'For the beauty of the earth'; 'God who made the earth'; 'Now thank we all our God'; 'Yes, God is good'; 'Every blade of grass'; 'God is so kind to us'; 'Come, you thankful people, come'; 'It's a good thing'; 'Give thanks to the Lord, our God and King'; 'Thank you, Jesus'; 'God made you and me' *Light for Everyone* CD (SU).

Songs based on Psalm 100 include: 'All people that on earth do dwell'; 'Come rejoice before your maker'.

Game

It may be that many in the congregation

do not know much about the story of the Exodus and settling into the Promised Land which is the basis of the **Bible talk**. To fill in some of the gaps, prepare four copies of the following events:

Jacob going into Egypt, taking all that he had with him; the people of Israel slaving on the building site; the people crossing the Red Sea as they escaped from Egypt; the people unpacking their bags in a place with background fruit trees etc. These images are available as a download (YearC.Harvest_2).

Hide the 16 pictures around the building before the service and just after the **Bible reading** of Deuteronomy 26, wonder to yourself about the stories of God's great deeds that were mentioned in the reading. Without an answer, ask the children to see if they can find 16 pictures. Bring the pictures to the front to sort into their four sets. Ask the children if they know what these pictures represent, and use that as a means of filling in the gaps of how God's people got to Egypt and got away.

Notes and comments

A service of Holy Communion is very easily incorporated into this harvest outline, as we thank God for what Jesus has done.

Visitors and fringe church people will come to a harvest service. Make sure that they are welcomed and that they are encouraged to explore why they might be thankful to God. Let everyone know of any activities which are particularly appropriate for those who are searching for God.

Harvest is a great time to sing songs of thanks to God, so let the music group lead in a joyful way. Percussion instruments will add to the enthusiasm.

Alternative online options

Visit www.lightlive.org for additional activities for children, young people and adults.

PROPER 22

READINGS: **2 Timothy 1:1–14; Luke 17:5–10**
Habakkuk 1:1–14; Psalm 37:1–9

Bible foundations
Aim: to learn from the example of others what it means to be faithful to Jesus

Timothy did not find it easy to face up to the prospect of suffering because of his loyalty to Jesus. So the apostle Paul uses various arguments to encourage him not to run away from his commission. First, Paul reminds Timothy that the Holy Spirit who lives in him is 'not a spirit of timidity, but a spirit of power, of love, and of self-discipline' (2 Timothy 1:7). Timothy does not have to face troubles on his own! The Holy Spirit will give him what he needs at just the right time. Second, Paul points to the gospel message. This good news is so wonderful and so important that it is worth giving up everything for. God has planned it all along and now at last the good news is clear to all – God will accept us when we trust in Jesus, not because of any good deeds we may do but purely because of his own unmerited favour.

And what if Timothy should have to face death for his loyalty to this gospel? There is still nothing to fear, for Christ 'has destroyed death and has brought life and immortality to light through the gospel' (v 10). Death for Timothy (and for us, if we remain faithful to Christ) will prove to be merely the beginning of new, fuller life. Finally, Paul uses his own example to encourage Timothy. Timothy has seen how Paul is 'not ashamed' of the disgrace that repeated beatings and imprisonment have brought; rather he sees his wounds as his trophies, 'the marks of Jesus' on his body (Galatians 6:17), and Timothy can learn to do the same. (We know in fact that Timothy was later imprisoned for his loyalty to Christ – see Hebrews 13:23.)

But serving the Lord faithfully is not meant to make us boastful. Jesus teaches his disciples that when we have done everything expected of us, our attitude should be, 'We are unworthy servants; we have only done our duty' (Luke 17:10). This is all about Jesus, not about us. But if we are willing to share his suffering here on earth, then one day we will also share his glory (Romans 8:17).

Beginning the service

With: a young plant or seedling

Begin by displaying your plant. Talk about how any plant (particularly when it is just starting to grow) is fragile and vulnerable to the weather, but under the right conditions it can gradually grow into a strong and healthy bush, tree or flower. (You'll need to know what your little plant will grow into to make the most out of this point. Expand appropriately upon the beauty, decoration, shade or fruit it will provide when it is full-grown.)

Compare our lives as Christians to that plant. We are vulnerable to all kinds of trouble, but under the right conditions, and most importantly with help from others, we can keep on growing as followers of Jesus, adding to the glory and beauty of the church, caring for people we meet, and helping even more people to follow Jesus.

This service will explain part of a letter written by Paul to his younger friend, Timothy. Explain that Timothy had stopped working with Paul to go and lead other followers of Jesus, taking responsibility for them. Paul wrote to Timothy to encourage him, telling him how much he appreciated working with him, and giving him some careful advice about how to work with and care for others. Encourage everyone to be ready to learn from Paul and Timothy about how to follow Jesus and care for others.

Bible reading

2 Timothy 1:1–14 introduces Paul's letter to Timothy. Explain how Paul has been like a father to him. Divide the congregation into five groups. Ask each group to listen out for what Paul is saying to Timothy when their particular few verses (as follows) are read and put their verses into their own words. The verses are 1 and 2; 3 and 4; 5–7; 8–10; 11–14. Ask for feedback from each group.

Bible retelling

With: two speakers or actors, prepared in advance

An excellent way of sharing the message and emphases of Paul's letter to Timothy would be to improvise a dialogue between Paul and his jailer (Paul was probably in chains while writing this letter) in which Paul asks the jailer to make sure Timothy gets his letter (or that one of the other early Christians passes the letter to Timothy), and they talk briefly about the contents of it. This will need confident and prepared volunteers who have read the passage (a Bible commentary would help in preparation), but should, if done well, help you 'get under the skin' of Paul's attitude to Timothy. This could follow immediately after the Bible reading. Some questions to help you are given below:

- Why (and how) does Paul care for Timothy so much? (2 Timothy 1:2–5; 3:14,15). Mention that Paul is feeling left alone by some of the people he had hoped would help him (see 2 Timothy 1:15; 4:9–11) but he trusts Timothy to pray and care for him.
- What does Paul think is involved in following Jesus? (See 2 Timothy 1:6–8, 11–14; 2:1–7; Luke 17:9,10.) Luke 17:5–10 is a story that Jesus told, which Paul may have heard from Matthew or another early follower.
- Why does Paul follow Jesus? (See 2 Timothy 1:9,10; 2:11–13; 4:6–8.)

Bible talk

With: copies of the 'celtic cross' diagram, available as a download (YearC.Proper22_1); pens or pencils

Copies of the image of the 'celtic cross' should be distributed or displayed via a data projector.

Begin by talking about the relationship between Paul and Timothy. Paul, with his experience and history of struggling to follow Jesus and share his good news with others, is passing on his work to the next generation. Paul saw Timothy's potential, took him under his wing, trained him, tested him and encouraged him. Now he can let Timothy take over this hugely important role. If appropriate, encourage everyone, both young and old, to share stories or memories of people who have helped them grow and learn as Christians. (Examples could include Sunday School teachers, family, friends, people who encouraged them to follow Jesus or showed them by their love and care what Jesus is like.)

Emphasise two parts of what Paul says: he wants Timothy to be ready and willing and courageous to look after the people he is going to lead and guide, using fully the gifts he has (2 Timothy 1:2,6,7,14) and he wants Timothy to be focused on Jesus, knowing who he is and always ready to share this with others (2 Timothy 1:9,10).

Learning from others about Jesus

Engage people in a discussion about learning from others to follow Jesus. Show Jesus at the centre of the cross shape, with the names of Eunice, Lois, Timothy and Paul placed around the circle surrounding the cross. Paul says he has learnt from Timothy and Eunice and Lois about what it means to follow Jesus, and Timothy has learnt from Paul and Eunice and Lois. They are (or have been) joined together in a circle of love, learning from each other, and passing on the message of Jesus. Distribute pens or pencils and encourage everyone to write a few key names on the circle around the cross on their sheets (adults may need to help younger children); these should be people they feel connected to as they try to follow Jesus, or just the people around them in church. In addition, they could write one word or phrase to describe what these people have done.

Empowered by the Spirit to follow Jesus

Next, talk about 'gifts', such as 'Kylie's honesty' or 'Josh's questioning'. Paul highlights the faith and courage Timothy has shown so far in trying to follow Jesus. He also mentions how the Holy Spirit gives power, love and self-control, and his own work as an apostle in passing on the message of Jesus to others. We could talk about all these things in different ways as 'gifts'. Gifts come in all kinds of shapes and sizes: the special ministry gifts that the Holy Spirit gives; the love and care we show our friends and family; the work we do or special talent we have that helps or inspires other people (give a range of examples). Just being yourself can also be a gift, because people like to know you and to be with you and that's important too. Encourage everyone to write or draw around the 'celtic cross' reminders of the gifts they have seen used or been given by others in the past. Adults and children should be ready to talk and engage meaningfully with each other as this goes on, giving help as needed.

It would probably be best to end this activity

with prayers of thanks – or move straight into the **Prayer activity**.

Prayer activity

With: bowl of very small seeds; bowl of sand or earth

Place the two bowls (ideally large ones) at the front of the church. Begin by referring to Jesus' words in Luke 17:5–10, which suggest that only a little faith is needed to follow him – we can trust him to help us and guide us as we struggle to grow and try to follow him. Relate this to 2 Timothy 1:7 and 8 where Paul encourages Timothy not to be overwhelmed but to share fully in the 'big' work of passing on the good news of who Jesus is to others, and caring for the people of Jesus' church.

As quiet or meditative music is played, invite everyone to come forward (a few at a time, adults accompanying and praying with children) and take a seed to 'plant' in the bowl of sand or earth. As they do so encourage them to say a quiet or silent prayer, asking Jesus for courage to follow him.

End by saying the Lord's Prayer together, or use the **Statement of faith**.

Ending the service

With: 'flower petals' cut from coloured paper; bookmark-shaped card; sheets of paper; glue or sticky tape

Returning to the idea of Christians growing like a plant, introduced in **Beginning the service**, say that you're going to thank God for the good things you have learnt from or seen in other Christians. Compare this to seeing a flower coming into bloom. Distribute the craft materials listed above. Everybody uses their sheets of paper to make a picture of a flower by drawing leaves and a stem and then sticking the 'petals' as decoration on the card, to remind them all week of what has been explored in the service.

Helpful extras

Music and song ideas

Songs that focus on guidance or commitment for the future include: 'I know not why God's wondrous grace' (using words from 2 Timothy 1); 'I'm not ashamed to own my Lord or to defend his cause'; 'I do not know what lies ahead'; 'Give me oil in my lamp'; 'O Jesus, I have promised'; 'When you walk through the waters'; 'Father, hear the prayer we offer'; 'Guide me, O thou great Jehovah'; 'Brother, sister, let me serve you'; 'God's Spirit' from *Bitesize Bible Songs 2* CD (SU), which uses 2 Timothy 1:7 as a Learn and remember verse.

Statement of faith

It is set for four voices, who should ideally be a mixture of children and adults (perhaps alternating, so that the idea of faith in Jesus being passed on through a chain of his followers, young and old, is reinforced).

The rest of the congregation should join in at the end with a loud 'Amen!' A PowerPoint presentation is available as a download (YearC.Proper22_2).

> **Statement of faith**
>
> Voice 1: We follow Jesus, just as Paul and Timothy did,
>
> Voice 2: As friends helping each other to grow and care.

> Voice 3: We commit ourselves to learn from them and from the rest of the Church around us,
>
> Voice 4: And to share their faith and trust and love, based on these truths:
>
> Voice 1: That God, because he is kind, has saved and chosen us to be his holy people, when we did nothing to deserve this;
>
> Voice 2: That Jesus Christ has come, as part of God's plan, to show us who God is and what he is like;
>
> Voice 3: That this Jesus is our Saviour, who has defeated death and brought us good news;
>
> Voice 4: That this good news is so good, it is like a bright, shining light – it is God's offer of life to us, life that never ends.
>
> All: Amen!
>
> Based on 2 Timothy 1:9,10

Notes and comments

The idea of seeds and growth would be appropriate for a harvest celebration. Other harvest ideas can be found in the four volumes of the *All-Age Service Annual* (SU).

If the service includes Holy Communion, someone could be invited to share how joining with others in remembering Jesus' death has helped them follow him.

One church encouraged everyone to write a message in ink using a sharp-ended stick as a pen. They put a cardboard (loo roll) manacle around their wrist. The message was addressed to God or to someone they wanted to thank. This helped everyone to identify with Paul who was writing to Timothy in prison. This could make an alternative **Ending the service** or could be incorporated into the **Bible talk**.

Alternative online options

Visit www.lightlive.org for additional activities for children, young people and adults.

PROPER 23

READINGS: **2 Kings 5:1–3,7–15; Luke 17:11–19**
2 Timothy 2:8–15; Psalm 111

Bible foundations
Aim: to thank Jesus for the healing and salvation he brings

Imagine what it must have been like to have an infectious skin disease like leprosy. The sores and scars, and the gradual disappearing of fingers, noses and other bodily parts, must have been bad enough. Apart from the bodily pain, imagine what it would have done for your self-image! Then there was the social ostracism. No longer could you mix with friends and family. If they ever came at all close you would have to cry out to warn them, 'Unclean! Unclean!' Finally, there was the lack of hope. All you could look forward to was that things would get steadily worse until eventually death brought the suffering to an end. In 2 Kings 5, Naaman did not appear to be an outcast. This may have been because his disease was in the early stages. But he would know what awaited him unless he was healed.

The ten men in Luke 17 were outcasts. How wonderful for them to hear that the prophet Jesus was healing people of leprosy, along with other diseases. No wonder they went to meet him and begged him to heal them. As they obeyed Jesus' command, they were healed. But only one, a despised Samaritan, came back to say 'Thank you!'

Leprosy is a picture of the sin that gradually ruins the lives of each of us. Gradually, like a cancer, it ruins our moral character, our health and our relationships. If we come to him and cry for mercy, Jesus can deliver us from the power of sin, giving us a new nature and his Spirit within us to enable us to live a life that is healthy and wise. But how grateful are we for the salvation we have experienced? The apostle Paul warns us to be faithful to our Lord and Saviour. If we turn our backs on him, then he will one day turn his back on us (2 Timothy 2:12b). Rather, what we need to do is show how grateful we are to him for transforming our lives and giving us hope by living for him and, if necessary, dying for him.

Beginning the service

With: a handbell

Begin by ringing a handbell (or any reasonably loud bell!) and asking the congregation to imagine how far away they would have to go to be out of earshot. Explain that today's story is about some men suffering from a skin disease that may have been leprosy, and that at times in the past such people were made to carry bells and shout 'Unclean!' so that everyone who heard them could get out of the way. Discuss the loneliness of being that far away from everyone and being unwanted.

Bible reading

As the story in Luke 17:11–19 is read, ten people could mime calling to Jesus, and dash to the back of the church to go to the priests, while just one solitary man returns.

The story of the healing of Naaman in 2 Kings 5:1–15 lends itself to being read with a narrator, the girl, the king, Naaman, Elisha and servants.

Bible talk

With: music (see below); cards each with one word from part of John 3:16 on them (optional)

Use any song that expresses thanks to God for our life and health and body, and perform suitable exercises or movements of the body. There are a number that would work well with under-5s – see **Music and song ideas**. Talk about the amazing things our bodies can do but recognise that some people are disabled in some way so are limited in what they can do.

Then ask what we most wish for. For example, ask children what they most want for their next birthday/Christmas. Then ask what would be the first thing they would do if somebody gave them that wish?

The dearest wish

In the story from Luke's Gospel, ten people were given their dearest wish – to be made well from a terrible disease. Paint a picture of the men with the skin disease rediscovering the wonder of a healthy body that they had thought they would never have again. Explain that the first thing that nine of them did was to race back to the priests and confirm that they were no longer unclean. They had to get permission to re-enter society. Imagine what they did next – did they go home to their long-lost families and friends, get their dream jobs or perhaps go into the town and enjoy being among people again? The first thing that the tenth man did was to go back to Jesus, the person who had given him this amazing gift, to say thank you. Jesus was able to send him on his way with a blessing and a promise that his faith had healed him for ever.

The greatest gift

Ask what the greatest gift is that God has ever given us. At this point, ask volunteers of mixed ages to put the large cards in order, each bearing one word of the sentence 'God so loved the world that he gave his one and only Son', helped by the congregation. Explain that in the reading from Timothy, Paul says that Jesus is his 'gospel', which means 'good news'. Just as Jesus healed the lepers from the disease that kept them apart from others, he has healed us from the sin that kept us apart from God.

You could make more detailed reference to

Christ's death on the cross to achieve peace between God and human beings. This is good news! Referring to 2 Timothy 2:11–13, explain that thankfulness for the gift of being freed from sin is demonstrated by turning to and following Jesus. The tenth leper physically turned around and followed Jesus in order to say thank you. If we believe that Jesus has spiritually healed us and saved us from the wrong things in our lives, we need to take opportunities to 'turn' and give thanks to him.

Finish by explaining that, if we say thank you for a present someone gives us but then put it into a drawer and forget it or give it to the nearest charity shop, it shows that we were not really grateful to receive it. Our thankfulness for God's gift of healing and salvation will be shown, not just in our words and songs of praise, but also in how we respond to it.

Prayer activity

With: small card counters, each carrying a smiling face, enough for everyone; large bottles, jars or other containers

This activity could take place after the **Bible reading** or **Bible talk**, or may be appropriate after the **Prayer of confession**. Encourage everyone to think of something for which they wish to thank God – a person who has helped them, a difficulty they have recovered from, the fact that they believe in Jesus and are trying to follow him. Everybody takes one of the counters. Explain that the smiling face is like the thankfulness of the man healed from his skin disease. People then hold their counter and decide what they want to thank Jesus for.

As quiet music is played, everyone comes to the front to place their counter into one of the bottles or jars, as an outward sign of their thanks, just like the leper's journey to find Jesus to say 'Thank you'. Conclude by praying:

Father, we offer you our prayers of thanks for all the ways you have helped us in our lives; most of all we thank you for the gift of your Son, Jesus, because through him we can come to you.

Alternatively, people write their prayers of thanks on pieces of paper and put the paper into the jars or fix them to a notice board.

Continue with a more intercessory tone, by encouraging silent prayer for someone (personally known or unknown to them) who does not have the help or blessing that they thanked God for. (You could remind them that if they have thanked Jesus for dying for them, they could pray for someone known to them who does not yet know Jesus.)

Prayer of confession

Begin by introducing the idea that sin, like the skin disease mentioned in the Gospel reading, separates us from God and others. Alternatively, ask people to reflect on things during the week for which they need God's forgiveness.

Invite the congregation to turn so that they are facing away from the front or from a cross in the building, or to turn outwards so that they are facing away from each other, as you say:

Father, the things that we have done have separated us from you and from each other. We have let in the sickness of sin.

Invite everyone to pause to think of specific

things for which they would like to say sorry. When they are ready, invite them to turn back to the front, or to turn inwards to face each other again, as you say:

Thank you for your promise of forgiveness. We turn to you for our healing. Have mercy on us and make us whole. Amen.

Prayers of intercession

In view of the emphasis in the stories on those who have a skin disease, it would be appropriate to pray for those who are sick.

Helpful extras

Music and song ideas

Appropriate songs and hymns for this service could include: 'I am a new creation'; 'There is a Redeemer'; 'The Lord is gracious and compassionate'; 'Thine be the glory'; 'King of glory, King of peace'.

The Taizé chants 'Laudamus Omnes Gentes' or 'Cantate Domino' could be used as background music during the **Prayer activity** or as a response between prayers. A more lively option would be 'Venite, Exultemus'. Some of these can be found on the Taizé website: www.taize.fr.

Suggestions for songs about the body to use at the start of the **Bible talk**: 'Head, shoulders, knees and toes'; 'If you're happy and you know it'; 'One finger, one thumb, keep moving'; the 'Hokey Cokey'.

Statement of faith

The theme of thankfulness for salvation naturally leads to a statement of faith in what Jesus has done for us. This could include testimonies from a few forewarned people, especially if there are any baptisms. Alternatively, encourage people to speak out with single, personal statements. Use your usual creed or use the following adaptation of 2 Timothy 2:8–12:

> Let us remember our healing and salvation, and be thankful:
> We remember Christ Jesus, the son of David,
> who for our sake died and was raised from the dead.
> He is our good news
> and in him is salvation with eternal glory.
> If we have died with him, we will also live with him,
> and if we endure, we will also reign with him.
> Amen! (based on 2 Timothy 2:8–12)

Ending the service

Remind the congregation that the man healed of a skin disease was able to go on his way and begin a full life. In the same way, our salvation gives us 'life to the full' (John 10:10). End with the words of Jesus to the leper, 'Get up and go on your way; your faith has made you well.'

Notes and comments

If this service includes Holy Communion, you could emphasise that it represents our invitation, through Jesus, into the kingdom of God.

Alternative online options

Visit www.lightlive.org for additional activities for children, young people and adults.

PROPER 24 (suitable for Bible Sunday)

READINGS: **Genesis 32:22–31; 2 Timothy 3:14 – 4:5**
Psalm 121; Luke 18:1–8

Bible foundations
Aim: to explore what it means to persist in being faithful to God

Jacob had cheated his brother, Esau (Genesis 27:41–44) and had run away to live with his uncle Laban. He had cheated his uncle too and had become rich on the proceeds of his deception. (His uncle has also cheated him many times!) But years later, on his eventual journey home, it was as though his past caught up with him. He spent the night before meeting up with his brother, on the river bank, anxious and fearful. (He had already sent all his family (33:1–3) and possessions (32:13–21) to the other side to face the wrath of Esau without him.) Here he wrestled with the unknown man and in the process his hip was damaged permanently, which meant that he had to cling on to prevent himself from falling. He was now dependent upon the unknown man whom he discovered was God. God then gave Jacob a new name, the one by which he and his people would always be known. Jacob would not give up and his dependence upon God changed him for ever.

It is this perseverance, refusing to give up, that the apostle Paul urges upon Timothy in his second letter. Timothy needed to be reminded to be faithful to what he had been told in his youth. The Scriptures would remind him of how God wanted him to live. His God-given task was to teach others faithfully the truth about God, even though they may not wish to hear it (2 Timothy 4:3). The Gospel parable similarly emphasises the importance of not giving up as we talk and intercede with God.

May everyone in this all-age service be inspired to persist in their dependence upon God and in being faithful in prayer and engagement with the Scriptures. This service outline would be especially useful for Bible Sunday.

Beginning the service

With: a downloaded image of Jacob Epstein's alabaster sculpture of 'Jacob wrestling with an angel' (1940), or Rembrandt's painting (1659) or Gustave Doré's illustration (1855), both with this title

Welcome everyone and then display one of the images above. Ask what people notice. What is most striking about the sculpture is that Jacob is held and appears to be almost passive. It is a strange sort of wrestling! Of course, we do not know whether or not it was an angel. Genesis 32:24 says it was a man, and verse 28 that it was God himself. As Genesis 32:22–31 is read, you could ask what error the artists appear to have made.

Explain that in the service you are going to hear this story of Jacob and see what it means to persevere in being faithful to God.

Bible reading

Genesis 32:22–31 lends itself to an expressively read narrative reading with a narrator, Jacob and the man. A drum or cymbal could be struck at the point where Jacob's hip is struck. The person being Jacob could limp back to their seat, having walked to the front with great confidence.

Alternatively, one person could read this while an actor mimes the actions of Jacob, shadow miming his wrestling with God. This would need to be practised to get the timing correct. The **Bible retelling** tells this story in a challenging way.

Introduce the reading of 2 Timothy 3:14 – 4:5 by explaining that Paul was writing to his friend and follower Timothy, who had a Christian mother and grandmother and was naturally somewhat shy. Remind people of other parts of the letter that have been read in the past two weeks.

Bible retelling

With: six named parts; a loud audience; copies of the scripts (The full script is available as a download (YearC.Proper24_1).)

A drama: Runner or Winner?

The 'Presenter' needs to be a confident reader. Give them a script and a whistle, if you have one. 'Hunter' could be played by someone who finds reading a challenge. They will just need prompting on their entrance and on their two lines at the end. 'Runner/Winner' and 'Shadow' wrestle during the drama. If possible, copy and cut out their scripts and put them round their wrists so they can read their lines while 'wrestling'. The 'Assistant' is a non-speaking part. Give them one blank card like the presenter's script cards.

The 'Prompter' holds up the audience prompt cards, written on separate sheets of card: BIG CHEER, QUIET CHEER, BOO, SNORE, BOO HOO, MASSIVE CHEER, SSSSHHH, GASP, 4 HOURS LATER.

Start up a 'Gladiator'-style clapping rhythm (from 'We will rock you', Queen). When the children are joining in, introduce your drama by saying these words to the beat. Invite the children to join in with, 'We will watch you'.

Jacob, you're the man, with a plan
to get the best out of any situation.
But you feel out of place,
A big disgrace,
And now your brother you're going to face.

We will, we will watch you. (x2)

Then perform the drama and encourage everyone to join in with the audience response.

Bible talk

With: two large thought bubbles either on flip chart paper or use an OHP; markers; five strips of paper labelled as below (How Jacob changed) to be stuck on the second thought bubble; glue or sticky tack

Jacob had cheated his brother, Esau, and had run away. Briefly tell the story from Genesis 27. But he was really scared when the time came for him to meet his brother. In the time that Jacob had been away both he and his brother had become very rich. But could he give his brother enough gifts to ensure that Esau would not kill him?

How Jacob felt

Ask for suggestions for how Jacob would have felt. These might include: scared stiff, anxious, curious, proud, or scheming to save his skin. You could ask just for words that begin with the letters that spell JACOB, to tie in with the second part. These might be: jumpy, jaded, anxious, afraid, anticipating, cowardly, curious, overwhelmed, bothered or bewildered. Write these words on the first thought bubble.

Despite all this, Jacob cried out to God. Read Genesis 32:7–12. Comment that he remembered that God was the God of his grandfather, Abraham and his father, Isaac. He reminded God of his promise and how generous God had been to him. Had he been talking with God like this while he had been away, or was this panic praying?

How Jacob changed

Having set everything up so that he might escape the wrath of his brother, Jacob wrestled with an unknown man all night on the river bank. Finally, he discovered who this man was and was changed. Stick the five labels (without the bracketed comments) one at a time on the second thought bubble, explaining the story as you do so. They spell the word Jacob.

Jacob (a new name)
Agonising injury (he always walked with a limp afterwards)
Changed life and still alive (he had seen God face to face and survived)
Open communication with God (he had been devious and scheming all his life)
Back in touch with his brother (meeting Esau was not as bad as expected (33:4))

After persisting throughout the night, Jacob was never the same again and the damaged hip was a constant reminder. Refer back to Paul's instructions to Timothy. Timothy was also fearful but Paul urged him to remember what he had learnt in the Scriptures and to allow them to have an impact upon him. Paul wanted to reassure Timothy that God was with him and he had an important task to do.

How the Bible changes us

Ask at least one person to share what the Bible has meant to them, beginning with when they were children, right up to the present day.

You could ask them:
How did you read the Bible or hear Bible stories when you were a child?
How has the Bible helped you know God?
How do you read the Bible now?

What advice would you give parents to help their children to read the Bible?

If you are using this outline on Bible Sunday, emphasise the importance of reading the Bible. Provide sample material of Bible reading guides. For details of Scripture Union Bible reading resources visit www.scriptureunion.org.uk. You could provide parents with Bible storybooks and resources that they can use with their children. There is no more important task for a parent than to help their child know God.

Follow this with the **Prayer activity** below.

Prayer activity

With: three pairs of people of similar build and strength

Invite three pairs of people (chosen beforehand so that they are equal, rather than wait for volunteers) to come forward to engage in three bouts of arm-wrestling. You may need a table and chairs for this. Ask how frustrating this was and if it was obvious who the winner was. Comment that God said that Jacob had won, although it did not look as though he had.

Invite everyone to get into pairs and think of something that they really want God to do, something that they have wanted him to do for ages and ages. You should give some suggestions. Each pair shares what they have thought of, then they clasp each other's right hand, as though about to arm-wrestle. Either out loud or in their own minds, they tell God what it is that they long for him to do.

Alternatively, ask three pairs to prepare to do this in advance for the benefit of everyone else, sharing their prayer need with everyone before they wrestle and speak with God.

Prayers of intercession

With: whatever props help you to pray in a fresh way for a persistent long-term prayer need; the three questions for each group written on a card

Since persistence in praying and growing in faith is the focus of this service, it would be appropriate to name topics for prayer that have regularly featured over the past few weeks or months. But think how you could approach these topics in a fresh way. For example, have you been praying for someone to get better for many weeks, or for a house sale to go through, or a church building project to make progress?

Split into smaller groups and give each group one topic to consider how God has been answering prayer. Give each group three choices, written on a piece of card:
- Have you seen answers to prayer?
- Have you been praying for the wrong thing?
- Is God calling you to persist?

Invite feedback and then, having prepared in advance, pray for one of the topics in a different way from usual. For example, you could show a photo of someone who is chronically ill if this is not your usual custom and specifically ask God to do something different. Remember to thank him that he hears our prayers and always answers, although not in the way we might expect.

Ending the service

With: drums to beat out a simple rhythm; other percussion instruments

Distribute the instruments. Practise a simple beat such as stamp-stamp-stamp bang-bang (**kee-e-ep** – stamp the foot three times; **go-ing** – slap the thigh twice). Begin the rhythm and invite people to make the emboldened response. You should perform a 'bang-bang' after 'faith', 'heard' and 'care'.

Leader: When it's a struggle, to keep the faith…
All: Kee-e-ep go-ing!

Leader: When you are suffering, to keep the faith…
All: Kee-e-ep go-ing!

Leader: When God seems silent, has he now heard?
All: Kee-e-ep go-ing!

Leader: When all around you, don't seem to care.
All: Kee-e-ep go-ing! Kee-e-ep go-ing!

Send people out confident that God has heard their prayers, has met with them in the service and will be with them during the week. Challenge them to read the Bible this week.

Helpful extras

Music and song ideas

'Everything' from *Bitesize Bible Songs* (SU), which is the words of 2 Timothy 3:16 in a format to learn and remember; 'Here, oh my Lord, I see you face to face'; 'We will seek your face'; 'Pray, pray without ceasing'; 'Nearer my God to thee'; 'We will give ourselves no rest'; 'Blessed be your name, oh Lord'; 'Be bold, be strong'.

Notes and comments

If this service includes Holy Communion, you could emphasise that just as you meet with God in a special way as you take the bread and wine, so Jacob also met with God in a dramatic way. Meeting God changes us.

If you are using this on Bible Sunday you could focus on Bible translation or distribution agencies such as Scripture Union, Bible Society or Wycliffe Bible Translators.

Providing opportunities for personal testimony about how the Bible has impacted people, or how they have persisted in praying for a situation, would fit very comfortably into this service outline. Make sure that those speaking are aware of the context of the learning in this service and have prepared, so that what they say is easily accessible for people of all ages and stages of faith.

Suggestions for fresh ways of praying can be found in *Top Tips on Prompting prayer* (SU) – see page 309.

Alternative online options

Visit www.lightlive.org for additional activities for children, young people and adults.

PROPER 25

READINGS: **2 Timothy 4:6–8,16–18; Luke 18:9–14**
Jeremiah 14:7–10,19–22; Psalm 84:1–7

Bible foundations
Aim: to learn to rely on God and not on what we have done or who we are

To us the Pharisees are the villains, but it is important to realise that in the time of Jesus they were the heroes. These were the people who treated the Scriptures with the greatest possible seriousness, and who were determined to do God's will in every area of life. They had worked out that there were 613 divine commands and they discussed endlessly how these should be obeyed. If anyone was going to be saved, surely it was them! There could be no hope for the tax collector, considered a traitor to his people and nation, a collaborator with the Gentile oppressors! But Jesus turns people's expectations upside down. In the story that he tells in Luke 18:9–14, there is no doubting the Pharisee's dedication or his sincerity. But somehow there is something seriously wrong. His main concern is to compare himself (favourably, of course) with others. Moreover, he has no sense at all of having fallen short of what God required of him. In contrast, the tax collector is all too aware of his sins. He has no thought of what others may think about him, beating his breast. His one concern is that God might have mercy on him. Jesus says that it is this man whom God the Judge will declare to be righteous!

The apostle Paul looks forward to a 'crown of righteousness' from the Lord (2 Timothy 4:8). Is he, then, like the Pharisee? No, for Paul knows that his righteous standing before God depends not on his own good deeds or obedience to God's law, but depends solely on God's unmerited favour and what Christ has achieved for sinners by his sacrificial death and victorious resurrection. Like the psalmist, his strength is in God (Psalm 84:5) as he walks the pilgrim way (2 Timothy 4:17). He gives the glory to God, and does not boast about his own achievements as the Pharisee does. He knows that it is those who are 'confident of their own righteousness and look down on everybody else' (Luke 18:9) whom God is unwilling to accept.

Beginning the service

The following shout of praise (based around Psalm 84) can be led from the front, or from individuals in the congregation. It should be used with enthusiasm and the response should be equally enthusiastic and inspirational. This shout of praise is also available as a download (YearC.Proper25_3).

The shout of praise can be used with imagery, using images such as sunsets, magnificent churches, open blue skies, birds nesting and snow-capped mountains.

> Leader: How I love your Temple, Lord Almighty!
> I long to be in your Temple.
> With my whole being I sing for joy to the living God.
> **All: How I want to be there!**
> Leader: Even the sparrows have built a nest,
> and the swallows have their own home; they keep their young near your altars, Lord Almighty, my King and my God.
> **All: How I want to be there!**
> Leader: How happy are those who live in your Temple,
> always singing praise to you.
> **All: How I want to be there!**
> Leader: How happy are those whose strength
> comes from you, who are eager to make pilgrimage to your mountain.
> **All: Lord God, Heavenly King, Mighty One!**
> **One day we will live with you**
> **And see you face to face.**
> **How we want to be there!**
>
> Based on Psalm 84

Bible reading

Before reading 2 Timothy 4:6–8 and 16–18, ask people to listen out for what Paul was looking forward to, as he came to the end of his life.

Two men could mime the reactions of the two men in Luke 18:9–14 or use the **Bible retelling**.

Bible retelling

In addition to the **Bible reading** and **Bible talk**, you could perform the sketch that is available as a download (YearC.Proper25_1). The sketch involves the whole congregation. Very little rehearsal is necessary and it can be used with quite a lot of improvisation.

Bible talk

With: running shoes and clothes; running magazines; a list of interesting facts about runners; a medal or trophy; a chair or a bike; a bunch of bananas hidden in a cardboard box

A runner who is a cheat

Show the items above, one at a time, asking people to guess who might use them. With as much interaction as possible, help them to think about how each item could be used. It should become clear, first, that these are all items a runner might use, and second, that some of the items are not what you would expect. Is this runner a cheat?

(The chair could be for when a runner gets tired – ask if a runner should sit down mid-race. The bike might be used to cheat, but the runner could alternatively take a short cut. The bunch of bananas could be for energy, but could also be used to throw the skin under the feet of other competitors to slip them up.) Such a runner might think that they have all the right things, possess all the knowledge by reading the right magazines… and be prepared to cheat if they need to so that they can win and be better than anyone else. In their own mind they have won the race before they have even started. Of course, no runner like that ought ever to win the prize.

A runner who lives for God
In contrast, speak about the runner who is described in 2 Timothy 4. They will live for God with what God has given them and will not try to be someone they're not; it's a long and tough race and there's no cheating or resting (refer to the chair, bike, bunch of bananas, and also drugs).

For a runner there is a pain barrier to get through. It is like that for Christians, as sometimes it is tough going. God gives strength – (see verse 17). As Christians, we should encourage one another. Emphasise that in the Christian race there is a prize for every runner, not just a medal for the fastest. Conclude by saying that for a truly dedicated runner there is no cheating, and you can't just win by looking good or knowing the right things – you have to 'just do it' and run. It is the same for someone who decides they want to 'run as a Christian', and rely on God's strength to help them to stay in the race to the end.

Prayer activity

With: images or drawings of a road, a crowd cheering on a runner, a tired runner needing help, the sky

Use the images above to decorate your worship area or display them on a large board or flip chart. Alternatively, obtain electronic picture files and display them as a PowerPoint presentation. A sample PowerPoint presentation is available as a download (YearC.Proper25_2). As each image is shown, guide the congregation in the following meditation using suitable words, examples of which are given below. Where possible try to include all ages:

The road image: A runner will look back on where they have already come from. What has happened in your life so far? Do you remember specific times when God has been with you?

The crowd image: Look at the people around you, or remember the stories you may have heard of people in the Bible who have trusted in God, or of any Christians who have followed God in the past. These are the cloud of witnesses, the people who cheer us on as we try to run the race. How might we encourage one another to keep going, by what we say and do for one another?

The tired runner image: It might be hard. What disappointments and struggles do you face? Is school or work difficult? How about your family? Jesus is there with you, and you can ask him to help you. Take time to do that now; imagine those situations and imagine that Jesus is standing there by your side.

The sky image: End by reading 2 Timothy 4:6–8.

Ending the service

With: laurel leaves prepared earlier from paper (enough for one per person), each with the words from 2 Timothy 4:7 written or printed on it

Talk about how laurel leaves were awarded

as a crown to the winner of races in ancient games. Explain that each person is going to receive a leaf to take home to remind them that we are running a race and can be sure from scripture that 'on the day of judgement he (the Lord) will give a crown to me and to everyone else who wants him to appear with power' 2 Timothy 4:8 (CEV).

Play some appropriate music while the leaves are distributed or collected from the front.

Helpful extras

Music and song ideas

Songs reflecting themes of discipleship and pilgrimage include: 'Every day I run this race'; 'Jesus, lover of my soul'; 'Trust and obey'; 'Amazing grace'; 'To God be the glory'; 'He who would valiant be'; 'How lovely is your dwelling place' ('Better is one day in your house').

Notes and comments

People may still have memories of the London Olympics in 2012; at **Beginning the service**, ask what people can remember of the running events.

Interview a real marathon runner. Many of the UK marathons have a prize for every runner. If you know a marathon runner or have one already in your congregation, ask them questions about why they do it, what it feels like, at what point they feel like quitting, whether they get paid anything for it, and what encourages them to keep going when they get tired. Weave these responses into the **Bible talk**. Rather than simply showing the items you could have someone dressed up as a runner carrying them.

In the **Bible talk**, you could also make a link to the reading from Luke about the Pharisee and the tax collector. The Pharisee thought that he had 'made it' already and was accepted into heaven because of what he wore, what he knew, and how he never made mistakes. He was pleased that he wasn't like the tax collector who had nothing in comparison. The tax collector, however, knew that without God's strength he didn't have a chance of doing what God wanted him to.

If this service includes Holy Communion, it is worth emphasising that in taking the bread and the wine we recognise that we cannot do anything to win God's acceptance – no good deeds and so forth. Only Jesus' death has made this possible.

Alternative online options

Visit www.lightlive.org for additional activities for children, young people and adults.

ALL SAINTS' DAY

READINGS: **Ephesians 1:11–23; Luke 6:20–31**
Psalm 149; Daniel 7:1–3,15–18

Bible foundations
Aim: to explore how we can live as 'saints' who trust in Jesus

In Luke's version of the Beatitudes, Jesus sets out the character, values and attitudes his followers are to have. In verses 20 to 26 we see that there is a real contrast with normal human ideas. Like the 'humble poor' who depend on God, frequently mentioned in the psalms, Jesus' disciples seem to risk missing out on all life has to offer: money to spend, good food, laughter and popularity. But Jesus teaches that it is those who enjoy such things now, but have no hope for the future, who are truly 'sad'. Meanwhile, verses 27 to 31 outline the attitudes Jesus' followers should exemplify. This is truly radical! 'Love your enemies, do good to those who hate you … give to everyone who asks you' – only those indwelt by God's Spirit could possibly begin to live in this way.

In Ephesians 1:11–23 we see that such power is indeed available to help all members of the Church, the body of Christ, in their struggle to live for him. This power is the gift of the Holy Spirit, marking out believers as people of the future, living the life of heaven here on earth (vs 13,14). God's people need to move on from the basics of trusting in Jesus and loving one another (v 15) to experience 'the Spirit of wisdom and revelation', who will enable us to know God better. So, trusting in the gift of a new status and destiny, and experiencing the same mighty power that brought Jesus out of the grave (verses 19,20), we can take our place in the body of Christ, and live for his glory. God's purpose is extensive; since Christ is 'the fullness of him who fills everything in every way' (v 23), we need to get out into the world and demonstrate through our countercultural lifestyle that God's rule can come to every area of life.

Beginning the service

With: several pictures or images of different people who could be described as 'saints' – a mix of historical figures, modern 'heroes' and ordinary Christians

Show the pictures. Ask the congregation if they would describe these people as 'saints'. Explain that the word 'saint' means 'holy', which is another way of saying that someone or something has been given to God in a special way. Some adults may be used to the phrase 'set apart' to express the same idea.

Ask whether anyone feels that this idea (that being a 'saint' means being given, or giving yourself, to God) changes how they were thinking about the pictures. The apostles often talked about Christians as being 'the saints'. Talk about whether we would feel comfortable to be described in that way – if not, is it that we don't feel worthy? Explain that we do not earn the title 'saint'; it is God who calls us, forgives us, and equips us to serve him. Being a saint is not an achievement, but a gift from God to everyone who believes in Jesus.

Bible reading

Luke 6:20–31 could be read by four readers, as below, using the CEV. Readers 1 and 2 could stand to one side, some distance from readers 3 and 4. This is also available as a download (YearC.Allsaints_3).

> Reader 1: Jesus looked at his disciples and said: God will bless you people who are poor.
> Reader 2: His kingdom belongs to you!
> Reader 1: God will bless you hungry people.
> Reader 2: You will have plenty to eat.
> Reader 1: God will bless you people who are crying.
> Reader 2: You will laugh!
> Reader 1: God will bless you when others hate you and won't have anything to do with you. God will bless you when people insult you and say cruel things about you, all because you are a follower of the Son of Man.
> Reader 4: Long ago your own people did these same things to the prophets.
> Reader 2: So when this happens to you, be happy and jump for joy! You will have a great reward in heaven.
> Reader 3: But you rich people are in for trouble.
> Reader 4: You have already had an easy life!
> Reader 3: You well-fed people are in for trouble.
> Reader 4: You will go hungry!
> Reader 3: You people who are laughing now are in for trouble.
> Reader 4: You are going to cry and weep!
> Reader 3: You are in for trouble when everyone says good things about you.
> Reader 4: That is what your own people said about those prophets who told lies.
>
> Luke 6:20–31 (CEV)

Bible talk

With: four presents wrapped in silver paper – a bag of chocolate money, a large chocolate bar, a water pistol or toy gun, a large badge saying, 'Look at me!'

What money, food, power and fame can buy

Invite four volunteers to come to receive one of your four gifts. As each gift is opened, talk about how these different gifts symbolise the things valued by 'the world' – money, food, power and fame. (The water pistol or toy gun is meant to symbolise the power and threat of people who bully others.)

Now discuss these gifts again. Observe that we might think that gifts are always good things, but, sadly, gifts are sometimes not good. Using appropriate language for your context, help the congregation (particularly younger children) to discuss and understand the idea that all these 'gifts' have negative sides – too much money can lead to manipulation, too much food can lead to obesity, people who want power over others are never satisfied, fame and celebrity can actually be very unpleasant if everybody wants to know about you all the time! So often these gifts mean that those who have them exploit and damage others. Saints are people who don't live like that – not that being rich or famous inevitably means you can't please God.

What poverty, hunger, sorrow and persecution can buy

Read Ephesians 1:18 – this was what Paul was praying for the Ephesians. Then read Luke 6:20–22 again.

- People who live to please God will be generous towards others.
- They will share what they have, including food.
- They will hunger to know God for themselves.
- They will weep with others and grieve over the state of the world.
- They will cope when everyone seems to turn against them.
- Saints experience God's presence now on earth, but their final reward will be in heaven.

Talk about how all the unearned things that we are given, which come from what God has done in Jesus' life, death and resurrection, give us real significance, hope and security, whether we are rich or poor, full or hungry, powerful or powerless, famous or insignificant. Finish by talking about how people who believe and trust in Jesus (all of them sometimes referred to as being 'saints') have God's power to live as God's people and spread this world-changing way of living – Jesus' way of living – among the people they meet and know.

Prayers of intercession

With the references to those who are mocked and persecuted, it would be appropriate to pray for those who are bullied. This could be for children in school, or those bullied at work or those treated unjustly for their faith in other parts of the world. Ask a group of people to prepare as appropriate. Conclude by reading Luke 6:22.

Alternatively, as it is All Saints' Day, pray for Christians (the saints) in another part of the world or in a country that you have links with. Display photographs and, if possible, provide a live link with them.

Ending the service

With: a bowl of olive oil

Oil was used in the Bible as a way of indicating

that someone or something was 'set apart' for God (eg anointing kings or objects used in worship). Invite everyone to think about whether we live as if we were 'set apart' for Jesus – are we aware of our special calling to serve him in our homes or workplaces?

As a final act of blessing, invite members of the congregation to dip their fingers in the oil (perhaps going on to sign one another with the mark of a cross on the hand) as a way of marking their willingness, as they go out from the service, to live as 'saints' in the world.

Helpful extras

Music and song ideas

Songs relevant to the themes of this service include: 'All I once held dear'; 'At the name of Jesus'; 'Beauty for brokenness'; 'I will offer up my life'; 'O God of burning, cleansing flame'; 'Seek ye first the kingdom of God'; 'The kingdom of God is justice and joy'.

Game

With: the 'Beatitude Cards', available as a download (YearC.Allsaints_1)

Print off, or create your own versions of, the 'cards' provided to play a game that explores issues relating to this service's Gospel reading. There are eight different cards. Each card has one word and a score: 'Poor' (minus 2), 'Rich' (+1), 'Hungry' (minus 2), 'Fed' (+1), 'Weeping' (minus 2), 'Laughing' (+1), 'Hated' (minus 2) and 'Popular' (+1). Ensure you make enough to give each person three cards. Shuffle them well beforehand.

Give each person their three cards. Explain that the aim of the game is to end up with as high a positive score as possible. In order to achieve this, you will need to use opposite cards to cancel each other out. In other words, if you have a 'Rich' and a 'Poor', these two cards cancel each other out and your score is calculated by looking at your remaining card. You can only use cards to cancel each other out in appropriate pairs. In other words, 'Fed' pairs with 'Hungry', 'Laughing' with 'Weeping' and 'Popular' with 'Hated'.

Everyone starts by adding up the points on their three cards. (So 'Poor', 'Rich' and 'Hungry' score minus 2, and 'Fed', 'Laughing' and 'Hated' score 0, but 'Hated', 'Popular' and 'Fed' score 1.) In order to increase their score, each person needs to swap cards with other people. Give them a couple of minutes to see how well they can do.

Then ask if anyone has scored 3. If they have, that is probably because they started with three 'blessings' and no 'woes'; so why would they choose to swap? Has anyone managed to increase their score? How did they manage it?

Now explain that if they wish to, people can form groups and see if they can increase their score by sharing their cards together. Can any group get a full set of 'blessings'? Give everyone a couple of minutes to see how well they can do. Finish by drawing attention to the way these 'blessings' and 'woes' are from Jesus' teaching in Luke 6:20–26. Talk briefly about how the kingdom of God is not about individual gain, but about how we care for each other – the blessings God gives us (even the poorest or hungriest among us) are meant to be shared. This is what it means to be a saint, someone who lives as God desires.

Statement of faith

The following declaration of Jesus' purposes for the 'saints' of his church, based on Luke 6:20–31, is also available as a download (YearC.Allsaints_2). Display it for several seconds so that people have a chance to own what they will be saying. Remind everyone that it is only through the grace of God and the empowerment of the Holy Spirit that we are able to fully live out the attitudes expressed here.

> God will bless us, when we trust in him instead of money.
> God will bless us, when we give food to the hungry before we get fed.
> God will bless us, when we share his love instead of laughing when others get hurt.
> God will bless us, when Jesus is more important to us than how important the world thinks we are.
> God will bless us, when we live his way!
>
> Based on Luke 6:20–31

Notes and comments

Both the *Revised Common Lectionary* and *Common Worship* suggest that the readings for All Saints' Day may be used on the following Sunday, in place of the readings set for the Fourth Sunday before Advent.

Alternative online options

Visit www.lightlive.org for additional activities for children, young people and adults.

FOURTH SUNDAY BEFORE ADVENT

READINGS: **2 Thessalonians 1:1–12; Luke 19:1–10**
Isaiah 1:10–18; Psalm 32:1–8

Bible foundations
Aim: to celebrate the surprising glory of Jesus' return

How surprised Zacchaeus must have been when Jesus looked up to the tree where he was perched, addressed him by name, and said 'I must stay at your house today.' Surely he was the last person Jesus would want to have fellowship with! He was not only a collaborator with the Romans, but as a chief tax collector he may also have been using his position to fleece his fellow countrymen for personal profit (and even if he was not, this would have been assumed to be the case by his neighbours). He was the last person one would expect a holy man to associate with!

But from Jesus' point of view he 'must' eat with Zacchaeus. There is a divine necessity here, related to his mission, which is to look for and to save people who are lost (Luke 19:10). He has 'not come to invite good people to turn to God. [He] came to invite sinners (Luke 5:32). And indeed Zacchaeus does experience salvation and repentance – proved by his readiness to give restitution to any who have been defrauded, and by his generosity to the poor (Luke 19:8,9).

The coming of Jesus in power and glory at the last day will come as a surprise to many. The small group of Jesus' disciples might seem pathetic, without power or status, and indeed always seem to be suffering in one way or another (2 Thessalonians 1:5–7). If a king were to come to their city with all his glory, they would be the last people he would want to meet. But the apostle Paul assures Christians in the Greek city of Thessalonica that they are the ones – rather than powerful politicians, wealthy business people or proud philosophers – whom this true Emperor is coming to visit. They are the ones who have recognised him as Lord when others mocked him. The tables are turned, and it is the persecutors who are excluded while the Church of Jesus receives a right royal welcome into his eternal kingdom. What 'songs of deliverance' (Psalm 32:7) they will sing on that day.

Beginning the service

With: green paper 'fig leaves', available as a download (YearC.4Sunb4Advent_1)

The 'sycamore' referred to in some translations of Luke 19:4 would in fact have been a 'sycamore fig'. These have very distinctive leaves. Make enough fig leaves out of green paper for every member of your congregation to have one each. Make sure that these are distributed as people arrive.

Explain that you will be hearing a story about when Jesus came to visit a town called Jericho, and a surprising thing that happened there. (The fig leaves everyone has are a reference to that surprising thing – ask everyone to be ready to look out for when the sycamore fig tree is mentioned as the Bible is read, later in the service.) When Jesus came to visit surprising things often happened – and, as Jesus' followers, Christians should be ready for surprises. Invite everyone to take part in the following response or praise shout, waving their leaves in the air, praising Jesus as they respond each time. The response is: **We are ready for you to surprise us!**

Jesus, thank you that you came to be with us.
We are ready for you to surprise us!
As we worship, show us more about who you are:
We are ready for you to surprise us!
Help us to celebrate your good news and face the challenges you bring:
We are ready for you to surprise us!

Bible reading

As Luke 19:1–10 is read, show a simple outline of one of three faces (happy, sad, curious) and ask for suggestions for which face fits the different characters as the story progresses.

Introduce 2 Thessalonians 1:1–12 by explaining that Paul was writing to a church he had helped to found, but they are now going through a lot of trouble.

Bible retelling

The following storytelling activity should help you celebrate some of the surprising aspects of Zacchaeus' story with your congregation. You will need a number of volunteers (at least three, preferably more) to prepare and deliver three presentations which imagine the emotions of the 'eyewitnesses' involved in the story. Short details are given for improvised delivery below. Each individual or group should focus on engaging the congregation with their perspective on events – encouraging boos or cheers for their particular 'heroes' or 'enemies', each time.

The people of Jericho (one to three people)
Tell the story of how excited the residents of Jericho were when Jesus came through. Was he the Messiah? Would he do healings? Would he throw out the Romans? *(Encourage booing for the Romans.)* Maybe he would help honest and hardworking people *(cheers)* get their own back on the wicked people who did the Romans' dirty work for them – like the tax collectors! *(More booing.)* Describe the crowd pressing round Jesus, full of expectation, as he walked through the town. Then, he suddenly stopped by a fig tree and called up to someone sitting in the branches, inviting himself round for dinner and to stay – describe your confusion and anger when it turned out that this was the chief tax

collector, who everyone thought the worst 'sinner' in the town! End with a phrase such as, 'It wasn't what I was expecting when Jesus came to town'.

Jairus' fellow tax collectors (one or two people)

Describe how it's very hard to survive with everybody's suspicion and distrust – everyone in the town thinks you are taking money off them unfairly, just because you work for the Romans. Some people seem to think that that means they can cheat you in return! Express resentment, distrust, hatred of your fellow Jews, but also of the Romans too. But at heart you're just like ordinary people – and you were as excited as anyone when Jesus arrived. You joined the crowd.

Describe some unkind comments you got from those around you – encourage booing. And then you saw Jesus stopping to talk to Zacchaeus, your boss – the most hated man in town – and offering to stay at his house! *(Encourage cheers.)* Here was a religious teacher who didn't condemn people like you just because they talked to the Romans. Try to convey the surprising release that you felt on hearing Jesus' words in Luke 19:9,10. End with a phrase such as, 'What Jesus did when he came to town and ate and drank with someone like us … that was the best surprise we'd ever had!' (They might also have been jealous of Zacchaeus and may have felt condemned by his actions at the end of the story – might they also be expected to give away their ill-gotten gains?!)

Jesus' disciples (one to three people)

If two or more people are involved here, they need to take sides. One or two should loosely represent those of Jesus' disciples looking to throw the Romans out by force, if necessary, while another should appear to have a history similar to that of Zacchaeus or Levi/Matthew (see Luke 5:27–32). If you are giving this presentation alone, try to reflect some of the ambiguity in the disciples' attitudes to the Romans as best as you can, revealing that Zacchaeus' turning to Jesus could be controversial for them.

Describe the arrival in Jericho – all those people coming to see your teacher and his followers. What were they expecting? Comment that you'd learnt that if you hang around with Jesus, strange things can happen. Describe the surprise when Jesus suddenly looked up into the tree – reveal the mixed feelings in your group when you found that you were going with Jesus to spend time with Zacchaeus. *(If there is more than one of you, invite simultaneous boos and cheers for tax collectors from the congregation, before realising the disunited front this presents – see above.)* Perhaps remark that you're getting used to spending time with 'sinners' but it still makes some of you feel odd. Describe Zacchaeus' speaking of Jesus as 'Lord' and offering to give half his money to the poor – suddenly, you recognised someone who, like you, would do anything to follow Jesus, whatever happens. Emphasise Jesus' words in Luke 19:10 – express both excitement at what you understand and confusion at what you don't understand in what he says. End with words such as, 'If you decide to follow Jesus, you have to always be ready for surprises!'

Bible talk

With: flip chart, marker pens, pictures of Jesus available as a download (YearC.4Sunb4Advent_2)

(If you are using the **Bible retelling**, this activity would work well immediately afterwards. If not, use this talk following the **Bible reading**.) Display the pictures from Jesus' life showing him 'coming to visit' people in different ways or you could source your own images as follows:

His birth (Luke 2:1–7)
His visiting the Temple, aged 12 (Luke 2:41–50)
His coming to Zacchaeus' house (Luke 19:1–10)
His arrival in Jerusalem for the Passover (Luke 19:35–40)
His appearing in the upper room after his death (Luke 24:36–44)
His promised return (2 Thessalonians 1:1–12)

Either discuss these all together, or ask the congregation to gather into small groups, each with a printout of a different picture. In either case, encourage a brief discussion between people of all ages about the pictures, focusing on the following points:

What can people remember about this story or promise that is or was surprising?
What can they remember that is special or wonderful about Jesus?
What is there that they would want to celebrate (share and enjoy with other people)?
Write up the results of your discussions for each picture on a sheet of flip chart paper (if you are using small groups, ask for feedback after the discussion). Jesus often surprised people and acted in ways they didn't expect. In Jericho, he ate with Zacchaeus, a hated tax-collector, and declared him to be a true follower of God because of his readiness to give to the poor. Jesus also often did things that were special or wonderful – we could say he showed his 'glory'. He spoke and acted with power and authority that came from his identity as 'God among us'.

Finally, Jesus' story – as well as the hope that he will come again – is worth celebrating! Make reference to Zacchaeus' generous acts that celebrated Jesus coming to his house, and to the joy and wonder that Paul suggests Jesus' followers will share in when he returns (2 Thessalonians 1:7,10). Encourage people to find different ways in their daily lives to share and enjoy Jesus' story.

Prayer activity

With: one large dice

Number everyone 1 to 6, then invite people where they are sitting to briefly chat with their neighbours about what it is they find surprising about Jesus' story. Encourage children to think creatively and seek help from adults and young people around them. Invite adults to listen to what the children around them are saying and to take their responses seriously.

Then, each time you roll the dice, call out the number rolled. Everyone with that number stands up and speaks a sentence that praises Jesus for the surprising things he does, or the surprising truths he shows us about God. (Give examples which could include: 'Thank you, Jesus, for being ready to forgive'; 'We praise you, Jesus, for listening to ordinary people'; or 'Lord God, help us to be ready for Jesus' second coming'.) If people don't want to speak out loud, they can stand and pray in silence. The whole congregation should be ready to respond with a loud 'Amen!'

End with a closing prayer – if you have confident children and young people, ask two or three younger members of your congregation to prepare in advance to lead everyone in the Lord's Prayer, particularly appropriate as it contains Jesus' own teaching on prayer, and includes reference to the future coming of God's kingdom.

Ending the service

The following prayer of commitment could be read by two or three volunteers of mixed ages (reading alternating lines) or said by the whole congregation together. It is also available as a download (YearC.4Sunb4Advent_3). This prayer is partially based on ideas and phrases from the GNB translation of 2 Thessalonians 1:1–12 (although the idea of 'marvelling' at Jesus comes from the NIV version of verse 10):

We belong to Jesus –
We are looking forward to the day when he will be revealed again.
On that day, he will come from heaven to punish cruelty and rejection of God
And receive honour from his people, who will marvel at his glory.

We belong to Jesus –
We ask God to make us ready for the life Jesus calls us to live.
We need his grace and power to bring about all our desires for goodness,
So that he will receive glory from us, and we from him.
Amen.

Helpful extras

Music and song ideas

Songs and hymns that celebrate Jesus coming to us and his promised return include: 'All heaven waits with bated breath'; 'In majesty he comes'; 'Lo, he comes with clouds descending'; 'All glory, laud and honour'; 'Born in the night, Mary's child'; 'Heaven opened and you came to save me'.

Notes and comments

If you are using this material in the context of a Communion service, draw attention to Jesus' words in Luke 19:5, where he declares that he must stay with Zacchaeus and drink and eat with him. In communion, Christians celebrate Jesus' coming to meet with them and rescue them from sin, in the form of a meal (which itself remembers the 'surprising glory' of the events leading up to his death and resurrection). Make this link as you invite your congregation to share in Communion.

Alternative online options

Visit www.lightlive.org for additional activities for children, young people and adults.

THIRD SUNDAY BEFORE ADVENT

READINGS: 2 Thessalonians 2:1–5,13–17; Luke 20:27–38
Job 19:23–27; Psalm 17:1–9

Bible foundations

Aim: to look forward to Jesus' second coming and the new life he will bring for those who have died

The Sadducees were the most influential group among the Jews; most of the chief priests came from their party. They had a vested interest in protecting their privileged status under the Romans; their fear was that if Jesus continued stirring up the people then the Romans would 'come and take away both our place (ie the temple) and our nation'. They themselves did not believe in a bodily resurrection as the Pharisees did (Acts 23:8), and their story is intended to make Jesus look ridiculous in the eyes of the people.

In his reply Jesus quotes a verse from the Law of Moses, the only part of the Hebrew Scriptures that the Sadducees accepted. He shows that he has meditated more deeply on the Scriptures, and that he knows God better than they do. He is the living God, and having entered into relationship with people he will not just let them perish for ever.

The apostle Paul's teaching about the second coming of Jesus in 2 Thessalonians 2 contains some things that are hard to understand. Who is this 'man of lawlessness' he speaks of (v 3)? What does it mean that he will 'set himself up in God's temple, proclaiming himself to be God' (v 4)? But some things are clear. The coming of Jesus will be a public, dramatic affair (compare Revelation 1:7). Don't let anyone tell you that it happened secretly and you missed it! The significance of his coming for Christians is that after it has happened we will share in his glory (v 14). This is meant to give us a powerful incentive to keep going in our struggle to try to be holy, and to be patient in the midst of any trials we may experience. In the gospel God has given us, we find both 'eternal encouragement and good hope' (v 16). Our vindication will come from him one day soon (Psalm 17:2).

Beginning the service

Ask three people of mixed ages and backgrounds to bring with them to church an object that represents one of the cruel things in life that they struggle with or find difficult to understand. This may be better explained to children in terms of representing anything in the world that they feel God will not allow in heaven.

Explain what these volunteers were asked to bring; then invite them to show their objects and talk briefly about what they brought and why. Explain in a few words that as we go through life we will all find some things difficult and troubling. But despite such worries or cruelties, there is still hope. Today you will be exploring some words of Jesus that encourage us not to give up and instead to look forward to the future. Then read this prayer:

Lord God, we come here to worship you.
We bring with us our worries about the cruel things in life.
Help us to lay them down before you today.
As we pray and hear from your Word, may we find new hope and inspiration in you and in your Son, Jesus.
May we come to look forward to the future with hope.
Amen.

Bible reading

Explain that the Sadducees, religious leaders, wanted to trick Jesus. Then read Luke 20:27–38 with a narrator, Sadducees and Jesus.

Before reading 2 Thessalonians 2:1–5,13–17, remind people how much Paul longed to see the Christians in Thessalonica grow in their faith.

Bible talk

With: the words of Luke 20:38 (The Lord isn't the God of the dead, but of the living) on slips of paper (each at least 22 cm x 4 cm), to act as wristbands or bookmarks – available as a download (YearC.3Sunb4Advent_1)

Arrange for someone to play a practical joke either on another person in church or on yourself. Make it as visually funny as possible, but do not humiliate anyone. Then draw out the fact that often practical jokes can make the person they are played on look stupid or silly – ask whether everybody agrees with this. Does anybody in the congregation feel that such jokes can go too far? Talk about why this is so.

Explain that in Luke 20:27–38 a group of people are trying to play a trick on Jesus. They are the 'Sadducees', Jewish leaders who had big disagreements with Jesus. It seems that they didn't like the idea that people might be beginning to trust him more than they trusted them. One of the things that made them different from Jesus was that they believed that once you were dead, you were dead for ever. The Sadducees tried to make Jesus give a silly answer and make him look silly, along with everyone else who believed that there was life after death.

Briefly outline, in all-age friendly language, the basic points of the Sadducees' 'trick', and how Jesus turned it back on them (use the **Bible foundations**). Say that Jesus showed that what is important is not just that God has acted in the past (which these Sadducees believed), or that we know we need to trust and follow him now (this, too, is something the Sadducees believed). It's also important that we believe in God's promise that he has good plans for us for the future.

Share with everyone the amazing promise contained in Luke 20:38 '… the Lord isn't the God of the dead but of the living.' This is a really important truth for understanding God and trusting in him. Emphasise the importance of remembering such vital truths and promises from the Bible for times when we find life difficult. (Draw out this theme further if you wish to make reference to 11 November being Remembrance Sunday). All Jesus' followers shared this belief that God can free people who trust in him from the fear of death.

We know that Paul, who saw Jesus after he had died and risen from the dead, thought that this was a very important part of believing in Jesus. Paul talks about Jesus coming back, in a way everybody will see, to save people who trust in him and give them a share in his glory (2 Thessalonians 2:14). 'Sharing in his glory' includes rising from the dead. Encourage everybody to look forward to these promises being fulfilled.

Distribute a sheet of paper to every member of the congregation, and encourage them to decorate it and use it either as a bookmark or as a wristband to help them remember this important truth and promise from Jesus. Have sticky tape available to make wristbands for people who wish to make them.

Prayers of intercession

With: paper, pens (optional)

Use the following prayers to lead intercessions, which ideally should be read by an adult and an older child together, in alternating parts. These prayers use ideas from Luke 20 and 2 Thessalonians 2.

Lord God,
You are the Father, who spoke to your special people in the past.
You are the Son, who met us in Jesus and died so that we might live.
You are the Spirit, who helps us believe in the truth.
We can meet you in so many ways.
Help us to listen to you, as you speak to us.
You have good plans for the future.
Help us to look forward with hope.

We pray for Christians around the world, and for their leaders:
Where they are in trouble or in danger, or giving up for any reason,
Help them to look forward to a future when you will put things right.
Help them to look forward with hope.

We pray for the people of the world, particularly victims of wars:
Remember them when we forget them and their suffering.
Help them to know you properly and trust in you.
Help them to look forward with hope.

We pray for the people we know who need your hope:
Because they are ill; because they are hurt or worried;
Because they are unhappy when they remember people who have died.
Help them to believe that you can turn their sadness to happiness,
And give new life to people who have died.
Help them to look forward with hope.

Ending the service

Join together in the following prayer, with people repeating the emboldened response.

Let us go in peace, trusting in God and looking forward to the future,
Because Jesus isn't the Lord of the dead but of the living!
May Jesus give us hope, in all the days of our life,
Because Jesus isn't the Lord of the dead but of the living!
May we see those whom Jesus loves risen again from death at the end of time,
Because Jesus isn't the Lord of the dead but of the living!

Helpful extras

Music and song ideas

Songs appropriate to the themes of trusting in God, the resurrection and the second coming include: 'All my hope on God is founded'; 'In Christ alone'; 'Lord, for the years'; 'O Lord, my God' ('How great thou art'); 'O God, our help in ages past'; 'There's a sound of the wind'; 'Soon and very soon'; 'There's a place where the streets shine'; 'What a friend we have in Jesus'; 'There is a hope that burns within my heart'; Oh my soul, arise and bless your maker'.

Statement of faith

With: several very large sheets of paper; marker pens

Break into groups and ask each group to complete the following sentences, writing their answers on a large sheet of paper. Remind everyone that the Sadducees were questioning what it was that Jesus believed in. One of the small groups could be especially geared for young children, who might want to make statements about who Jesus is or what he has done.

'We believe that God is … Amen!'
'We believe that Jesus, God's Son, is … Amen!'
'We believe that people who follow Jesus [are/can/will] … Amen!'
'God [or Jesus] has promised that … Amen!'
'We are looking forward to … Amen!'
'Because of all these things, we will put our trust in Jesus – Amen!'

Invite each group to then stand and make a group declaration of their faith.

Notes and comments

If you are using this service outline on Remembrance Sunday, the cruelty items used in **Beginning the service** would tie in here as you commemorate those who have died and fought in wars around the world, in the First and Second World Wars and more recently. Use this modified version of the opening prayer:

Lord God, we come here to worship you and remember the victims and survivors of war.
We bring with us our worries about the cruel things in life,
And our sadness at the pain that wars still bring.
Help us to lay them down before you today, and as we pray and hear from your Word,
May we find new hope and inspiration in you and in your Son, Jesus,
And come to look forward to the future with hope. Amen.

Since you have been reflecting on

resurrection life, it would be appropriate to pray for any who have recently been bereaved.

Alternative online options

Visit www.lightlive.org for additional activities for children, young people and adults.

> Now is the time for people of all ages to get their Bible reading guides. Provide attractive information to encourage everyone in the congregation to take the Bible seriously in the coming year!
>
> For details of Scripture Union's Bible reading guides visit www.scriptureunion.org.uk or see page 154.

Top Tips on Prompting prayer
978 1 84427 322 5

What does the Bible say about prayer? How can you use all the senses to stimulate a relationship with God? This readable and practical guide is packed with wisdom and ideas that will inspire anyone wanting to strengthen children's and young people's conversations with God.

For more details, visit www.scriptureunion.org.uk

SECOND SUNDAY BEFORE ADVENT

READINGS: **2 Thessalonians 3:6–13; Luke 21:5–19**
Malachi 4:1,2; Psalm 98

Bible foundations
Aim: to make a commitment together to follow Jesus in the tough times

Probably most of us would not tend to see the coming of the Lord to judge as something to look forward to! But for the psalmist, the coming of the Lord to 'judge the world in righteousness' (Psalm 98:9) is something to get excited about! Actually, for many people in the world who are oppressed and long for justice this may ring bells. The hope of justice one day helps us to persevere when times are tough. Jesus warns his disciples that difficult times are coming their way. In Luke 21 he speaks of the destruction of the Temple and the rest of Jerusalem (which happened about 40 years later in AD 70) and also of the end of the age. The trials of the one historical event foreshadow the coming judgement. Before the end comes there will be numerous wars, revolutions, earthquakes, famines and plagues.

False prophets will arise and will deceive many. Jesus' disciples will be persecuted and put on trial. But even if their families reject them, they must still stand firm in their faith (vs 16–19). Paul emphasises another aspect of what it means to follow Jesus. We should never think that because Jesus is coming back we have an excuse to down tools and give up earning our living. When he comes he expects to find us busy with the tasks he has assigned us. And these include ordinary everyday duties as well as more 'spiritual' activities like prayer or witnessing. We need a whole-life discipleship that sees every part of life as under God's direction and that never tires of 'doing what is right' (2 Thessalonians 3:13). Our basic attitude in life must be that we revere the Lord's name (see Malachi 4:2). We do everything we do as under his eye, and with the aim of pleasing him. As Paul says elsewhere, we are to 'serve wholeheartedly, as if … serving the Lord, not men' (Ephesians 6:7), determined that whatever we do, whether in word or deed, we 'do it all in the name of the Lord Jesus, giving thanks to God the Father through him' (Colossians 3:17).

Beginning the service

With: four or five pictures of well-known political leaders, sporting figures or pop stars

Show your collection of pictures, one at a time. Ask for suggestions as to who is depicted and what people know about their life. Each time a picture is shown, organise a vote by show of hands to discover whether people feel that person to be 'good', 'bad' or 'indifferent'.

After this, point out that these are very shallow judgements, made on the basis of only a little information. We cannot really know, based on just what we have heard or read through the media, whether such people are 'good' or 'bad' people. Neither can we really know what are the struggles or difficulties a famous politician or sports star might have gone through to get to where they are, or how honest they really are over their expenses or in their relationships. This would be a glib and lazy judgement to make. It is God who knows, not us. We all tend to form opinions about other people, based on very little – emphasise that where such opinions are negative, repeating them carelessly can be hurtful and cruel, and that we should be careful to avoid passing on nasty gossip about others. Others will form the same kind of impressions about us.

In both of today's Bible passages we will hear about believers in Jesus who were preparing to face tough times. They knew that how they reacted would affect both the way in which others saw them and what they thought about Jesus. They also knew that many people would not understand their difficulties, and would take any opportunity they could get to criticise or make more trouble for them. They had to make a commitment to follow Jesus closely and be faithful to him, whatever the difficulties.

Bible reading

On this occasion introduce each reading with a brief explanation of where it fits in the chronology of the Bible, preferably reading the Gospel passage first. The Scripture Union *Bible Timelines* are always a helpful visual guide for children. The **Bible foundations**, as well as a good commentary, should help you.

Luke 21:5–19 could be read as follows: two people read verses 5 and 6; two people read verse 7 and one person reads verses 8–19 in a chatty, reassuring style.

2 Thessalonians 3:6–13 calls for a similar chatty yet firm style.

Bible talk

With: a large world map; cards with country names and information about struggling Christians; sticky tack

Start this **Bible talk** after the **Game** or **Beginning the service** and the **Bible reading**. Expand upon the simple ways in which these activities have tried to illustrate the troubles of the disciples of Jesus as they struggled to follow his way in the years after his ascension into heaven: the suspicion, nastiness, scrutiny and jealousy that may have come from people around them, the attempts to 'catch them out' in not living up to the claims they made about Jesus and the new life he offered them (see Luke 21:12,17; 2 Thessalonians 3:12,13).

Alternatively, begin by chatting to people about whatever the most recent reality TV game shows may be. Emphasise the fact that while we may find it entertaining, there is a cruel aspect to these kind of shows – often involving the newspapers, radio and TV, as journalists look for gossip about contestants and try to 'catch them out' – and move into making the points outlined above. (Emphasise that there are differences between the early church and reality TV – we should not trivialise what the early church endured and survived.)

Talk about how Christians around the world still suffer because of their commitment to following Jesus through tough times. Use a map, displayed at the front of the church, to show where followers of Jesus face difficulties. You could use country names written on cards distributed before the service. Ask volunteers to come forward with a card, identify the country on the map and attach the country name to the right place on the map with sticky tack before sharing information about the situation of Christians in that country. Some suggestions are given below to help you seek out further information and more information is given in **Notes and comments**.

China. Although it is no longer illegal to be a Christian, it is illegal to teach the Christian faith to children; there is a shortage of Bibles.

The Middle East. Christians of many different kinds (Arabs, Messianic Jews, immigrants) may struggle through poverty, government restrictions, suspicion from other faiths, wars or other conflicts.

Eritrea. Ministers and members of certain churches are frequently arrested and can be held for months or years without trial.

Be careful to think through what information you will share with children, and make the level of detail appropriate to your audience's understanding. End by emphasising the amount of care and love, and the great promises, expressed in Jesus' words to his disciples that we hear in today's Gospel reading (see Luke 21:14,15,18,19). He has not abandoned his followers!

We follow the same God and we can be confident that he will be with us and our fellow Christians around the world, that he will help us as we seek to follow Jesus, and that he will hear and act (although maybe in ways we cannot see or immediately understand) when we pray to him for Christians in tough situations.

Briefly look ahead to (or review) other parts of your service (such as the **Prayer activity** or **Ending the service**) where people will be encouraged to make or renew a commitment to following Jesus through tough times, or to act on that commitment by praying for others who face difficulty.

Prayer activity

With: lengths of ribbon, string or coloured wool

How you structure this time of prayer and the amount of time it takes will depend on the layout of your church or room and how much space there is for movement and forming smaller groups. The aim is for individuals or groups to take a length of string to symbolise the link between people in church as followers of Jesus, so that they can pray for each other's concerns. These could include tough times they personally are facing, or situations they are aware of in others' lives. Ensure that adults and children can interact and pray together honestly and with confidence.

Each person is given a piece of string/wool/ribbon, which stands for one prayer need. As the pieces of string are tied together, people explain what this need is. If people are in groups they pray for the different needs. One long piece of string is then joined to another piece of long string from another group until there is just one long piece of string made up of everyone's prayer needs. We are joined together in praying for one another.

End the prayer time with a short prayer that recognises your church's links to other churches and Christians around the world. Then encourage everyone to say the Lord's Prayer together, a prayer that links Christians from around the world.

Ending the service

Pray a commissioning prayer asking for God's help in caring for each other as you seek to follow Jesus even when times are tough. Use the prayers below, which are also available as a PowerPoint download (YearC.2Sunb4Advent_1). Let people see or hear what you are going to say beforehand so they can decide whether they will respond with an '**Amen!**' If you wish, follow these prayers with a further simple prayer of blessing.

Father God, we seek always to follow your ways. Send the Holy Spirit to bring each one of us a life full of faith and hope. May we follow your commands to love and care for those around us.
Amen!

Lord Jesus, you warned us that following you would not be easy. Help us to live with your mercy and compassion, and to support one another in love when times are hard.
Amen!

Holy Spirit, Jesus commanded us to tell others about him. Help each one of us to share the good news of Jesus with people we know.
Amen!

Helpful extras
Music and song ideas

Songs or hymns with relevance to the Church's commitment to love and support one another include: 'A new commandment'; 'Bind us together'; 'For I'm building a people of power'.

The theme of finding encouragement in God, despite trials, is pursued in hymns and songs such as 'I'm gonna worship my God' (*Reach Up!* CD, SU); 'It is good, it is good, it is good to give thanks to the Lord on high' (particularly the third verse); 'There is a voice that must be heard'; 'The Church's one foundation'; 'What a friend we have in Jesus'.

Game

With: a table; a straightforward task to complete such as an easy jigsaw puzzle; a ball of string to unravel or a simple household task; prizes

Ask for volunteers of mixed ages to come forward and inform them that they have to complete an otherwise simple task in tough circumstances. All eyes are on them, checking their every move. The volunteers have to work together as a team to finish their task, with the twist that they have to work under the table! The rest of the congregation will call out if they touch the table legs or top at all, or if they put a foot or an arm outside the area of the table. (Note that this activity will only work if you have a table that is suitable for people to sit under without knocking their head on any protruding parts. To work well, you will need a mix of ages and sizes of people and enough volunteers to make it slightly uncomfortable – though not impossible – to move around.)

If the volunteers complete their task (you may wish to give them two or three goes), reward them appropriately. Draw a parallel with the believers Paul writes to in Thessalonica, whose task was to follow Jesus, knowing that all eyes were on them and that people would be quick to criticise if they did not live good lives. Mention that they weren't left on their own. Paul is careful to reassure them of the many ways in which God will bless and help them and make it possible for them to follow Jesus (see 2 Thessalonians 1:11,12; 2:13–16; 3:3–5,16–18) – which is reassuring for us, too! If appropriate this explanation could merge straight into the beginning of the **Bible talk**.

Notes and comments

As an alternative to **Beginning the service**, you could use part or all of Psalm 98 as either a call to worship or an affirmation. This psalm works particularly well in this context as it carries a reminder that Christian belief in God's ultimate coming to judge the earth is a positive hope, which those in trouble can look forward to as they struggle to follow Jesus (see **Bible foundations**).

The **Bible talk** includes details of parts of the world where the church is under pressure. Websites that have current information about the persecuted, minority or struggling Church include: www.csw.org.uk; www.opendoors.org; www.tearfund.org. Note that Scripture Union does not take any responsibility for the content of websites maintained by external organisations.

If this service includes Holy Communion, it would be appropriate to refer to the injustice that Jesus experienced in his trial and death.

Alternative online options

Visit www.lightlive.org for additional activities for children, young people and adults.

SUNDAY NEXT BEFORE ADVENT/ CHRIST THE KING

READINGS: **Colossians 1:11–20; Luke 23:33–43**
Jeremiah 23:1–6; Psalm 46

Bible foundations
Aim: to praise Jesus as our King, and look forward to the coming of his kingdom

The notice above Jesus' cross proclaimed, 'This is the King of the Jews' (Luke 23:38). Herod, who was supposed to be the 'king of the Jews' and Pilate, who served the Roman emperor, wanted to mock this man who had none of the trappings of kingship. But Jesus is a different sort of king, who uses his power not to oppress or control but to liberate and redeem. His concern is not to protect what he has, but to 'save others' (v 35), even at the cost of his own life. The world had never before seen a man who would pray for the forgiveness of his enemies even as they tortured and killed him (v 34). This is truly the King of Love. One of the criminals crucified with Jesus shows some key characteristics of those who would belong to God's kingdom. He acknowledges his guilt (vs 40, 41). He recognises that Jesus is a King, despite all the seeming evidence to the contrary, and asks to be remembered when he begins his reign (v 42). He models the repentance and faith we all need.

Paul describes 'the kingdom of the Son [God] loves' as a 'kingdom of light' (Colossians 1:12,13), and his emphasis is on God's action in allowing us entry. God has 'qualified us', when we could not hope to qualify ourselves; he has 'rescued us' from a pit we could not climb out of; and he has 'brought us' into his kingdom: like an asylum seeker entering a new country, we live under new authority. Set free from the past, with all our wrongdoings forgiven, we certainly have every incentive to 'joyfully give thanks to the Father' (vs 11,12). Jesus is 'The Lord our Righteousness', a king who reigns wisely and brings us salvation (Jeremiah 23:5,6). One day soon he will make all wars cease as he is exalted among the nations (Psalm 46:9,10). Our privilege is to bow the knee to him now, although he is despised by the world, and to start living now by his values of justice and love even before his kingdom comes in its fullness.

Beginning the service

With: a box containing a passport, a coin, stamps (or large cardboard cut-outs depicting these items)

Ask volunteers to take an item out of the box (or pick up a cut-out). Ask people to identify the items as each appears, and to suggest what the connection between these items is. There may be more than one correct answer here – do acknowledge all correct answers!

If no one has already said it, explain that they are all things that might give a sign about a person's nationality – if you met someone with a French passport, a pocket full of euros, and some French stamps in their wallet, you might expect them to be French. Ask for suggestions of other ways in which you might identify what country a person is from (some answers might be their language, the way they shake hands, clothes).

Jesus often speaks about the kingdom of God – but there's no passport for it. Ask for suggestions as to how people will know if we are part of the kingdom of God. Explain to people that in this service we will be exploring what it means to call Jesus a 'king' and belong to the kingdom he spoke about.

Bible reading

Psalm 46 could be read accompanied by appropriate sound effects.

Colossians 1:11–20 forms the **Statement of faith** available as a download (YearC. Sunb4Advent_1). This is for everyone to say all together or just the emboldened response.

Bible talk

With: prepared list of 'kings' with associated pictures (optional)

Expectations of a king

Before the service, meet with a group or groups of people to brainstorm a list of usages of the word 'king' in our culture, including a youth group or children's group. You should be looking for a good and eclectic range of readily recognised answers (eg Elvis – 'The King'; King Kong; Leonardo Di Caprio's line, 'I'm the king of the world!' from *Titanic*; *The Lion King*; *Lord of the Rings: Return of the King*, a historic or contemporary king, King's College, Martin Luther King etc) that show the many different uses of or meanings we put on the word 'king'. If there is time, collect pictures that illustrate these examples. An Internet search will help.

Begin by sharing the list and displaying any pictures you found. Talk about what people think a king is or does. Most of us now live in countries where if there is a monarch, he or she is little more than a figurehead. They don't do much, and certainly don't command the same kind of awe, reverence and fear that a king would have done in Jesus' time. Ask what the word 'king' is being used to suggest in each of these cases (or any others that members of the congregation can think of). Discuss how the word 'king' is used widely by people and organisations today.

Expectations of a king in New Testament times

Talk about the **Bible readings**, particularly the Gospel passage. Draw out how provocative it was to be called 'king' in Jesus' time, and what the expectations people around Jesus would have had of someone who called themselves a king. Questions to ask yourself as you prepare to deliver this part of the talk include: what would the Herods, who ruled in Jesus' day, expect a king to do (see Matthew 2)? What would Pilate expect a king to do (see also John 18:33–37)? What did the Jews expect that a king would do? Convey the fear or uncertainty that a new person calling themselves a 'king' would create in a land under foreign rule, largely based around understandings of 'king' involving violence and war-leadership – particularly among the people who thought they should be in charge! (As Christmas is close, you could explain the three 'Herods' in the Bible: Herod the Great, ruling at the time of Jesus' birth; his son, Herod Antipas, active during Jesus' adulthood; and Herod Agrippa, grandson of the first Herod, who met Paul at the start of his imprisonment.)

Expectations of Jesus, the king

As Christians, we call Jesus the king, but we do this knowing that he is different from all other 'kings' – not strong and violent like *King Kong*, and not a fragile, idolised pop star like Elvis (go through your list as appropriate). He suffered and died on the cross, and lived a hard, travelling life, sometimes hiding from those in authority. And his 'kingdom', too, is different. Our readings today make it clear that anyone can be a part of it, if they follow Jesus. Even someone as wise and as devoted as Paul is not part of the kingdom of God by his own efforts – he counts himself among those whom God has 'rescued' and 'brought in' (Colossians 1:13). Even the thief on the cross, about to die, and with no opportunity to do anything at all in the few remaining hours of his life – is welcomed into the kingdom (Luke 23:43). Paul's statement that 'all beings in heaven and on earth' can be brought back to God by Jesus' love and sacrifice (Colossians 1:20) suggests that we can look forward to a time when there will be no doubt about Jesus' glory and power and authority. This is what we mean when we pray, 'your kingdom come'. Jesus is our king now, if we trust in him, but the full glory of his kingdom is yet to come.

As Christians we should use every opportunity we have (in worship, in prayer, in talking to others about Jesus) to celebrate Jesus' special and different 'kingship' and praise him for it.

Prayer activity

With: small, prepared sheets of paper with the words 'Lead us not into…' and 'Deliver us from…' with space to complete the sentences; pens; a basket

The Lord's Prayer mentions the kingdom of God twice. We pray 'Your kingdom come, your will be done' at the start and close with 'Lead us not into temptation … for yours is the kingdom, the power and the glory'. (The final phrase is a later addition to the biblical account of Jesus' teaching on prayer, yet widely used and consistent with the intent of the rest of the prayer.)

It's easy to pray about 'the kingdom' without thinking what it actually means – like the thief on the cross, we can find it easy to assume that 'your kingdom come' means something just 'happens' in the future. But God's kingdom comes in part when we choose to live in the way he asks us to – it's something that we can enter into now. Pass round pens and the sheets of paper.

Ask everyone to think of ways in which they find it hard to live as God wants them to. Write their thoughts in the spaces on the first part of the sheet of paper (such as 'Lead us not into… jealousy' or 'Lead us not into… being greedy' or even 'Lead us not into… pornography'). Next, ask everyone to think of aspects of life that are not in God's kingdom and from which people might need to experience deliverance and write these down (such as 'Deliver us from… bullying' or 'Deliver us from… famine' or 'Deliver us from… terrorism').

What people choose to write on their sheets of paper may depend on how you structure the activity. It can be organised individually or in groups, or a mixture of the two. Younger children will need someone to help them. When people have finished, allow them either to keep their slips or to place them in a basket to offer up to God, asking him to answer their prayers. End by saying the Lord's Prayer together.

Ending the service

With: jars or bags of real pennies or cut-out card 'pennies'

At the end of the service, give each person a penny. (Because of the health and safety implications of handing out small, easily swallowable metal objects to children, instead of giving pennies to younger children, either use pre-made cardboard 'pennies' as an alternative, or give family groups a clear plastic bag of pennies.) This week, each time someone uses a coin, ask them to think about what in their life shows that they are part of the kingdom of God, a follower of Jesus. (You may choose to clean the pennies by soaking them in vinegar or lemon juice the night before, rinsing them afterwards.)

Helpful extras

Music and song ideas

Some songs that touch on the kingdom of God and Jesus as King include: 'The kingdom of God is justice and peace' (Taizé chant); 'King of Kings, majesty'; 'From heaven you came' ('The Servant King'); 'Reign in me'; 'Prince of Peace you are'; 'Our Father in heaven' (Brian Doerksen).

Statement of faith

The following **Statement of faith** and praise is also available as a download (YearC.Sunb4Advent_1). It is based on Colossians 1:9–20. The repeated line, 'Jesus, we praise you!' (in bold) could be said all together by your congregation. It could also be used as part of the **Bible reading**.

> **Jesus, we praise you!**
> You are our king, and as we follow you,
> You bring us into a new kingdom:
> A kingdom of light, not darkness;
> A kingdom of forgiveness;
> A kingdom of freedom from evil.
> **Jesus, we praise you!**
> You show us the God we cannot see,
> And you rule over all of creation, which was made through you:
> The things we know about and do not know about;
> Everything in heaven;
> Everything on earth.
> **Jesus, we praise you!**
> You are the leader of our new family, the church:

> You have made it possible for all beings in heaven and earth,
> To come back to God, making peace with him through your sacrifice.
> We look forward to a time
> When your kingdom is known throughout the world.
> **Jesus, we praise you!**
>
> Based on Colossians 1:9–20

Notes and comments

There are many more things that can be talked about with regard to the kingdom of God. Note that the kingdom of God is barely mentioned in the Old Testament, but there is plenty about kings and kingdoms. Jesus uses the concepts of kings and kingdoms that the people around him were familiar with to communicate something about the nature of following God; but remember, God's people were initially nomadic and only settled down later. Their concept of kingdoms was much less focused on land ownership than is our Western understanding of the word following several hundreds of years of feudal rule. The word 'kingdom' (Hebrew: malkuth; Greek: basilea) was more about a group of people who were led by a king rather than an area of land owned by one. The physical 'kingdoms' are based on who or what this king can control; the spiritual kingdom, the kingdom of God, is based on who will willingly follow this king.

The New Testament is also clear that although the kingdom is coming, it has also in some senses already come! It has come because Jesus has brought it within our reach, in all its fullness. It is still coming because it requires us to respond, to enter into the kingdom. Also, the kingdom is unlike any other kingdom the world has seen, because in this kingdom the king serves his subjects as well as them serving him!

With an older congregation or home group you could explore some of the puzzling questions in more depth such as: In what ways can we see that the kingdom of God has come? In what ways can we see that the kingdom of God is coming?

Alternative online options

Visit www.lightlive.org for additional activities for children, young people and adults.

London SW6 3TN
www.boldwoodbooks.com